MILLER'S

TWENTIETH-CENTURY
ceramics

There is only ONE
CORNISH KITCHEN WARE

MILLER'S

TWENTIETH-CENTURY
ceramics

A COLLECTOR'S GUIDE TO BRITISH AND NORTH AMERICAN FACTORY-PRODUCED CERAMICS

PAUL ATTERBURY

ELLEN PAUL DENKER

MAUREEN BATKIN

MILLER'S TWENTIETH-CENTURY CERAMICS

by Paul Atterbury
Ellen Paul Denker
Maureen Batkin

First published in Great Britain in 1999 by Miller's, a division of
Mitchell Beazley, imprints of Octopus Publishing Group Ltd,
2-4 Heron Quays, London E14 4JP
Reprinted 1999, 2000
Revised edition 2005

Miller's is a registered trademark of Octopus Publishing Group Ltd

ISBN 1 84533 081 1

A CIP record for this book is available from the British Library

Set in ITC Century Light

Colour reproduction by Hong Kong Graphics.
Printed and bound in China by Toppan Printing Company Ltd

Executive Editor **Alison Starling**
Executive Art Editor **Vivienne Brar**
Senior Editor **Anthea Snow**
Designer **Jane Parry, Christine Keilty**
Editorial Assistant **Stephen Guise**
Picture Researcher **Maria Gibbs**
Illustrator **Amanda Patton**
Production **Paul Hammond**

JACKET PICTURES

Front, clockwise from top: Zambesi dish by Jessie Tate (c.1956); Platter by Petra
Tilly (2004); Nora water server (c.1980); Lily Maid by Gilbert Bayes (c.1930);
Secessionist ware vase by Léon Solon and John Wadsworth (c.1904); Highfield
cream jug by Lorna Bailey (2004).

Back, left to right: Dish by John Piper (1982); China coffee set by Victor Skellern
(1935); Football pattern jug by Clarice Cliff (1930s).

Spine: Free-form vase by Poole Pottery (c.1958).

CONTENTS

BRITAIN

Throughout the 20th century the British ceramics industry mirrored public taste. The early years saw an industry fixated by the word 'art'. Advertisements in magazines offered the public artistic pottery of every conceivable form and style, reflecting both the lasting impact of William Morris and the Arts and Crafts Movement, and the excitement generated by a new enthusiasm for European Art Nouveau. At the same time potters responded to the contemporary fashion for the 18th century and the Adam revival, the continued interest in orientalism and the taste for French styles. World War I brought dramatic changes, notably the sudden removal from the British market of cheap, popular ware imported in huge quantities from Germany. British manufacturers were quick to fill the gap.

An influx of new wealth and new tastes marked the 1920s. Most of the popular styles in ceramics came from France and the USA as potters struggled with the colourful, decorative modernism of the Jazz Age. Other styles of the time included Egyptian and a new exotic orientalism with the emphasis on bright glazes and lustre finishes. There was also a strong element of fantasy and escapism, underlined by the success of products such as Wedgwood's Fairyland Lustre.

The 1930s witnessed the arrival of a style now known as Art Deco: cool, elegant, modern and with an emphasis on round, streamlined forms, pastel colours and matt glazes. The influence of the USA was again paramount. With the 1940s came a new challenge: British potters were compelled by government restrictions to make only undecorated ware for the home market, and therefore to explore for the first time on a grand scale the relationship between style, shape and function. The 1950s were a reaction to this style; ceramics were now full of colour, pattern and excitement, though marked with a clear hangover from the 1930s. Ideas were drawn from Scandinavia, Italy, the USA and the world of science, with textiles the principal source of pattern design, but there was an overriding determination to be contemporary and avoid historicism. The 1960s brought strong colours, tall shapes and a sense of confidence as British styles and attitudes briefly dominated the world.

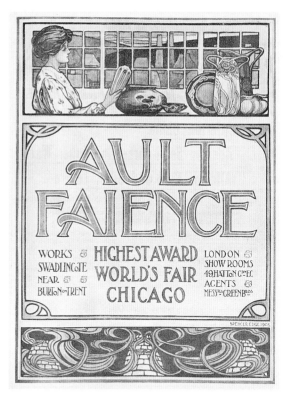

◆ Ault Faience advertisement, 1905
The impact of Art Nouveau was considerable during the early 1900s, affecting potters great and small. This stylish advertisement for the Ault potteries in Derbyshire was published in *The Pottery Gazette* in November 1905. It shows how potters wanted to associate themselves with avant-garde trends in both ceramics and graphics. It also reveals the importance of the international exhibition as a showcase for minor manufacturers. 1

◆ Lenox teapot, c.1906
Lenox's earliest tableware was made for wealthy customers who could afford to pay for the best hand gilding and painting. This pattern, which is typical of Lenox's earliest tableware, is rendered in raised gold paste and delicate hand painting. The pattern suits the shape superbly. 2

◆ **Wedgwood Fairyland Lustre, 1925**
Fairyland Lustre, designed by Daisy
Makeig-Jones, established a new look
for Wedgwood in the 1920s, and set
the fashion for decorative lustre ware
with exotic, fanciful and fairy themes.
Bright and cheerful, the vase reflects
the spirit of the Jazz Age. 3

☛ **Ruskin vase, c.1915**
Experimentation with shapes and
glazes was a feature of the early
years of the 20th century. One of
Britain's greatest experimental
potters was William Howson Taylor;
his Ruskin Pottery was renowned
for Orient-inspired high-temperature
flambé glaze effects. 4

This confidence evaporated in the 1970s and 1980s, and the result was
the introduction of softer colours, quieter patterns and a growing use of
florals to suggest a romanticism, albeit contrived. Design was increasingly
driven by retrovision, with the styles of the past seeming more attractive
than any commitment to the future. At the same time niche markets
expanded, as makers aimed products at new generations of collectors. A
more dynamic sense of design characterized the 1990s. The focus of
interest shifted away from the traditional large manufacturers towards
smaller, more flexible and more adventurous producers.

Useful though it is, a design-led history such as that outlined above
tells only half the story. It ignores the fact that many manufacturers had
little interest in modernism and were only half-hearted followers of style
trends. For every modern pattern produced there were large numbers
of traditional and conventional ones. Indeed, the century's best-selling
patterns have been wares such as Minton's Haddon Hall and Royal Albert's
Old Country Roses – not designs by Susie Cooper, Eric Ravilious or other
names revered by design historians and collectors.

Ultimately it is technology rather than design that forces changes in
style. In the ceramics industry in Britain and North America alike, the
most significant technological advance of the 20th century was the
replacement of the bottle oven, fired periodically with coal, by the tunnel
kiln, fired continuously with gas or electricity. This evolution made possible enormous improvements in consistency and quality control, along
with a hugely increased output. Product quality was radically improved by
advances in clay and glaze technology, which led to the introduction of
oven-to-table ware, and microwave-, freezer- and dishwasher-proof ware.
Also important was the application to domestic products of the great
advances in science and space technology.

Design was revolutionized not by style but by the wholesale adoption
of lithographic printing. Decoration by coloured lithography first
appeared in the late 19th century, and the printed transfers (known as
decals in North America), mostly made in Germany, were widely used to
decorate cheaper wares until World War I. The war closed German markets, and, with no alternative source of supply, British potters reverted to
conventional printing and hand-decorating techniques. In the 1920s and
the 1930s lithography was considered expensive, unreliable and of indif-
ferent quality, even though the results achieved by pioneers of the

process, such as Susie Cooper, tended to suggest otherwise. At the time there was, in any case, a fashionable preference for wares apparently decorated by hand. Lithographic decoration did not begin to dominate the industry until the 1950s, but since then its march has been inexorable, and through the second half of the century it became universal, thanks to its quality, reliability, speed of application and ability to imitate adequately all other decorative methods. Other printed processes also made an impact, notably silkscreen and various rubber-stamping techniques. Elsewhere in the industry, technology made little impact. Mechanization was applied where possible, but by its nature ceramics production remains a labour-intensive craft-based industry.

During the 20th century the most powerful force for change in the industry was marketing. In crude terms, potters exist only to sell their wares, and their ability to achieve sales is dependent upon market forces. In short, the potteries that have survived in a healthy state into the 21st century are those that are able to recognize and respond most rapidly to market shifts and social changes.

For much of the 20th century the British ceramics industry depended upon its export markets. The old colonial markets remained strong, in many cases outliving the British Empire itself, and the USA was for decades a huge market. As a result, the fortunes of British potters have long been linked directly to events in the USA. For example, the Wall Street Crash and the Depression imposed trading difficulties and bankruptcy upon British potters. By contrast, World War II and its aftermath brought success, thanks to the national drive for exports and the need to earn foreign currency. The stability that this produced continued through the 1960s and into the 1970s, but then the global oil crisis again severely damaged the US market. The last decades of the century witnessed a steady decline in Britain's ceramics industry, as a result of increasingly effective competition in traditional markets from Japanese and other Asian manufacturers. This drove some major manufacturers to set up production plants in Indonesia and other Far Eastern centres that offered the irresistible combination of cheap labour and good-quality products.

The traditional British response to competition is the merger. Potters have always joined forces with their rivals, but in the second half of the 20th century this strategy grew beyond recognition as major, and often incompatible, companies came together, in many instances under the umbrella of some large industrial conglomerate. Increasingly, the industry was controlled by organizations that knew little about making pottery. By the 1970s three large groups had emerged and seemed likely to dominate the field: Wedgwood, Royal Doulton and Royal Worcester/Spode. But after that the composition of the industry changed again, thanks to two decades of frenetic mergers, regroupings, closures and management buyouts. Today the traditional big names face increasing pressure from imported products, falling export business and unpredictable markets. They are also under attack by smaller and more dynamic companies whose products can more quickly adjust to the demands of a volatile, fashion-conscious and increasingly niche-based market.

➤ **Moorcroft pottery, c.1930**
While retaining the traditional slip-trailing technique, William Moorcroft developed designs in the 1920s and 1930s that were adventurous in both style and colour. [5]

➤ **Keith Murray vase, c.1932**
The New Zealand architect Keith Murray was one of a number of outside designers employed by Wedgwood in the 1930s to create a new look in tune with contemporary styles. [6]

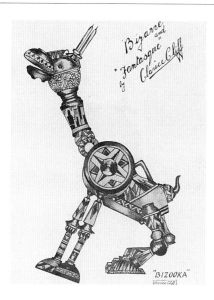

NORTH AMERICA

In the USA at the beginning of the 20th century potteries were making a
hodgepodge of wares for large and small markets. Aesthetically speaking,
the art potteries that began tentatively in the early 1880s had blossomed
through the 1890s. By 1900 potteries such as Rookwood, Weller and
Roseville, all in Ohio, were employing large numbers of painters to decorate earthenware vases and speciality items in underglaze slip for the gift
market. Art porcelain was also making news. Two large ironstone factories
in Trenton, New Jersey, the Etruria Pottery and the Willets Manufacturing
Company, had set the standard for Belleek-type ware in America in the
1880s with a few artists working from small studios. Walter Scott Lenox
and Jonathan Coxon took a chance that art porcelain alone would sustain
a pottery when they opened the Ceramic Art Company in 1889.

However, for the most part US potteries concentrated on mid-range
tableware and sanitary goods for the consumer market and sturdy utilitarian pottery. Consumers sought out inexpensive but stylish wares in china
shops and department stores. Manufacturers of general wares responded
by making serviceable white earthenware (called semi-porcelain or semi-
vitreous) dinner and toilet sets with Limoges-type decorations, while utilitarian potteries made stoneware jugs and jars, red clay flower pots and
large quantities of drainage pipes.

By the end of World War I French porcelain was hardly in the market;
British china began to reclaim its previously held lion's share, and Lenox
tableware had been ordered for service in the White House by President
Woodrow Wilson. Most US consumers were still shopping for good decal-
decorated white earthenware, hoping to find goods that would not craze in
use. Factories making fully vitreous china were, for the most part, supplying the institutional rather than the home market.

Because British imports dominated the Canadian market, domestic
potteries, such as those in Medicine Hat, Alberta, concentrated on filling
the most utilitarian requirements for ceramics. Only occasionally did they
aspire to produce commercial artware such as that made by the Ecanada
Art Pottery, of Hamilton, Ontario.

During the early years of the 20th century, US art potteries such as Hampshire, Roseville and Peters & Reed proliferated as consumers moved away from ornamental ware of highly decorated porcelain in favour of earthenware vessels with art glazes. About 1930 a relaxed attitude towards interior decoration was translated into dinnerware made to suit a more casual lifestyle. The first colourful crockery tableware was made for Californian buyers by the J. A. Bauer Pottery in 1930, but the taste for bright colours and simple, informal shapes quickly spread eastwards. Homer Laughlin's designer Fred Rhead put solid primary colours on his Century shape to make Riviera, in 1931, and brought his famous Fiesta to the national market in 1936. This early casual style set the stage for designers such as Russel Wright, whose fluid American Modern pattern (1939-59) was said to be the most popular dinnerware ever made.

Special decorative kitchen items also became an important part of the US potter's repertoire. As fewer servants were employed, kitchens were redesigned and the use of labour-saving appliances grew. Accessories that harmonized with these surroundings were essential, and potteries were kept busy producing bowls, baking dishes, pitchers, teapots, cookie jars, refrigerator jugs and the like. Much of this stylish earthenware was sold through mass-market department and variety stores, as well as mail-order catalogues such as those of Sears, Woolworths, Kresge's and McCrory's. The buyers for these chains had a huge impact on what was made in the burgeoning Ohio potteries. In addition, they worked directly with decal makers to develop colours and styles for patterns that suited the market.

Designers also became important in successful pottery operations during the first half of the 20th century. Previously most ceramic design was conceived by pottery owners, modellers and decorators, but after 1900 professional designers such as Frank Holmes at Lenox, Frederick H. Rhead at Homer Laughlin and Viktor Schreckengost at Salem surveyed the market for consumers' needs and desires and translated them into new products.

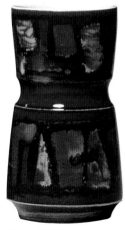

◆ Poole Delphis vase, 1970s
With its bright colours and individual hand-crafted designs, the Poole Pottery's Delphis range captured the spirit of the 1960s. First produced in the early 1960s, this cheerful pottery remained in production until the mid-1970s. Cheap at the time, it is now keenly collected. 11

◆ Bridgewater Black Cat plate, 1998
Set up in 1985 by Emma Bridgewater and Matthew Rice, the company brought a new look and approach to ceramics in Staffordshire, making popular again in a modern idiom traditional techniques such as sponging and stencilling. 12

◗ Beswick animals, 1993
Famous since the 1930s for its animal models, Beswick, now part of the Royal Doulton group, has continued to concentrate on this popular area of production. The Pig Promenade is a typical modern range and was introduced in 1993. 13

Designs in every historical and modern style could be found in china shops and department stores during this period. The work of companies such as Lenox tended to be more conservative. Some British china factories were mimicking this pottery's patterns by the 1920s, and there were certainly many US companies that made similar patterns in opaque wares. At the same time US dinnerware design could be very modern; even Lenox made some colourful Art Deco patterns during the 1920s. However, most of the radical shapes and patterns of the period can be seen in earthenware or stoneware rather than fine china. Examples include Frank Irwin's Mobile (1950s) for Metlox Potteries, Russel Wright's American Modern (1939) for the Steubenville Pottery and Eva Zeisel's Town and Country (1947) for Red Wing Potteries. Freelance designers also contributed greatly to potteries whose output was in transition from utilitarian goods to tableware, and among them were Belle Kogan at Red Wing Potteries, Ben Seibel at Pfaltzgraff and Eva Zeisel at both the Western Stoneware Company and the Hall China Company.

Before World War II coal-fired bottle kilns were gradually replaced by gas-fired tunnel kilns. While most clay-handling techniques did not change greatly in North American factories during the first half of the century, many of the materials did. Chemists strove to create vitreous bodies, with glazes to suit them, so that crazing virtually disappeared. The early 1940s were critical for US potteries because fuel and materials were rationed during World War II, and many of the factories that survived these years were quick to develop products to support the war effort. After the war, increased competition from potteries in the Far East forced North American factories to adopt new clay-handling techniques in order to survive. Mechanized systems eventually replaced much of the workforce.

Post-war Far Eastern competition in the domestic tableware market also greatly affected the types of clay product made in the USA. Several potteries stopped making consumer goods in favour of institutional china, while others simply closed. Similar pressures have grown in the institutional china market in recent years as trade with China has begun. Chinese potters are able to supply hotel and restaurant ware at extremely low cost. Several of the large US producers of these goods, for example Mayer and Shenango, have closed in recent years. Competition in the fine-china market has been equally fierce, involving Britain and other European countries as well as Japan.

WILLIAM ADAMS & SONS

From the late 18th century, Adams was renowned for quality earthenware, blue-and-white ware, ironstone, basalts, stoneware, jaspers and parian. In the 20th century the firm has been known mainly for toilet ware and tableware, often with printed patterns. From early in the century regular features have been historical subjects and the reissue of earlier designs; an example is the Cries of London series. Also typical was ware decorated with printed scenes and lustre in the style of traditional Sunderland pottery, made until at least the 1960s. Similar are prints of ships, compasses, mottoes and rural scenes, and Victorian-style monochrome prints used on children's ware.

Adams introduced hand-painted tableware in the 1920s. Notable are the modern versions of traditional 19th-century painted and sponged cottage ware: fruit and flowers boldly and simply applied on cream or coloured grounds. Also hand-painted was the Titian Ware range, made until the 1960s. Perennially popular are traditional patterns, usually hand-enamelled over prints, and the best known of these is Calyx Ware. At this time the main products were blue printed ware, colourful enamelled ware, semi-porcelain and utility ware, along with plain tableware with moulded borders, typical of the 1930s; these were made until the 1970s. During the 1940s the firm concentrated on exports.

In 1966 Wedgwood (see p.230) took over Adams, which continued to blend the modern with the traditional. Wedgwood designers helped it to develop new styles and ranges, such as the modernist Greensleeves pattern on the Wayfarer shape, Toys children's ware and Castella tableware.

◆ **Shakespearian scenes, 1913**
This selection of pieces is from an earthenware range decorated with finely engraved scenes from plays by Shakespeare, a popular subject with a number of manufacturers during the early years of the 20th century. This range, with 11 subjects, was advertised in *The Pottery Gazette* in April 1913. 14

🖌 **Lancaster tableware, 1990s**
Traditional shapes and decorative styles have always been part of the Adams range. 15

◆ **Calyx Ware, 1946**
Oriental designs in hand-enamelled colours on a greenish porcelain glaze are the distinguishing characteristics of Calyx Ware, a very popular and long-lived Adams pattern, shown here in a *Pottery Gazette* advertisement of December 1946. 16

KEY FACTS

Location: Tunstall and Stoke, Staffordshire, UK.
Important dates: Founded 1769. Joined Wedgwood Group 1966. Now closed.
Production: Earthenware tableware, toilet ware and children's ware.

MARKS

Many Adams marks incorporate crown and date '1657' (William Adams inherited a much older pottery). Most 20th-century marks printed, sometimes with pattern name or type of ware. Impressed marks generally found on jasper ware.

ADAMS
ESTᴰ 1657
ENGLAND

ADDERLEY

The firm of Adderley, which succeeded Hulse & Adderley (1869–75) and William Alsager Adderley & Co. (1876–1905) at the Daisy Bank Pottery in 1906, manufactured bone-china tableware and floral ornaments, along with durable hotel and restaurant ware made under the brand name Steelite China. A conventional Staffordshire maker of bone-china tableware for the general market, Adderley produced a wide range of wares, most of which were printed, in standard designs. The firm also made children's ware, notably the Zoo Alphabet pattern of 1939. During World War II production ceased under the Concentration Scheme but restarted immediately the factory was released from Government control.

Adderley is probably best known for its floral novelty items, made under the Royal Adderley and Floral China names at a separate factory, in Sutherland Road, Longton. China flowers were used originally to decorate ornamental pottery made at Bow, Chelsea and Derby, and by other 18th-century porcelain manufacturers, and it was not until soon after World War I that Staffordshire potteries such as Adderley began to make florals as ornaments.

The pottery's output included trinkets, fancies and jewellery decorated with hand-modelled and hand-painted flower sprays in naturalistic forms. Particularly popular are its floral shoes. Among other Adderley products are bone-china figurines, animals, wine labels and presentation ware.

◆ Drink labels, 1970s
With their floral sprays, these labels for alcoholic drinks are typical of the printed novelties made by the pottery from the 1960s. The inspiration came from pottery and silver decanter labels made in the early 19th century. 17

◆ Flower sprays, from 1972
Adderley has always been best known for the elaborate ranges of hand-modelled florals, as popular today as in the 1930s and 1950s. Flowering, the modelling of these sprays, is a traditional Staffordshire process. 18

KEY FACTS

Location: Daisy Bank Pottery, later renamed Gainsborough Works, Longton, Staffordshire, UK.
Important dates: Founded 1906. Joined Ridgway Potteries 1947. Later owned by Lawley Group. From 1964 part of Allied English Potteries and later of Royal Doulton Group. Now closed.
Production: China and earthenware.

MARKS

This printed mark used in 1970s. 'Adderley' or 'Adderleys' usually incorporated in backstamp.

HENRY ALCOCK POTTERY

The pottery was based at the Elder Pottery, Cobridge, from 1861 and Clarence Works, Stoke, Staffordshire, from 1910 to 1935. The products ranged from ordinary domestic wares to toilet wares and fancies to rich cloisonné decoration on coloured grounds. In the early 1920s the firm reintroduced the multicoloured Pratt prints of the 1840s after the original engravings were discovered at the historic Pratt works at Fenton.

MARKS
Printed mark showing company name, armorial shield and 'semi-porcelain'.

CHARLES ALLERTON & SONS

This pottery, specializing in tableware in china and earthenware, was in production from 1859 to 1942 in Longton, Staffordshire. It also made children's china, notably the Noah's Ark pattern of 1926. The company was taken over in 1912 by Cauldon Potteries Ltd (*see* p.40), and later became part of the George Jones Crescent Potteries Group (*see* p.100), when it was renamed Allertons Ltd.

MARKS
Printed marks often include crown and firm's claimed founding date, 1831.

ALLER VALE ART POTTERY

This pottery used local clays to produce terracotta and slip-decorated ware. After merging with the Watcombe Terracotta Company around 1900 it developed a series of individual shapes and a few principal styles of decoration, giving the ware a distinctive character. Typical of this period is Crocus pattern. The Watcombe Pottery Co. was established by the earlier Watcombe firm around 1875 as a terracotta works producing classical forms, including finely modelled figures and some contemporary subjects, and painted plaques. By 1904 the merged companies, based in Newton Abbot, Devon, were advertising a wide range of decorated, grotesque and mottoed ware, high-class artware, richly coloured and glazed; teasets, pots and pedestals, vases and flower pots, many of them aimed at the burgeoning tourist trade.

By 1934 the Royal Aller Vale and Watcombe Art Pottery was advertising its 'new speciality, Mosaic Ware, a lovely light blue ground with bright interlay decorations ...; Original Alexandra Rose Ware; plain coloured ware – blue, green, tangerine; and Decorated Ware: Kingfisher, Marine, Mosaic Ware, Pitcher Ware, Coloured Tops and a large variety of Other Decorations'. Until its closure in 1962, the pottery in Torquay continued to make distinctive slipware for the tourist market.

ORIGINAL DEVON MOTTO WARE

◆ Devon motto ware, 1952
Motto ware has long been the most characteristic production of the Devon potteries, and its popularity with visitors has endured since the late 19th century. [19]

◗ Aller Vale vase, c.1910
The traditional technique of slipware decoration, associated with the West Country since at least the 17th century, was exploited in more modern styles at Aller Vale, such as in this Art Nouveau-inspired vase. [20]

KEY FACTS

Location: Newton Abbot and Torquay, Devon, UK.
Important dates: Founded c.1887. Closed 1962.
Production: Redware, ornaments, artware and motto ware.

MARKS

Mark used c.1958–62. 'Royal Aller Vale', printed or impressed in capitals, also used from c.1901.

ROYAL WATCOMBE TORQUAY ENGLAND

ARKINSTALL & SONS

The firm was founded by Harold Taylor Robinson, primarily to make souvenir and crested china in the Goss (*see* p.77) style. It seems to have been taken over around 1906 by his old firm, Wiltshaw & Robinson, and Robinson became a partner. From as early as 1903 he had begun to acquire other china and earthenware firms, and he merged Robinson & Leadbeater with Arkinstall around 1908. In 1910 he formed a new company which operated as J. A. Robinson (*see* p.178). Arkinstall itself was later taken over by J. A. Robinson.

In 1920 Robinson bought Cauldon (*see* p.40) and under the trade name Cauldon Ltd began to amalgamate most of the firms he owned or in which he had a controlling interest. Cauldon Potteries was advertising Arkinstall products until at least 1921 but had probably disappeared by 1925.

KEY FACTS

Location: Trent Bridge Pottery, later at Arcadian Works, Stoke, Staffordshire, UK.
Important dates: Founded c.1903. Closed 1925.
Production: China fancies.

MARKS

Printed marks usually include Arcadian China trade name.

◗ Souvenir badged ware, c.1920
Many potters produced badged ware during the early part of the 20th century, making the most of the expanding holiday trade. Such novelties are popular with collectors today. [21]

ASHBY POTTERS' GUILD

The Victoria Pottery in Woodville was originally a typical Victorian Derbyshire manufacturer of stone bottles and domestic ware. The making of decorative pottery there by the Ashby Potters' Guild, which took its name from the nearby town of Ashby-de-la-Zouche, was inspired by enthusiasm for the Arts and Crafts Movement and the Guild revival.

Production started in 1909 with a range of shapes designed by Thomas Camm, with coloured glazes developed by Pascoe Tunnicliffe. Marketed under the name Vasco Ware, the pottery was widely exhibited, winning gold medals at Brussels in 1910 and Turin and Ghent in 1911. Glazes, often orientally inspired, included deep blues and greens, the Goldstone aventurine, and, from 1913, flambé effects. In addition to vases, the pottery made bowls, jars, biscuit barrels, tobacco ware, cake stands, ink-wells, candlesticks and altar ware. The production of separate Ashby ware ceased after the merger with the Ault Faience Pottery in 1922.

KEY FACTS

Location: Victoria Pottery, Woodville, Derbyshire, UK.
Important dates: Founded 1909. Merged with Ault Faience Pottery and production ceased 1922.
Production: Earthenware, artware.

MARKS

Usually impressed and including 'Ashby Guild'.

◆ **Vase, c.1912**
The Art Pottery movement was very successful from the 1870s , with distinctive potteries in all parts of Britain. In Derbyshire the Ashby Potters' Guild produced ware with typical oriental shapes and rich, experimental glazes. 22

ASHTEAD POTTERS

Ashtead Potters gave employment and support to disabled ex-servicemen and their dependants. Its characteristic style blended Arts and Crafts and Art Deco influences in a soft earthenware body hand-painted in a wide range of colours. The pottery's first success was at the Wembley Exhibition in 1924, and in its short life it produced over 300 catalogued items, all available with a wide range of decorative finishes. As well as tableware shapes, there were vases, tankards, covered boxes, lamp bases, candlesticks, jam and mustard pots, ashtrays, ink-wells, condiment sets, bulb bowls and toilet ware. Notable were the wide range of modelled ware, which included animals and birds, figures, plaques and character jugs. The sculptor and medallist Percy Metcalfe created at least 15 models, while some of the best modelled figures were after Phoebe Stabler's designs. Ashtead also made nursery ware, notably the Christopher Robin service from 1928, and much commemorative and advertising ware.

KEY FACTS

Location: Victoria Works, Ashtead, Surrey, UK.
Important dates: Founded 1923. Closed 1935.
Production: Earthenware ornaments, figures and domestic ware.
Principal designers: Percy Metcalfe, Phoebe Stabler, William Reid Dick, Joan Pyman, Donald Gilbert, Allan Wyon.

MARKS

Usually printed and incorporating a stylized tree.

◆ **Ashtead ware, 1920s and 1930s**
Although short-lived, Ashtead Potters produced an extensive range of domestic pottery, ornaments and figures, many of which featured the characteristic coloured glazes seen on these pieces. 23

G. L. ASHWORTH & BROTHERS

Formerly Francis Morley & Co. and then Morley & Ashworth, G. L. Ashworth & Brothers was a large 19th-century manufacturer of conventionally decorated tableware, whose designs showed a strong dependence on oriental styles. In the era of Francis Morley & Co. the firm had acquired the famous Mason's Ironstone name, and throughout the latter part of the 19th century and into the 20th century it constantly experimented to improve the ironstone body. Its efforts were rewarded with numerous awards at national and international exhibitions. In the 1920s the company successfully revived Mason's original amber glaze and introduced a series of shapes based on early-19th-century originals, commencing with Romney and including Milburn, Mason's Gadroon and Oak. Throughout its history the company has made extensive use of Mason-style designs and shapes and the Mason name. This pattern has continued to the present day, to the extent that the Ashworth name completely disappeared in 1968, when the firm became Mason's Ironstone China Ltd.

Although the oriental style has had an enduring appeal, Ashworth products were essentially functional rather than collectable. The firm was a leading manufacturer of butchers' and dairymen's sundries, hospital ware and scale plates, in addition to making kitchenware and tableware, jugs and mugs. Exceptions were the multicoloured lustre-decorated Lustrosa range of artware, produced briefly during the first decade of the 20th century, and, perhaps, the Circusland nursery ware of the 1950s, originally designed for export. Today the pottery, which joined the Wedgwood (*see* p.230) Group in 1973, makes an extensive range of ornaments and novelties in modern and traditional styles, including the Mason-type oriental patterns. At various times it has also made series of decorative collectors' plates.

▲ **Mason's Masterpiece plate, 1990**
First produced in 1990 in a limited edition, this finely made piece draws its inspiration from the oriental styles of the Regency period. 24

▲ **Magnolia tableware, 1990s**
This traditional Imari-style pattern on the Bedford shape links modern Mason production with the decorative styles of the early 19th century, and shows the lasting popularity of such ware. 25

◆ **Pink and blue Vista tableware, 1990s**
Traditional-style printed tableware has always been popular, and modern demand is reflected in this current Mason's pattern on the Gadroon shape. 26

KEY FACTS

Location: Hanley, Staffordshire, UK.
Important dates: Founded 1862. (Formerly, from about 1858, Francis Morley & Co. and then Morley & Ashworth.) Renamed Mason's Ironstone China Ltd 1968. Became part of Wedgwood Group 1973. Pottery closed, production moved to Wedgwood's Barlaston factory.
Production: Earthenware and ironstone tableware and ornaments.
Trade names: Ashworths, Mason's, Leeds, Patent Ironstone, Lustrosa.

MARKS

Versions of this mark, or Mason's mark, incorporating 'Mason's' above crown and 'Patent Ironstone China' in cartouche, used until 1960s, when Ashworth name dropped.

AULT FAIENCE/AULT POTTERIES

In 1887 William Ault began producing ware inspired by the Arts and Crafts Movement, in particular by the work of Christopher Dresser. Vases, plant pots, pedestals, plaques and teasets decorated with rich glazes established the pottery's reputation, helped by displays at the Chicago World's Fair of 1896 and elsewhere. In the early 20th century grotesques and novelties dominated production, along with an ever-increasing range of dramatic and often orientally inspired glazes. Production of artware continued for a while after Ault retired in 1922, but in the 1930s the emphasis switched to domestic ware, including tableware, cookware, kitchenware and garden ware in more conventional shapes and colours. This pattern of production, in both stoneware and bone china, continued until the firm closed in 1974.

◆ **Ault vase, c.1910**
Art Nouveau styling and mottled glazes are typical of Ault artware produced during the early part of the 20th century. `27`

KEY FACTS

Location: Swadlincote, Derbyshire, UK.

Important dates: Founded 1887 as Ault Faience. Merged with Ashby Potters' Guild 1922. Reformed as Ault Potteries 1937. Joined Pearson Group 1962. Closed 1974.

Production: Earthenware artware, novelties and grotesques, kitchenware, tableware and toilet ware. Fireproof ware.

Principal designers: Christopher Dresser, Pascoe Tunnicliffe.

Trade names: Ault, Aultcliff, Mauresque Ware.

MARKS

Printed vase mark 1887–1923. After 1923 'Aultcliff' in script used.

AVON ART POTTERY

This company was a relatively large producer of decorative tableware, including salad ware, fruit sets, jugs, teapots, comports, sweet dishes and dessert trays and other ornamental ware and fancies in matt glaze, both self-coloured and variegated. Its velvet-glazed Avon Art Ware, advertised throughout the 1930s, was also made with painted and other handcraft decoration in vogue at that time. The epitome of popular design of the period, this sold well in Britain and in other parts of the world, including South Africa, Canada, Australia, South America and The Netherlands.

Avon's strong export market helped it in its efforts to remain in production under the Government's Concentration Scheme introduced during World War II. It was given the status of a nucleus factory, and Elektra (*see* p.63), which was making similar lines, transferred its production to the Avon works for the rest of the war. Each company continued to trade under its own name. In 1946 the Avon catalogue included animal jugs, vases, bulb bowls, flower pots, garden pottery, novelties and ornamental teapots and bowls.

➡ **Avon Ware advertisement, 1938**
By the late 1930s Art Deco styles with their geometrical shapes, which were at their peak during this decade, had become universal in the pottery industry, even among the smaller companies. `28`

KEY FACTS

Location: Jubilee Works, Edensor, Longton, Staffordshire, UK.
Important dates: Founded 1930. Closed mid-1960s.
Production: Earthenware ornaments, fancies and tableware.

MARKS

Usually printed; this example used 1939–47. Round version, with lighter lettering, used 1930s. After 1947 oval mark introduced. Both include Avon Ware name.

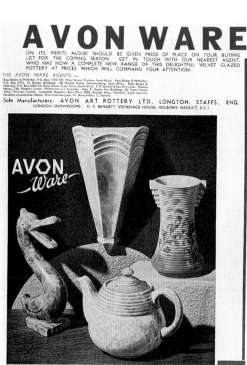

H. AYNSLEY & CO.

The firm produced ordinary domestic earthenware, including kitchen and chamber ware, tableware, fancies and ornaments, as well as hotel ware and printed and decorated toy teasets displayed in boxes. It also supplied the Admiralty, War Office, Indian Government and leading steamship companies. From the 1940s it introduced new ranges reflecting contemporary trends, such as Vogue Moderne from the mid-1950s, and various patterns with a studio handcraft look, promoted in the late 1960s.

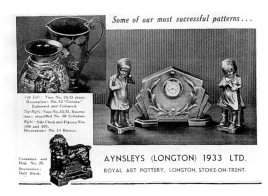

◆ **Advertisement, 1934**
Published in *The Pottery Gazette*, this advertisement shows how smaller potteries depended for their survival on both traditional and modern styles. 29

JOHN AYNSLEY & SONS

The first pottery operating under the Aynsley name was opened in 1775, but three generations later it was John Aynsley who founded the present company, which remained a family business until 1970, when it was acquired by Waterford Crystal. Concentrating at first on bone-china tableware, the firm gained a reputation for quality and traditional design that was maintained into the 20th century. Finely painted ornamental ware in traditional French-inspired styles, by artists such as R. J. Keeling and Micklewright, expanded the range. Pierced dessert ware, crested dinner services and children's ware, often decorated with patterns inspired by nursery rhymes, have been a major part of Aynsley's output. Also important were commemoratives, particularly after 1911, when the firm made items for the Coronation of King George V and Queen Mary.

In more recent times the Aynsley name has become synonymous with finely decorated ware in traditional styles, presentation and sporting trophies, including those made for the Grand National horse race, commemorative ware, hand-painted figures, florals and animal models, the best of which were known as the Aynsley Animal Kingdom. Other ranges have included oven-to-table ware.

▲ **Art Deco teaware, 1930s**
Well-made and stylish tableware, including this modernist pattern from the 1930s, has long been the Aynsley hallmark. 30

▼ **Diana, Princess of Wales, plate, 1998**
Aynsley was not alone in making limited editions to commemorate the life of Diana, Princess of Wales. 31

BARKER BROS

Originally, Barker Bros was a manufacturer of advertising ware and a full range of 'medium class' domestic goods, including chamber pots in earthenware or cream-coloured, kitchenware such as milk and pudding bowls, basins, bakers and blancmange moulds, dinnerware, trinkets and fancies, nursery china and dainty afternoon-tea services. The company offered the full range of standard decorations, including 'Derby' and chintz patterns. Trade names included Tudor and Tudor Royal.

In 1919 Barker Bros launched Teddy Tail nursery china by arrangement with Charles Folkhard, the originator of the *Daily Mail* comic-strip character. The following year, at the British Industries Fair, it launched a range of fancies with a striking kaleidoscopic underglaze decoration. The company was granted nucleus status in 1941 through concentration with its own firm, Sampson Smith (*see* p.207). Post-war designs include Popeye nursery ware, advertised shortly after the company was taken over by Alfred Clough in 1959, and modern-shape tableware such as Mayfair, introduced in the mid-1960s and marketed in a choice of patterns. By the 1970s Barker Bros' main output was reduced to domestic tableware in ironstone.

◆ **Teddy Tail nursery ware, 1919**
Launched in 1919, the Teddy Tail range is probably Barker's most collectable product. 32

BARKERS & KENT

At the Foley Pottery the firm made full ranges of basic earthenware for the kitchen and the hospital, in addition to teaware and fancies. In the early 1930s it launched an innovatory 15-piece set for salad and cream or fruit and cream with salad servers and deep plates with recessed rims to hold individual cream jugs. At least one early printed pattern, School, was reworked and reissued by Adams (*see* p.12) in the 1960s.

BARLOWS (LONGTON)

Under the trade name Melbar Ware, this firm manufactured ordinary domestic earthenware and late-Victorian-style ornamental ware, including vases, jardinières and stands.

During World War II the pottery's production was concentrated with that of Crown Staffordshire under the Board of Trade's scheme. Since Barlows did not propose to make earthenware, this arrangement put it out of business from the early 1940s until the end of the war. Despite reassuring its customers that its plant was intact and ready to recommence production, the company never really recovered from the period of enforced inactivity.

◆ **Rose jardinière, 1920s**
This decorated jardinière, made during the 1920s, is typical of Barlows' rather conventional approach to design. 33

BARRATT'S OF STAFFORDSHIRE

The Royal Overhouse Pottery is one of Burslem's oldest, having belonged for more than two centuries to Wedgwood (*see* p.230). Throughout its history there Barratt's has specialized in kitchen and domestic earthenware for the popular market, along with a limited amount of ornamental and nursery ware. Typical designs include Oriental Vase tableware, featured on the cover of *The Pottery Gazette* in December 1946, and Rupert Ware, introduced in 1972. More recently the firm has helped to establish the mug as an essential Staffordshire product.

◆ Lincoln tableware, late 1980s
Introduced in 1988 and still in production, this range is based on a set of late Victorian moulds; some pieces, such as the coffee pot, reproduce the original shape exactly. 34

KEY FACTS
Location: Royal Overhouse Pottery, Burslem, Staffordshire, UK.
Important dates: Founded c.1943. Sold 1987. Merged with Royal Stafford China 1994 and now trading as Royal Stafford Tableware.
Production: Earthenware.

CORONA

J. A. BAUER POTTERY COMPANY

From 1909 the company made utilitarian earthenware and stoneware, including jugs, jars, kitchen crockery and flower pots. By 1916 the modeller and turner Louis Ipsen had joined the pottery and probably contributed greatly to the development of an art-pottery line that won a bronze medal at the Panama-California International Exposition in San Diego in 1916. In 1919 the factory was enlarged to four kilns.

Victor Houser was hired in 1929 as a ceramic engineer to improve the firm's colour formulas and glaze quality. By 1930 his new colours and the decision to experiment with tableware resulted in America's first brightly coloured casual dinnerware. Bauer lines popular today include Ring (about 1931), Monterey (1936–45), probably designed by Ipsen, and La Linda (1939–59). Bauer's ollas (oil jars) are extremely desirable.

KEY FACTS
Location: Los Angeles, California, USA.
Important dates: Founded 1909. Closed 1962.
Production: Utilitarian stoneware, florists' crockery, dinnerware, ollas.

MARKS
Impressed variations of 'Bauer, Los Angeles, USA'.

BAUER MADE IN USA LOS ANGELES

◆ Ring group, c.1931
Bauer's Ring, simply designed and brightly coloured, set the style for casual dinnerware in the American market for the next decade. Colours included black, burgundy, orange-red, chartreuse, Chinese yellow, dark and light blue, grey, ivory, jade green, light brown, olive green, red-brown, turquoise and white. 35

FRANK BEARDMORE

From 1903 to 1914, at the Sutherland Pottery in Fenton, Staffordshire, this firm made stylish and well-designed tableware and toilet ware in earthenware. It drew inspiration from traditional and contemporary sources, including Art Nouveau. After it closed, many of its best-selling shapes and patterns were eagerly sought by rivals such as A. J. Wilkinson (*see* p.239), British Anchor Pottery (*see* p.33) and Swinnertons (*see* p.214).

MARKS
Either impressed 'F.B. & CO.' or this printed circular mark with name in full.

J. & M. P. BELL & CO.

In the 19th century Bell's Glasgow Pottery was one of Britain's greatest manufacturers of tableware, particularly spongeware and blue-printed ware for export markets. Bell excelled in the production of fine bone china with decal and other printed patterns. One of its best-known blue-and-white printed patterns was the Warwick Vase pattern, registered in 1850 and again in 1890. Inspiration for this pattern came from the vase itself, which now forms part of the Burrell Collection in Glasgow. By the 20th century the pottery was already in decline, and it made little after World War I. Production until that time included tableware, toilet ware and hotel ware and a limited range of ornamental goods made in traditional styles. Transfer printing and sponging were still carried out.

KEY FACTS

Location: Glasgow Pottery, Dobbies Loan, Glasgow, UK.
Important dates: Founded 1842. Closed c.1928.
Production: China, earthenware.

MARKS

Printed or impressed and usually incorporating bell.

◆ **Gouda tureen, before 1912**
Made during the Edwardian period, this blue-and-white tureen has echoes of both Dutch Delft and French faience, which were fashionable styles at the time. 36

BELLEEK POTTERY

The pottery traded from 1863 as D. McBirney & Co., noted for its fine-quality, cream-coloured porcelain body with an iridescent glaze that was developed with the assistance of William Bromley, a Staffordshire potter, and others who also moved from the W. H. Goss (see p.77) factory, where they made similar porcelain paste. Bromley travelled to America in 1883, joining first John Hart Brewer and then Willets Manufacturing Co. to supervise the development of American Belleek Ware. The reputation enjoyed by Belleek for highly decorative and finely made ornamental parian and porcelain, which was established in the 19th century by displays at international exhibitions and by support from Queen Victoria and other members of the Royal family, was continued into the 20th century.

The characteristic Belleek product, extravagantly modelled, inspired by natural and marine forms, and featuring basketwork, delicate piercing and the use of eggshell-thin clays with lustrous glazes and gilding, is still made, thanks in part to the pottery's great success in export markets. As recently as 1980, 85 per cent of its production was exported.

Belleek's emphasis on craftsmanship, delicacy of design and manufacture, as well as the pottery's continued use of traditional shapes, has ensured the perennial popularity of its products. Alongside traditional designs such as Shamrock, Killarney and Limpet, the company has produced highly elaborate limited-edition models for the collector. Until 1946 it also made a more basic range of earthenware, including tableware, domestic ware and toilet ware.

◆ **Neptune teapot, c.1910**
Maritime motifs have always been popular with Belleek. The shell and coral forms of this teapot are emphasized by the lustre finish. The teapot was made in three sizes, and with green or pink colouring. 37

KEY FACTS

Location: Belleek Pottery, County Fermanagh, Northern Ireland, UK.
Important dates: Founded 1863. Still active.
Production: Ornamental parian and porcelain, domestic earthenware.

MARKS

Variations of this mark, either printed or impressed, used since the early 1860s.

◆ **Shamrock trefoil basket, c.1900**
Baskets are one of the most famous Belleek forms. From the 1860s the pottery produced them in at least six versions, to designs by William Henshall. 38

BENNINGTON POTTERS

David Gil started the Bennington Potters in 1948, choosing for its site a Vermont town already renowned for its distinctive pottery. During the 19th century several significant local potteries had produced utilitarian stoneware and redware, as well as a wide variety of fancy domestic articles in the mottled Rockingham glaze that was popular in the second half of the century. The name of Bennington Potters is identified with this long tradition, which is traced by exhibits in the local museum.

Gil's designs, made in stoneware and terracotta, are classically modern, combining streamlined contemporary forms with colour and design references to historic ceramic types. His company of 25 craftsmen produces more than 250 shapes in consumer dinnerware, cookware and garden accessories, as well as custom work, including museum reproductions, artist's murals, commercial mugs and dinnerware. Gil has designed hundreds of shapes to satisfy modern tastes. His best-known design is perhaps the trigger mug, a cylindrical body with a handle of two circles stacked vertically that comfortably and securely admits two fingers. The handle has been widely copied.

↞ **Cookware, 1990s**
Contemporary styling and convenience combined with traditional decorative treatment are the hallmarks of David Gil's designs for Bennington. 39

JOHN BESWICK

James Wright Beswick started in business in 1894 with a five-year lease on the Baltimore Works in Albion Street, Longton, Staffordshire, manufacturing majolica, tableware in jet and Rockingham, toilet sets, gilt jugs, figures, flower pots and pedestals, comports and domestic ware such as spittoons. Before the end of the century he had two other factories, the Britannia Works in Longton High Street and the Gold Street Works. Illustrated brochures from this period show well-modelled figures, including Staffordshire flatback dogs, horses, cattle, generals and milkmaids, all competitively priced.

Beswick died in 1921, leaving the business in the control of his son, John, who brought the pottery into the 20th century, phasing out the elaborate and old-fashioned styles and replacing them with more modern cottage ware and embossed salad ware. Like most businesses, Beswick

♦ **Horses, 1950s and 1960s**
The typically diverse collection of horses shown here underlines Beswick's long-established reputation as a maker of high-quality animal models. 40

◆ Art Deco wall mask, 1930s
Inspired by French models, many British potteries produced decorative wall masks during the 1930s. Beswick examples are rare and very collectable today. 41

◆ Marmalade pot, 1930s
Beswick was always a remarkably diverse pottery, making a huge range of domestic and decorative goods. From the 1930s to the 1950s fruit ware was popular. 42

◆ Advertisement, 1934
This advertisement from *The Pottery Gazette* reflects Beswick's long involvement in the market for novelties and decorative domestic ware. Cottage ware, naturalistic salad ware, and vases and jugs in typical Art Deco styles are all Beswick pieces of the 1930s now sought by collectors. 43

experienced lean times after the Wall Street crash of 1929, but it soon recovered a strong market position. In the 1930s modern shapes and matt glazes reflected both contemporary tastes and the design skills of Jim Hayward, who, after being trained by Gordon Forsyth, became decorating manager in 1934. More than 50 young women, known as Beswick's Matt Glaze Girls, were employed to meet the demand for these new styles. Popular modernism became the defining style for Beswick, underlined by ranges such as Sundial Ware.

However, animal models remained an important part of the pottery's production, and in 1938 it launched Bois Russell, its first naturalistically modelled horse. This model was the work of Arthur Gredington, a graduate of the Royal College of Art. He joined the company in 1939, becoming the first resident sculptor and producing models of horses, foals, farm and wild animals, dogs, birds and figures. By the mid-1940s these items, together with novelties and ornaments such as wall masks and character jugs mostly made for export, became the mainstay of Beswick's production. From the 1950s the pottery employed many highly skilled modellers to create designs for model horses, and items such as a rearing Lipizzaner stallion and rider from the Spanish Riding School in Vienna remain very popular with collectors.

Modelling has always played an important part in Beswick's success, and authenticity in this respect has always been the pottery's aim when producing animal models. This is especially true of its fine horses, to produce which the modeller must know the subject intimately enough to be able to capture its bearing and proportions, whether it be a hunter, a work horse, an Arab thoroughbred or a moorland pony. Fidelity is achieved by observing all the horse's movements and translating these first into sculpture and then into the ceramic creation.

The original model, usually made in a relatively soft clay, is cut into its constituent parts, which often amount to several dozen pieces, and from these moulds are made. The ceramic casts are taken from the moulds and then assembled and given the first, or biscuit, firing. The biscuit-fired casting is then decorated before receiving its final glaze.

Of all Beswick's ranges, none has attracted such widespread admiration as the distinguished Connoisseur Series. These include racehorses such as Red Rum, made both with and without its famous jockey Brian Fletcher, Arkle and Grundy; typical horse studies such as Hunter, Thoroughbred and Arab; the Charolais Bull; wild creatures such as Tawny Puma and Golden Eagle; and champion dogs. The series has a growing appeal to collectors throughout the world.

Prominent among important artists and designers associated with Beswick are Albert Hallam, Eric Owen and, more recently, Colin Melbourne, a graduate of the Royal College of Art, and Harry Sales. Melbourne was responsible in the 1950s for the contemporary CM range, one of a number of Beswick's contributions to popular 1950s modernism.

Another successful line has been Beswick's Beatrix Potter characters, first produced about 1947 under licence from Frederick Warne & Co., the publisher of Potter's popular children's books. By 1966 the number of characters in this series had risen to more than 30. The firm has also produced animals based on characters in A. A. Milne's story of Winnie the Pooh. Another collaboration, beginning in 1975 and an immediate success, was with Kitty MacBride, a freelance potter. Her Happy Mice series, made exclusively for Beswick, contained one-off figures of mice in human situations, with titles such as 'I'll trim that hedge tomorrow'.

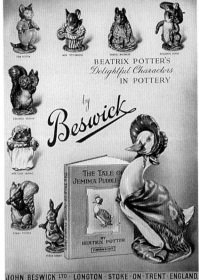

◤ Beatrix Potter animals 1960s, advertisement 1950
The best-loved Beswick product is the extensive range of Beatrix Potter models. 44

◆ Vases, mid-1950s
Flowing abstract shapes and dynamic fur-inspired patterns were typical of the 1950s. This ware, its shapes by Albert Hallam and the pattern by Jim Hayward, show Beswick leading popular taste. 45

KEY FACTS

Location: Longton, Staffordshire, UK.
Important dates: Founded 1894. Taken over by Royal Doulton Group 1969. Production ceased 2004.
Production: China and earthenware tableware, novelties, ornaments, animal models and figures.
Principal designers: Jim Hayward, Arthur Gredington, Albert Hallam, Eric Owen, Colin Melbourne, Harry Sales, Kitty MacBride.
Trade name: John Beswick, Beswick Ware. From 1969 some pieces marked 'Studio of Royal Doulton'.

MARKS

This script mark used from c.1936. Other backstamps, impressed or printed, round or oval, usually include company name in capitals.

Beswick Ware.
MADE IN ENGLAND

BILTONS

In its early years the company, known as Biltons Ltd from 1901 to 1912, was an earthenware manufacturer producing practically nothing but teapots. However, after World War I it diversified into ornaments, novelties, figures and fancies for the popular market. New ranges advertised in 1919 included well-modelled figures such as Pierrot and Pierrette, grotesques and flower holders, tubes, bulb bowls, fern pots, candlesticks and night-light holders, supplied in a large variety of self colours, including green, pink, heliotrope, yellow and tangerine, along with ecclesiastical ware and devotional statuettes.

Biltons was closed in 1941 under the Government Concentration Scheme, and after the war the company re-entered the market as a producer of mass-market tableware. Its advertisements of the 1960s show the influence of new decorating techniques, such as rubber-stamp machine printing and multicolour machine printing. During the mid-1960s and the 1970s Biltons advertised widely its new ranges of printed ware with either geometric or floral designs, along with Galaxy Two Tone tableware and cookware. In the 1980s the company introduced a new surface which made it possible to bring out new designs, including some in which the pattern is burnt into the body.

Fragrance tableware, 1997
In recent years Biltons has concentrated on tableware aimed at a popular market, with decorative floral patterns in soft colours. 46

Mug, 1990s
While operating as a major concern, Biltons has developed new techniques to give a handcraft look. 47

KEY FACTS

Location: London Road Factory, Stoke, Staffordshire, UK.
Important dates: Founded 1901. Bought by Coloroll, renamed Coloroll Biltons 1986. After management buyout 1990, new company, Staffordshire Tableware Ltd, formed with Staffordshire Potteries. Sold again 1995 and 1998 to Portmeirion Pottery.
Production: Domestic earthenware and fancies.

MARKS

Biltons' script mark introduced 1947. Later, square-shaped 'B' with 'Finewhite Tableware' used.

Biltons MADE IN ENGLAND

BIRKS, RAWLINS & CO.

The company was at its peak in the early 1920s, when its well-modelled and finely decorated ceramic novelties included small figures, naturalistic bird, animal and butterfly models, ornamental ware, bird centres for floating bowls, commemoratives and souvenir items. Miniature architectural models of cottages, town halls, cathedrals and colleges were an enormous success, encouraging the company to offer to execute models of any well-known building to order.

At the British Industries Fair in 1920, the firm showed ornamental tobacco jars, figure models, and, in its Grotesques range, Bairnsfather's immortal Ole Bill, Sunny Jim, Weary Willy, Artful Eliza, Saucy Sue, Peter Pan, Conchy, Blighty and C.3.

Bird models, 1920
Shown in an article in *The Pottery Gazette*, these well-finished models highlight an unfamiliar and therefore collectable aspect of Birks, Rawlins & Co.'s production. 48

KEY FACTS

Location: Vine Pottery, Stoke, Staffordshire, UK.
Important dates: Founded 1900. Closed 1933.
Production: China tableware and novelties.

n he was over
ssed with the
purposes was
the contrary,
almost every
ss was now to
ere the opinion
avour; indeed,
t had not yet
ass was one of
idly become a
which led the
g agencies of
ssware. It is
sorts of ways,
se. The idea
is being ex-
ise both to the
Co. and the
their require-
osed of almost
ers are coming
have had the
feature of the

[Photo. by "*The Pottery Gazette*."]
BIRKS, RAWLINS & CO., STOKE: SOME GOOD BIRD CENTRES FOR FLOATING BOWLS.

BISHOP & STONIER

In its early years this company, which used the trade name Bisto, specialized in high-quality tableware, including dinner, tea and dessert services, toilet and trinket sets, and a wide range of novelties and children's ware. Patterns often had an Eastern inspiration; examples are the range of Oriental Ivory Ware with printed and enamelled on-glaze decoration.

During World War I the pottery diversified and introduced more small fancies and ornaments for the popular market, including many new examples of children's ware and toy teasets which were widely advertised and sold by shops such as Harrods. Also of interest are children's beakers and mugs from the late 1930s with handles modelled in the form of characters from nursery rhymes.

KEY FACTS

Location: Hanley, later Burslem, Staffordshire, UK.
Important dates: Founded 1891. Joined George Jones Crescent Potteries Group 1932.
Production: Earthenware and china tableware, ornaments and nursery ware.

❧ FOR THE KIDDIES

Rainbow colours are employed for the beehive honey jar. Father Christmas supplies the handle for the tumbler, while the handles of the mugs represent an appropriate nursery-rhyme figure.

—*Bishop & Stonier.*

◆ **Children's ware, 1939**
This advertisement in *The Pottery Gazette* illustrates Bishop & Stonier's new children's ware: distinctive mugs with character handles. 49

BLYTH PORCELAIN CO.

This company, specializing in earthenware and stoneware, was well known for the quality of its trade-name Diamond China body and practically leadless glaze. In the 1920s its modern and well-equipped factory, Blyth Works, enabled it to aim its goods at the expanding middle-class market, and it produced traditional designs based on rich ground colours and gold-stamped patterns used on the Tudor and Trent shapes.

KEY FACTS

Location: Longton, Staffordshire, UK.
Important dates: Founded c.1901. Taken over by A. T. Finney 1935.

BOEHM PORCELAIN STUDIO

Boehm designs and makes porcelain sculpture collectables as open stock, limited editions and special commissions. Among the most famous commissioned pieces is Birds of Peace, a group of life-size mute swans, presented by President Richard Nixon to Chairman Mao Zedong in 1972.

Edward Marshall Boehm, having become interested in making porcelain sculptures of animals, flowers and birds, established a small home studio in 1950. Rapid expansion followed, and by 1960 the company was represented in a dozen museums, including the Metropolitan Museum of Art, Buckingham Palace, the Elysée Palace and the Vatican. Today more than 100 museums, botanical gardens and institutions display its sculptures.

➡ **Birds of Peace, 1972**
Only two examples of this life-size group of mute swans survive. One, a diplomatic gift of the USA, is on display in China; the other is outside the Sistine Chapel in the Vatican, Italy, a gift from E. M. Boehm's wife to Pope Paul VI in 1976. 50

KEY FACTS

Location: Trenton, New Jersey, USA; Malvern, Worcestershire, UK.
Important dates: Founded 1950. Still active.
Production: Porcelain sculpture.
Principal designer: Edward Marshall Boehm.

BOOTHS & COLCLOUGHS

The late 1940s saw the merger of two well-established Staffordshire potteries: Booths, whose Church Bank Pottery was established in Tunstall in 1868, and Colclough China, formerly H. J. Colclough, china and earthenware manufacturers, established at the Vale Works, Longton, in 1897.

By the 20th century Booths was a major maker of domestic ware in popular styles for all levels of the market, with an emphasis on orientally inspired designs. Also famous was its Silicon China, made for shipping lines and hotels, and its copies of 18th-century Worcester ware. Historicism was also the inspiration for Roma Bronze Ware, launched at Olympia in London in 1937. Later Booths concentrated on tableware patterns for the North American market, the most popular of which were Wild Rose, Wildflower, Maple Leaf, Victoria, Chinese Tree, Tulip and Larkspur, and Tapestry.

Colclough China, by contrast, was one of the largest manufacturers of bone-china tableware, with a reputation established in the late 19th century for a wide range of patterns from simple prints to elaborate 18th-century and Derby-style designs. The firm also made heraldic and view ware, commemoratives and items for the tourist and souvenir markets, advertising ware and a wide range of novelties. After the merger in 1948 of Booths and Colclough China, the emphasis was on bone-china tableware.

In 1948 two Hungarian refugees, Endre Hevezi and Dr Gyula Bajo, were taken on as labourers at the company's works in Tunstall, acting as carriers between the plate-making shops and the kilns. Both were trained in the arts and architecture, and during their spare time they produced pottery designs. The two men were provided with a studio at the factory and given virtually a free hand. The result was Bajo Ware, a range of interesting and unusual designs for tableware and ornaments with painted and printed decorations based on historical, mythological and modern themes.

In 1954 Booths & Colcloughs merged with Ridgway (*see* p.176), part of the Lawley Group, and was renamed. From 1955 the firm traded as Ridgway Potteries, and in 1965 it was taken over by Royal Doulton (*see* p.187).

Square earthenware dish painted with engobes on the wet body, greyish-matt glaze. Designer: Dr Gyula Bajo. Makers: Booths & Colcloughs Ltd (GB)

◆ **Bajo Ware, mid-1950s**
Together with many of its contemporaries, the pottery tried to capture the taste for modernism in the 1950s. Typical is this piece decorated by Dr Gyula Bajo. [51]

◆ **Elephant teapot, 1950s**
A number of companies have made novelty elephant teapots, some inspired by films such as Walt Disney's *Dumbo*, or the story of Sabu the elephant boy. [52]

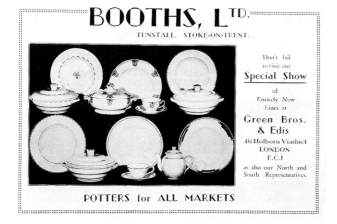

BOOTHS, L^TD**.**
TUNSTALL. STOKE-ON-TRENT.

Don't fail to visit our
Special Show
of
Entirely New
Lines at
Green Bros. & Edis
46 Holborn Viaduct
LONDON
E.C.1
as also our North and South Representatives.

POTTERS for ALL MARKETS

◆ **Art Deco tableware, 1934**
While not in the first rank of potteries whose products are now collectable, Booths always had a taste for the contemporary. This *Pottery Gazette* advertisement shows the company's interpretation of Art Deco style. [53]

BOVEY POTTERY CO.

With a tradition stretching back to the era of creamware, the pottery produced a wide range of ordinary tableware and toilet, kitchen, hotel and hospital ware, as well as fancies, motto ware, toy and children's ware, commemoratives and souvenirs. Most collectable are the simple handcraft-style 1930s tablewares, the Wemyss ware with Plichta designs made here from 1930 and a series of figures of wartime military and political characters sculpted by Gwyneth Holt and Fenton Wyness from 1940. Finished in a smooth, soft cream glaze, the models were known as Our Gang or On Parade. Fenton Wyness was also the designer of the 'decal-decorated children's nursery rhyme series designed for export about 1947.

In 1996 William Bavin launched the Dartmoor Pottery on the site of the Bovey Pottery.

KEY FACTS

Location: Bovey, Devon, UK.
Important dates: Founded 1894. Closed 1957.
Production: Earthenware,
Principal designer: William Clayton.

MARKS

Printed and impressed marks from late 1930s usually include Bovey name.

♦ **Our Gang figures, early 1940s**
The Pilot, Stalin and The Sergeant Major, from the Our Gang or On Parade figures made at the Bovey Pottery from designs by Gwyneth Holt and Fenton Wyness. Particularly rare are the figures representing Hitler and Mussolini. [54]

E. BRAIN & CO.

In the early years of the 20th century this pottery pursued a modern image, echoing Art Nouveau style and advertising ware in 'modern art styles, specially suited for art furnishers etc'. Among its art-pottery lines was Harjian faience, and Coon Ware was a typical contemporary range. During the same period early tableware patterns such as Checker Border, Torch, Hillington, Pelham, Rocester and Tudor helped to establish the Foley style. In later decades the company maintained its reputation for modernism while producing well-conceived and well-made ware in bone china in more traditional styles. Tableware patterns including Ming Rose and Cornflower satisfied this sector of the market, along with richly painted and gilded vases, christening mugs and the like.

During the interwar years, however, it was the impact of the modern movement that above all determined the pottery's design philosophy. This influence was evident in an emphasis on simplicity of shape and the avoidance of unnecessary decoration. Patterns such as Cubist Landscape and Cubist Sunflower, launched in about 1928, are good examples of this style. In 1934 the pottery was involved, with A. J. Wilkinson (*see* p.239), in Harrods' well-publicized Exhibition of Contemporary Art for the Table, an attempt to marry art and industry by commissioning tableware designs from contemporary artists. Among those invited to take part were John Armstrong, Paul Nash, Graham Sutherland, Vanessa Bell, Duncan Grant, Laura Knight, Ernest Proctor and Alan

◤ **Gay Nineties dishes, 1956**
This range of Gay Nineties dishes designed by Maureen Tanner shows Brain's desire to capture some of the current market. At the same time, contemporary figures modelled by Donald Brindley were produced, reinforcing this aim. [55]

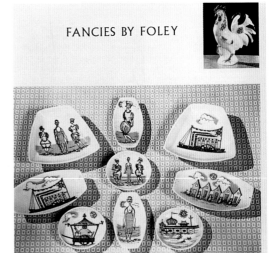

FANCIES BY FOLEY

Walton. Brain pattern books show 51 designs for the exhibition by various artists. The experiment was not a commercial success, merely serving to confirm that good artists do not necessarily make good tableware designers. Nevertheless, the publicity, both at the time and later, gave the name of Brain an important place in design history.

About 1950 Peter Cave and Hazel Thumpston joined the pottery as in-house designers, both having studied at the Stoke-on-Trent Schools of Art and the Royal College of Art in London. By the middle of the decade they had been joined by the sculptor and modeller Donald Brindley and the designer Maureen Tanner. The latter's contemporary-style designs such as Gay Nineties and April were well received by critics of the day.

In the early 1960s, following the pottery's merger with Coalport (*see* p.47), the Brain name disappeared from the market-place.

◀ Artist tableware, 1934
Made for the Harrods exhibition of 1934 entitled Art for the Table, this tableware is highly collectable today. On the left are pieces by Milner Gray, and on the right examples by Gordon Forsyth. In the middle is Circus by Laura Knight, an earthenware service made by A. J. Wilkinson. 56

C. H. BRANNAM

The company was founded in 1879 when Charles Herbert Brannam, son of the potter James Brannam, took over his father's works in Litchdon Street, Barnstaple, Devon. The pottery still occupies the same premises. Charles Brannam studied at the local school of art, and his interest in art pottery seems to have begun at this time. When he first operated the pottery he continued the production of redware with sgraffito decoration in traditional local styles. By the 1890s he was using carved and sgraffito decoration and painted slip together under coloured glazes, such as a green or a blue, which he himself had developed.

In the 19th century Brannam was well known as one of the leading manufacturers in the south-west of England of slip-decorated artware, novelties and souvenir motto ware. Barum Ware, named after Barnstaple's Roman name, was introduced in the early 1880s. After receiving royal patronage in 1885 it was often referred to as Royal Barum Ware. This range of artware, with its imaginative designs, soft colours and adventurously fluid decoration, was initially sold in London exclusively through Howell & James and remained in production until around the outbreak of World War II. Tableware, toilet ware, brooches and animal novelties were made in forms and styles which remained popular into the 1920s and 1930s. Toy teasets were also among Brannam's regular lines. Of special interest is the range shown at the British Industries Fair in 1933 and purchased by the Duchess of York, a

▲ Barum Ware vases, 1904
With their fish-and-seaweed decoration in coloured slips, these vases carry on the lively styles developed by Brannam in the late 19th century but show a hint of Art Nouveau. 57

generous patron of children's ware. A move into more domestic areas of production was reflected in the 1946 catalogue, which included bread crocks, flower pots and garden pottery, poultry fountains, jugs, vases, ornamental bowls, table lamps, mixing bowls, seed pans and nest pans. The company has maintained this pattern in recent times, and today concentrates on a wide range of redware and glazed terracotta vases and bowls, terrace and flower pots, as well as kitchen, oven and cottage ware, some of which is made in the Far East. Brannam ceased firing its bottle oven in the 1980s. Until that time it had been one of the very few potteries in England to retain a traditional bottle oven in regular commercial use.

KEY FACTS
Location: Litchdon Pottery, Barnstaple, Devon, UK.
Important dates: Founded 1879. Took over works of W. L. Baron in 1939. Still active.
Production: Redware and earthenware with slip decoration.
Trade name: Castle Ware, Royal Barum Ware.

MARKS
This mark used from 1929 as well as impressed mark giving company name in capital letters.

◆ **Terracotta garden pots, 1990s**
Although much of Brannam's glazed ware is made overseas, the firm is still a large-scale producer of terracotta garden ware such as these strawberry pots. ⬚58

SASCHA BRASTOFF

The whimsical humour of Sascha Brastoff's early sculpture comes through in the playful and colourful ceramics he designed and made in the 1950s and 1960s. Figurines, lamps, vases, flower bowls, masks and wall plaques all show his flamboyant style, but perhaps the most popular of his offerings were his smoking accessories.

A native of Cleveland, Ohio, Brastoff was working in New York City by 1939, but in 1945 he moved to California, where Winthrop Rockefeller financed a pottery in West Los Angeles. A small staff was assembled to make, decorate and sell goods made according to Brastoff's designs. Vases, bowls and ashtrays were the earliest products. Figurines were first made about 1950. In 1953 Brastoff and Rockefeller built the factory, studio and gallery on West Olympic Boulevard that became a famous tourist attraction. Of the 80 employees, half were decorators because almost all of Brastoff's production was hand-decorated. Earthenware and fine-china dinnerware lines were launched in 1954, Surf Ballet being the most successful pattern.

Brastoff retired in 1963, but production continued for ten more years. His work is held by the Metropolitan Museum of Art, the Guggenheim Museum and several other prominent US art museums.

KEY FACTS
Location: Beverly Hills, California, USA.
Important dates: Founded 1948. Closed 1973.
Production: Figurines, lamps, vases, flower bowls, plaques, smoking accessories.

MARKS
Often give name only, or 'Sascha B.' without including drawing of cock.

◆ **Brastoff mug, c.1960**
Brastoff employed a large number of decorators to embellish his designs by hand. The sprightly horse, rendered with only a few energetic lines, is typical of Brastoff's manner. ⬚59

BRENTLEIGH: see HOWARD POTTERY p.94

BRETBY ART POTTERY

Bretby Art Pottery (formerly known as Tooth & Co.) was one of the more adventurous of the late-19th-century art potteries, thanks initially to its dynamic leadership by Henry Tooth, who, with William Ault, co-founded it for the production of decorative earthenware. The pottery was always known for the extraordinary diversity of its products, which ranged from early simple vases to art vases in exotic shapes and colours, drawing inspiration from all corners of the world. Figures, garden ware and novelties characterized the firm's output in its early days, and ensured its survival in later periods when other art potteries were closing. Of special interest to collectors is the series of large rustic figures and statuettes, moulded and hand-finished in limited editions around 1900.

Early-20th-century advertisements feature bulb bowls, window boxes and ranges of goods imitating bamboo, bronze and oriental lacquer. One from 1928, promoting Zuyder Zee Ware, also shows the great variety of wares then in production. This included jardinières, vases, pedestals, umbrella stands, candlesticks, ashtrays, pin trays, tobacco jars, plaques, bulb bowls and window-boxes, decorated in transparent or matt self colours, carved bamboo, Ivorine, cloisonné, veined effects, shaded colours, mottled glazes, bronze and Clanta in various natural effects. The firm won many awards at international exhibitions, notably for its tall, stylish vases and other colourful items with mottled and splashed glazes.

By the 1930s some of this rich diversity had disappeared as the pottery tried to be both artistic and competitive. Modernism appeared in matt glazes, Art Deco shapes and the blue-and-white KK range of kitchenware, but references to garden ornaments and peasant pottery showed that old habits lingered on. Many of the goods produced in the 1930s continued to be made into the post-war era. The pottery advertised animal models, wall vases, lamp bases, ashtrays and novelties, as well as a series based on characters from Dickens.

◆ **Advertisement, 1921**
This advertisement from *The Pottery Gazette* shows ranges of orientally inspired Bretby ware made since the late 19th century. [60]

◆ **Nut dish, 1900–1910**
Highly naturalistic *trompe l'oeil* novelties were a Bretby speciality in the late 19th century. Nuts, fruit, biscuits and even cigarettes were included in the range, which continued to be made in the early 20th century. [61]

KEY FACTS

Location: Woodville, Derbyshire, UK.
Important dates: Established as Tooth & Ault in 1883. Continued as Tooth & Co. from 1887. Closed 1997.
Production: Artware and ornaments in earthenware.
Principal designers: Henry Tooth, Florence Tooth.

MARKS

Printed or impressed Bretby's Sol trade mark, showing half sun above Bretby name, registered in 1884, is most common 20th-century mark.

◆ **Wall pocket, 1940s**
With its matt glaze and stylized shell shape, this wall pocket was designed in the 1930s and was still in production in the early 1950s. [62]

BRIDGEWATER

Founded in 1985 by Matthew Rice, a furniture designer, and Emma Bridgewater, the pottery pioneered, initially on a small scale, the revival of spongeware and other traditional decorative techniques for tableware and domestic ware. Success bought rapid expansion and a move to Staffordshire from Fulham, London, and by 1991 the company was producing spongeware mugs, kitchen dresser ware – mugs, plates, dishes, bowls, jugs, cups and saucers, teapot and tureen, butter dish, jam jar and candlesticks – lettered ware for kitchen and nursery, bedroom and bathroom ware and Christmas ware. All of the pottery's shapes are designed by Emma Bridgewater and are intended to work together.

Since moving into the former Johnson Brothers factory in Hanley, the company has developed full tableware ranges which feature traditional printed spongeware, stencilled and textile-inspired designs, and lettered ware and mugs.

◆ Toast and marmalade plate, 1998
Inspired by the lettered ware of the early 19th century, this recent Bridgewater design has been much copied by other manufacturers. The version with black lettering was introduced in 1992. 63

◆ Blue stars teapot, early 1990s
Made in two sizes, this teapot reflects the lively Bridgewater approach to design, a blend of traditional and modern elements. 64

◆ Clover mug, 1998
Emma Bridgewater revived the old techniques of sponging and stencilling. This is one of over 50 patterns in production. 65

> ### KEY FACTS
> **Location:** Eastwood Pottery, Hanley, Staffordshire, UK.
> **Important dates:** Founded 1985. Still active.
> **Production:** Decorative earthenware.
>
> ### MARKS
> Spongeware backstamps, as shown, vary slightly each year. Marks for decal-decorated ware change less frequently.
>
>

SAMPSON BRIDGWOOD & SON

The Anchor works and mill, built by Sampson Bridgwood and his son in 1853, remained in the Bridgwood family until the business became insolvent in 1890. The Aynsley family bought the factory and operated it until 1965, retaining both the Bridgwood name and its style. The pottery produced good-quality china teaware and ordinary domestic tableware decorated in traditional styles, including refined decal patterns in rich colours and oriental-style patterns. At its peak in the 1930s Bridgwood also made more colourful Art Deco-inspired patterns, and supplied white ware to A. E. Gray (*see* p.78) to decorate.

> ### KEY FACTS
> **Location:** Anchor Pottery, Longton, Staffordshire, UK.
> **Important dates:** Founded 1795. Part of Churchill Group 1984.
> **Production:** China and earthenware.
>
>

BRITANNIA POTTERY CO.

This traditional tableware pottery, formerly known as Cochran & Fleming, maintained the transfer-printed design styles of many 19th-century Scottish companies. Patterns included Willow, Canton and Delft. Also made were sponged and cream-coloured kitchenware, and goods for hotels and shipping lines. These, advertised in the early 1920s, featured recessed knobs and rolled edges (the latter were claimed to be unchippable). In 1923 the firm introduced an ivory body and some more colourful jazz-age patterns, as well as a series called Omar Khayyam, with vividly coloured oriental scenes.

Toilet ware, fancies, including floating bowls, and children's ware were also made. A 1927 review stated: '"Moyen" is ... well engraved, the printing being nicely executed ... The old "Blue Willow" pattern offered in either light or dark blue, is another stock pattern for which the firm has been noted for many years. The Canton "Delft" pattern is another stock line, but there are three or four new underglaze designs in sponged ware ... these are quite equal in their execution to a print ...'

KEY FACTS

Location: St Rollox, Glasgow, UK.
Important dates: Founded 1920. Closed 1935.
Production: Earthenware tableware.

MARKS

Variations of this mark used 1920–35, sometimes with 'B.P. Co. Ltd.' and 'Made in Scotland'.

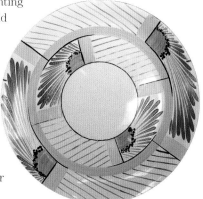

◆ **Plate, c.1930**
In the 1920s and 1930s Britannia Pottery produced a large number of striking products, often using the vivid colours that are associated with the Art Deco Movement. The pottery's commitment to modernism and the handcraft revival finds ready expression in this piece, painted in five on-glaze colours on a blue ground. [66]

BRITISH ANCHOR POTTERY CO.

In the first half of the 20th century the pottery produced a full range of tableware, toilet sets, kitchenware, ornamental ware, commemoratives, fancies and nursery ware, usually decorated in traditional styles. More inventive and stylish were Cottage Green kitchenware introduced in the 1930s and Noah's Ark nursery ware from the 1950s.

During the 1950s British Anchor also developed a more modern image, producing contemporary tableware shapes with coupe plates, decorated with litho patterns or with monochrome coloured glazes, such as the Montmartre range, first introduced for export and available in chartreuse, French grey, caramelle and Parisian green. From 1965, with the development of the Hostess Tableware name, the firm specialized mainly in tableware.

➡ **Cottage Green advertisement, 1939**
This advertisement shows British Anchor's Cottage Green range, one of the many examples of banded kitchenware produced in the shadow of T. G. Green's Cornish Ware. [67]

KEY FACTS

Location: Anchor Road, Longton, Staffordshire, UK.
Important dates: Founded 1884. Closed 1982.
Production: Earthenware.

MARKS

Anchor with monogram or full company name.

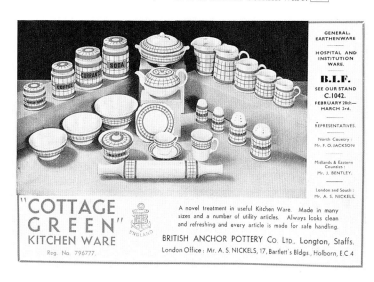

JAMES BROADHURST & SONS

In its early years the firm produced a full range of domestic tableware for both export and the mass market at home. By the 1920s it was making mainly cheap printed dinner sets, half teasets with transfer-printed or decal borders, white and gold teaware, toilet sets and other useful goods. Later it specialized in boxed sets of teaware, dinnerware and giftware, and presentation sets aimed at the growing catalogue and chain-store markets. Patterns included the usual on-glaze and underglaze banding, painting and printing.

From the 1950s and into the 1970s styles were more distinctive, thanks to a rubber-stamping technique which enabled handcraft-style contemporary patterns to be made in huge quantities. These became the pottery's hallmark, primarily through the creativity of Kathie Winkle, its in-house designer.

"MIKADO" ROSETTA
POMELLA ORCHARD
JAMES BROADHURST & SONS LTD
PORTLAND POTTERY · FENTON · STOKE-ON-TRENT
★ We cordially invite you to visit us at the
Mount Royal Hotel, Room 428

♦ **Advertisement, 1964**
Advertising for Broadhurst's contemporary printed and rubber-stamped ranges, the latter designed by Kathie Winkle. 68

A. W. BUCHAN & CO.

At the start of the 20th century the firm, already established as a maker of basic stoneware, began producing more ornamental ware. This included whisky flagons, hot-water bottles, meat-extract pots and patented designs such as the Easo Phild Footwarmer of 1909 and the Portovase cemetery vase of 1922. By the mid-1940s the firm's products included acid containers, insulators, advertising ware, stoneware bottles, casseroles, jam jars, mugs, ointment jars, pickling jars, spirit jars and vases. New glazes were developed by the chemist Lady Milne, and a decorating shop was set up where women hand-painters or designers created the decorative stoneware range known as Thistle Ware. This, with its variety of hand-thrown shapes with hand-painted underglaze decoration in floral or symbolic styles, was shown at the Festival of Britain in 1951. In 1960 the pottery launched oven-to-table ware in patterns such as Brittany, a fruit design, Edinburgh and Tuscany. These supplemented its standard stoneware range, which included decanters, butter dishes, bowls, beakers, baking dishes, casseroles and beer mugs.

♦ **Stoneware, 1950s–1960s**
The distinctive hand-thrown and hand-decorated look of Buchan stoneware was particularly popular during the 1950s and 1960s. The pottery's contemporary look was inspired partly by Scandinavian ceramics. 69

BUFFALO POTTERY COMPANY

John D. Larkin founded the Buffalo Pottery Company in 1901, and by 1903 it was making soap premiums and other goods for retail sale. The body of the earliest products was semi-porcelain. Blue Willow was a popular pattern for many years. From 1905 to 1909 Buffalo made a wide variety of collectable pitchers with transfer-printed and filled decorations ranging in style from traditional Imari to Art Nouveau, many featuring historical figures or fictional characters such as George Washington and Cinderella.

In 1908 the company developed the Deldare line, which had printed and filled decorations, based on illustrations of colonial-revival subjects by Ralph Stuart in the Arts and Crafts style, that were applied to a sage-green body developed by William Rea. Thematic series included Fallowfield Hunt, Ye Olden Days and Dr Syntax. In 1911 only, the pottery also made a line called Emerald Deldare that had a lot of green in the decorations and a special mark. Abino Ware was made from 1911 to 1913 using the same shapes as Deldare and Emerald Deldare. Seascapes and some pastoral scenes were transfer-printed and filled in green on a rust-coloured body.

Buffalo introduced a vitreous china body in 1915 and supplied this to the US Government during World War I. After the war institutional ware gradually replaced premium items. Many custom services were made for US and Canadian hotels, restaurants, hospitals, railways and steamship lines. Notable was the set of service plates with a Gilbert Stuart portrait of George Washington made for the Chesapeake and Ohio Railroad in 1932.

When the company was reorganized as Buffalo Pottery Incorporated, in 1940, the factory was streamlined and fewer custom orders were accepted; such work was eventually discontinued. During World War II, however, much ware was made again for the US Government. Goods for institutional use have been the company's mainstay since then. In 1956 the pottery became Buffalo China, Incorporated, and today it still thrives as a maker of vitreous institutional ware under Oneida's ownership.

◀ **Deldare Ware, 1908–25**
The Deldare lines were characterized by complex decal decorations applied to a sage-green body and filled with colour by hand. By 1925 the small market for such costly ware could no longer support its production. [70]

➤ **Roycroft cup and saucer, c.1910**
One of Buffalo's many custom services, this was made for the Roycrofters of East Aurora, New York, a small Arts and Crafts-style colony who used this insignia on their books, furniture and metalwork. [71]

➤ **Blue Willow plate, c.1915**
Nearly every pottery in the USA has contributed a version of the Blue Willow design to the market-place. Buffalo's variation is on heavy, institutional food-service china. [72]

KEY FACTS

Location: Buffalo, New York, USA.
Important dates: Founded 1901. Still active.
Production: Artware, dinnerware and hotel ware.
Principal designers: Ralph Stuart, Charles Harris, W. E. Simpson, August Riehs, Perry Doncaster, Frederick Krausen.

MARKS

Early marks have 'Buffalo China'. This mark with drawing and 'Buffalo Pottery' introduced by 1907.

BULLERS

This company, a maker of high-temperature porcelains for the electrical industry, established an experimental art studio at its factory in the 1930s. The idea came from Gordon Forsyth, who had encouraged students at the Burslem School of Art to experiment with Bullers' porcelain insulator clay, and from the company's chemist, Guy Harris, who was interested in re-creating a range of oriental high-temperature glazes, notably celadons, aventurines, crackles and flambés. Examples were shown at the Royal Academy, London, in 1935, and a small studio was established under Anne Potts, making vases, tableware and rolled-clay figures inspired by the work of 18th-century Staffordshire potters.

World War II interrupted further progress, but when peace returned the studio was reopened under the Danish potter Agnete Hoy, who had studied with Gordon Forsyth. A large range of ornamental ware, tableware and figures was produced in small quantities, featuring Hoy's shapes, Harris's glazes and hand decoration in a variety of styles by young artists such as Robert Jefferson, James Rushton and Michael Leach. Attempts to develop quantity production failed, and the studio closed in 1952. Hoy left to work with stoneware at Royal Doulton's (*see* p.187) Lambeth factory.

▲ **Agnete Hoy dish, 1940s**
The shape is by Danish potter Agnete Hoy, and the dish has a typical freely drawn floral decoration. 73

◀ **Oriental vases, 1940s (far left) and 1930s (left)**
Typical hand-thrown shapes with a crackle glaze and a flambé effect. 74

BURGESS & LEIGH

The company, which has been a family-owned business since the 1860s and is one of the few Staffordshire potteries still to enjoy this independent status, is a manufacturer of good-quality everyday ware, and specializes in underglaze decorated earthenware. For most of its long history its output has consisted mainly of printed bowls, jugs and mugs, dipped bowls and mugs, Broseley teaware, kitchenware and printed dinnerware with traditional patterns such as Blue Willow, Cottage Pheasant and Dove Rine. Moulds and copper plates acquired with Samuel Alcock's (*see* p.13) Hill Pottery in the 1860 were still in use in the 1950s. From 1862 the pottery traded as Burgess, Leigh & Co., and in 1877 it adopted the name Burgess & Leigh.

On its impressive stand at the 1921 British Industries Fair the firm showed a variety of tableware and toilet ware, including new and established patterns and shapes and the new Rhodian Ware with a double colour effect in grey, achieved through heavy and light engraving. Tableware patterns were produced en suite, so that other sets of ware in the same design, such as tea, fruit and salad sets, could be collected. In 1927 the pottery took out a full-page advertisement to announce the

▲ **Fantasia side plate, 1959**
Harold Bennett's design reflected a widespread fascination in the 1950s with contemporary imagery. 75

arrival of its newest designer, Charlotte Rhead (*see* p.173), daughter of Frederick Rhead. This described her as an accomplished lady artist who had produced for the pottery a number of original decorations, all of which were pure 'handcraft' with beautiful underglaze colourings.

After maintaining production throughout World War II, the firm relaunched its full range of traditional wares in the 1950s. Production continued until 1999 when the pottery closed. It was later bought by William and Rosemary Dorling and production was resumed. (*See* p.245.)

◆ **Chanticleer cup and saucer, 1990s**
This range shows the recent enthusiasm for sponging and stencilling. 76

KEY FACTS
Location: Middleport Pottery, Burslem, Staffordshire, UK.
Important dates: Founded 1862. Closed 1999. Relaunched as Burgess Dorling & Leigh.
Production: Earthenware.

MARKS
Initials or name of company in full printed on early ware. Printed Burleigh Ware mark used from 1930s.

◆ **Calico kitchenware, 1990s**
Today's designs include a number of kitchenware ranges, currently of strong interest in the British ceramics industry. This design brings up to date the pottery's traditional association with blue-and-white printed ware, and shows the continuing enthusiasm for overall textile patterns that began with chintzware. 77

CANONSBURG POTTERY COMPANY

This pottery, established by John George in 1901, made standard semi-porcelain dinnerware, hotel ware and toilet ware. In 1959 it acquired moulds from the Steubenville Pottery (*see* p.213), producing two of that firm's most popular patterns, Rosepoint and Adam Antique, well into the 1960s. A fire closed the factory in 1975, and it never reopened. The George family sold it in 1976, and its remaining physical assets were dispersed through bankruptcy proceedings in 1978. The design of Canonsburg's products was generally rather conservative. For example, Washington Colonial (introduced as Priscilla in 1931) was based on 18th-century salt-glaze stoneware patterns found in colonial homes. However, a number of modern designs were also produced. The Art Deco-style Westchester shape can sometimes be found with decoration recalling the Wiener Werkstätte.

◆ **Washington Colonial platter, 1930s**
The bicentenary of George Washington's birth in 1932 inspired many patterns based on 18th-century taste. Archaeology at Washington's birthplace, Wakefield, Virginia, revealed salt-glazed stoneware and reintroduced consumers to the classic style. 78

KEY FACTS
Location: Canonsburg, Pennsylvania, USA.
Important dates: Founded 1901. Closed 1976.
Production: Semi-porcelain dinnerware, toilet ware, hotel ware.

MARKS
May include image of a canon or pattern name with firm's name.

BURLEIGH: see BURGESS & LEIGH p.36
BURSLEY: see CHARLOTTE RHEAD p.173 and WOOD & SONS p.241

CARLTON WARE

The firm of Wiltshaw & Robinson was established in 1890 and from the mid-1890s used the Carlton Ware trade mark. Harold Taylor Robinson (*see* p.178) began as a representative for the firm in 1899, and was a partner from 1906 to 1911. He merged it with Robinson & Leadbeater, which he also controlled. Throughout his partnership with J. F. Wiltshaw he maintained the independence of his own company, Arkinstall & Son (*see* p.14), which he had established to make porcelain novelties and souvenirs.

Wiltshaw & Robinson specialized in decorative items, toilet ware, teaware, ornaments and novelties and was advertising crested porcelain goods from the early years of the 20th century, if not before. From 1920 the firm began to gain a reputation for its orientally inspired shapes, glazes and patterns, including lacquer and lustre effects. Ground colours included powder-blue *rose du Barry*, decorated in gold and other finishes. Next came the range of twelve lustre colours, including mother-of-pearl and shades of orange, turquoise, black and red. In the mid-1920s the range was expanded to include animal models, Toby jugs and female figures, children's china and decorative ware for table use. The latter, among which were a lettuce and tomato dish, lobster dish, grapefruit holder, cucumber dish and covered Java preserve pot, had embossed patterns illustrating the purpose for which they were to be used.

In the late 1920s Wiltshaw & Robinson suffered financially and decided to diversify. While continuing production at the Carlton earthenware works, it took over the Vine Pottery, a china works. Here it began making china teaware and dinnerware marked with a Carlton China backstamp. Among the first series were some fine-china teaware and dinnerware with popular patterns such as Springtime, Delphinium and Sunshine.

Successfully established in the market-place since the early 1930s, the Carlton name became synonymous with lavishly decorated vases and coffee sets with rich gilding and enamel-relief work. It was also well known for its lustres and ornamental tableware designed by Violet Elmer, the first of a number of women designers employed by Cuthbert Wiltshaw over the next 20 years. The Carlton Works continued production throughout World War II. An impressive list of modellers and designers worked for the firm in the post-war years and into the 1960s, and their work reflects design

◆ **Chinoiserie vase, 1920s**
In the 1920s Carlton Ware followed contemporary trends and introduced lustre and coloured-ground ware with exotic patterns in gold. This chinoiserie design was inspired by the Willow pattern. Better known was the Rouge Royale series. 79

◆ **Apple Blossom dish, 1930s**
This popular Carlton moulded pattern was applied to many shapes, including teapots, mugs, cups and bowls. 80

◆ **Guinness Toucan, 1960s**
Carlton produced a wide range of Guinness-related items in the 1960s. Best known, and most collectable, is this free-standing model, also made as a lamp base. Three sizes were made. Recently, fakes and copies have been produced, and so collectors need to buy with care. 81

If he can say as you can Guinness is good for you

advances of the period. Typical was Ken Coxon, modeller for Carlton from just after the war until his death in 1978. Another was Chris Boulton, a textile designer before he worked for Carlton from the late 1940s to the mid-1950s. Among his pattern designs were Kingfisher and Peking. Other designers were Angela Fox and Vivienne Brennon, responsible for some of the later novelty money boxes.

After being taken over by Arthur Wood & Son (*see* p.240) in 1967, Carlton continued to make its traditional tea and coffee sets, fancy tableware, boxed giftware and ornamental ware until the late 1980s, concentrating in the 1970s and early 1980s on a wide range of novelties. The takeover by County Potteries in 1987 was followed by receivership and closure. A few years later the trade names, pattern books and some moulds were bought by Grosvenor Ceramic Hardware, of Stone, Staffordshire, who relaunched the Carlton Ware name on lustre ware and novelty teapots. Grosvenor also made a limited-edition centenary vase, commemorating the founding of Wiltshaw & Robinson in 1890. Production ceased in 1992.

The Carlton Ware name was relaunched in 1998, and today various manufacturers are making, under licence, limited-edition collectors' pieces, some from original moulds and styles. Advertising ware with the Carlton name is particularly popular with collectors today, notably pieces made for Guinness and other drinks manufacturers. This popularity, and the high prices achieved by the Toucan series, has recently led to the production of fakes, some cast from original moulds and bearing a backstamp.

◆ **Advertisement, 1960**
Published in *The Pottery Gazette*, this shows the popular Windswept Ware, a twin-tone series in a range of shapes and colourings. 82

◆ **Red Baron teapot, early 1990s**
Carlton Ware production in the 1970s and 1980s concentrated on novelty items, notably teapots, storage jars and other kitchenware. This ware pioneered the great vogue for the novelty teapots that were a feature of the 1990s. 83

KEY FACTS

Location: Carlton Works and Vine Pottery, Stoke, Staffordshire, UK.
Important dates: Founded 1890. Renamed Carlton Ware 1957. Taken over by Arthur Wood & Son 1967 and by County Potteries 1987, when it was renamed Carlton & Kent. Closed 1987. Carlton Ware name relaunched late 1980s and 1998.
Production: Tableware and ornaments in china and earthenware.
Principal designers: Violet Elmer, Ken Coxon, Chris Boulton, Angela Fox, Vivienne Brennon.
Trade name: Carlton Ware (relaunched 1998 specifically for the collectors' market).

MARKS

Wiltshaw & Robinson's Carlton Ware script mark, dating from 1920s, continued, with and without addition of 'Handpainted', by company's new owners, Arthur Wood & Son, from 1967.

CARTER, STABLER & ADAMS: see POOLE POTTERY p.159
GEORGE CARTLIDGE: see SAMPSON HANCOCK & SONS p.89

CARTWRIGHT & EDWARDS

This pottery, a large producer of china and earthenware for the popular market, using two separate factories, was well known for its progressive outlook. At the outbreak of World War I it took over and reconstructed the Heron Cross Pottery to enable the works 'to produce on a large scale a class of earthenware that is cheap, attractive, and universally saleable'. The firm made useful and decorative teaware in fashionable patterns, and the range was expanded after it took over Holdcrofts Ltd about 1940. More recently, it has specialized in good-quality, ordinary domestic tableware and kitchenware and, to a lesser degree, nursery ware. In the 1970s it turned to large-scale mug production.

CAULDON POTTERIES

About 1904, Brown-Westhead, Moore & Co., one of Europe's largest potteries, was incorporated under the Cauldon name. Later this company was bought by Harold Taylor Robinson (*see* p.178). From 1920, as Cauldon Potteries, it became the flagship of his rapidly expanding pottery empire, particularly after it gained a Royal Warrant following the success of its display at the British Empire Exhibition in London in 1924.

The factory was known for its 'moderate priced artistic productions to meet the needs of the Modern Home of distinctive taste'. Extensive tableware ranges in the early 1920s featured rich decoration and acid-gold detailing, with many finely painted service plates aimed at the American market. From about 1929 Cauldon's art director was Frederick Rhead, who introduced contemporary styles and highly finished ware. Throughout this period the factory could, at its best, rival the finely painted china of Minton (*see* p.132), Doulton (*see* p.187) and Derby (*see* p.184). Among its artists and modellers were Donald Birbeck, S. F. Nixon and Stephen Pope, specialists in landscape, fruit, cattle and game subjects.

Cauldon was also a major producer of ordinary tableware for all markets. More unusual, in the 1930s, was its production of cafetières, coffee pots and milk boilers. In 1985 the Perks Ceramic Group re-established the Cauldon name as Cauldon Potteries Ltd, taking over production facilities at the former Kingston and Ferrybridge Potteries in Yorkshire.

Rose bowl, c.1905
The making of fine porcelain in traditional styles became a Cauldon hallmark in the early 1900s. With its apple-green ground and rich gilding, this French-style bowl is a fitting rival to the type of ware usually associated with great names such as Minton, Doulton and Derby. 84

CAVERSWALL CHINA

est known for its prestigious ornamental ware and special-edition plates, thimbles and cups and saucers aimed at collectors, Caverswall acquired in 1983 the moulds from Fielding's (*see* p.66) Crown Devon factory. More popular were children's ware featuring Rupert Bear and a range of Easter Bunny ware.

The takeovers of the mid-1980s led the company to develop a more aggressive marketing strategy intended to create a stronger image. As a result the factory began to make goods aimed at a broader domestic market, including tableware, giftware, mugs and promotional ware. Decorative treatments included some striking effects, with the emphasis on black, white, grey and platinum. In 1993 the company took over the pottery owned by the modeller Michael Sutty and incorporated it into the Caverswall factory.

Caverswall China has had various owners, including Thomas Goode & Co. and Bullers (*see* p.36). Thomas Goode, whose name has appeared on pottery since about 1860, acquired the company in 1994, and continued to produce its own exclusive range alongside Caverswall lines. The Caverswall name ceased to be used for a short time, but it has since been relaunched, and now Caverswall produces its own ranges in conjunction with Thomas Goode's manufacturing division. Among recent Caverswall products are personalized promotional and commemorative china, tableware and richly decorated giftware, including plates decorated with butterflies, birds, flowers and ships.

◆ **Rupert Bear plate, early 1980s**
The Rupert Bear range was introduced to capture a larger market share. 85

◆ **Roman Gold jar, 1996**
Since its revival the firm has focused on fine and decorated porcelain. This jar has hand-applied 22 carat gold. 86

KEY FACTS

Location: Berry Hill Road, Stoke, Staffordshire, UK.
Important dates: Founded 1973. Still active.
Production: Fine china and giftware.

MARKS

This Caverswall trade mark used on its own or incorporated in more elaborate backstamps of named patterns or series.

Caverswall
FINE BONE CHINA
ENGLAND

CHURCHILL

ritain's largest family-owned manufacturer of ceramics, Churchill has wide interests in all types of tableware, hotel ware, giftware, children's ware, mugs and character ware. Initially this group of companies, established in 1984, comprised Sampson Bridgwood (*see* p.32), James Broadhurst (*see* p.34) and Wessex Ceramics, but more recent additions include Crownford, a maker of bone-china tableware, and Wren giftware. The Churchill China name was registered in 1992, and the group operates three factories in Staffordshire, in Longton, Cobridge and Tunstall.

Churchill produces goods for specific markets, including tableware patterns such as Briar Rose for the bridal market. The company is also one of the largest suppliers to Ikea, the international home furnishings store, for which it has produced many exclusive designs. In recent years Churchill Tableware has introduced Wild Life wall plaques in a series of 19th-century colour print reproductions. The series also includes six Herring's Hunt English fox-hunting scenes and four Currier & Ives famous American sailing ships. These have been reproduced, using Churchill's new four-colour printing technique, for Heritage Mint, USA. A range of

◆ **Animal Farm mug, 1997**
Many firms have added interest and variety to mug production, currently a popular sector of the market. 87

English-style giftware has also been launched, using the traditional technique of tissue-printing. The same technique was used for the reproduction of the archive design Bermuda, a single-colour all-over floral design that was included in the company's 1994 range.

Despite extensive automation, many traditional skills are maintained at the company, namely jollying of oval dishes, banding and lining, and the application of decals by hand. The process of hand-dipping has also continued alongside the spray-glazing machines.

Churchill's catalogue today includes a wide range of tableware, such as the lobed shape Buckingham, made in a super-vitrified body, suitable for commercial use in its undecorated form and for which over 50 tableware patterns have been produced. There are also many colourful tableware ranges for casual dining, such as the popular Wallace & Gromit Ware.

◆ **Wallace & Gromit plate, 1997**
Following the huge success of the Wallace & Gromit animated films during the mid-1990s, Churchill has made under licence a number of ranges of mugs and tableware featuring the films' characters. 88

GEORGE CLEWS & CO.

Although well known as a teapot maker, Clews also produced a wide range of fancy and ornamental ware such as animal figures, bulb bowls, cigarette boxes, flower pots and garden pottery, table lamps, artistic vases and novelties. Notable was the Chameleon range of decorative and artistic vases, candlesticks and other items of the 1930s, with their richly coloured and semi-abstract patterning based on stylized natural forms. In common with other teapot makers, the company produced Cube (*see* p.56) tableware under licence, notably for the *Queen Mary* and the *Queen Elizabeth*. Those made for the latter were in stoneware in a matt pale 'oatmeal' finish which was heralded as an achievement in the application of an artistic glaze for useful and inexpensive articles.

Clews continued production of most of its normal range throughout World War II, and also took over production for the teapot manufacturers Lingard, Webster & Co. In the early post-war years it brought out a number of new lines as part of the export drive. Among these was an interesting children's pattern, Animaland, introduced in 1950 and based on characters created by David Hand for the J. Arthur Rank Organisation.

◆ **Advertisement, 1952**
This advertisement illustrates a range of contemporary products, some of which clearly have their roots in the 1930s. Particularly popular with collectors today are the pottery's stylized animal figures. 89

CLARICE CLIFF

The colourful and brashly modernistic pottery of Clarice Cliff was a marketing phenomenon in its time and has since become the epitome of British Art Deco. Of all the pottery produced in Britain in the 20th century, it is probably the most familiar and the most collectable. In Cliff's early upbringing there was no clue to her later success. Born in 1899, one of eight children of an iron moulder, she went to school in Tunstall, Staffordshire. In 1912 she started her apprenticeship as an enameller at a local tableware pottery, Lingard, Webster & Co. Three years later she joined Hollinshead & Kirkham (*see* p.91) to learn lithography. Her next move was to A. J. Wilkinson (*see* p.239), where she qualified as a lithographer and gained experience of modelling, decorating, designing and gilding. At the same time she began to attend evening classes at Tunstall, and later Burslem, Schools of Art. Wilkinson, owned and managed by Arthur Shorter (*see* p.204) and his sons, was an ambitious company with an expanding output of styles aimed at the new market for decorative and inexpensive tableware and ornaments in modern styles.

In 1920 Cliff started work alongside Wilkinson's two designers, John Butler and Fred Ridgway, and after a few years was able to put her name on her work. Towards the end of the decade Arthur Shorter's son Colley, who became her protector, sponsor and eventually lover, set her up in a small studio in the Newport Pottery, which Wilkinson had bought in 1920. Here, aided by the paintress Gladys Scarlett, she tried out new designs on old stock shapes from the Newport warehouse, and adapted them to fit current production ranges. From the start these patterns were colourful, brash and outrageously modern, and designed to be rapidly applied freehand by teams of factory paintresses. Cheap to produce and aimed at the popular market, these bold reflections of contemporary taste, which were backstamped 'Bizarre' by Clarice Cliff, were tested on the market in 1928. To Wilkinson's surprise they were an immediate success; within a year the Newport Pottery was given over to the production of Clarice Cliff ware, and the team of 25 paintresses was rapidly increased to 150.

Cliff became art director in 1931. Initially the geometric and stylized abstract Bizarre patterns had been painted onto existing shapes, but by 1929 her own range of matching geometric shapes was in production. Conical was followed by Biarritz and Le Bon Jour, and the patterns poured out in a rich profusion: Crocus, Fantasque, Honolulu, Rhodanthe, Forest Glen, Capri, Harvest, Latona, Secrets, Appliqué, Blue Chintz, Ravel, Rainbow and many more. Hundreds were created by Cliff herself; others

🔺 **Monsoon wall plaque, c.1930**
Hand-painted plaques by Clarice Cliff illustrate a variety of designs, from geometric patterns to elaborate stylized landscapes, and floral and tree motifs. Shown here is Monsoon from the Appliqué series, one of the first to include individual pattern names with its own identifying marks. 90

🔺 **Sugar shaker, 1930s**
Painted with the Secrets pattern, this is a particularly desirable Clarice Cliff shape of the 1930s, but one that is prone to damage. It reflects the contemporary fascination with geometrical forms. 91

◀ **Swirls pattern teapot, c.1932**
As well as the swirling abstract pattern, inspired by French Art Deco designs, this Bizarre teapot reflects Clarice Cliff's extensive use of applied geometry in her shapes. 92

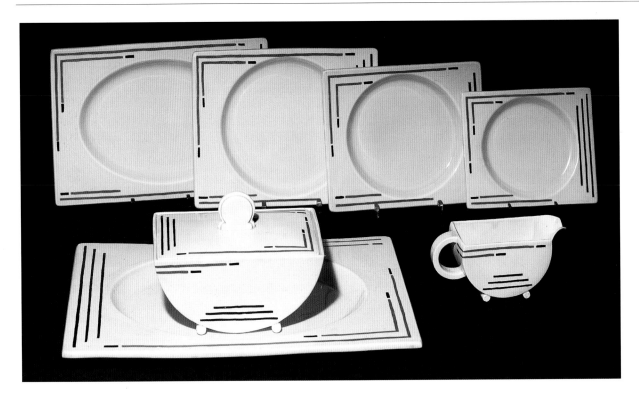

she developed from ideas created by the paintresses. Taking the lead from Cliff, the paintresses projected a modern, colourful and decorative image, and were known throughout the Potteries as the Bizarre Girls.

Cliff's great skill was in capturing the taste of the moment. She was not a great designer, and much of her work is crudely repetitive. Her inspiration, as was common at the time, came from textiles and French flat-pattern portfolios, but the result was both wildly successful and very influential. Soon all the potteries in Britain were producing Cliff-type designs in their desire to capture a section of this market. The emphasis was on tableware, but the Bizarre range also included vases, wall pockets, teapots, figures, book-ends, candlesticks, table centres and other fancies, some of which fulfilled Cliff's love of the outrageous, the extravagant and the grotesque.

Although hand-painted, the wares were consciously aimed at the mass market. They were not artware but inexpensive items intended to sell in huge quantities. For example, an early morning teaset retailed for eight shillings (40p/65c) in 1931. At the same time the decorative modernism of these pieces secured for them an artistic status and following. They were featured in design exhibitions, such as Dorland Hall in 1933 and the British Art in Industry exhibition in 1935, and were sold by Liberty and Woolworth alike. Cliff played a major role in the famous Harrods tableware exhibition of 1934, organizing the adaptation of the artists' designs for production of Wilkinson's earthenware.

However, Cliff never shared the status enjoyed by Susie Cooper (*see* p.49) as a modernist designer. No awards came her way, and despite the efforts of Colley Shorter she never became part of the design establishment. She was widely disliked, on both moral and artistic grounds, but no one could doubt her success, which was envied throughout the industry. After all, Bizarre ware had rescued the Newport Pottery from oblivion and greatly improved Wilkinson's balance sheet. Cliff's greatest assets were

◆ **Biarritz dinner service, 1934**
This stylish and elegant design shows Clarice Cliff's more restrained side. The square plates are characteristic, but highly impractical, like so many of her shapes. 93

◆ **Tulip Lotus vase, c.1935**
With its ribbed body, single handle and simple, stylized tulip pattern, this vase shows how industrial potters were imitating the styles of studio pottery during the 1930s. 94

▲ **Football pattern jug, 1930s**
A typical Clarice Cliff-shape jug decorated with the abstract pattern known as Football. 95

▲ **Summerhouse pattern clog, 1930s**
Clarice Cliff patterns were widely applied to tableware, ornaments and fancies. Particularly popular were the clogs. 96

◗ **Yoo Yoo coffee set, 1930**
Unusual and dramatic in their dark and rich colours, these pieces show the more experimental approach to decoration that Clarice Cliff developed in the mid-1930s. 97

her eye for fashion, her taste for decorative frivolity and fun, her sense of colour and her ability to be in tune with popular taste. In this regard, design was less important than marketing, and an instinctive understanding of the power of marketing, advertising and self-promotion seemed innate in Cliff. Indeed, the success of Bizarre and her other ranges probably owed more to marketing than to design. From the start Wilkinson planned clever and entertaining advertising campaigns to support these goods. Quite early on Cliff appreciated the marketing potential of her paintresses, sending them out to take part in painting demonstrations in major retailers and other outlets. In fact, she pioneered this selling technique, which was quickly copied by other companies, for example Shelley (*see* p.200) and Carter, Stabler & Adams (*see* Poole Pottery, p.159), and is still widely used today.

At first some retailers were hesitant to stock her extravagantly modern ware, but they were soon convinced by the volume of sales being enjoyed by their less cautious rivals. A writer in *The Pottery Gazette* in 1930 emphasized this point: 'Retailers … who said it was too advanced for their particular market … were quick to change their minds when they saw how the bold colourings and whimsical decorations were finding a market in the shops of their more courageous competitors.'

Cliff's creativity was at its peak in the 1930s, and her reputation properly belongs to that decade. In 1940 she married Colley Shorter, and around the same time World War II temporarily brought her creative activities to an end. She worked through the 1950s and into the 1960s, but she had lost the spark and her designs were by now dated and repetitive. Ironically, her death in 1972 came as a new generation of collectors was discovering her work. Their enthusiasm made Cliff into an icon and turned her mass-market 'bold colourings and whimsical decorations' into ridiculously expensive works of art. As a result she has belatedly achieved the artistic standing she never enjoyed during her lifetime.

KEY FACTS

Important dates: Apprenticed to Lingard, Webster & Co. 1912. Joined Hollinshead & Kirkham 1915. Joined A. J. Wilkinson 1916. Worked at Wilkinson's Newport Pottery 1927, with a brief interval for study of modelling and figure drawing at Royal College of Art, London. Production of Clarice Cliff ware by Newport Pottery began 1928. Became art director of Newport Pottery 1931. Played major role in Harrods tableware exhibition 1934. Retired 1965. Brand name still active as part of the Wedgwood Group.
Production: Earthenware.
Trade name: Bizarre.

MARKS

Signature incorporated in printed backstamps, or stamped in relief, on earthenware produced by Wilkinson's and Newport Pottery from late 1920s to early 1960s. Bizarre Ware mark used from c.1928.

CLIFTON POTTERY

Chemist Fred Tschirner and potter William A. Long established the Clifton Pottery in 1905. This was a small operation, with never more than a dozen workers, specializing in artware. Its first product was a line of vases, with a dense white body, called Crystal Patina for its green crystalline glaze similar to bronze oxidation. In mid-1906 the company introduced Clifton Indian Ware, a line of red earthenware vessels reproduced or adapted from historic and prehistoric American Indian pottery.

Clifton's forms for the general market included vases, jugs, mugs, jardinières, pedestals, fern dishes, candlesticks, umbrella stands, souvenirs and cooking vessels. It also made Robin's-egg Blue, a pale luminous glaze, on the same forms as Crystal Patina, and Tirrube Ware, a redware body with slip-painted flowers and unglazed finish. Some of the Tirrube Ware pieces are signed by artists such as Albert Haubrich.

By 1911 artware had been abandoned in favour of high-fired porcelain wall tiles and vitrified floor tiles using glazes invented by Charles Stegmeyer, and in 1914 the firm's name was changed to the Clifton Porcelain Tile Company.

KEY FACTS

Location: Newark, New Jersey, USA.

Important dates: Founded 1905. Became Clifton Porcelain Tile Company 1914.

Production: Artware and floor and wall tiles.

MARKS

This cipher used on Indian Ware. Crystal Patina had slightly different version.

◀ **Indian jug, c.1910**
Pottery from Four Mile Ruin in Arizona inspired the decoration on this jug. While the forms of Clifton Indian Ware were familiar to its consumers, the overall finish and decoration evoked Indian pottery. [98]

ALFRED CLOUGH

After working as a wholesaler from 1905, in 1913 Alfred Clough established the Waterloo Works and Mill Street Works, Longton, Staffordshire, trading as the Royal Art Pottery Company & St Louis Fine Art Pottery Company. By 1915 his advertisements included vases, clock sets, pots and pedestals, bulb bowls, flower holders and rose bowls. Clough also made, at both his St Louis Works and Garfield Pottery, china and earthenware tableware and ordinary domestic ware in white, white and gold and printed, printed and gilt, blue band and litho and gilt. Largely for the popular market, these goods were widely advertised in the 1930s.

The company continued in production during World War II, although two of the factories – the Garfield Pottery and the Smithfield Works – were closed, and production was limited to utility lines such as jugs, mugs, pudding bowls, toilet ware, chamber pots and roll-edge canteen plates. The firm also made nursery ware for export, including babies' plates and a delightful set with a Ducks and Drakes pattern which was advertised in *The Pottery Gazette* in 1949.

When Government restrictions were lifted in 1952, production was greatly expanded to include a full catalogue of dinner, tea, kitchen and nursery ware, as well as domestic and fancy items for both home and export markets. During the 1950s and 1960s the company brought out many new lines and pursued an aggressive advertising campaign. Among other lines advertised during this period was the contemporary-style Gaytime tableware range and a newly modelled Seymour

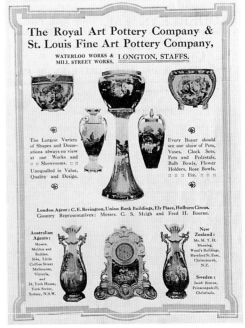

◀ **Advertisement, 1915**
This advertisement shows the wide range of generally over-elaborate ware produced by many Staffordshire companies at this time. [99]

tableware shape, launched in 1960, which was brought out in plain white or decorated. The Royal Art Pottery was renamed Clough's Royal Art Pottery in 1961 and became a holding company for a number of companies with which Clough had merged or which he had acquired. Among those which came under his control were Barker Bros (*see* p.19), Cartwright & Edwards (*see* p.40), W. H. Grindley (*see* p.84) and Sampson Smith (*see* p.207). In 1973 the much-expanded Alfred Clough Group merged with Royal Stafford China (formerly Thomas Poole; *see* p.162)) and the British Anchor Pottery (*see* p.33). Some of these companies have remained with the group to this day, whereas others have closed or changed hands more than once. The group changed its name to Grindley of Stoke (Ceramics) Ltd in 1978, and in 1982 it became the Federated Potteries Co. (*see* p.65).

KEY FACTS

Location: Waterloo Works, Mill Street Works, St Louis Works, Garfield Pottery and Smithfield Works, Longton, Staffordshire, UK.
Important dates: Founded 1913. Later became Alfred Clough Group, which became Grindley of Stoke (Ceramics) 1978 and Federated Potteries Co. 1982.

MARKS

Printed 'ROYAL ART POTTERY' above crown.

◆ Gaytime advertisement, 1957
Although not known as a style leader, Clough made some interesting ware in the 1950s. This smart advertisement shows its version of the popular plaid, or tartan, design. 100

COALPORT

Coalport's reputation was built in the 18th and 19th centuries on its ranges of extravagantly decorated ornaments and tableware. In the 19th century Coalport was noted for its fine painting and gilding in the manner of 18th-century Sèvres, Meissen and Chelsea porcelains, especially the much-admired *rose du Barry* ground that was used on a prize-winning dessert service shown at the Great Exhibition in London in 1851. Many well-known artists specializing in fruit and flowers, landscapes, exotic birds, fish and other traditional subjects were drawn to the factory and this type of ware has remained a characteristic Coalport product. Despite its renown as a maker of high-quality ware, the pottery experienced a steady decline in the latter part of the 19th century, brought about in part by its increasingly isolated location on the banks of the River Severn. However, new patterns and the continual revival of more traditional ware combined to ensure the company's survival into the 20th century.

About 1920 Coalport was bought by Cauldon Potteries (*see* p.40) and about 1926 it was moved to Staffordshire, although it retained its own name and a degree of autonomy. Around this time the Coalport showroom displayed many of the old favourites from

◆ Coffee cup and saucer, 1912
Coalport made its name in the 19th century for its high-quality Sèvres-style tableware and ornaments. Fine painting, rich gilding and the apple-green ground make this a good example. 101

◆ Coronation chalice, 1902
Made to commemorate the coronation of Edward VII in August 1902, this wonderfully elaborate porcelain chalice brings the traditional French style into the Art Nouveau era. 102

its period in Ironbridge in the 18th century. These included rich patterns on gadroon edge shape and a full range of service plates, desserts, tea and coffee services and vases, as well as souvenir and coronation ware and a wide range of miniatures, many with hand-modelled flower encrustation.

In the 1930s another famous name in the Victorian pottery industry, George Jones (*see* p.100), was acquired by Cauldon, and from about 1936 until 1950 Coalport, Cauldon and George Jones operated as Crescent Pottery, the George Jones trade name. In 1958 Coalport and George Jones were bought by E. Brain & Co. (*see* p.28), while Pountney of Bristol bought Cauldon Potteries, and by 1963 the Coalport name had been reintroduced and was applied to all the group's products.

The Wedgwood Group (*see* Josiah Wedgwood & Sons, p.230) took over Coalport in 1967 and streamlined the production of both tableware and ornaments while maintaining the output of traditional richly decorated and flower-encrusted ware. Wedgwood also expanded the production of high-quality limited-edition ware and commemoratives, a Coalport speciality throughout the 20th century, along with reproductions of earlier ware. The new owner also continued to produce a full range of tableware, including Ming Rose, the best-known Coalport pattern, ornamental ware and some floral groups and figures, as well as introducing nursery ware. Many nursery series have since been produced, some of the more recent examples featuring Postman Pat and Paddington Bear.

In 1975 the old Coalport factory at Fenton (formerly E. Brain's Foley Pottery) was modernized, and the Coalport Museum was opened in Coalport the following year. The company's production since then has included Walt Disney figurines and the Peter Jones collection of miniatures. In the 1980s tableware production was reduced, and in 1988 the production of some Coalport tableware shapes was transferred to the Wedgwood trade mark. Coalport has since then concentrated on the production of figures and giftware. The old Coalport works and the adjoining new Coalport factory both closed in 1992.

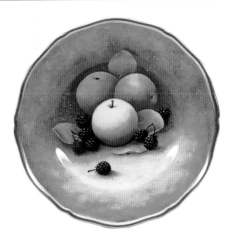

⬥ Hand-painted service plate, 1980s
Lusciously painted fruit subjects in the manner of Chivers have been popular for decades, and are still made in limited editions. [103]

⬥ Anne Boleyn, c.1985
This bone-china figure was made from 1979 to 1992 as part of the Henry VIII collection. [104]

⬥ Floral vase, 1990s
Hand-modelled floral ornaments have been made by Coalport for at least two centuries, and are still popular. [105]

KEY FACTS
Location: Coalport, Shropshire, and, from about 1926, Foley Works, Fenton, Staffordshire, UK.
Important dates:, Founded c.1795. Still active, as part of Wedgwood Group.
Production: Ornamental porcelain and tableware.
Principal designers: Donald Brindley, Susan J. Cashmore, Graham Coates.
Trade names: Coalport, Coalbrookdale, Royal Cauldon.

MARKS
Usually include crown and 'COALPORT'. 'Made in England' added to backstamp c.1920.

COLCLOUGH & CO.

During its early years the company specialized in red-body teapots. By 1920 it was able to offer a wide range of standard lines in Rockingham, jet, Samian and rustic teapots in addition to the Marne-shape green-glazed teapot, with a sunk lid, designed for use by the hotel and restaurant trade. Around this time Colclough expanded production to include white-body teapots with on-glaze red-blue-and-gilt Derby or Imari style of decoration, as well as highly ornamental teapots and five-piece teasets, tableware, novelty ranges and ornaments such as colourful wall masks featuring young ladies in contemporary dress.

Colclough & Co. was, in the 1920s and 1930s, one of a number of smaller manufacturers to bring out eye-catching designs in response to commercial pressures. In many cases the wall masks and other inexpensive items were produced in response to similar designs originating from manufacturers on the European mainland. The wall decorations, in particular, were also attempts to fill a gap in the production of mantelshelf ornaments at a time when the vogue for modern fireplaces was growing.

In 1928 the firm was renamed the Stanley Pottery, but trade was badly affected by the slump that came after the Wall Street Crash, and it closed in 1931.

KEY FACTS

Location: Stanley Pottery and other sites, Longton, Staffordshire, UK.
Important dates: Founded 1887. Became Stanley Pottery 1928. Closed 1931.
Production: Earthenware and china.
Trade names: Stanley, Royal Stanley.

MARKS

Impressed mark 'C & Co' or printed mark with initials and 'Royal Stanley Ware'. These marks continued after pottery renamed in 1928.

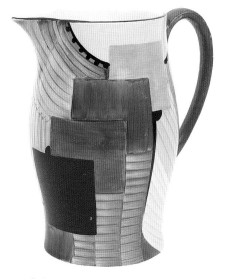

◆ **Wall mask, c.1930**
Following the route pioneered by European manufacturers such as Goldscheider, wall masks became a popular phenomenon in Britain in the 1930s. Particularly stylish are those in contemporary dress, often inspired by films. [106]

SUSIE COOPER

One of the leading tableware designers of the 20th century, Susie Cooper was one of the few women in the history of British ceramics to own and control a large pottery factory. A creative but practical designer, with a keen understanding of the market, and a fashion leader, she was also a clever businesswoman.

Born in 1902 into a comfortable Staffordshire family, she began to study at Burslem School of Art in 1919. At the same time, following the death of her father, she gained valuable experience in helping to maintain the family retail business. At Burslem, Gordon Forsyth took her under his wing and in 1922 secured for her a job as a decorator with A. E. Gray (*see* p.78), working initially with Forsyth on the new Gloria Lustre range.

Cooper always intended to be a designer, and by the end of 1923 her name was appearing alongside the Gray backstamp. From the start she was associated with the newly popular freehand and craft styles, establishing an approach to design and decoration that she was to retain throughout her professional life. At Gray she was one of a number of designers, and so not all her early work can be easily identified. However, her known work from this period reveals a taste for the decorative modernism and stylized abstraction that were becoming fashionable following the Paris Exhibition of 1925: a style referred to by *The Pottery Gazette* in 1926 as 'mild futurism'. Pieces designed by Cooper were shown in Paris, as they had been at Wembley the previous year. A typical Cooper motif from this period is the leaping deer. She also pioneered another style that was to become universal: hand-painted banding.

◆ **Cubist pattern, 1928–9**
In the late 1920s Susie Cooper was already well known for her modernist designs, many of which drew on popular abstract decoration. Typical are the so-called 'Cubist' patterns, inspired by contemporary French flat-pattern portfolios. [107]

Determined to fulfil long-held ambitions, Cooper left Gray in 1929 and in partnership with her brother-in-law Jack Beeson established in Tunstall a decorating studio with six employees. A few weeks later her landlord went out of business, and the venture ceased production while she sought new premises. Despite the adverse trading conditions caused by the Wall Street Crash, she leased the Chelsea Works, in Burslem, from Royal Doulton (*see* p.187), and her pottery was soon in production again, with an enlarged workforce. Blanks were bought from a number of suppliers, including Wood & Sons (*see* p.241) Doulton (*see* p.187), Grimwade (*see* p.83) and Grindley (*see* p.84), and Cooper's reputation for good modern design applied by hand to practical small services aimed at the growing domestic market steadily increased. Production was on a commercial scale, but the ware managed to retain the freshness of studio creations. Apart from vases and fancies, the production was mostly tableware, and Cooper quickly laid the groundwork for her policy of making the kinds of service that buyers really wanted. These included early morning sets for two, breakfast services, 21-piece tea services, coffee services, 15- and 26-piece dinner services, soup services, salad services, hors-d'oeuvres services, buffet services and game services.

Responding to an ever-greater demand for the undecorated ware, the pottery soon outgrew the Chelsea Works. In 1931, after forging close links with Wood & Sons (*see* p.241) via its subsidiary Bursley Ltd, Cooper moved into the Crown Works, Burslem, owned by Wood. At the same time Wood became the main supplier of the undecorated ware, giving her a greater control over the design of the shapes. Design and production were backed by a clear understanding of marketing and retailers' needs. Cooper always had well-equipped modern showrooms in London, and she exhibited at the British Industries Fairs, international exhibitions and modern design displays such as Dorland Hall in 1933 and the British Art in Industry exhibition in 1935. Particularly successful was her stand at the British Industries Fair in 1932, which featured her immediately popular Kestrel and Curlew shapes, with their blend of modernism and practicality.

Over the next few years the distinctive Susie Cooper style of decoration emerged, featuring banding, crayon, polka dot and stylized flowers, often in soft colours on the rounded shapes. Incising and tube-lining were also used, but the emphasis was on the handcraft studio look. At this time Cooper was producing up to 200 new designs a year, as well as running a major industrial enterprise. Correct in her analysis of the tastes of the

◆ **Service plate, c.1938**
Large service plates, made to decorate the table before the serving of the food, were a surviving Victorian idea, brought up to date by Susie Cooper with this stylish sgraffito design. 108

◆ **Coffee pots, 1930s**
Three typical Cooper shapes and styles are shown here: left, a Rex-shape pot with typical late-1930s sgraffito decoration; middle, a Kestrel shape pot with the decal pattern Gardenia first made in 1932; right, a Falcon-shape pot with the simple hand-painted Maroon Feather design of 1939. 109

Stars pattern coffee ware, 1939
Simple star patterns were a favourite
Cooper motif; this one is shown on the
Curlew shape. The design was made in
a number of colourways. 110

Toast rack, c.1938
Susie Cooper's confirmed liking for
simply painted repeating patterns is
shown here. A five-bar toast rack was
also produced. 111

newly emerging middle-class and younger markets,
she enjoyed an ever-increasing reputation as a daring
but successful innovator, able to sell her ware widely
in both home and export markets. As well as being
decoratively modern, her tableware was essentially
practical and affordable.

In 1935 the pottery produced its first decal-decorated pattern, Dresden Spray, whose success led to
many more at a time when most firms were barely considering this new process of mechanical decoration.
New shapes followed, Falcon and Spiral, and new
designs featured aerographic and sgraffito patterns,
along with hand painting. By this time Cooper was
famous all over the world as a remarkable woman designer and successful
pottery owner. Her products were in every major store, and were used by
Imperial Airways. In 1940 she received the accolade of Royal Designer for
Industry, but by that time World War II had already limited production.

After a fire in 1942 the pottery closed for the rest of the war, even
though it was licensed by the Government to maintain production.
Afterwards, production of pre-war ranges, including tableware, fancies,
ashtrays, vases, cruet sets, eggcups, fruit sets, sandwich sets, mugs and
teapots, started again, but output and decoration were still limited by
Government restrictions. However, Cooper was looking to the future and
designing new patterns that featured flowers and leaves in greens, blues
and pinks in hand-painted and sgraffito techniques. In 1950 she took control of Jason China, a move that enabled her for the first time to expand
into the bone-china market. This new material demanded a different
approach to design, for both shape and pattern, and she rose to the challenge, creating the Quail shape and patterns in clear, modern colours that
showed off the white porcelain. The 1950s represented a period of growth
and development, with many new patterns and shapes, and a new emphasis on transfer printing and decal decoration of mainly floral designs. The
straight-sided and elegant Can shape set the style for the future.

In the late 1950s the firm finally phased out earthenware, but by then
many popular patterns had been adapted for bone china. Its floral designs
became more abstract in the early 1960s, with a modernism that showed
the influence of Scandinavia, and then in 1966 Susie Cooper Ltd was
taken over by the Wedgwood Group (*see* Josiah Wedgwood & Sons, p.230)

Starburst bachelor set, 1946
Shown here on the Kestrel shape, this
version of the Starburst pattern was
first made for the export market. 112

and allied with another Wedgwood company, William Adams & Sons (*see* p.12). Cooper remained the sole designer, creating new ranges such as the matt-coloured Contrast series. In 1969, 60 of her patterns were still being produced, but by now she was losing management control and decisions were being made elsewhere. She continued to produce exciting and distinctive designs, such as Corn Poppy, but the number that went into production steadily diminished. In 1972 she resigned as a director, although she continued to design on a freelance basis for Adams and other Wedgwood companies. In 1980 Wedgwood closed the Susie Cooper pottery in Burslem, bringing to an end 50 years of remarkable achievement.

Cooper died in 1995, by which time a number of retrospective and celebratory exhibitions had made her a figure of international renown whose ware is appreciated by collectors all over the world.

◆ **Black Fruit breakfast cups, c.1957**
With its polychrome mix and match interiors contrasting with the black print, this popular pattern is more commonly found on straight-sided coffee cups. 113

KEY FACTS

Important dates: Worked for A. E. Gray 1922–9. Started Susie Cooper Pottery in Tunstall and soon after moved to Chelsea Works, Burslem, Staffordshire, 1929. Moved to Crown Works, Burslem, 1931. Merged with Bursley Ltd (a subsidiary of Wood & Sons) 1933, with Jason China 1950 and R. H. & S. L. Plant 1958. Became part of Wedgwood Group 1966. Resigned as director and became freelance designer 1972. Brand name still active as part of the Wedgwood Group.
Production: Tableware in earthenware and bone china.

MARKS

Painted monograms used in A. E. Gray period. Crown Works marks from 1932; this version used to c.1965. Also, 'Susie Cooper design' marks.

ELIJAH COTTON

Before the 1930s, Elijah Cotton was above all a specialist in jugs, claiming to be the largest manufacturer of them in the world. Later the firm broadened its range to include kitchenware, tea, breakfast and dinner services, toilet ware, nursery ware and useful fancies. Although it expanded the range of decorated ware and brought out some new designs in the 1930s in contemporary styles, including heavy floral Art Deco patterns, it continued to specialize in goods for the utilitarian middle-class household.

In the 1930s Elijah Cotton brought out a number of new ranges with a wash band and printed border design. Notable among these were June, with a blue or ivory wash band, and Cairo, with an ivory wash band, both launched in 1932 and sold, like most of the pottery's products, under the Lord Nelson trade name. Production continued throughout World War II, and after the war the full range of domestic and fancy tableware, vases, packaged giftware, kitchen sets, pudding basins, jugs, hotel and catering ware was produced.

◆ **Advertisement, 1932**
This *Pottery Gazette* advertisement shows typical patterns produced by a company that played safe by marketing both modern and traditional designs. 114

KEY FACTS

Location: Nelson Works, Hanley, Staffordshire, UK.
Important dates: Founded 1880. Closed 1980.
Production: Earthenware.
Trade name: Lord Nelson.

B.C.M. / NELSON WARE

W. T. COPELAND: see SPODE p.208

COWAN POTTERY

A member of an old Ohio pottery-making family, R. Guy Cowan was already producing utilitarian pottery when he went to study in Alfred, New York, with Charles Fergus Binns at the New York School of Clayworking and Ceramics, which was at that time a relatively new academic clay programme.

In 1908 Cowan returned to Cleveland to teach ceramics and design at Cleveland Technical High School, and in 1912 opened his first pottery in that city, the Cleveland Pottery and Tile Company. Ware from this pottery, which was equipped with three kilns, was made of red clay with coloured and lustre glazes. In 1917 Cowan was awarded the First Prize at the prestigious International Show at the Art Institute of Chicago, but he closed the pottery that year to join the Army.

Cowan went back to Cleveland once again in 1919, to reopen the pottery, and the following year moved to nearby Rocky River, Ohio, where he had nine kilns. The redware body was replaced with a high-fired porcelain body, and the emphasis of design shifted to sculpture produced with moulds. 'The duplication of good design,' Cowan believed, 'does not of necessity injure the product from an art standpoint.' Guided by this philosophy, he gathered a number of young artists around him at the Rocky River pottery to design sculpture and artware that could be produced in multiples. Waylande Gregory, Arthur Baggs, Thelma Frazier, Edward Winter, F. Luis Mora, Richard O. Hummel, Alexander Lazys, Paul Bogatay, Whitney Atcheley, Walter Sinz, Viktor Schreckengost, Jose Martin, Raoul Josset, Margaret Postgate, Elmer L. Novotny, Elizabeth Anderson and Russell Aitkin each contributed one or more significant models to the pottery's output. Hummel created vase shapes and glaze formulas, including a successful Asian ox-blood colour.

While the Cowan Pottery offered some limited editions, most of its output was mass-produced and widely distributed. The company had plans to expand in 1929, but these were never carried out because of the severe worldwide economic depression which was beginning to make itself felt in the autumn of that year.

In 1931 Cowan closed the pottery. He moved to Syracuse, New York, where he became art director of the Onondaga Pottery Company (*see* p.145), makers of Syracuse China.

◆ **Vase, c.1920**
This large porcelain vase was wheel turned by hand and covered with a finely mottled plum-and-turquoise glaze. Cowan may have been inspired by Asian models, but he gave the ware his own contemporary styling. 115

◆ **Group of lustre vases, late 1920s**
Cowan's pottery was carefully made and covered with brilliant glazes in fashionable colours. His ware offers the collector an exceptional variety of glazes, including matt, glossy and lustre finishes. 116

KEY FACTS

Location: Cleveland and Rocky River, Ohio, USA.
Important dates: Founded 1912. Closed 1931.
Production: Artware.

MARKS

'Cowan Pottery' impressed or printed on early ware. This version, including stylized 'R. G. Cowan', impressed on later ware.

CRESCENT POTTERY: see GEORGE JONES & SONS p.100

G. M. CREYKE & SONS

Originally a partnership between G. M. Creyke and a Mr Boulton, this firm was owned by the Creyke family after Boulton's death in 1897. In 1919 Creyke & Sons took over the Bell Pottery, and became known for practical domestic earthenware. Its specialities were pudding bowls, pie dishes, mugs, transfer-printed and decal-decorated tableware, tableware fancies, jugs, cheese stands and toilet ware. By 1923 it was advertising as a teapot manufacturer, with a full range in Rockingham, Samian, solid green and semi-porcelain. In the same year it advertised its G.M.C. teapot, which it claimed to be a perfect non-drip teapot with an unbreakable spout, suitable for the hotel, restaurant and liner trade. Better known today is the T-Flo teapot.

During World War II Wood & Sons (see p.241) took over production. Creyke reopened after the war but never recovered, closing about 1948.

◆ Advertisement, 1937
Patent teapots in modern shapes were a feature of the 1930s, with many potters trying to capture the market. Creyke's T-Flo, advertised here for the first time, exploited the fashion for streamlining. [117]

KEY FACTS

Location: Bell Works, Broad Street, Hanley, Staffordshire, UK.
Important dates: Founded 1897. Closed c.1948.

MARKS

Marked with monogram or initials 'G.M.C.' in script from 1930.

CROOKSVILLE CHINA COMPANY

The company made good-quality semi-porcelain dinnerware in a variety of traditional and modern styles, with solid colours, embossed patterns and colourful decals. It was one of the first potteries to make decorated kitchenware.

Pantry Bak-in Ware was first marketed in 1931, and an extensive line was quickly created. Crooksville made batter sets, fruit juice sets, refrigerator jugs and containers for leftovers, and cereal sets and spice sets consisting of four jars each. Batter sets, for making and serving waffles at the table, included a covered batter pitcher and covered syrup pitcher usually having a matching tray. Breakfast dishes could be purchased in the same shape and with decal patterns that matched the batter set, and a tray.

KEY FACTS

Location: Crooksville, Ohio, USA.
Important dates: Founded 1902. Closed 1959.
Production: Semi-porcelain dinnerware and kitchenware.

MARKS

Company name used alone or with body type (such as 'IVO-GLO', late 1920s), pattern name or product line.

◆ China platter, mid-1930s
Crooksville's Euclid shape was introduced in 1935. The example here shows the Autumn pattern in a brown palette; Euclid can also be found with Vegetable Medley, Flower Shop and others. [118]

CROWN DEVON: see S. FIELDING & CO. p.66
CROWN DUCAL: see A. G. RICHARDSON p.175

CROWN STAFFORDSHIRE

The company earned its reputation at the beginning of the 20th century for its well-made replicas of Chinese porcelain. These featured famous oriental glaze effects such as powder-blue and rouge flambé, recreated after painstaking research. Successful copies were also made of other Chinese ware such as *famille rose* and *famille verte*, along with the work of English porcelain artists such as William Billingsley.

Normal production lines were also of a high standard, aimed at the upper end of the market. These included dainty ornamental ware, trinket sets, teasets, based on the Swansea period, breakfast and dessert services hand-painted with birds, caricature figures and true-to-life oriental figures, as well as an interesting line of ivory bone-china pieces in open basketwork, with applied hand-made and hand-painted encrusted flowers, which appeared in company notes in 1916.

Nursery ware has always been an important part of the company's output. Early examples were the decal-decorated patterns made in the first decade of the century and R. R. Tomlinson's finely drawn imps for the Brownies or Merry Elves nursery ware designs registered in 1916.

Production continued during World War II and after the war expanded in the areas of both tableware and more traditional ranges such as flowered ware, modelled jewellery and china earrings. During the 1950s and 1960s the Crown Staffordshire name became associated with contemporary design. Under David Queensberry's direction, new styles of tableware, nursery ware and ornamental ware gave the firm a modern image which enhanced its reputation. Successful patterns included Queensberry's Lines and Starburst, and Musicalia by Tom Taylor.

In the early 1970s the company was advertising a full range of bone-china tableware, individual teacups and saucers, birds, flowers, jewellery, fancies, figurines, presentation ware, and promotional and advertising ware. Today, however, the name is in use only for special productions.

BONE CHINA SOUVENIRS

Chief item in the range of Coronation souvenirs by Crown Staffs. China Co., Ltd., is an 8-inch-tall loving cup heavily gilded and bearing an ornamental groundlaid decoration near the rim. It is founded by laurel embossed work, the handles taking the form of ornamental lions. Other pieces consist of a mug, beaker, hand-bell, and bridies set (cigarette box and four ash trays). Only a limited number of the loving cups are to be manufactured.

◆ **Coronation range, 1953**
Along with almost every other pottery, Crown Staffordshire celebrated the coronation of Queen Elizabeth II. 119

◆ **Musicalia, c.1956**
Designed by Tom Taylor, this pattern is one of a number of striking contemporary styles created for the company by Taylor and David Queensberry. 120

♦ **Robin, 1970s**
Modelled by John Bromley, this colourful robin shows the lasting popularity of traditional bird and animal models. 121

KEY FACTS

Location: Minerva Works, Fenton, Staffordshire, UK.
Important dates: Founded 1889. Formerly T. A. & S. Green and owned by the Green family until c.1965. Name changed from Crown Staffordshire Porcelain Co. to Crown Staffordshire China Co. 1948. Taken over by Semart Importing Co. 1964. Became part of Wedgwood Group 1974.
Production: China.
Principal designers: David Queensberry, Tom Taylor, J. T. Jones.
Trade names: Crown Staffs, Queensberry Tableware.

MARKS

Many versions show crown above 'Staffordshire' or 'Staffs'. From c.1961, 'Queensberry' used on specially designed tableware.

CUBE TEAPOTS

The Cube teapot was the creation of a Leicester entrepreneur who patented the design and licensed production to pottery companies and metalware manufacturers. As a result, Cube ware is found in the catalogues of some of the best-known makers of china, earthenware and stoneware, and in most cases its backstamps incorporate Cube Teapots Ltd's square licence mark. Also produced under licence were Cube hot-water jugs, compact teaware, eggcups and other articles of this shape. Among firms licensed by Cube were E. Brain (*see* p.28), George Clews (*see* p.42), Gibson & Sons, T. G. Green (*see* p.80), Grimwade (*see* p.83), Jackson & Gosling (*see* p.97), A. B. Jones (*see* p.99), Minton (*see* p.132) and Wedgwood & Co (*see* p.230).

Cube Teapots Ltd was a master of self-promotion, describing its innovation as 'the brilliant climax in teapot construction' and 'the essence of efficiency'. The principle behind the design was the avoidance of projecting spouts and handles, in order to create a range which could be easily stored and stacked, and which resisted chipping. Helped by winning a gold medal at the Nation's Health exhibition and the certificate of the Institute of Hygiene, and by widespread use by ships such as the *Queen Mary* and the *Queen Elizabeth*, the Cube teapot and related items were very successful. In 1928 Cube Teapots Ltd claimed in advertisements that its product had the largest sale of any patent teapot in the world.

◆ Cube teapot, c.1930
This version was produced by Gibson & Sons of Burslem, one of the patentees of the Cube design. The colourful pattern is rather out of keeping with the modern shape, a not uncommon phenomenon. 122

◆ T. G. Green catalogue, 1930s
Cube teapots and other patented cube ware were made by a number of British potters from the late 1920s onwards. It was only the shape that was patented, and so manufacturers could decorate them in any way they wished. A major producer of Cube ware was T. G. Green, the Derbyshire kitchen and domestic potter, whose range can be seen in this early 1930s catalogue. 123

KEY FACTS

Location: Campbell Yard, Leicester, Leicestershire, UK.
Important dates: Founded 1917. Closed 1951.
Production: Designers and patent holders of teapots and tableware.

MARKS

Goods simply marked with 'CUBE'. Ware made under licence by other factories may carry identifying marks.

CUBE

CYBIS

Polish artist Boleslaw Cybis travelled to the USA in 1939 to paint two frescoes in the Polish Pavilion at the New York World's Fair, but he was prevented from returning to Poland by the German invasion of his native country that year and the world war that followed. In 1942 he set up an art studio in Trenton, New Jersey, and by the end of the war he had made his home in nearby Princeton.

Before his death in 1957 Cybis had established a style which is still being followed by the studio today and remains popular with collectors of porcelain sculpture. Indeed, many contemporary pieces originate from drawings and paintings executed by Cybis. For example, 'The Bride' of the early 1980s was based on an oil painting of the same title that he did in 1937. Others who have designed sculptures for the studio are Marja Tym Cybis and Marylin Kozuch Chorlton.

MARKS

Bird and company name used on every piece.

→ Cybis group, c.1980
Dutch Crocus Golden Goblet is typical of the affordable range of Cybis's popular porcelain sculpture. 124

DART POTTERY

The renowned potter Bernard Leach's original workshop at Shinners Bridge, Dartington, Devon, is now part of the Dart Pottery, established in 1984 by Stephen Course, Peter Cook, Peter Hazel and Janice Tchalenko to manufacture Tchalenko designs. Her colourful work was immediately popular and in 1988 won the first Manchester Prize for Art in Production. Today the pottery makes earthenware by hand and machine.

MARKS

Ware usually marked with this logo combining letters 'D' and 'P'.

DARTMOUTH POTTERY

Established in 1947 in the Devon town from which it takes its name, this pottery has produced earthenware ornamental ware, teapots, jugs, mugs, teaware and fancies, including motto ware for souvenirs. The company's 1950s catalogues illustrate a number of contemporary-style dishes as well as a self-coloured range of vases and flower holders such as the London bowl and the Classic corner vase, which were available in ivory and light green. However, Dartmouth's main output has been traditional Devon-style ware, echoing the work of the Aller Vale Pottery (see p.14), especially motto ware and other slip-decorated patterns, notably Cottage, Seagull and Polka Dot. Dartmouth pottery is made for sale to local tourists as well as for the rest of Britain and for export.

In 1997, when the Honiton Pottery closed, Dartmouth bought the name and made Honiton designs marked as 'Honiton ware made at Dartmouth Pottery'. Production ceased in 2002.

→ Advertisement, 1953
A wide range of typical south Devon slipware for the tourist market. 125

KEY FACTS

Location: Dartmouth, Devon, UK.
Important dates: Founded 1947. Bought Honiton Pottery name 1997. Closed 2002.
Production: Ornamental ware, teaware and fancies.

DEDHAM POTTERY

Hugh C. Robertson, an English potter who settled in the USA in the 1860s with his father and brothers, experimented with glazes and in the late 1880s created a white crackle glaze in the Chinese taste. After the family's Chelsea Keramic Art Works failed in 1889, investors urged Robertson to develop this glaze commercially. He became the pottery director of the Dedham Pottery (founded as the Chelsea Pottery in 1891) in 1895, when the operation was moved from Chelsea to Dedham.

Dedham prospered for many years with a single product: tableware with an overall white crackle glaze decorated with painted blue borders which featured more than 50 repeating patterns of animals, birds, flowers and ornament. The pottery's rabbit is its most familiar design, but among the many others it produced are elephants, crabs, birds, butterflies, cats, chicks, swans, dolphins, ducks, fish, apples, azaleas, clover, cosmos, magnolias, mushrooms, owls, pineapples, polar bears and poppies. Patterns were created by persons inside and outside the company, including decorators Maud and Charles Davenport and Charles Mills, teacher J. Lindon Smith and history professor Denman Ross.

▲ Peacock pattern plate, c.1896
Dedham's pottery has been collected since the company ceased business, perhaps because of the cheery stylized borders and the classic blue-and-white palette. The example shown is decorated in the rare Peacock pattern. [126]

KEY FACTS

Location: Dedham, Massachusetts, USA.
Important dates: Founded 1895. Closed 1943.
Production: Tableware and artware.
Principal designers: Hugh Robertson, Maud Davenport, Charles Davenport, J. Lindon Smith.

MARKS

This mark printed in blue from 1896; 'Registered' added 1929.

DENBY POTTERY

In the early years of the 20th century Denby continued to build on the high reputation it had enjoyed since 1809 for its famous leadless glazed stoneware. At first production was concentrated on utilitarian domestic items. More exceptional were the ornamental flower vases and bowls, including some interesting scratch blue sgraffito items and Butterfly Ware vases by Horace Elliot and James Wheeler made around the turn of the century. Denby was an innovative company, always adding new lines to its catalogue. In the mid-1920s, as well as introducing new ranges such as Chef's Ware, it made a dripless teapot patented as 'Nevva-drip'.

However, during the early 1920s many of Denby's domestic lines had become either outmoded or obsolete and, in an effort to establish a new identity, it expanded its ornamental ranges. In 1923 it established a decorating department under the pottery decorator Albert Colledge. A series of hand-painted pieces, including tube-lined artware, was produced, some

▲ Oriental Ware vase, c.1926
Denby's enthusiasm for colourful 'art' glazes with mottled effects came to a head in the late 1920s. The glazes included Electric Blue and Antique Green as well as Oriental Ware. [127]

◆ Pastel Blue Ware, c.1933
Donald Gilbert masterminded the decorative ranges of the early 1930s, which featured contemporary pastel glaze effects. [128]

of which were shown at the British Empire Exhibition at Wembley, London, in 1924. There followed successes with the Danesby stoneware ranges, with tube-lined decoration and 'art' glazes such as Electric Blue, Antique Green and Meadow Green, and Oriental Ware.

Like many other potteries, Denby felt the impact of the slump in trade after the Wall Street Crash in 1929. Moreover, its outdated equipment made it difficult to diversify; but a turning point came in 1931 when Norman Wood joined the company and energetically modernized the works. Tunnel kilns replaced the old bottle ovens, and Denby changed the main emphasis of its production from industrial ware to more general domestic lines. The first success from this period was the Cottage Blue tableware. This encouraged the company to bring in Donald Gilbert, a graduate of the Royal College of Art, as a freelance modeller and designer.

In 1934 the firm reintroduced some of its 1920s novelty footwarmers and launched a new nursery series of ornamental ware, including book-ends, love-birds, flying fish, a sea lion, a rabbit, a group of three geese and a Scottie dog, along with footwarmers modelled on animal subjects created by Gilbert. By this time Gilbert had also designed the Epic and Manor Green ranges of oven-to-table ware. Manor Green and Cottage Blue were both still made in the 1980s. Their production stopped during World War II in favour of Utility Brown Ware, but they were reintroduced in the 1950s, along with the Homestead Brown range. Over the next few years,

as well as employing highly skilled in-house designers, Denby recruited prominent freelance designers. Among these were the Austrian Alice Teichtner and the Hungarian Tibor Reich. Reich had a small pottery studio in Stratford-upon-Avon, Warwickshire, and in 1953 he proposed to Denby that it should produce his original pottery. The firm appointed him as a consultant and merged his small Tigo company with Denby. The result was Tigo Ware, a contemporary range of functional, stark black-and-white ware launched in 1956. During this decade Denby moved into the dinnerware and more sophisticated tableware market; Greenwheat, designed in 1956 by Albert Colledge, was one of its most successful lines.

The company was floated on the Stock Exchange in 1970 and renamed Denby Tableware Ltd in 1976. It was taken over by Crown House in 1981, and later developments included takeover by the Coloroll Group in 1987 and a management buyout in 1990. Today Denby is a major independent producer of distinctive tableware and stoneware for the domestic market.

KEY FACTS

Location: Denby, Derbyshire, UK.
Important dates: Founded as Bourne's Pottery 1809. Still active.
Production: Stoneware. Introduced porcelain range 2003. Production outsourced abroad.

MARKS

Pottery with pattern or designer's name.

➡ **Harlequin and Spice tableware, c.1993**
The fashion for casual dining is reflected in recent Denby ranges. [131]

DEVONMOOR ART POTTERY

Started by Mr Hope, an American potter, the company quickly became known for innovative novelty ware and individualistic creations, decorated in good-quality coloured glazes with unusual multicoloured effects, which could loosely be called artware.

Output was mainly vases, fern pots, bowls and novelties, plus some utilitarian ware such as tea and breakfast-table sundries, including cruet sets, eggcups, jam jars, mugs, jugs and teapots, and toilet ware. Novelty ware included Toby jugs, a teapot, sugar and cream representing Simple Simon, Old Mother Hubbard and Georgie Porgie, and an amusing Judy jug. After World War II the pottery relied increasingly on the tourist trade.

KEY FACTS

Location: Liverton, near Newton Abbott, Devon, UK.
Important dates: Founded 1913. Closed c.1914. Reopened 1922. Closed c.1981.
Production: Earthenware.

MARKS

Impressed or printed name of pottery.

DEVONMOOR
MADE IN
ENGLAND

◆ **Devonmoor eggcup set, 1930s**
Made from local red earthenware, and covered with thick slip glazes in soft colours, this decorative tableware was made with the tourist trade in mind. [132]

DERBY: see ROYAL CROWN DERBY p.184

DICKER POTTERY

From around 1843 the pottery made its name as a manufacturer of utility and country ware, such as bread pans, wash bowls and milk pans, in red earthenware. These continued in production well into the 20th century, alongside ranges of utilitarian ware decorated with metallic and lustre effects which were sold under the name Sussex Iron-glazed Art Ware. Many Dicker shapes were inspired by Roman or medieval forms; others were reminiscent of Chinese and Japanese bronzes. A black ironstone lustre effect predominated, although the pottery also used numerous coloured glazes, principally greens and amber.

KEY FACTS

Location: Hellingly Pottery, East Sussex, UK, 1946–59.
Important dates: Founded c.1843 as Uriah Clark & Nephew. Closed 1959.
Production: Earthenware.

DUDSON BROS

This major pottery has remained in the same family since its foundation in early Victorian times. Early products included mosaic and jasper ware, and crested and badged ware. In 1891 the Dudson factory became one of the first in Britain to concentrate exclusively on tableware for the developing hotel and restaurant trade, and for shipping and railway lines.

During World War I Dudson Bros introduced a type of bronze-green ware, its stoneware body being particularly suitable for the company's production, and modelled a range of additional articles, including a cafetière which was supplied to the UK hotel trade.

The company underwent sustained expansion after World War II. In the 1950s it acquired the Albert Potteries in Burslem, renamed J. E. Heath Ltd (*see* p.91), and created a new range of vitrified hotel ware for the UK under the Armorlite trade name. Later it acquired the Grindley Hotel Ware Co., along with its Duraline trade name. The leading designer of this period was Helen Cooper, who created many of the most popular patterns.

Further technical achievements followed in the 1960s and 1970s, resulting in the Super Vitrified products. A more recent technical advance was Dudson's Fine China, which placed the pottery among the world's leading producers of tableware for hotels and the catering industry.

◆ **Nevada, 1980s**
A dramatic design from Dudson's modern range of service plates. 133

◣ **Corinth Amber tableware, 1970s**
This pattern is typical of the ware made by Dudson in the 1970s, aimed at both domestic and hotel ware markets. 134

◆ **Sun Moon Stars, 1990s**
In the 1990s Dudson promoted its contemporary look with a collection of decorative service plates for use in hotels and restaurants. 135

KEY FACTS

Location: Hanover Works, Hope Street, Hanley, and later Burslem and Tunstall, Staffordshire, UK.
Important dates: Founded 1838. Still active.
Production: Earthenware and stoneware.
Principal designer: Helen Cooper (née Dudson).

MARKS

Impressed or printed marks usually include Dudson name.

DOULTON: see ROYAL DOULTON p.187

DUNOON CERAMICS

This pottery, established in Scotland in 1973, started by producing stoneware, using studio pottery glazes and styles and etched designs. Later it added direct screen-printed floral patterns to its range. It began making bone china in 1974, having established a studio in Staffordshire and employed three full-time designers from the Martin Hunt group, Jack Dadd, Martin Hunt and John Clappison. Also around this time, Dunoon extended its production to include tableware and kitchenware, concentrating in particular on making mugs for the domestic market.

In the early 1980s the company set up a second factory in Staffordshire for the manufacture of fine bone china, and current production at this site consists mainly of mugs and kitchenware.

◀ **Dunoon mugs, 1999**
With factories in Scotland making stoneware and their English counterparts producing bone china, Dunoon has made an impact on the mug market. Typical are Living World, which is on the Windsor shape, and Bears, which is on the Devon shape. 136

ECANADA ART POTTERY

Jasper ware is closely identified with Wedgwood (*see* Josiah Wedgwood & Sons, p.230), but other potteries sprigged contrasting decorations on solid stoneware bodies in the Wedgwood manner. George Emery's Ecanada Art Pottery took this design concept and expanded its traditional range, using Canadian subjects and a contemporary style. The ware was slip-cast of solid colour bodies in dark green, pale and dark blue, dusty pink, white, chocolate brown and, most rarely, black. Contrasting, usually white, moulded ornaments were sprigged on the slip-cast form in its leather-hard state before firing. A variety of ornament on vases, jardinières, teasets, smoking sets, candlesticks and lamp bases was invented by Emery, including figures of Indians and explorers, chinoiserie pagodas, Canada geese and roses.

Born in Staffordshire, UK, Emery learned mould-making as an apprentice at Wedgwood and emigrated to Canada in 1912. By 1926 he was making sprig-decorated stoneware in his home workshop. In 1944 he set up a separate pottery. Some 20 employees, including his son George, made the ware. Emery Jr directed the works from 1949 until 1952, when production ceased.

◀ **Jasper ware vase, c.1930**
George Emery's jasper ware offers a delightful Canadian counterpoint to Wedgwood's typical neoclassical patterns. He supported himself by making moulds for electrical porcelain, but developed the jasper ware in his home workshop. 137

ELEKTRA PORCELAIN CO.

The pottery made ornamental tableware accessories, novelties, jugs, figures and statuettes, garden pottery, table lamps, vases and flower holders, animals, clock sets and cellulose fancies. In 1931 its catalogue included embossed designs in willow, Cries of London, Dutch and other familiar styles of decoration. However, Elektra is probably best known for its Zanobia and Vulcan ware, typical examples of popular commercial Art Deco modernism. Many of the lines that the pottery was making in the 1930s were similar to those produced at the Avon Art Pottery (*see* p.17), and therefore, as part of the Board of Trade's Concentration Scheme introduced during World War II, it was decided in 1941 to close the Edensor Works and transfer Elektra's production to Avon's Jubilee Works. Elektra continued to trade under its own name during the 1940s, making cellulose fancies for export, but the company never really recovered from the effects of the war and by 1950 had ceased trading.

Please the Customer

KEY FACTS

Location: Edensor Works, Longton, Staffordshire, UK.
Important dates: Founded 1924. Closed 1940s.
Production: Earthenware.
Trade names: Zanobia, Vulcan.

MARKS

Usually show name of range only. This printed mark introduced c.1924; similar mark identifying Vulcan range from c.1940.

⬥ **Zanobia Ware advertisement, 1939**
Elektra Porcelain's Zanobia Ware, seen here advertised in *The Pottery Gazette*, was typical mass-market Art Deco. [138]

ELLGREAVE POTTERY CO.

This large-scale producer of teapots, good-quality domestic earthenware, red-body ware and some tableware was established in 1921 by Wood & Sons (*see* p.241). About two years later Charlotte Rhead, Wood's art director since 1912, modernized the designs. Her typical tube-lined trellis patterns were sold under the Lottie Rhead Ware name, and she may have designed red-body dinner and teaware, vases and bowls made in the 1920s.

The pottery continued production throughout World War II and was one of the first makers of white teapots designed to fit under an insulated metal cover. These insulated goods became a major part of Ellgreave's production, but it also made figurines, lamp bases, vases, coffee ware, oven-to-table ware, and Bonzo and other money banks. Attempts at a contemporary look included the Apollo teaset in matt white and gold, part of the Tiko range, in 1967. The pottery closed in 1981.

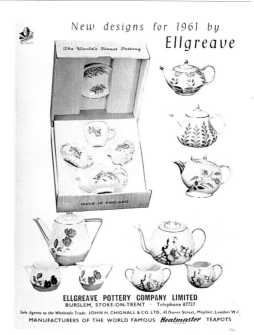

New designs for 1961 by Ellgreave

ELLGREAVE POTTERY COMPANY LIMITED
BURSLEM, STOKE-ON-TRENT · Telephone 87727
Sole Agents to the Wholesale Trade: JOHN H. CHIGNALL & CO. LTD., 43 Dover Street, Mayfair, London W.1.
MANUFACTURERS OF THE WORLD FAMOUS *Heatmaster* TEAPOTS

KEY FACTS

Location: Ellgreave Pottery, Ellgreave Street, Burslem, Staffordshire, UK.
Important dates: Founded 1921. Closed 1981.
Production: Earthenware.
Trade names: Lottie Rhead Ware, Heatmaster.

MARKS

Usually printed and include name of firm. Addition of 'Lottie Rhead Ware' in script indicates ware by designer Charlotte Rhead.

⬥ **Advertisement, 1960**
Ellgreave's dominance of the popular teapot market is reflected by this advertisement in the December 1960 issue of *The Pottery Gazette*. [139]

EMPIRE PORCELAIN CO.

From its early years this pottery specialized in new decal-decorated ware. Among the first items it advertised were toilet sets and nursery ware, but it also produced substantial quantities of both ornamental and useful ware for the popular market. Between the wars and after World War II the firm made dinner, tea and hotel ware. The 1950s saw the introduction of contemporary-style teaware such as Polka Dot spotted ware on coupe shape, familiar tartan patterns in bright underglaze colours, and stylized animal figures known as Fantasies. In the early 1960s Tom Arnold joined Empire; he designed several tableware shapes, including Mirage. The pottery closed in 1967, when owned by the Qualcast group.

KEY FACTS
Location: Empire Works, Shelton, Staffordshire, UK.
Important dates: Founded c.1896. Closed 1967.
Production: Earthenware.

MARKS
Printed mark incorporating Empire name or monogram.

♦ Tartan tableware, mid-1950s
Hand-painted tartan, or plaid, tableware was a popular Staffordshire product in the mid-1950s. The Empire version had a distinctly contemporary flavour and exploited the American-inspired mix-and-match approach. 140

EWENNY POTTERY

Long associated with the slipware tradition, and using local red clays and glazes based on local minerals, this country pottery, owned by the Jenkins family since about 1800, is well known for its puzzle jugs, dishes, wassailing bowls and other domestic slipware.

The Ewenny Pottery became part of the widespread art-pottery movement that flourished from the late 19th century, producing ware with sgraffito decoration and a more adventurous use of coloured glazes. These styles dominated production in the 20th century, thanks to the expanding tourist trade, and carried echoes of the similar artistic slipware being produced in profusion by the North Devon potters. At the same time the pottery made traditional Welsh forms, often decorated with Welsh mottoes and inscriptions. Traditional domestic ware from the late 18th and early 19th centuries, such as bowls, vases, jars, platters, jugs and wassailing bowls, continued in production, in familiar slipware colours and with rich new glazes: deep blue, lime green, buff, dark green, metallic black and a multicoloured effect called Autumn Tints, developed in 1953. More recently the pottery has concentrated on domestic ware and souvenirs, but still makes slipware in traditional styles.

➥ Jug, 1930s
With its antique form, which evokes both German stoneware and early slipware, and mottled finish, this jug maintains Ewenny's links with traditional country pottery. 141

KEY FACTS
Location: Near Bridgend, Glamorgan, UK.
Important dates: Founded c.1800. Still active.

MARKS
Variation of this mark from early 20th century still used today.

Ewenny Pottery 1904

FALCON: see THOMAS LAWRENCE p.113 and J. H. WEATHERBY & SONS p.229

FARNHAM POTTERY

Founded by Absalom Harris in 1860, this family-owned pottery originally specialized in Farnham Green Ware, inspired by 16th-century green-glazed ware and designed from 1890 by W. H. Allen. Contemporary catalogues list fern pots, baskets, flower stands, wall pots, casks, dishes and pitchers and later, tableware, toilet ware and hearth tiles. After World War II garden pottery dominated production, as it still does.

KEY FACTS

Location: Farnham, Surrey, UK.
Important dates:
Founded 1860. Still active.
Production: Earthenware.

FEDERATED POTTERIES CO.

The story of this group of companies, which at its peak employed about a thousand people, illustrates the battle for survival among smaller Staffordshire potteries in the 1980s and 1990s.

Probably the most significant event in the group's history was the setting up of a design studio under the direction of Roy Midwinter (*see* p.129), and the resultant launch of Federated Potteries Designer Collection, low-priced tableware with a radically modern look. Midwinter gathered about him young designers, notably Dave Harper, who were able to meet the challenge. The result was a range of stunning and largely abstract co-ordinated patterns and shapes which could be mixed and matched, and which were not only attractive but also suited to the new informal dining habits of the young generation. Patterns in this range are noted for the use of strong colours such as black, red, yellow and green and include Tropicana, Safari, Banjo, Calypso and Fireball.

Ahead of its time, the Federated Potteries, experiment failed, but it anticipated the move to casual dining that has determined the nature of the pottery industry's production in the late 1990s.

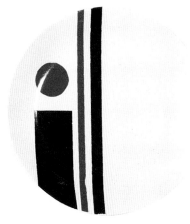

◆ Midwinter plate, early 1980s
Refreshingly simple, this plate depicts one of a series of exciting patterns noted for their vibrant colours produced by Roy Midwinter's studio in the early 1980s. [142]

◆ Safari pattern tableware, 1984
Samples of a small range of 12 new shapes introduced by Federated Potteries in 1984 as part of the already successful Designer Collection created by Roy Midwinter. Coloured mugs were co-ordinated to go with any of the patterned saucers in the series. [143]

KEY FACTS

Location: Woodland, Tunstall, Fenton and Meir Park, Staffordshire, UK.
Important dates: Founded 1982 from merger of W. H. Grindley, Cartwright & Edwards and Weymek. Group dissolved in 1987, when Grindley acquired by Churchill and Cartwright & Edwards by Coloroll. Closed 1992.
Production: Tableware.
Principal designers: Roy Midwinter, Dave Harper.

MARKS

Include pattern name and 'Roy Midwinter Designer Collection' on special pieces.

'BANJO'
Roy Midwinter
Designer Collection
by
Federated
Potteries
Staffordshire
England

J. T. FELL & CO.

Cyples was a well-known pottery in Staffordshire between 1794 and the 1840s, producing tableware in earthenware, drabware and redware. However, J. T. Fell's only connection with Cyples was its use of the company's old factory in Market Street. Not alone in the pottery industry in exploiting a rather tenuous historical link, Fell produced ornamental ware, tableware, toilet ware, vases, flower bowls, jugs and tableware fancies for the popular market, and a range of embossed lustre ware which it marketed under the trade name Embossa Ware from the 1920s. During World War II the firm sold its production quota to the North Staffordshire Pottery Co. About 95 per cent of the North Staffordshire Pottery Co.'s production was for government contracts and for hotel and canteen ware for essential services. Fell opened again after the war and continued to operate until 1957.

◀ **Planter, 1920s**
This planter, with a moulded, embossed swan design, painted purple-blue lustre-glazed exterior and orange lustre-glazed interior, is a typical example of Fell's Embossa Ware of the 1920s. It is also characteristic of the ornamental useful ranges introduced by potteries as an alternative to majolica production, which had diminished due to pressure to reduce the lead content in glazes. [144]

S. FIELDING & CO.

The company was founded by Simon Fielding in 1870 to produce majolica and black, brown and green-glazed ware, hand-painted ware and a wide range of domestic earthenware. He was joined by his son, Abraham Fielding, in 1878 and there followed a period of expansion. In the early 1880s the pottery produced a range of relief modelled tableware in the Japanese taste. For this range, which was called Majolica Argenta, the company used its new white body and glaze and majolica colours. It continued to make embossed tableware of this kind until well into the 20th century.

From the beginning the Crown Devon trade name offered an extensive range of all classes of ware, including children's and nursery lines. By the early 1920s the firm had earned a considerable reputation for glaze effects and lustre finishes, notably its range of vellum-grounded domestic utility ware, and the Crown Devon name was becoming well known. The firm also made an enormous range of earthenware.

Crown Devon

Economic prices ; delightful colour schemes harmonising with modern designs are just a few outstanding qualities which contribute to the speed with which CROWN DEVON moves from your shelves.

S. FIELDING & CO., LTD., DEVON POTTERY, STOKE-ON-TRENT

◀ **Crown Devon advertisement, 1930s**
This leaflet shows a typical range of richly decorated teaware, ornamental useful ware, ornaments and figures in the prevailing Art Deco style. [145]

Cubist jug, 1930s
During the 1930s Crown Devon favoured the modernist style pioneered by Clarice Cliff and Susie Cooper. 146

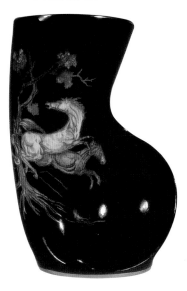

Free-form vase, 1950s
With its curved abstract shape and printed and enamelled decoration, this is a typical 1950s product. 147

Hors d'oeuvre dish, 1950s
The dynamic shape, soft colour and stylish marine decoration reflect the powerful influence of Poole pottery in the 1950s. Crown Devon, always with an eye on current taste, was not alone in copying the ware of the Dorset trendsetter. 148

Pattern books from the mid-1920s include fine Art Deco tea and coffee services and tableware accessories with sunbursts, stylized floral and geometric patterns in bold colours, such as black and green, and lustres. New shapes in tableware in the same period include the octagonal form Era, which was brought out with print and enamel patterns such as Poppy and Iris. Other productions worthy of note are Silverline ware with a black handle finish, and figure models, some extremely realistic, in Devon Ivrine and Bronzine treatments.

A new line in painted panels was also introduced in the early 1920s, featuring fruit subjects by F. Cole and bird subjects by J. Coleman. In the same period the pottery also expanded Willow Lustrine ware to include Rustine, with a russet-brown background and black border, and a Chinese lantern theme in oriental colours. The latter was supplied right through the ranges, from small fancies to toilet ware.

By the late 1920s the Crown Devon catalogue included salad ware in both green and straw colour in the form of savoy cabbage leaves, as well as many other novelties. These included a honey pot in the shape of a bee-hive, a marmalade jar shaped like a Jaffa orange and tomato trays with high-relief modelled tomatoes. From 1930 embossed dinnerware, teaware and breakfast ware were produced in floral patterns treated with a primrose glaze. Notable among these patterns was Belle Fleur, which featured modelled poppies, pansies and other flowers.

In 1932 Abraham Fielding died and his son, Arthur Ross Fielding, took control of the pottery. A very productive period followed this change, and soon the Crown Devon name was predominant in the company's advertisements and catalogues. By 1934 Crown Devon, while continuing to offer a full range of domestic ware, kitchenware and other items, was also advertising a greater range of new models, including presents for men such as smokers' sets consisting of cigarette box, four coffees cups and saucers, and two ashtrays, in a plush-lined case, as well as 'wonderful lines in figures, suitable as gifts for ladies'. Typical named examples of these well-modelled contemporary-style figures are A Windy Day and Rio Rita. Kathleen Parsons created many of them as a freelance designer. The pottery also introduced a cheaper range of smaller figures, known as Sutherland Figures. These were fired once, painted and aerographically sprayed with cellulose. The company also made table lamps, door stops, musical cigarette boxes, in the form of a grand piano, and musical jugs.

From the 1930s to the 1950s Crown Devon established its reputation for distinctive, stylish and modern ware, including tableware such as the Checks pattern. The company continued production throughout World War II, and after the war embarked on a period of sustained reconstruction and development, planned before the war and carried out under Reginald Ross Fielding, who succeeded his father in 1947. In 1951 a fire

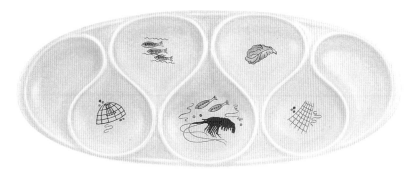

destroyed most of the company's premises, and although production resumed within twelve months, rebuilding of the factory was not completed until 1957, when the name Devon Phoenix Pottery was adopted.

The pottery remained until 1966 in the control of the Fielding family, which had acquired Shorter & Son (*see* p.204) two years earlier. Sold in 1966 and again in 1976, the Crown Devon name became associated with novelty items, including cheese stands, gourmet ware and tableware, kitchenware, bathroom ware and boxed giftware, nursery ware and ornamental teapots, until 1982, when the Crown Devon Pottery was closed. The factory and its moulds were bought by Caverswall China (*see* p.41) early in 1983, and then sold to the retailers Thomas Goode & Co. in 1984. After being sold again in 1987, the pottery was demolished.

(*see* p.204) ... (*see* p.41)

KEY FACTS

Location: Railway Works (until 1905, when name changed to Devon Pottery), Sutherland Street, Stoke, Staffordshire, UK,
Important dates: Founded 1879. Closed 1982.
Production: Earthenware.
Trade names: Crown Devon, Royal Devon.

MARKS

Incorporate crown, 'Fieldings' or company's initials. From c.1913 'Crown Devon' included.

♦ **Novelty teapots, late 1970s**
Devon pioneered the novelty teapot revival in the 1970s. In their shapes and colours these examples are typical of the last years of the decade. 149

E. B. FISHLEY & W. FISHLEY HOLLAND

George Fishley was the first of a famous dynasty of North Devon potters, making traditional slipware, harvest jugs and domestic and garden pottery. Of his descendants, the best known is Edwin Beer Fishley, who continued this pattern of production until his death in 1906 and was also responsible for following contemporary trends and introducing ranges of artistic pottery, inspired both by historical models and by the impact of local art schools. The pottery was then taken over by William Fishley Holland, who had been working with his grandfather from 1902. Artware, tourist and souvenir ware and traditional slipware were produced in quantity until 1912, when Fishley Holland sold the pottery and set up a new one in Somerset.

From the 1920s there was a great revival of interest in traditional slipware and other country pottery styles and techniques. The Fishley Hollands responded by making large quantities of harvest jugs and chargers, along with ware in more modern styles.

KEY FACTS

Location: Fremington, near Barnstaple, Devon, UK; later at Clevedon, Somerset, UK.
Important dates: Founded late 18th century. Traded as E. B. Fishley 1861–1906. Closed 1959.
Production: Earthenware.

MARKS

Incised mark with 'E. B. FISHLEY', 'FREMINGTON' and 'N. DEVON' on early ware. Later ware marked with incised initials or signature.

♦ **Mottled glaze vase, early 1920s**
The dramatic colours of this vase are evidence of Fishley Holland's move away from traditional slipware at this time. 150

FIFE POTTERY: see WEMYSS p.237

FLINTRIDGE CHINA COMPANY

The company was founded by Tom Hogan and Milton Mason in 1945, when European manufacturing was struggling to recover from World War II. While many US manufacturers of fine china succumbed to intense competition in the 1950s and early 1960s, Flintridge was successful throughout this period because its designs were marketable.

In 1970 the Gorham Manufacturing Company, an old American silversmith known for its quality flatware, bought Flintridge. Within eight years it expanded the operation from four kilns to eight and more than doubled its manufacturing space. In 1985 Gorham decided to have its china made by manufacturers worldwide, and ceased production in California. Black Contessa was the firm's biggest seller.

KEY FACTS

Location: Pasadena, California, USA.

Important dates: Founded 1945. Taken over by Gorham 1970. Closed 1985.

Production: China dinnerware.

MARKS
Backstamp in green on-glaze.

◀ **Miramar Platinum demitasse, 1950s**
The contrasting blue-grey colour on the outside of the cup and top of the saucer is a layer of coloured clay rather than a glaze. It co-ordinates with the rose decal and harmonizes with the platinum striping. [151]

THOMAS FORESTER & SONS

Active from 1883 to 1959, this Longton, Staffordshire, pottery made traditional and contemporary ware for the popular market. In 1921 it showed decorated vases, flower pots and fancy goods in earthenware, and china services with patterns based on oriental, Persian and Egyptian art. The mid-1930s saw Art Deco ware, including Seville bowls, jugs and vases, and the mid-1950s contemporary patterns such as Stardust Decoration.

MARKS
Usually include phoenix and company initials.

FRANKOMA POTTERY

Dinnerware, collectors' plates, vases and planters, novelty items and giftware have been produced by this company for many years. Founded by John Frank in 1933 as the Frank Potteries in Norman, Oklahoma, the Frankoma Pottery moved to Sapulpa in 1938.

By 1954 Frank was employing a distinctive red clay dug in the local Sugar Loaf Hill to make all of Frankoma's output. This clay is covered with a variety of glazes in the green and brown families. The design of these items draws on American Indian motifs, American pioneer artefacts and flora of the south-western USA. The Wagon Wheel pattern, for example, was among the most popular in giftware and dinnerware.

KEY FACTS

Location: Sapulpa, Oklahoma, USA.

Important dates: Founded 1936. Still active.

Production: Earthenware dinnerware and giftware.

MARKS
Early ware stamped in black; most marks impressed or raised.

◀ **Pottery, 1960s**
Mayan-Aztec, the pattern of the mug on the left, was introduced in 1945 and continues to be made. Besides dinner and giftware, the pottery is also known for collectable Christmas plates, figural sculpture, flower containers and other novelties. [152]

FOLEY CHINA: see E. BRAIN & CO. p.28
FRANCISCAN: see GLADDING-McBEAN COMPANY p.73

FULHAM POTTERY

Best known for its remarkable stoneware made by the late-17th-century potter John Dwight, the principal pottery in the Fulham area of London had a rather chequered history after that period. From 1864 C. J. C. Bailey made a wide range of decorative stoneware there, echoing Royal Doulton's (*see* p.187) Lambeth artware.

In 1889 Bailey sold the pottery to George Cheavin, a producer of water filters, laboratory and sanitary ware, jugs, bottles and other basic domestic stoneware, and the firm became known as the Cheavin Filter Co. From the 1920s Cheavin's output expanded to include, in addition to its utility ware, moulded garden ornaments, such as vases and bird baths, and other ornamental lines. In 1933 the pottery also produced a special line for children: a boxed set of Christopher Robin with half a dozen assorted animals, modelled by A. R. White. This series was also made in larger sizes as garden ornaments.

After World War II the pottery, which became the Fulham Pottery in 1948, produced undecorated wall brackets, bowls, and vases in modern styles, designed by W. J. Morriner and A. R. White. Also made were more utilitarian ranges such as acid containers, ashtrays, stoneware bottles, bread crocks, cigarette boxes, jugs, table lamps, mugs, ointment jars, poultry fountains, screw stoppers, spirit jars and vases, as well as figures and statuettes, ornamental bowls and novelty items. A typical novelty was the five-piece children's Clown set of the late 1950s, the pieces of which fit together to form a clown.

Changes of ownership and the site's redevelopment brought production to a close. However, in the early 1980s there was a Fulham revival, in which contemporary artists made unusual and decorative ware, and traditional materials and production techniques were used. Among the well-known figures who participated in this brief but exciting experiment were John Piper, Quentin Bell and Philip Sutton.

▲ **Philip Sutton plate, 1980s**
Artist Philip Sutton adapted his free and decorative painting style to ceramics in this period. 153

▲ **Quentin Bell plate, 1980s**
There have been many links between Bloomsbury and pottery, and Quentin Bell, son of the Bloomsbury artist Vanessa Bell, kept that tradition alive at Fulham in the 1980s. 154

◀ **John Piper dish, 1982**
Piper came to pottery late in life but enjoyed the new medium, painting ware at Fulham that added echoes of Picasso to his familiar style. 155

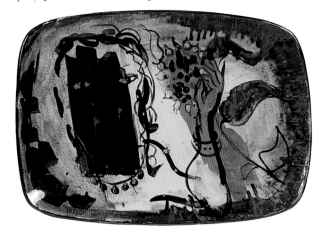

KEY FACTS

Location: Fulham, London, UK.
Important dates: Founded 1864 as C. J. C. Bailey. Became Cheavin Filter Co. 1889 and Fulham Pottery 1948. Moved to Battersea, London, c.1987. Pottery production ceased c.1989. Continues as supplier of pottery materials and equipment, operating as Potterycrafts Ltd.
Production: Stoneware.
Principal designers: A. R. White, W. J. Morriner, John Piper, Quentin Bell, Philip Sutton.

MARKS

Impressed or incised, usually incorporating 'FULHAM POTTERY' and 'LONDON' or 'ENGLAND'; marks showing 'LONDON' sometimes arranged in oval.

FULPER POTTERY COMPANY

In 1860 Abram Fulper bought Samuel Hill's pottery in Flemington, New Jersey, where Fulper had been making utilitarian redware and stoneware for Hill. After Abram died in 1881, his sons Charles, William, George and Edward took over management and production. In 1899 the Fulper Pottery Company was incorporated, but the popularity of heavy stoneware vessels was passing in favour of lighter materials such as glass and the company was adversely affected by these market changes.

In 1909 Fulper introduced a new Vasekraft or Vase-Kraft line of art glazes applied over its traditional stoneware clay body fired at a lower temperature. The forms were decorative rather than strictly utilitarian, and included vases, jardinières, blossom cups, bowls, book-ends, tobacco jars, candleholders, clock cases, desk sets, lamps, mugs and decanters. Many shapes were based on ancient Asian and European forms exhibited in museums in New York and Philadelphia. These were simplified somewhat to accommodate the heavy stoneware body and thick glazes.

Glazes were given exotic names such as 'elephant's breath', a luminous black; 'Alice blue', from the song about Theodore Roosevelt's daughter Alice; 'leopard skin', a crystalline lustre on slate or mauve; 'cat's eye'; 'mission matte', a brown-black flambé; 'café au lait', a chocolate colour; and 'famille rose', a matt pink in several shades. J. Martin Stangl, a German glaze chemist, made significant contributions to the art line through the development of a wide range of crystalline, matt and flambé glazes after he started working for the pottery in 1911. In 1915 the Fulper display won an award at the Panama-Pacific Exhibition in San Francisco.

In 1928 a second factory was opened in Trenton, New Jersey, in the old Anchor Pottery. The original Fulper factory in Flemington continued to be used for artware even after a serious fire the next year. In Trenton, however, Stangl was setting up tableware production with a red clay body. He bought the firm in 1930 and eventually phased out production of artware at Flemington, closing the factory in 1935.

KEY FACTS

Location: Flemington, New Jersey, USA.

Important dates: Founded 1860. Closed 1935.

Production: Utilitarian stoneware, artware and florist's crockery.

Principal designer: J. Martin Stangl.

MARKS

Also horizontal version.

◆ **Pottery vase, c.1915**
The trade name for the glaze on this classical baluster-form vase was Ashes of Roses, a fitting description for this flowing semi-matt finish. 156

◆ **Pottery bowl, c.1920**
There is so much variety in Fulper's glazes that it would be difficult to collect an example of every one. Many of the open forms, like this bowl, have beautiful glaze effects inside as well as outside. On this example, the brown flows from the rim over ochre outside and sky blue inside. 157

FURNIVALS

This manufacturer of tableware and utilitarian printed and decorated ware began production in 1890 in Cobridge, Staffordshire. Dinner, tea and toilet ware predominated, but the firm also made ranges in a good-quality semi-porcelain body toughened for hotels and restaurants. Typical products were brightly coloured Art Deco tableware ranges featuring hand-painted florals, made in the early 1930s. The factory closed in 1968.

MARKS

One of many different marks used; all include Furnivals name.

FURNIVALS
(1913)
ENGLAND

W. S. GEORGE POTTERY COMPANY

In 1898 W. S. George leased the East Palestine Pottery Company from the Sebring brothers, who were active in the pottery business in the region. About 1904 George bought and renamed the pottery. He made hotel china and semi-porcelain dinnerware in a great variety of shapes and decorations for sale in department stores and 'five and dimes' – small shops selling a wide range of inexpensive goods. Shapes were decorated with solid colours as well as many different colourful decals. Eventually there were four factories – another in East Palestine, and one each in Canonsburg and Kittanig, Pennsylvania. W. S. George died in 1925, and management devolved to his son W. C. George, who greatly improved production methods and equipment. The company closed around 1960.

W. S. George tableware has long been collectable because of its availability and variety. Many shapes were made and many decals designed to go on them, so the collector may be searching for the same decal on different shapes or the same shape with different decals. For example, Shortcake can be found on the Ranchero shape as well as on Times Square, while the Ranchero shape was also decorated with Wheat, Wampum, Iroquois Red, Indian Corn, Fruit Fantasy and other patterns. Similarly, the Bolero shape was made with Cherry Blossom, Gracia, Calico and other decals, while the Lido shape was decorated with, among others, Blossoms, Mexi-Lido, Mexi-Gren, Plain-Jane, Bouquet and Flower Rim.

Favourite shape lines with collectors are Lido, Rainbow, Georgette (sometimes called Petal) and Ranchero. These names, as well as George's many other shape lines, are included in the appropriate backstamp for each line, making shape identification quite easy. A single shaker shape, apparently designed originally for the Ranchero line, was used with several other shapes as well and can be found with many different decals.

Canarytone was the name for the firm's off-white glaze, a creamy yellow, made to compete with other earthenware makers who mimicked Lenox's (*see* p.114) ivory body. George also offered patterns on white.

▲ **Tulip plate, early 1930s**
Cheery red tulips were hand-painted in a matt finish on this Lido plate. First used in 1932, the Lido shape was made in white and Canarytone. 158

▲ **Dinnerware, 1930s**
The dinnerware shown here is in the Cherry Blossom pattern on the Lido shape in Canary-tone, W. S. George's version of the pale yellow tableware colour that was popular in the 1930s. 159

◆ **Striped platter, 1954**
'A good name is more to be desired than great riches,' declares the mark on goods honouring the company's fiftieth year. The George family took dinnerware seriously, making a variety of marketable patterns, both stylish and traditional. 160

KEY FACTS

Location: East Palestine, Ohio, USA.
Important dates: Founded 1904. Closed c.1960.
Production: Semi-porcelain dinnerware and hotel ware.

MARKS

Usually incorporate product line with company name.

> LIDO
> W. S. GEORGE
> CANARYTONE
> MADE IN U.S.A
> 1 8 4 A

GLADDING-McBEAN COMPANY

The Gladding-McBean Company has been a clever player in the American ceramics industry since its foundation in 1875. By 1926 it was the largest manufacturer of clay products in the USA. Its product line was diverse but concentrated on utilitarian clay products, including various speciality bricks (fire, enamel, face and coated), roof tiles, interior decorative tiles and architectural terracotta. From the 1930s to the 1970s the company made dinnerware in addition to these sturdy materials. Nowadays, as the market for fine tableware shrinks, the pottery is concentrating once again on the manufacture of utilitarian goods. However, in the heyday of the dinnerware business the name Franciscan was well known, and indeed Gladding-McBean's Desert Rose pattern, introduced in 1941, may well be the most popular dinnerware pattern ever made. The company gave a Desert Rose teapot to the Smithsonian Institute in 1964 as the 60-millionth piece made in that pattern. Much more of this line has been sold since then, and it is still being made today by the Wedgwood Group (*see* p.230).

When Charles Gladding, Peter McGill McBean and George Chambers, all of Chicago, founded the Gladding-McBean Company in California in 1875 for the manufacture of drainage pipes, they were attracted by the deposits of refractory clays in Placer County. In 1884 the firm added architectural terracotta, the product for which it is known throughout the world. Over the years other useful materials became part of its repertoire as a result of product development and the acquisition of other companies. For example, Tropico Potteries, known for tile and faience products, was bought in 1923, and tiles were produced for a number of years.

In 1934 Gladding-McBean introduced Franciscan Ware, a line of earthenware for gifts and tableware designed by Mary K. Grant, wife of Frederick J. Grant, the manager of the new plant. The new ware depended on Malinite, a talc body developed by Andrew Malinovsky and patented in 1928. When mixed with an amorphous flux, such as glass, the glaze materials fused with the Malinite body in relatively low heat. This chemistry produced a one-fire process which reduced costs considerably and resulted in a durable product that was virtually without crazing. The first tableware pattern, El Patio, featured eight bright solid colours in the

▲ Coloured bowl, 1930s
Following the lead of companies such as Bauer, Gladding-McBean's first ware was simply shaped and brilliantly decorated in the solid colours that were quickly becoming popular in the American market. 161

◆ Franciscan Apple dinnerware, 1940s
One of Franciscan's most popular patterns and, indeed, one of the most popular American dinnerware patterns of the 20th century, Apple, which was introduced in 1940, is very recognizable and highly collectable. 162

casual taste that was becoming fashionable at that time (*see* J. A. Bauer Pottery Company, p.20). New additions to the line in the mid to late 1930s included the Coronado, Avalon, Del Oro, Mango, Pueblo and Rancho patterns. From the late 1930s fruit and flower patterns followed, such as Hawthorne, Geranium, Ivy, Apple (1940) and Desert Rose (1941), the last three being the most popular of this group that survive today. Low-relief designs in the mould are painted with oxide stains by decorators to create a product hand-decorated under the glaze. Because Malinite cannot be fired with metallic glazes, no gold or platinum could be added to spoil the effect of informality achieved with these earthenware patterns.

In 1937 Gladding-McBean acquired Catalina Clay Products from the Santa Catalina Island Company and continued to make artware and dinnerware using the designs and moulds it had so acquired. In a region and an era in which the casual lifestyle was admired, a name like Catalina was an important marketing tool. Catalina Rancho, a solid-colour casual dinnerware, was popular from 1937 to 1941. The many art and table lines that followed under Gladding-McBean's ownership carried names that invoked casual life on the Pacific Rim, and included Nautical, Reseda, Saguaro, Coronado, Polynesia and Avalon. These goods had colourful monochrome and duotone glazes that featured blue, gold, agate and green. A group of art figures and flower holders covered in an ox-blood glaze on Chinese-style shapes designed by Dorr Bothwell was very popular. The last Catalina line, Angeleno artware, was introduced in 1942, and the whole line was discontinued shortly afterwards.

In 1939 New York's Metropolitan Museum of Art asked the Franciscan plant to produce a dinnerware shape designed by Morris B. Sanders that had been honoured with a prize in the 15th Exhibition of Contemporary American Industrial Art. It was the first entirely square dinnerware made in America and was renamed Tiempo in 1949. The first Franciscan hotel ware was developed for the Dohrman Hotel China Company of San Francisco in 1939. This high-fired body became the basis for the fine-china products that were added to Franciscan Ware in 1941. In 1947 the names Franciscan Fine China and Masterpiece China were used to differentiate between the two lines that the Franciscan plant developed with this body. The Masterpiece China line, made from 1941 until 1979,

▲ **Franciscan Desert Rose plate, mid-1940s**
Along with Apple and Ivy (introduced in 1948), Desert Rose, which first appeared in 1941, is one of those classic Franciscan patterns that never seem to go out of style. Covers have rose-bud finials, and matching glassware by Imperial Glass is also available. [163]

▲ **Franciscan Swirl demitasse, c.1950**
Collectors call this pattern Swirl, but the company called it Coronado. It was made from 1934 to 1954 and the pattern came in satin-matt (ivory, green, blue, white, turquoise, grey and yellow) and glossy glazes (copper, coral, maroon, yellow, green, ruby and white). [164]

◆ **Franciscan Starburst dinner plate, late 1950s**
The Starburst pattern (introduced in 1954) on the Eclipse shape, designed by George James, is the most popular of Franciscan's decal pattern lines. Duet (introduced in 1956) and Oasis (introduced in 1955), also on Eclipse, are collectable as well, but collectors pay less for them. [165]

eventually included nine basic shapes with 165 patterns designed by Otto J. Lund and George James. The Discovery line was introduced in 1958. Many patterns were created by a large staff of designers, including Francis Chun, Dora DeLarios, Jerry Rothman, Harrison McIntosh, Henry Takemoto, Rupert Deese and Helen Watson. When Mary K. Grant retired in 1952, Mary J. Winans became supervisor of the design department. Fan Tan, Tulip Time, Hacienda, Pebble Beach, Madeira and many others were produced during these years. Kaleidoscope was a solid-coloured line. In addition to the popular cream-coloured earthenware patterns that have carried through since the 1940s, the Franciscan plant also made Whitestone Ware, a white earthenware, during this later period.

The Lock Joint Pipe Company purchased the Franciscan plant from Gladding-McBean in 1962 and created the International Pipe and Ceramics Corporation, called Interpace, in 1968. Franciscan Ware made under this ownership also carries the name Interpace in the mark. However, as foreign competition for the middle range of dinnerware increased in the American market, Interpace chose to sell Franciscan Ware and its factory to Wedgwood in 1979. The company was renamed Franciscan Ceramics Inc. In 1984 Waterford-Wedgwood closed the California plant and transferred all manufacturing of the remaining Franciscan Ware patterns to England. Today these are produced in Staffordshire by Johnson Bros (*see* p.98).

♦ **Franciscan Fan Tan cream jug and sugar bowl, late 1960s**
Fan Tan, introduced in 1951, was a dinnerware pattern in the Whitestone Ware line. It was designed under the supervision of Mary J. Winans and continued to be made throughout the Interpace years. 166

GLADSTONE CHINA (LONGTON)

Formerly known as George Proctor & Co., Gladstone China produced fine-china teaware and dinnerware for the general market. The pottery claimed to have pioneered the use of 21-piece teasets instead of the more usual 40 pieces. It was closely linked with Thomas Poole (*see* p.162), an earthenware and china maker also operating in Longton. The Poole family were thoroughly involved in the running of Gladstone China, and Horace Poole, who joined in 1902, later owned the company.

During World War II the pottery was closed, but the Gladstone name survived at Poole's Cobden Works. Gladstone China and Thomas Poole were merged in the late 1940s and, after Government wartime restrictions were lifted, operated as Royal Stafford China. After many years of decay, in the early 1970s the Gladstone factory was converted into a 'living museum' for the Staffordshire pottery industry. The ceremonial final firing of a Staffordshire bottle oven took place on the site in 1978, and in 1994 the Gladstone Pottery Museum became part of Stoke's Potteries Museum.

GLIDDEN POTTERY

The pottery produced an imaginative range of one-fire stoneware tableware and cookware for the North American market. Indeed, the high standing of the work in the American industry led museums and universities to recognize its merit; the Museum of Modern Art gave awards to Glidden's production five times, and the pottery was a consistent winner at the Ceramic National Exhibitions held annually at the Syracuse Museum of Art, in Syracuse, New York.

Glidden Parker, a graduate of Alfred University's College of Clayworking and Ceramics, set up the pottery with his wife in 1940, with the backing of Eddie Rubel, a manufacturers' representative who eagerly financed and sold Glidden output. The workforce ultimately numbered 55 craftsmen, including designers Sergio Dello Strologo, who created an oven-to-table buffet line, and George Fong Chow, who designed appealing serving pieces, some of which mixed copper and wood with stoneware. Fern Mays and Kathryn Welch designed and executed Glidden decorations. The company's production is characterized by a variety of earthy ground colours, often with lively, sometimes incised, designs enhanced by sunny colours. Designs were based mainly on plants and animals, and include Menagerie, Mexican Cock and the leaf pattern shown here. Parker's interests elsewhere led to the pottery's closure in 1957.

◆ **Canapé dish, c.1950**
Using clays from New York, Kentucky and Tennessee to create a stoneware body that could be formed and decorated for one firing only, Glidden used 130 different designs before its closure. 167

KEY FACTS
Location: Alfred, New York, USA.
Important dates: Founded 1940. Closed 1957.
Production: Hand-crafted stoneware dinnerware, oven-to-table ware, hostess ware and giftware.
Principal designers: Glidden Parker, Sergio Dello Strologo, George Fong Chow, Fern Mays (decorator), Kathryn Welch (decorator).

MARKS
All marks incised from the mould with shape number.

GOLDSCHEIDER POTTERY

Marcel Goldscheider, a Viennese potter, modeller and creator of stylish Art Deco figurines and wall masks, arrived in England in 1939 as a refugee. Assisted by his wife Rosemarie and by other manufacturers, including Myott, who made artware for itself and for him, he began to manufacture a new range of figures and ornaments. When World War II was over he moved to his own premises in John Street, Hanley, Staffordshire.

Goldscheider specialized in bone-china figures but also made ornamental ware. His inspiration came from historical subjects, fairy stories and the Art Deco forms of his earlier productions. The 1951 catalogue included boxes, ware in the form of buildings such as St Paul's Cathedral, and other souvenirs.

KEY FACTS
Location: Newcastle and Hanley, Staffordshire, UK.
Important dates:
Founded c.1946.
Closed 1959.
Production:
Earthenware, china.

◆ **Catalogue, c.1951**
Marcel Goldscheider's Staffordshire range included over 800 models, some reflecting pre-war European styles and others aimed at more up-to-date domestic and gift markets. 168

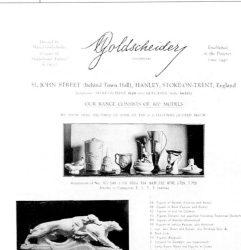

W. H. GOSS

William Henry Goss concentrated initially on making parian figures and ornaments, as well as domestic ware in terracotta. Later he turned to jewellery and other trinkets, such as openwork baskets, and by 1873 had patented a method of making impressions of 'jewels' in the wet clay before firing which enabled him to make a wide range of costume jewellery.

From the 1880s Goss pioneered the making of small pieces of heraldic ware and souvenirs, beginning with items bearing the arms of schools and colleges. Expanding this range for the popular market, he placed the coat of arms in a prominent position instead of on the base. This venture was an instant success, and the scope of the new range of items was prolific; it included shoes, vessels, table and domestic ware, kitchenware, lighthouses, fonts, cottages and buildings of interest, war souvenirs, horseshoes, animals and a myriad other miniature items, many of which were replicas of historical objects. Goss's success, which soon spawned many imitators, was also due to the rapid growth of the tourist industry. Children's china, lettered and painted ware, figures and a wide range of ornamental porcelains were also among the output, but it is for its crested and badged ware that Goss is best known and sought after today.

The firm remained in family hands until 1929, when it was taken over by George Jones Ltd (*see* p.100) and the factory was sold to Harold Taylor Robinson of Arkinstall & Sons (*see* p.14). For some years after this, crested ware made by Arcadian, Willow and others continued to carry Goss's goshawk trade mark. In or about 1934 the company was renamed Goss China and continued, through several changes of owner, to trade under its own name until about 1940.

After World War II the Goss assets were acquired by Coalport (*see* p.47) and then, about 1955, by Ridgway (*see* p.176) and Adderley (*see* p.13). The Lawley Group Ltd bought the moulds and engravings in 1956, and the Goss name came into the ownership of Royal Doulton (*see* p.187), which revived the trade mark in 1985.

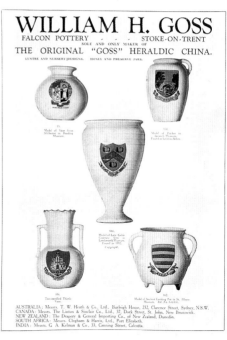

◆ Advertisement, 1926
Goss pioneered the heraldic china market, and this advertisement demonstrates the continued use of historical models. [169]

➤ Children's mug, c.1920
Children's ware was an interesting aspect of Goss production. This pattern, designed by Goss's daughter Margaret and entitled Shopping, is from a sequence featuring animals dressed as humans. [170]

◆ Cottage, c.1913
Goss models of famous buildings are particularly popular today. Shown here is Lloyd George's house. The inclusion of the annexe makes this a rare example. [171]

KEY FACTS

Location: Falcon Pottery, Stoke, Staffordshire, UK.
Important dates: Founded c.1858 (or 1862). Taken over by George Jones Ltd 1929. Renamed Goss China c.1934. Taken over by Coalport after World War II and by Ridgway and Adderley c.1955. Lawley Group bought Goss's moulds and engravings and Goss trade name became part of Royal Doulton Group 1972.
Production: Parian and china.
Principal designers: William Huntley Goss, Margaret Goss, Robert Leicester.
Trade names: W. H. Goss, Goss China Co.

MARKS

Early marks printed or impressed with 'W. H. GOSS'. Variations of this mark used from c.1862, with 'England' below from 1891.

A. E. GRAY & CO.

After beginning his career as a salesman in a glass and china shop in Manchester, A. E. Gray established a ceramics wholesale business in Stoke, Staffordshire, in 1907. His interests in design standards prompted him to set up a workshop specializing in the decoration of ceramics at the Glebe Works in Mayer Street, Hanley; this was in operation by 1912, when the name A. E. Gray & Co. Ltd was registered. Early pieces included novelties, miniatures, souvenirs and commemoratives; an example of the latter is ware with printed and hand-painted decoration commemorating Football Association teams. The pottery also made copies of early-19th-century Staffordshire figures, which were decorated in a non-traditional way using multicoloured lustres. By 1920 the company had almost completely abandoned decal-decorated ware in favour of bright, hand-painted patterns which echoed the growing importance of the handcraft movement. To carry out the painting, it drew on the skills of young women who had been trained in local schools of art.

Among the designers who worked for the pottery were Gordon Forsyth, John Guildford, Sam Talbot, Jack Bond, Nancy Catford and Susie Cooper (*see* p.49). Nancy Catford, a young woodcarver, was showing her work at the Maclellon Galleries in Glasgow, in an exhibition which ran from 1933 to 1934, when she met A. E. Gray. Gray persuaded her to move to the Potteries, where she worked for the firm as a freelance figure modeller until the outbreak of World War II. Among her first works was a series of life-size garden ornaments such as penguins, owls, rabbits and toucans. She was also responsible for a series of colourful wall ornaments and masks, notably a fox, a pair of love-birds, or budgerigars, an Old Salt, and Sunny Boy with blond hair and blue eyes.

Susie Cooper worked for Gray from 1922 to 1929 before she established her own company. When she was an assistant designer for Gray, some of her earliest work for the pottery was executing patterns for the Gloria Lustre ware, which had been designed by Gordon Forsyth in 1923. Among her own designs were patterns for Gray's large output of lustre ware, along with floral, abstract, banded and dotted Art Deco-influenced patterns, nursery ware and decal-decorated designs. Some of these carried her name incorporated in the backstamp.

In 1929 a showroom was opened at Hatton Garden, central London, which provided the firm with an excellent base for its London and overseas sales, and many new lines were introduced in the next decade. One interesting development was the introduction in 1932 of stoneware made from clay from Chesterfield, Derbyshire. Included in this range of goods were casseroles and stew pots in three sizes as well as flagons and other useful items, such as ashtrays and jugs and mugs, some with designs to

◆ **Biscuit barrel, early 1930s**
With its freehand Susie Cooper-style painting of flowers, this is a typical Gray product of the time. 172

◆ **Budgerigar wall ornament, mid-1930s**
This stoneware piece is one of a series of colourful hand-painted wall ornaments and masks modelled for the pottery in the mid-1930s by freelance modeller Nancy Catford. 173

◆ **Trellis fruit bowl, c.1928**
Designed for Gray by Susie Cooper, this pattern shows the characteristic freehand-painted style that she developed when she worked there. 174

Pottery of Distinction

GRAYS POTTERY

WHIELDON ROAD

STOKE-ON-TRENT

➤ **Teaware advertisement, 1949**
This stylish advertisement highlights
Gray's revival of English Regency
shapes and patterns. 175

➤ **Hunting jug, 1950s**
Transfer-printed with a conventional
hunting scene, this jug reveals Gray's
mass-market approach in the last
decade of the factory's existence. 176

match the colours or patterns used on the dinner tableware. Other decorations varied from simple coloured bands and abstract designs to freely painted floral lustre and enamel patterns. Animal figures and wall ornaments modelled by Nancy Catford were also made in stoneware from the mid-1930s.

By 1933 the Glebe Works was too small for the volume of production; the company moved to more spacious and more modern premises in Whieldon Road, Stoke, and began trading as Gray's Pottery. Three years later it secured an interest in Kirklands Pottery, which was primarily a maker of hospital ware, at Etruria. About this time Gray introduced a range of more serious and restrained ornamental ware with a matt-glaze finish which reflected a move towards the English modernist style just emerging. Included in the range were vases, lamp bases, candleholders, wall pockets and a cider/beer set, perhaps the only ordinary useful item made with this new glaze.

The company continued in production throughout World War II, and in the post-war period greatly expanded its output. Its extensive catalogue now included advertising ware, animal figures, animal troughs, drinking fountains, ashtrays, breakfast sets, bulb bowls, casseroles, chamber pots, cigarette boxes, coffee pots, coffee sets, cruet sets, dinner sets, eggcups, fancies, figures and statuettes, fruit sets, hospital ware, hotel ware, jugs, kitchenware, table lamps, lemon squeezers, morning sets, mugs, mixing bowls, novelties, ornamental bowls, pie dishes, pudding bowls, sandwich sets, supper sets, teapots, teasets, toilet ware and vases.

After the lifting of wartime restrictions the company introduced lustre-decorated stoneware designed by S. C. Talbot. It also applied its own print and enamel designs from this period to bought-in stoneware bodies made by Denby (*see* p.58) and Pearson & Co. (*see* p.150). However, from the late 1940s Gray progressively reduced the amount of detailed lustre painting it carried out, and often printed designs with hand-applied lustre surrounds, especially those based on traditional Sutherland splatter ware. Another form of decoration widely used by the firm during the years following World War II was the resist-lustre technique. In this process the liquid lustre is applied after the pattern has been drawn or stencilled to the piece in a resist medium. The design may be white or coloured after the resist is applied.

A. E. Gray retired in 1947 and was succeeded by his son and the artistic director S. C. Talbot, who became joint managing directors of the firm. In 1960 the pottery was purchased by the designer Susan Williams-Ellis and her husband Euan Cooper-Willis. In December of the following year the couple also bought Kirkhams (*see* p.105) and, operating as a new company under the name of Portmeirion Potteries (*see* p.163), they began production on 1 January 1962.

KEY FACTS

Location: Glebe Works, Hanley; later at Whieldon Road, Stoke;
Staffordshire, UK.
Important dates: Founded 1912. Closed 1961.
Production: Earthenware decoration.
Principal designers: Gordon Forsyth, John Guildford, Sam Talbot, Jack Bond,
Nancy Catford, Susie Cooper.

MARKS

Various marks
featuring galleon
used. Others
include sunburst in
gold and black and
'Gloria Lustre'.

T. G. GREEN & CO.

Thomas Goodwin Green bought a pottery in Church Gresley, Derbyshire, in 1864, in a region already well known for the manufacture of basic domestic and utilitarian ware from the local red and yellow clays. Under his direction the pottery became the nucleus of a larger and more important business. When he acquired the business Green was more an engineer than a potter, and he began to mechanize the works, leaving control of the pure pottery manufacturing to the workforce. For a while he was associated with William Ault (*see* p.17) and later, when Ault joined Henry Tooth at the Bretby Art Pottery (*see* p.31), he was assisted by Henry William King, who became joint director of the company.

There followed a period of expansion, and within 20 years Green had built a new pottery near the old works to make general earthenware of a utilitarian type, such as pudding bowls, jelly cans, mugs and churn jugs, and inexpensive kitchenware both in plain white and with sponged, banded and other simple forms of decoration. By the early years of the 20th century Green's two potteries, which were taken over by his sons after his death in 1905, had become a major enterprise, the largest in the area, and were producing an extraordinary diversity of wares.

A fire destroyed the new pottery early in the century, but this merely gave the family the chance to create a more modern and better-equipped works rivalling any in Staffordshire. Catalogues of this period include kitchenware, hospital and medical ware, mocha and banded ware, stamped measures, domestic stoneware, Rockingham, Samian and black lustre teapots and other ware, toilet ware and tableware with all kinds of printed and painted patterns in traditional and modern styles, with an emphasis on blue and white.

By the early 1930s T. G. Green had begun to develop its tableware trade significantly. The firm introduced a number of modern geometric shapes decorated with bright colour patterns, such as the Flora floral spray border pattern and Fairy Glen with its simple landscape design reminiscent of London Underground posters of the period. Also new were jugs painted in free and confident style in powerful colours, in keeping with contemporary trends. The pottery was particularly famous for its biscuit-coloured mixing bowls, still produced today. Novelties were also made, including ranges of the Cube (*see* p.56) teaware from the late 1920s, and children's ware such as the Happy Ark nursery series advertised in 1939.

However, Green's most famous and most imitated product is the blue-banded Cornish kitchenware, introduced in 1926 and still made today by the same traditional methods. Made from white earthenware, this familiar and much-loved pottery is dipped in blue slip; the bands are then cut through the slip on the lathe, revealing the white body underneath. From

◆ **Mixing bowl, 1930s**
In both traditional and modern styles, mixing bowls have always been a major feature of T. G. Green's production. [177]

◆ ◆ **Cornish Ware, 1920s**
Widely advertised and still popular today, Cornish Ware became, from the late 1920s, a style statement for the modern kitchen. Most familiar are the lettered storage jars and covered caddies. More than 100 contents names have been recorded. [178]

◆ Coffee-pot variations

While the basic techniques involved in the production of Cornish Ware remain unchanged, the pottery's designers have varied the shapes over the decades to reflect changes in fashion. Typical of this constant development is the coffee pot, whose design showed a marked evolution between the 1920s and the 1960s. On the far right is a coffee pot designed by Judith Onions in 1968; the other three designs span the 1930s to the 1950s. 179

its inception Cornish Ware was a great success, and at the height of its popularity it was considered indispensable for the modern home. Cornish Ware was modern, distinctive and clean to use, and, as a result, in 1928 it was awarded Britain's Certificate of Hygiene, the first of many. The range was rapidly expanded to fulfil all kitchen needs, embracing such rarities as a toast rack, a lemon squeezer and an egg separator. Best known are the lettered storage jars, made in a wide variety of sizes, but equally popular is the tableware. Cornish Ware continues to be successful, with new shapes and colourways still being added to the range, and is very collectable.

Linked to Cornish Ware in style and colour was Domino Ware, tableware and kitchenware with white spots on the blue slip ground. This range was introduced in the late 1930s and continued until the mid-1960s. A version was revived in 1993 using Cornish Ware shapes.

The popularity of these classic Green ware has tended to overshadow other areas of production, notably the full ranges of painted and printed tableware which have been made throughout the present century. While never a style leader, the pottery was always closely in touch with fashion, and its designs of the Art Deco period and the 1950s were notably up to date. Typical are the 1950s Gingham pattern on the modernist Patio shape and other contemporary designs by Colin Haxby, Audrey Levy and Judith Onions, who was also responsible for a major shape redesign of Cornish Ware in the 1960s.

◆ Gingham on Patio range, 1950s

The contemporary look was an important feature of the pottery's output in the 1950s. Typical was the Gingham pattern applied to Patio, a full range of kitchenware and tableware, including a clock. 180

In parallel with its manufacture of items with a contemporary look, the company also produced traditional designs and a variety of hand-painted and printed florals, as well as other kitchenware and cookware ranges. In the mid-1960s difficult trading conditions led to the closure of the pottery for a short period, after which it passed through a series of owners until 1987, when it joined the Cloverleaf group. Today T. G. Green continues to

◆ Yellow Cornish Ware, 1950s

Over the years the pottery has produced a number of colour variants for Cornish Ware, of which the most successful was the yellow range launched in the 1950s. More recently it has introduced green ranges. 181

produce traditional Cornish Blue and Cornish Green ware, but it also constantly updates and develops other lines, for both the casual dinnerware and kitchenware ranges, which are still made by traditional methods. The design team works with new artists to produce fashionable designs such as Jeff Banks's Ports of Call homeware collection, recently expanded to include two ranges of matt-glaze co-ordinated oven-to-table ware, Herat and Kabul. Among other notable lines are the Farm Animals co-ordinated range, the lettered Let's Eat tableware co-ordinates, the Duo two-tone oven-to-table ware and the Bistro casual dining collection, which combines Green's classic shapes with fashionable colours.

KEY FACTS

Location: Church Gresley, Burton-on-Trent, Derbyshire, UK.
Important dates: Founded 1864. Various owners since the 1960s, including Cloverleaf. Merged with Mason Cash in 2002, now run by the Tabletop Company.
Production: Earthenware and stoneware.

MARKS

This mark, showing a church above 'GRESLEY', registered 1888. Variations use company's initials or full name. Other backstamps give pattern names or ranges.

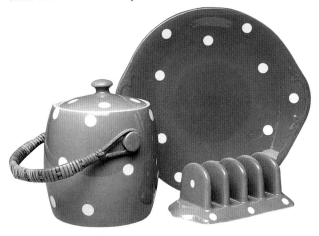

◆ **Blue Domino Ware, 1950s**
This biscuit jar, bread-and-butter plate and toast rack are unusual 1950s examples of Domino, and therefore popular with collectors. 182

GRETA POTTERY

Greta Loebenstein, who had been a designer at the Bauhaus school of art and design in Germany, and had made tableware with her first husband, fled the Nazi régime in 1933 and settled in England. She married Harold Marks in 1938, rented space in a series of factories in Stoke, Staffordshire, including Goss's (*see* p.77) Falcon Works, and developed her own approach to contemporary modernism, drawing on Bauhaus principles. She persuaded a number of British companies, among them Ridgway (*see* p.176) and Minton (*see* p.132), to manufacture her designs. However, probably because of their exaggerated geometric shapes and minimalist decoration, Marks's ware did not appeal to the nation's buyers, and as a result she gave up the enterprise in 1941. At the end of World War II she set up a pottery studio in London and continued her painting.

KEY FACTS

Location: Stoke, Staffordshire, UK.
Important dates: Founded 1938. Closed 1941.
Production: Earthenware.

MARKS

Hand-painted or printed monogram, sometimes with manufacturer's name.

◆ **Teaware, 1930s**
This teaware shows the influence of 1920s Bauhaus design. The exteriors of the three pieces at the back are decorated with semi-matt blue-grey glaze, the interiors with semi-matt pale yellow glaze. The geometric shapes of all four pieces were designed by Greta Marks, a designer of patterns for several pottery manufacturers. 183

GRIMWADE BROS

From its early years Grimwade produced a wide variety of good-quality domestic and ornamental ware for the general market, including advertising mugs with prints for children and other products. From the outset nursery ware was always important and included registered designs by leading artists and illustrators, along with massive quantities of coronation and other commemorative ware. Typical is nursery ware decorated with Palmer Cox's delightful Imps or Brownies, the Black Cats nursery ware and Peter Rabbit's china teaware based on Beatrix Potter's original drawings, first advertised in 1922.

Grimwade's rapid progress in the early years of the 20th century was helped by the purchase of other companies: J. Plant & Co.'s Stoke Pottery in about 1900, and six years later the Upper Hanley Pottery, formerly the famous Brownfield Works. By 1913 it had taken over the Rubian Art Pottery (see p.194), and later Atlas China. The interwar years were very productive. Previously well known for its ordinary domestic lines, toilet ware, flower pots, dinnerware and teaware, Grimwade began to expand in the 1920s and launched many new shapes and patterns as well as making more ornamental artistic ware. Typical are the plaques, vases, lamp stands and similar articles inspired by Urbino faience and featuring bright colours and lustre glazes. Another top-of-the-range series was mazarine blue background ware decorated with fine gilding and hand-painted butterflies. Classical themes were also popular in this period. Ornamental ranges included a series of six Dickens figures and the Cecil table centre, decorated with the new lustres in 50 varieties, floating bowls and other ware with modelled kingfishers, tits and swallows, advertised until well into the 1930s.

During World War II production was mainly utilitarian: breakfast sets, chamber pots, coffee pots and sets, eggcups, hospital ware, hot-water bottles, jugs, morning sets, mugs, pie dishes, rolling pins, sandwich sets, supper sets and teasets. Around this time Lily Markus, well known in Europe for her sculpture and large-scale ceramics, made a small number of individual pieces in association with Grimwade. More significant was chintzware, introduced initially for the export market but quickly becoming a major part of Grimwade's production under the Royal Winton name.

About 1964 the company moved to a new works at Norfolk Street, Shelton, where it made earthenware, tea and coffee sets, fancy tableware, musical ware, vases, bowls, teapots, ashtrays, nursery sets, hospital ware, lamp bases, plaques, character jugs, beakers and trinket sets.

GRIMWADES LTD., Winton Potteries, STOKE-ON-TRENT. London Showrooms, 11, ST. ANDREW STREET, E.C.1

▲ Advertisement, 1926
This *Pottery Gazette* advertisement shows table centres in typical contemporary styles. 184

▲ Rose vase, c.1910
With its print roses and soft colours, this is a typical Staffordshire product from the early years of the 20th century. 185

◆ Royal Winton Hazel teapot, 1934
Royal Winton, which was Grimwade's trade name, was a pioneer of chintzware in the early 1930s. 186

Grimwade became part of the Howard Pottery Group (*see* p.94) in 1979 and traded as Royal Winton. Also in 1979 Royal Winton was bought by Staffordshire Potteries (*see* p.210), which was taken over by Coloroll in 1986. Since then Royal Winton has had several owners. The name was revived in 1995, and in 1996 Royal Winton moved to Longton.

KEY FACTS

Location: Winton and Upper Hanley Potteries, Hanley and Elgin Potteries, Stoke, Staffordshire, UK.
Important dates: Founded 1886 as Grimwade Bros. Grimwades Ltd from 1900. Became part of Howard Pottery Group 1979, taken over by Taylor & Tunnicliffe in 1995. Still active.
Production: Earthenware and china.
Trade names: Stoke Pottery, Royal Winton, Rubian Art, Atlas China.

MARKS

Early ware marked with crown above 'Stoke Pottery'. This mark c.1934–50. Other marks include 'Winton', 'Rubian Art' and 'Atlas'.

▲ Cottage teapot, c.1934
Grimwade joined many other potters in the production of cottage teaware during the 1930s. Production of this pottery's version continued until the 1950s. [187]

W. H. GRINDLEY & CO.

Founded in 1880 in Tunstall, Staffordshire, this pottery made earthenware and ironstone, including good-quality morning, breakfast, tea, coffee, sandwich, fruit, dinner and supper sets, tableware accessories, cruet sets, eggcups and hotel ware. In 1982 it was one of three founder members of Federated Potteries (*see* p.65), but became independent again in 1988. Since then there have been further changes of ownership.

MARKS

Usually include name in full. Galleon marks used from c.1936.

HAEGER POTTERIES

Established in Dundee, Illinois, by David Haeger in 1871 as a brick factory, the original pottery began making giftware with brilliant glazes in 1914 under the design direction of J. Martin Stangl (*see* p.212). Dinnerware, especially tea and luncheon sets, followed in 1919. However, Haeger's reputation was defined by Royal Arden Hickman, who worked there from 1938 to 1944. He designed the highly successful Royal Haeger artware, offering stylish vases, figurines and flower containers in brilliant glazes. The stalking black panther, Hickman's single most popular and influential design, was copied by more than 30 other potteries. Most of the artware and lamps made between 1947 and 1972 was designed by Eric Olsen, who is famous for his Red Bull.

KEY FACTS

Location: Dundee and Macomb, Illinois, USA.
Important dates: Founded 1871. Still active.
Production: Figurines, florists' crockery, giftware and lamps.
Principal designers: J. Martin Stangl, Royal Arden Hickman, Sebastiano Maglio, Eric Olsen.

MARKS

Many different backstamps and labels in this style used from 1914.

Haeger

♦ Planter, c.1940
This double-shell cornucopia is typical of the decorative planters and vases that have been Haeger's mainstay. The 1983 *Guinness Book of Records* lists the 8ft (2.4m) tall vase outside the Dundee factory as the world's largest. [188]

HALL CHINA COMPANY

The Hall China Company's ware is among the most collectable in the American ceramics market because of the wide variety of shapes and patterns made. There are more than 2000 teapots from which to choose, in addition to the many consumer premiums (especially the pieces for the Jewel Tea Company), the streamlined Moderne refrigerator containers given away with refrigerators in the 1940s and 1950s, and the Hallcraft dinnerware line designed by Eva Zeisel. Indeed, today's collectors of old Hall pieces can even enjoy a stop at the Hall Closet, Hall's seconds shop next to the factory, to see what the company is making now and buy favourite pieces at bargain prices.

Founded in 1903 by Robert Hall out of the ruins of the East Liverpool Pottery Company, the Hall China Company struggled for years to make any profits from bedpans and combinets. Eventually, however, Hall's son Robert T. Hall developed a high-temperature leadless glaze that allowed the pottery to make one-fire ware with a non-crazing glaze. Production and sales grew enormously and rapidly. During World War I, when European potteries could not supply the common stoneware steam-table insets, coffee-urn liners and similar vessels for preparing and serving food in restaurants and institutions, Hall's potters developed casseroles, teapots, coffee pots, coffee-urn liners and similar institutional goods for sale to American buyers. After the war the Hall products were chosen in preference to the imports because of their superior finish.

By 1920 the teapot line had been greatly expanded through new production facilities and an educational advertising campaign that taught modern homemakers the proper way to brew tea. As a result, Hall claimed to be the largest manufacturer of decorated teapots in the world. Today a collector could amass all of the 2000 or so Hall teapots and never have a duplicate when shape, size, colour and decoration are taken into account. In 1930 Hall built a completely new factory to contain all manufacturing on the east side of East Liverpool, Ohio, and over the next 15 years it expanded that facility eight times. In the years between the wars the company gained a reputation for introducing new brilliant colours that greatly enhanced the streamlined institutional and utilitarian shapes that it designed. Decals were added to the goods in 1931, an innovation that opened new markets for premiums and tableware.

A few years later the company began making dinnerware in addition to its teapots, kitchenware and institutional specialities. Although Hall's dinnerware is not as collectable as its teapots and kitchenware, the

● **Crocus dinnerware, late 1930s**
Crocus was applied to a wide range of items. Perhaps its familiarity and cheerful aspect make Crocus desirable to collectors. In addition to D-line dinnerware, Crocus can also be found on kitchen and refrigerator ware, tea and coffee pots, casseroles and canisters. 189

● **Aladdin teapot, 1930s**
The Aladdin teapot came in 21 different colours, including black, pink, pale yellow, Chinese red, stock green, emerald and marine green, green lustre, ivory, stock brown, mahogany brown, maroon, orchid, rose, turquoise, warm yellow and light, medium and cobalt blue. 190

◀ **Autumn nesting bowls, 1940s**
Of the many coffee and tea premiums made by Hall China, Autumn Leaf, produced for the Jewel Tea Company is one of the most popular. The pattern can be seen on a wide variety of kitchen forms, and on the Ruffled D-line dinnerware. 191

Crocus pattern on an ivory background is a favourite with today's collectors. The pattern was used on a variety of standard shapes as well. The most sought-after pieces with Crocus include the Aladdin teapot, Bingo water bottle, Big Lip soup tureen and Kadota drip coffee pot.

Hall first entered the premium business in the early 1930s in association with coffee and tea companies, which were always looking for ways to entice buyers. The pottery made premiums for Best Tea, Cook Coffee, Great American Tea, Standard Coffee, the Grand Union Company and the Jewel Tea Company. The Red Poppy pattern for Grand Union, and the Autumn Leaf pattern for Jewel Tea are preferred by collectors. The same decals can be found on ware produced by other manufacturers because the tea and coffee companies frequently switched makers in response to the cost of supplying their contracts. However, collectors seem to prefer the Hall versions of these items. There are still plenty of examples of Hall's Autumn Leaf, one of the favourites, made for Jewel from 1933 to 1938, to be found in the collectables market. A few shapes have been decorated with it since 1978 as special items for the National Autumn Leaf Collectors' Club. The most expensive old Autumn Leaf items produced by Hall include butters, clocks, the Jordan drip coffee pot and the single-handled New England bean pot.

When, around 1940, electric refrigerators became new and desirable appliances for American homes, Hall made containers that were given away as premiums with the refrigerators. Butter dishes, leftover containers, water servers, casseroles and bowls were made for, among many other companies, General Electric, Westinghouse, Hotpoint, Sears, Aristocrat, Bingo, Montgomery Ward and Emperor. Collectors today, just like consumers 50 years ago, admire the streamlined designs and bright colours used by Hall. Cobalt, Daffodil, Chinese Red, Lettuce, Art Glaze Yellow, Delphinium, Ivory and Sunset are among the many colours that the pottery offered. Collectors are especially keen on the water servers for Aristocrat and Sears.

During the great American economic expansion after World War II, Hall sought to grow its dinnerware business by commissioning outside designers to develop new shapes and patterns. Englishman J. Palin Thorley designed Granitone for sale through Sears. This was a traditional neo-classical pattern, 'Designed in the Duncan Phyfe manner' according to Sears' advertising. Granitone was decal-decorated with delicate floral patterns bearing names like Monticello, Richmond and Mt Vernon, to evoke an early-American feeling.

Hungarian-born designer Eva Zeisel created the Hallcraft dinner service Tomorrow's Classic in 1949-50, and production began in 1952. Zeisel designed dinnerware for several American companies, including Red Wing Potteries (*see* p.170) and the Western Stoneware Company (*see* p.238),

▲ **Nora water server, c.1980**
Designed in the 1950s and made as a premium for McCormick Tea Co., the water server was demonstrated as an iced-tea pitcher in advertising. 192

▲ **Sundial casserole, c.1940**
Chinese Red is one of the most popular colours for Hall's kitchenware. The wind-swept cover handle gives this Sundial piece a streamlined look. 193

◄ **Refrigerator ware, 1940s**
Water servers – Phoenix (left) and Hercules – are seen with Pert salt and pepper pots. Lids and a larger size make the water servers the most valuable of the refrigerator premiums. 194

during the 1940s and 1950s, but the organic shapes and cheerful modern decorations on Tomorrow's Classic made it her most popular dinner set. Later she designed refrigerator jars (1954) and another dinner service for the Hallcraft line called Century (1956). Century is even more graceful than Tomorrow's Classic, and the pieces stack and nest beautifully, although the attenuation of the design made manufacturing difficult. Both lines are still affordable in today's market.

A few other Hall patterns and shapes are of interest to collectors. Blue Blossom and Blue Garden (both 1939), kitchenware and serving ware with a dark cobalt-blue glaze, were decorated with matt decals. Meadow Flower, Poppy, Poppy and Wheat, Red Poppy and Rose Parade are collectable floral patterns. The silhouette pattern called Taverne shows two old-fashioned gentlemen eating at a tavern table. Wildfire, a premium made for the Great American Tea Company, has a white body.

Little of Hall's recent work can be considered collectable, yet the company continues to make many of the same types of object as before: institutional cooking and serving pieces, refrigerator containers, premiums for all kinds of companies and organizations, and casual tableware.

♠ Eva Zeisel's Hallcraft Century bowl, 1956
The tear-drop shape of Century's handles is graceful but fragile. Zeisel's shapes are beautiful in white, but the decal patterns enhance the shapes. Fern is shown here. [195]

KEY FACTS

Location: East Liverpool, Ohio, USA.
Important dates: Founded 1903. Still active.
Production: Teapots, refrigerator ware, dinnerware and consumer premiums.
Principal designers: J. Palin Thorley, Eva Zeisel.

MARKS

All include 'Hall' or 'Hall's'. 'KITCHENWARE' added from 1932.

HAMMERSLEY & CO.

A specialist in high-quality, well-priced tableware for the home and colonial markets, Hammersley claimed in 1919 to be the first Staffordshire company to use the brown teddy-bear design in nursery ware. Its 1920s and 1930s catalogues ranged from ordinary stock patterns to sumptuous designs with hand painting and rich and raised gilt, and included giftware and fancies such as a handled strawberry-and-cream set, and an interesting cheese dish. During the 1940s production was mainly breakfast, coffee, morning, sandwich and teasets, but some fancies were reintroduced after wartime restrictions were lifted.

In 1972 Hammersley was bought by the Carborundum Co., owners of Spode (see p.208). Two years later Carborundum bought Royal Worcester (see p.191) and its subsidiaries, including A. E. Jones's (see p.99) Palissy Pottery.

The Hammersley factory closed in 1982, and Palissy took over the company's production and trade name. Both the Hammersley and Palissy trade names were discontinued in 1988.

KEY FACTS

Location: Alsager Pottery, Longton, Staffordshire, UK.
Important dates: Founded 1887. Closed 1982.
Production: China.

MARKS

Early marks show crown with or without 'H' and 'Co' above. Hammersley name added c.1912.

♦ Teaware, 1950s
In the 1930s Hammersley produced teaware and tableware with hand-painted decoration in traditional styles which were intended to rival those of better-known makers. This fine ware was still being made in the 1950s. [196]

HAMPSHIRE POTTERY

In 1871 James S. Taft established a flower-pot pottery, J. S. Taft & Co, on the Ashuelot River, New Hampshire. Soon afterwards he introduced a line of stoneware jugs, butter and cake pots, covered preserve jars, pitchers, churns, water kegs and spittoons. He continued to make flower pots and in 1874 bought a nearby pottery, expanding the range of earthenware goods to include hanging vases, bracket pots, florists' ware and Rockingham teapots. In 1879 Thomas Stanley joined the company from England and introduced majolica to Taft's earthenware repertoire, making mugs, pitchers, teasets and vases. This ware, with its hard white body and dark rich glazes, proved to be popular. The range of artware was further expanded in 1882 by the introduction of a version of Rookwood's (*see* p.179) standard mahogany glaze, artist-decorated by a small staff in the pottery. In the same period the artist Wallace L. King introduced a ware that imitated Royal Worcester's (*see* p.191) ivory ground. Using black transfer prints, Taft's pottery did a brisk business in souvenirs of this ware, which can be found today with scenes of places in eastern and southern states.

In 1904 Cadmon Robertson, brother-in-law of Taft and a chemist, joined the company. He introduced more than 900 new glaze formulas, especially the great variety of matt glazes in green-blue, grey, bronze, brown and yellow. These were applied to artware such as vases, flower holders, candlesticks, clock cases, lamp bases and bowls. Robertson also developed a semi-porcelain body that eventually replaced the earthenware body that the firm had been using since the 1880s.

King retired in 1908, Robertson died in 1914, and in 1916 Taft sold the pottery to George M. Morton. The new owner closed it in 1917, because of World War I, but reopened it in 1919, adding machinery to make common white china for institutions and clay presses to produce mosaic floor tiles. He did not convert the kilns to gas, and the pottery closed in 1923.

◆ Pitcher, c.1905
The solid matt-green glaze, one of many developed by Cadmon Robertson, covers a white semi-porcelain body, but the melon shape of the pitcher is late Victorian in its naturalism. 197

◆ Vases, 1905–15
The stylized low-relief leaves of the vase on the left, and the blue flowing matt glaze that breaks and falls down the body, copy a genre introduced by the Grueby Pottery, of Boston, Massachusetts. The entwined stems of the vase on the right, with green matt crystalline glaze, are original to the Hampshire Pottery. 198

KEY FACTS

Location: Keene, New Hampshire, USA.
Important dates: Founded 1871. Closed 1923.
Production: Utilitarian stoneware, flower pots, artware, hotel ware, souvenirs, majolica and floor tiles.
Principal designers: Thomas Stanley, Wallace L. King, Cadmon Robertson.

MARKS

Most include Taft's name and/or 'Hampshire'. Circle enclosing 'M' also used.

SAMPSON HANCOCK & SONS

This producer of tableware and fancies for the popular market expanded its production of ornamental fancies around the start of World War I. The firm also made children's ware, including some charming 1930s nursery-rhyme pieces by Molly Hancock and Edith Gater's Clown and Rabbit series. However, it is best known for Morris Ware, an ornamental range of the Edwardian era featuring elaborate, richly coloured tube-lined decoration in the style of William Morris and the Arts and Crafts Movement, designed by George Cartlidge.

Until 1920 this range was marked on the base with the artist's signature. By 1921 it had been taken over completely by the artist Frank X. Abraham, and new motifs and colour harmonies were added.

Between the wars the pottery introduced new lines in Corona toilet ware, teaware and dinnerware, including freehand-painted designs. It also continued to develop production of toy ware and novelties in crested ware, dolls' heads and earthenware mascots.

KEY FACTS

Location: Bridge Works and Gordon Pottery, Stoke, and other Staffordshire sites; later at Corona Pottery, Hanley, Staffordshire, UK.

Important dates: Founded c.1858. Renamed S. Hancock & Sons (Potters) Ltd 1935. Closed 1937.

Production: Earthenware.

Trade names: Duchess China, Royal Coronaware.

MARKS

Variations of this mark used from c.1900.

◀ **Morris Ware vase, c.1910**
George Cartlidge's flowing slip-trailed designs were sold by Hancock under the Morris Ware name. The style linked William Morris to Art Nouveau and used the technique associated particularly with Moorcroft. [199]

HARKER POTTERY COMPANY

When the Harker Pottery Company was incorporated in 1889, its products included semi-porcelain dinnerware, toilet ware, hotel ware, kitchenware and advertising pieces. In 1931 the company moved operations from its factory in East Liverpool, Ohio, to a newer plant across the river in Chester, West Virginia. By 1965 there were 300 employees making 25 million pieces annually. In the 20th century Harker made a limited number of popular shapes in both colonial revival and modern modes. Virginia, Gadroon and Royal Gadroon (1947) and Shell Ware or Swirl all have design references to colonial ware. Modern Age (1940), Nouvelle (1932) and Zephyr are streamlined and geometric in the modern idiom.

◀ **Hotoven custard cup, 1935–50**
Harker's Silhouette pattern was used on kitchenware and dinnerware. The pattern consists of two different vignettes: a woman watering her trellis garden, and two riders seated under a tree with a horse standing nearby. [200]

◀ **Engraved platter, 1955–60**
Cameo and its later variation, Engraved, were made by cutting away the solid-colour top layer to reveal the contrasting white body beneath. White Rose and Dainty Flower in Cameo are more commonly found today. The Engraved pattern shown here is Coronet. [201]

Harker claimed to be the first pottery to make decorated white kitchenware, and certainly was offering such goods by the 1920s. The company's first kitchenware was Hotoven, introduced in 1926 and very popular with collectors today. The kitchenware lines included batter sets (covered jugs for pancake or waffle batter and syrup), custard cups, rolling pins and pie pans, refrigerator jugs, mixing bowls, condiment shakers and teapots. Barbecue ware was developed for use outdoors.

Over the years the pottery offered a wide range and typical variety of decal patterns on its white earthenware. Many patterns were used on both dinnerware and kitchenware. Being matched in pattern, pieces could move easily between kitchen and dining table. Mallow, Ruffled Tulip, Petit Point Rose, Calico Tulip, Deco Dahlia, Countryside, Birds and Flowers were popular in the 1920, 1930s and 1940s. Harker had a cheery fruit-pattern kitchenware that featured an apple and a bright yellow pear popular in the 1930s and 1940s; it was called Red Apple.

Of particular interest to collectors is Cameoware. Created originally by George Bauer for the Edwin Bennett pottery in Baltimore, the Cameo process was later sold to Harker, who paid royalties to Bauer, and by 1941 it was used on both kitchenware and dinnerware. Dainty Flower and White Rose (made exclusively for Montgomery Ward) are the most common patterns. A set of shapes and patterns for children in Cameoware was called Kiddo and included a dog, a hobby horse, an elephant, a doll with a balloon, and a duck. The Cameo process continued to be used into the 1950s, although the patterns were referred to as Engraved, to distinguish them from the discontinued Cameo line. Engraved patterns included a rooster (Cock O' Morn), leaves (Coronet), birds on a branch (Country Cousins), dogwood, ivy wreath, wheat, a flower band (Petit Fleurs), a conventional tulip (Provincial) and stars (Star-Lite) in more colours than Cameo. Russel Wright designed a line called White Clover. Made between 1953 and 1958, this is among the least collectable of Wright designs.

▲ Royal Gadroon plate, 1947–63
Harker's most popular semi-vitreous dinnerware was made in the Royal Gadroon shape, shown here with ivy decals. 202

▲ Russel Wright clock, 1950s
Made as a companion to the White Clover dinnerware line by Wright, the General Electric clock has four pattern colours: Golden Spice, Meadow Green, Coral Sand and Charcoal. 203

◀ Historical pitcher, 1950s
This piece is a reproduction of a hound-handled pitcher made by Harker ancestors in the mid-19th century, but with a brown body glaze and frosty white drip glaze at the rim instead of the traditional overall mottled Rockingham glaze. 204

KEY FACTS
Location: East Liverpool, Ohio, and Chester, West Virginia, USA.
Important dates: Founded 1889. Bought by Jeannette 1972. Factory closed after being damaged by fire 1975.
Production: Souvenirs, dinnerware, consumer premiums and kitchenware.
Principal designers: Russel Wright, George Bauer.
Trade names: Cameoware, Hotoven, Bakerite, Harkerware.

MARKS
Name of line or pattern often included with Harker name.

THEODORE HAVILAND COMPANY (USA): see SHENANGO CHINA COMPANY p.203

J. E. HEATH

As part of its post-war reconstruction and development, Dudson Bros (*see* p.61) took over the newly formed Albert Potteries in Burslem, Staffordshire, in 1950. At first the new business was run by Bruce Dudson, who was joined by his brother Derek in 1951, when the name J. E. Heath was adopted. The Dudson brothers created a new range of Vitrified hotel ware, which they sold under the now well-known Armorite trade name. After the death of their father in 1964, Derek and Bruce Dudson were largely responsible for carrying on the Dudson Group's business. Derek was later succeeded by his sons Ian and Max, who have since managed the technical and aesthetic development of the Group's Armorite Super Vitrified Ware. Ian moved to the Heath factory in 1975 and Max in 1988, after training at the Group's Duraline factory.

➥ Maryse Boxer dish, 1990s
Unusual shapes and strong colours characterize recent designs by Maryse Boxer. These have introduced a powerful contemporary look and underline the design flexibility available to smaller companies. 205

KEY FACTS

Location: Albert Potteries, Albert Street, Burslem, Staffordshire, UK.
Important dates: Founded 1951. Later part of Dudson Group. Rebranded Dudson Armorlite.
Production: Vitrified hotel ware.

MARKS

Variations of this mark used from c.1951. Others include Dudson's Armorite Vitrified Ware mark.

HEWITT & LEADBEATER

From 1907, at the Willow Pottery in Longton, Staffordshire, Hewitt & Leadbeater specialized in making crested china and heraldic miniatures. In 1916 it was producing more than 200 different shapes, many of which were sold at a fixed price. In addition to these ornaments and fancies, the pottery manufactured classical parian busts, figures, groups and statuettes, and dolls' heads.

In the early 1920s the firm introduced new ranges, including glazed parian morning sets with nursery subjects as well as a self-coloured Willow pattern, and a range of lustres with decorated butterflies, miniature vases decorated with black cats designed by H. H. Hosband and a new series of souvenir items bearing lightly engraved views of holiday resorts. The pottery, renamed Hewitt Bros. in 1919, closed in 1926.

➥ Badged souvenir ware, 1916
Miniatures and fancies were made for the souvenir market, an important area for Hewitt & Leadbeater. 206

HEWITT & LEADBEATER: A SMART RANGE OF ARMS WARE MODELS.

KEY FACTS

Location: Longton, Staffordshire, UK
Important dates: Founded 1907. Closed 1926.
Production: Ornaments, fancies and figures.

HOLLINSHEAD & KIRKHAM

Founded in 1870 in Tunstall, Staffordshire, the firm made hospital, hotel, toilet, tea and dinner ware. In the early 1930s it translated some shapes for china teaware to its semi-porcelain range and decorated them with Art Deco-inspired designs and naturalistic cottage garden scenes. Also from the 1930s is Rougette Ware, decorated with artistic glaze effects. In 1956 Johnson Bros (*see* p.98) bought the factory.

MARKS

From 1900 marks incorporate company initials or name. This mark used 1924–56.

ROBERT HERON (& SON): see WEMYSS p.237

HONITON ART POTTERIES

The pottery at Honiton, Devon, established in 1881, was bought from James Webber around 1900 by Foster and Hunt, who produced the first identifiable Honiton ware, which was slip-decorated. In 1918 the firm was taken over by Charles Collard, who is noted for his exceptional hand-painted pottery, mainly with Jacobean and Persian designs. This was made from local clay and usually had painted decoration – predominantly in blue, red, green and purple – on a white or tinted opaque glaze. The designs were distinctive and all articles finished with a hand-dotted edge.

In 1945 Norman Hull and his wife Nancy arrived from Stoke to take over, introducing slip-casting and more industrial techniques. In response to the growth of local tourism they adapted Collard designs, which became the main area of production. Local clay ceased to be used, and the scale of production increased. Typical production in the 1950s included animal figures, teapots and vases, fancies and novelties, but giftware alone was too seasonal to keep a growing workforce busy. Therefore the firm, under Mr Cowell and Paul and Jennifer Redvers from 1960, launched many new ranges, including Craftsman tableware and ovenware. Made in matt brown and other colours, with hand-painted designs, this range was created by Paul Redvers, who also designed the traditional Devon Leaf and the Jennifer range. Other lines included Maryse Boxer's Japanese-style tableware and Jane Willingale's hand-painted Loudware. Vases in traditional patterns are among the pottery's most collectable products.

In 1992 the Honiton name was acquired by the Dartmouth Pottery (*see* p.57) and the main pottery-making equipment was moved from the site, but the Traditional Designs of Charles Collard are still painted.

▲ Woodland teapot, 1940s
Introduced in the 1930s, the Woodland design was used on a wide range of items, including lamp bases and vases. Most were painted in a semi-lustrous green or fawn brown. The stag's shape varies according to the type of pot and the decorator. 207

▲ Two-handled jar, late 1950s
Probably made in the late 1950s, during the Norman Hull era, this two-handled jar with lid is a particularly fine example of Honiton's skill in decoration. It shows the traditional Jacobean pattern of flowers with protruding stamens. 208

◀ Charger, early 1950s
This charger displays the Sweetcorn pattern, designed and applied to the piece by Jessie Banbury. In addition to the central sweetcorn motif, the decoration features a long tooth-edged leaf and a Persian flower. 209

KEY FACTS

Location: High Street, Honiton, Devon, UK.
Important dates: Founded 1881. Closed and name acquired by Dartmouth Pottery 1992.
Production: Earthenware freehand-painted ware, giftware, presentation items, oven-to-table ware.
Principal designers: Charles Collard, Norman Hull, Paul Redvers, Jennifer Redvers, Maryse Boxer, Jane Willingale.

MARKS

This printed or impressed mark used from 1956. Early ware usually unmarked. Various marks incorporating 'Honiton' used from c.1915. Collard Honiton mark 1918–47. N. T. S. Hull mark 1947–55.

MADE IN HONITON DEVON POTTERY ENGLAND

HORNSEA POTTERY CO.

Desmond and Colin Rawson began operating the company at their home in Hornsea, East Yorkshire. Initially they produced miniature Toby jugs, but after moving premises in 1954 they advertised modern slipware, contemporary-shape vases, tableware accessories and fancies.

Hornsea was one of the pioneers of direct printing, at that time an unusual way of screen-printing a resistant substance directly on to the biscuit ware. In the later stages of glaze dipping and firing the glaze runs off the pattern and produces the effect of glazed areas of one colour and contrasting semi-matt areas in another colour. The thicker glaze also produces an attractive relief effect.

In 1970 the company acquired a second, large factory site in Lancaster, Lancashire. Always aware of the value of good design, from the mid-1970s the company brought in consultants such as Martin Hunt, who designed the successful Contrast and Concept tableware shapes. Many other designers, including graphic specialists such as Philip Turner of Eurographics, helped to create Hornsea's modern image. The most important was John Clappison, who first designed for the pottery in the late 1950s and later became its design director. The design department developed many new items, including special pieces for Queen Elizabeth II's Jubilee in 1977. Most early pieces are highly collectable, including animal figures (such as the leopard inset right).

In 1984 the pottery was bought by clothing manufacturers Alexon and relaunched in 1985. That same year it was sold again, to Peter Black Holdings, a Yorkshire-based homeware group, and the Lancaster plant was closed. Production at the Hornsea site continues.

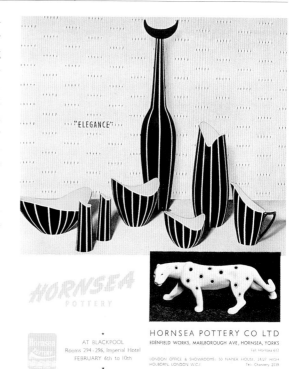

"ELEGANCE"

HORNSEA POTTERY

AT BLACKPOOL
Rooms 294-296, Imperial Hotel
FEBRUARY 6th to 10th

HORNSEA POTTERY CO LTD
EDENFIELD WORKS, MARLBOROUGH AVE, HORNSEA, YORKS
Tel: Hornsea 613

LONDON OFFICE & SHOWROOMS: 50 NAPIER HOUSE, 24/27 HIGH HOLBORN, LONDON W.C.1   Tel: Chancery 2539

Elegance tableware, 1956
Contemporary-style tableware accessories feature widely in Hornsea advertisements of the 1950s. Typical of the products is the Elegance range, designed by John Clappison. 210

Concept tableware, 1977
A close collaboration between Martin Hunt, the designer of the range, and Colin Rawson, the company's managing director, who was responsible for technical developments, led to the creation of Concept tableware. Hunt was also the designer of Hornsea's Contrasts, a range of bold, modern, two-tone ware introduced two years earlier, in 1975, that was a great success both in Britain and overseas. 211

KEY FACTS

Location: Hornsea, East Yorkshire, and Lancaster, Lancashire, UK.
Important dates: Founded in 1949. Bought by Alexon 1984. Bought by Peter Black Holdings 1985. Lancaster site closed 1985.
Production: Earthenware.
Principal designers: John Clappison, Martin Hunt, Philip Turner.

MARKS

This mark first used 1951. Representations of company name continued in use as printed or impressed marks until 1962. After 1962, trade mark in curl design or sail-like logo used.

HORNSEA POTTERY

Studiocraft planter, 1960–62
This range of planters and vases used colour inlay, mainly in black, red and blue. The moulded, patterned surface was coloured and then wiped clean, leaving colour in the recesses. 212

HOWARD POTTERY

This pottery made useful ware and ornamental fancies, including animal models, children's ware, figures and statuettes, table lamps, jugs and vases. In 1947 it was joined by Alan Luckham, who created a range of ornamental useful pottery for the Royal Norfolk section and became the factory's general modeller. Among his work was the Highlight series: vases, bowls, sweet dishes and candlesticks in two-tone semi-matt glazes of lime green, terracotta, peacock green, Cornish grey and mushroom to harmonize with contemporary interiors.

In the 1970s the pottery made oven-to-table ware and kitchenware and continued to make teapot sets and useful ornamental ware.

KEY FACTS

Location: Shelton, Staffordshire, UK.
Important dates: Founded 1925. Closed 1970s.
Production: Earthenware.

MARKS

Brentleigh Ware mark incorporated in Howard Pottery marks 1925. This printed mark used from 1950.

♦ Andy Pandy Ware, 1954
Characters from children's television have influenced designers of children's china since the 1950s. Brentleigh's Andy Pandy nursery ware is an attractive example. 213

HUDSON & MIDDLETON

The company was a partnership between William Hudson and J. H. Middleton, two independent manufacturers. From the late 1880s, at their Sutherland and Delphine potteries respectively, both firms made for the middle market teaware and dinnerware in traditional styles with painted, transfer-printed and decal-decorated patterns. Between the wars they also made small quantities of children's china and toy ware.

The partnership was formed in 1941, when production was concentrated at the Sutherland Pottery under the Government's wartime regulations. Hudson took over the manufacture of Middleton's range, with the exception of similar shapes that were made by both companies, and in the early stages of the merger both retained their individuality. Output was largely confined to tea, coffee and breakfast sets and associated tableware accessories; more recently beakers, coasters, collectors' cups and saucers, wall plaques and specialized giftware have been added.

In 1982 Hudson & Middleton was taken over by its parent company, Jesse Shirley & Son Ltd, but continues to trade under its own name.

KEY FACTS

Location: Sutherland Pottery, Longton, Staffordshire, UK.
Important dates: William Hudson and J. H. Middleton established late 1880s. Merged 1941.
Production: China and earthenware.
Trade names: Delphine, Sutherland China.

MARKS

This mark in current use. From 1941 both Hudson's Sutherland China mark with lion rampant and Middleton's Delphine china mark used. H. and M. Sutherland China mark introduced 1947.

♦ Nick Holland mugs, 1998
Surface designs created by Nick Holland in 1998 decorate these two mugs in the established Regent pattern. Striking decoration such as this is a key element in Hudson & Middleton's output. Other patterns used on the Regent shape cover the handle as well as the body. 214

EDWARD HUGHES & CO.

Founded in 1889 in Fenton, Staffordshire, the company originally made teasets, tableware and related items, and pieces bearing local views and coats of arms. From Edward Hughes's death in 1908 it concentrated on finely potted fashionable tea, coffee and breakfast services. By the mid-1920s Eusancos china, with its unusually white body, was selling very well. The firm occasionally made toy and nursery ware. It closed in 1953.

MARKS
Variations of basic globe mark used 1912–41. This mark introduced 1914.

A. E. HULL POTTERY

Although the company is best known among collectors for a large line of pastel artware, its range also includes Mirror Brown dinnerware and the Little Red Riding Hood novelty line. Founded by A. E. Hull in 1905 to make utilitarian stoneware, it purchased Acme Pottery Company, a maker of semi-porcelain dinnerware, in 1907. Artware, florists' crockery, kitchenware and tiles were added over the years. In the late 1930s Hull introduced the matt pastel artware for which it is best known. After a flood and fire in 1950 destroyed the glaze formulas for the artware, a new character for this was invented, with glossy glazes and more complex thematic motifs. Many of these were designed by Louise Bauer, the company's chief designer and modeller from 1949 to 1985. Bauer designed Little Red Riding Hood, introduced in 1943, and her Gingerbread line of the 1980s, featuring a gingerbread man, is also popular with collectors.

By the early 1980s Hull's entire production was dinnerware, especially Mirror Brown. The company supplied Woolworths and McCrory for many years. Penneys was a major buyer of dinnerware, but during a long strike in 1978, left Hull, whose fortunes declined until it closed in 1985.

Cookie jar, 1930s
Most of the company's dinnerware, kitchenware and novelty lines included cookie jars. These colourful containers enliven many kitchens, while their great variety encourages collecting. 215

Little Red Riding Hood, 1940s
Hull distributed this popular line, made by Regal China, from 1943. Cookie jars, casseroles, teapots, cream jugs, sugar bowls and butter dishes are among the pieces on which the character's distinctive clothing appears. 217

♦ **Mirror Brown dinnerware, 1960–85**
The Mirror Brown range eventually included plates, bowls, casseroles, platters, cups and saucers, mugs, canisters, coffee jugs and other forms. 216

KEY FACTS
Location: Crooksville, Ohio, USA.
Important dates: Founded 1905. Closed 1985.
Production: Artware, stoneware, dinnerware, kitchenware, tiles.

MARKS
Early marks show 'H' in circle or diamond; later marks show 'Hull' in combination with 'Art' or 'Ware' and 'USA'.

IROQUOIS CHINA COMPANY

The pottery was founded in 1905 and retrieved from bankruptcy in 1939. Its early products were unremarkable. Earl Crane bought the business in 1939 and made only hotel ware until 1946, when Russel Wright approached the company about producing a line of casual china for the mass market. Wright was already famous as a dinnerware designer because of the success of his American Modern, made by the Steubenville Pottery Company (*see* p.213) from 1939. However, despite the popularity of American Modern, there were many complaints about its fragility. Consequently, Wright sought a pottery making high-fired vitreous china for his second dinnerware pattern, hoping to find a body with thermo-shock properties that could be marketed as oven-to-table ware.

Wright introduced Casual China in 1946, but there were many early difficulties to work out: the body was a little thick, the glazes did not always fire properly, and the distribution contract had to be renegotiated. These problems were eventually solved, and Casual China continued to break its own sales records for more than ten years. Like American Modern it has a smoothly modern look developed from the coupe shape. However, American Modern's knob handles were replaced in Casual China with recessed handles designed to be moulded into the body. In 1951 the handles were redesigned as knobs, but the pinch-style handles continued to be made. Casual China was available in Sugar White, Lemon Yellow, Ice Blue, Nutmeg, Avocado Yellow, Parsley Green (later Forest Green), Oyster, Charcoal, Ripe Apricot, Pink Sherbet, Lettuce Green, Canteloupe, Aqua and Brick Red.

In the 1950s Ben Seibel designed five more lines of general market tableware for Iroquois: Interplay (1954, rare), Impromptu (1956), Informal, Inheritance and Intaglio. The last two are difficult to find today, but Impromptu and Informal are relatively easy to collect and come with a wide variety of decals, including florals, geometrics, conventionalized and naturalistic. Some of the many patterns on Impromptu are Aztec, Blue Doves, Country Garden, El Camino, Fjord, Grapes, Lazy Daisy, Luau, Pompon, Pyramids, Stellar and Wild Rose. Informal patterns include Blue Diamond, Bombay, Old Orchard, Rosemary and Teuton (also known as Thane). The pottery closed in 1969.

▲ **Russel Wright's Casual China, late 1940s**
Collectors of Casual China have much to look for, including restyled shapes, a variety of solid-colour glazes and decals, which were added in 1959. [218]

▲ **Ben Seibel's Informal bowl, 1950s**
Patterns of Informal have co-ordinating solid colours on the reverse side (the Autumn Leaf bowl shown here has a cinnamon brown exterior). Plates have the solid colour on the bottom; cups have it on the inside; pieces without decal decoration have solid colour inside. [219]

◆ **Ben Seibel's Impromptu teaware, late 1950s**
Typical Impromptu handles are seen here (the pattern is Jardinieres). Shapes for the dinner table were also made, including a condiment set. [220]

ISLE OF WIGHT HANDCRAFT POTTERY

This pottery was founded by Samuel Edgar Saunders, whose manager, Frederick S. Mursell, had suggested the use of the good local red clay to make glazed pottery. The company launched its products at the British Industries Fair of 1928, with an impressive show including handcraft vases, pots, bowls, jugs, eggcups and candlesticks. Also made were garden pottery, flower pots, lawn vases, pedestals and edging tiles. Output was always small, with never more than eight people employed. In 1930 Mr Laye, a Staffordshire potter who had helped establish the pottery, left, and in 1932 Edward Jervison Bagley became manager. Bagley was also the chemist and sometimes carried out his own design and decoration. Among other modellers and designers associated with the pottery were Reginald A. Davies, who became a decorator and designer in 1930, and William M. Baker, who had worked for his father, who ran the Upchurch Pottery.

KEY FACTS

Location: Carisbrooke, Isle of Wight, UK.
Important dates: Founded 1926. Closed 1938.
Production: Earthenware.

MARKS

Incorporate former mark of S. E. Saunders in central monogram.

◀ **Catalogue, 1930s**
This range of vases displays typical Isle of Wight shapes and the characteristic monochrome glazes that linked the pottery to the Arts and Crafts Movement. [221]

JACKSON & GOSLING

The company manufactured a full range of table services, nursery ware, toy ware and useful tableware accessories in its Grosvenor China range. Also produced were teaware, dinnerware and tableware, and accessories such as moustache cups and saucers, covered muffins, two-handled tea and breakfast cups, coffee jugs, jugs with lock lids, sweet dishes, sardine or wedge-cheese dishes, triple trays, covered honey pots with fast or loose stands, toast racks, meat pots, milk horns, broth bowls and stands, sick feeders, tea infusers, hair tidies, salad plates, jelly saucers, fruit saucers, butter pads, oatmeal saucers, sherbet cups, rose bowls and spills. Many of these items were available in more than one size. The pottery's specialities include reproductions of Lowestoft, Nant Garw, Rockingham, Chelsea and other scenes. In 1936 the company provided cube teasets for the RMS *Queen Mary*.

Under Government regulations the factory closed during World War II, and its production was combined with that of the adjoining Shelley Potteries (*see* p.200). The company continued to trade under its own name, but its registered office was transferred to Spode (*see* p.208), which had purchased it in 1932. Around 1953 the factory was bought by Shelley Potteries, and by 1954 most of the site had been demolished.

KEY FACTS

Location: King Street, Fenton, later at Grosvenor Works, Longton, Staffordshire, UK.
Important dates: Founded c.1860, Moved to Grosvenor Works c.1909. Closed c.1953.
Production: China.

MARKS

Grosvenor China mark used, sometimes with company name or initials added.

◀ **Advertisement, 1928**
Jackson & Gosling was a competent pottery with a traditional approach to design. This French-style Sèvres-inspired ware was advertised in *The Pottery Gazette* under the Grosvenor China trade mark. [222]

At the beginning of the 20th century Johnson Bros owned four factories at Hanley, one at Tunstall and one at Cobridge, and made large amounts of ironstone china, Royal semi-porcelain sanitary ware (white and decorated) and white and decorated tiles for various uses.

Johnson Bros is not known for hand-painted ware, but it supplied A. E. Gray (*see* p.78) with 'blanks' (undecorated and unglazed shapes) for decoration. It specialized in good-quality undecorated ware and ware with simple transfer-printed, stamped or decal-decorated designs. These products combined beauty with utility and were affordable for the mass market. As a result the firm was unaffected by wartime restrictions and the general slump; nor did it need to advertise widely until the 1960s, when it launched the Contempo shape range with a series of ten decorations featuring abstract designs. These designs include Marakeesh, with persimmon and grey fleur-de-lis border, and fruit and flower patterns such as Persian Rose and Royal Sovereign; the others were Castanet, Bramble, San Remo, Greencroft, Cannes, Bush Fire and Marguerite. The firm continued to produce children's ware and a full range of tableware, white and decorated, into the 1970s and 1980s, and, like other manufacturers, moved into the casual tableware market, introducing new trade names such as Goldendawn, Greydawn, Greendawn, Pareek and Snowhite.

Johnson Bros became part of the Waterford-Wedgwood Group (*see* p.230) in the early 1980s. A period of rationalization followed as Johnson Bros absorbed several factories and operated under various names. In 1992 Wedgwood closed Johnson Bros and centralized all its design groups at Barlaston. Four years later Wedgwood had three Johnson Bros patterns made in Malaysia and a Johnson stoneware range made in Japan.

Sauce boat, 1930s
In the late 1930s Johnson Bros caught up with the elegant styles of American-inspired Art Deco. 223

Happy Clown set, late 1970s
This is one of a series of colourful ranges for children made by Johnson Bros from the mid-1970s. 224

Willow ware, 1990s
The lasting popularity of the traditional willow pattern is endorsed by its inclusion in Johnson Bros' current range. 225

KEY FACTS

Location: Hanley, Tunstall and Cobridge, Staffordshire, UK.
Important dates: Founded 1883. Taken over by Wedgwood 1968. Became part of Waterford-Wedgwood Group early 1980s. Johnson Bros name revived 1991, discontinued by Wedgwood 1992 and revived 1996. Production outsourced in China.
Production: Earthenware and ironstone.
Principal designers: Colette Bishop, Marie Bennett, Susan Kennedy, Ursula Williams, Jessie Tait, Julie Holland.
Trade names: Johnson Bros Creative Tableware, Bull in a China Shop.

MARKS

Variations of this crown mark used from 1900. Marks usually printed. These incorporate 'Johnson Bros. and, in some cases, pattern names.

Johnson Bros. England.

A. B. JONES & SONS

The pottery specialized in badged ware, crested ware, view ware and souvenirs, the range including jugs, cups, vases and trays, figures and models of buildings in ivory bodies, decorated with coats of arms. By 1920 the firm had built up a comprehensive list of Grafton China heraldic and view ware, miniature mascots, animal figures and grotesques, as well as elegant border patterns in tea, breakfast and dessert ware. The pottery's tableware patterns were mainly traditional. Throughout the 1940s it made hotel ware for export only, and tableware. In the 1950s it brought out television sets, with saucers/plates recessed for cups, as well as the Capri shape coffee cup in six patterns designed by Henri Cole.

➤ Refreshment sets, 1956

This *Pottery Gazette* article shows a 1950s favourite: the television set. This combination ware had already enjoyed a long life, having been known in the Edwardian era as 'croquet cups and saucers'. 226

A selection of three of the wide range of refreshment sets made with floral designs by Alfred B. Jones and Sons Ltd. The patterns seen here include rose buds and harebells

Two more of the large round-shaped sets made by Josiah Wedgwood & Sons Ltd. The top design has the table mat in dark green with scattered white daisies. Below, an all-over grained pattern in a warm beige

KEY FACTS

Location: Grafton Works, Longton, Staffordshire, UK.
Important dates: Founded 1876. Bought by Crown House 1966, Crown Lynn Potteries 1971, management 1985; renamed Royal Grafton Bone China Ltd.
Production: China and earthenware.

GRAFTON CHINA MADE IN ENGLAND

A. E. JONES

After making bone china for a time the pottery concentrated on dinnerware in earthenware and semi-porcelain, for the home and export markets. In the early 20th century it was noted for its well-modelled shapes and patterns, including some strongly influenced by Chinese and other oriental styles used by Crown Derby, such as Pekin. The firm also produced toilet services, trinket sets, miscellaneous pottery for the table, teapots, cocoa jugs, hot-water jugs, fruit dishes, butter dishes, sardine boxes and other useful accessories. By 1946 it was making ashtrays, breakfast sets, bulb bowls, chamber pots, coffee pots, coffee sets, cruet sets, dinner sets, eggcups, fruit sets, hotel ware, jugs, morning sets, mugs, pie dishes, pudding bowls, sandwich sets, supper sets, teapots, teasets and toilet ware. Also launched after the war, the Thames River Scene series of hand-engraved and underglaze-printed patterns proved an export success and by 1965 accounted for almost half of the firm's output.

KEY FACTS

Location: Palissy Pottery, Longton, Staffordshire, UK.
Important dates: Founded 1905. Renamed Palissy Pottery 1946. Bought by Royal Worcester 1958. Closed 1988.
Production: Earthenware.
Trade name: Palissy.

MARKS

Printed or impressed marks include trade name Palissy. Mark depicting artist's palette and brush used for hand-painted patterns c.1936–1941.

Palissy ENGLAND

◆ Teaware, 1930s

Although Jones was not a major manufacturer its Palissy brand name was well known, and the products reflected both modern and traditional styles. This set displays the influence of Susie Cooper in its design, while the shape is typically 1930s. 227

GEORGE JONES & SONS

The company earned a reputation in the last quarter of the 19th century as a manufacturer of high-quality majolica ware and other artistic lines, including *pâte-sur-pâte*, mainly drawing inspiration from its near neighbour Minton (*see* p.132).

In the 20th century George Jones & Sons expanded its production for the domestic market, launching new ranges of dinnerware and toilet ware as well as rich bone-china tea services. In 1919, when the pottery opened a showroom in London, among its first displays was china teaware with a kaleidoscopic border pattern of circles, crescents and dots. The following year the show included nursery ware and many new earthenware shapes and patterns designed exclusively for the firm's ivory-body ware, and a new, richly coloured ornamental range decorated with sailing ships.

[Photo, by "The Pottery Gazette."]

◆ **Sailing ship advertisement, 1920**
This colourful ornamental range, decorated with variety of sailing ship motifs, was illustrated in *The Pottery Gazette* in March 1920. It shows the Crescent Pottery's determined attempt to bring itself up to date. 228

◆ **Abbey cereal dish, c.1910–20**
George Jones's Abbey pattern, a revived early-19th-century design, was made in huge quantities from the 1920s as a premium for Shredded Wheat. 229

KEY FACTS
Location: Trent Pottery c.1861–1907, Crescent Pottery 1907–57, Stoke, Staffordshire, UK.
Important dates: Founded c.1861. Jones name ceased 1950.

MARKS
Variations of crescent mark and 'GJ' monogram most often used. Mark usually printed or impressed.

JUGTOWN POTTERY

Jacques and Juliana Busbee were searching for quaint indigenous pottery to use for both serving and decoration in their tearoom in the bohemian Greenwich Village area of New York City in 1917 when they came upon the traditional stoneware and bright-orange earthenware still being made in rural North Carolina. The ware that the couple 'imported' to New York proved to be so popular in the tearoom that they began selling them as well in an adjacent gift shop.

In 1921 the Busbees founded their own Jugtown Pottery to produce custom giftware and dinnerware according to Jacques' concepts. Traditional ware continued to be made. Jacques also conceived, at the suggestion of Tiffany Studios, a hybrid style which combined traditional Chinese and Korean shapes. These pieces were made in native

◆ **Dish, c.1930**
This dish shows Jugtown's typical use of Asian design references. 230

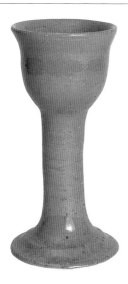

stoneware and decorated with various glazes, including a thick white, a mirror black, a greenish 'frogskin' of salt glaze over Albany slip, and a transmutational red/turquoise called Chinese Blue. Charles Teague was the first potter to work in the pottery, followed in 1923 by Ben Owen, who stayed for 36 years. In 1926, when the market for the ware was well established, Juliana closed the New York shop and moved to Jugtown.

Jacques Busbee died in 1947. Juliana and Owen continued the business until 1959, when Owen left to establish his own pottery. Brothers Vernon and Bobby Owens, who lived nearby, and Charles Moore kept the pottery going from 1960 to 1966 under various arrangements with the estates of Juliana Busbee and the subsequent owner, John Mare (both died in 1962), but their goods suffered from many production problems. In 1968 Country Roads, Incorporated, a non-profit corporation that fosters traditional arts, acquired the pottery and began to improve and standardize the products. In 1971, when US Food and Drug Administration regulations prohibited low-fired lead glazes on ware sold for food preparation and service, bodies and glazes were reformulated. With renewed marketing and new technical direction, the Owens and Charles Moore have continued to run the pottery. In 1983 Vernon Owen bought the pottery, which still makes a mix of folk ware and artware.

◆ Redware footed wine cup, c.1925
Traditional redware bodies were glazed to give a pumpkin-orange colour. 231

◗ Two-handled vase, c.1950
The thick white engobe on this vase stopped just short of the foot rim as it ran down the body. A fine salt glaze is just visible on the surface. 232

◆ Vase, c.1930
With its strong baluster form and dramatic transmutational red/turquoise glaze, this vase is reminiscent of Chinese bronzes. 233

KEY FACTS

Location: Jugtown, North Carolina, USA.
Important dates: Founded 1921. Still active.
Production: Red earthenware and stoneware dinnerware and artware.
Principal designers: Jacques and Juliana Busbee, Ben Owen, Vernon and Bob Owens, Charles Moore.

MARKS

Impressed stamp with jug in middle used throughout company's history. After 1977, date sometimes included. Pitcher sometimes substituted for jug 1960–77.

KEELE STREET POTTERY CO.

The firm was founded to make earthenware novelties, figures, traditional tableware, toy and children's ware and fancies, thus filling the gap in the domestic market caused by restrictions on German imports during World War I. Later this ware was widely marketed both at home and abroad.

In the late 1940s the company acquired several other potteries and formed the Keele Street Pottery Group. In 1949 the South Western Industrial Corporation Ltd took a 49 per cent share in the group, which then converted Meir Airport into a modern factory. By 1955 South Western had segregated the pottery companies from its other concerns, and Staffordshire Potteries (Holdings) Ltd was formed. Other pottery companies owned by the Keele Street Pottery Group were moved to Meir, which offered modern equipment and an efficient layout. The Keele Street Pottery Co. continued to trade under its own name until at least 1965.

Pottery produced by Keele Street was made mainly for the mass market. Production was concentrated on inexpensive lines such as ornamental cottage teaware, traditional teaware in earthenware with simple decal decorations, such as the Wildflower pattern of around 1954, boxed circus miniatures, bird and animal models and wall plaques. The latter included sets of three flying birds – for example, the Golden Oriole and Shoveller series. Colourful litho-decorated mugs, eggcups and novelties based on children's television characters must have been a large part of Keele Street's output from the mid-1950s. Among the subjects were Andy Pandy, Sooty, the Magic Roundabout, Lenny the Lion and Pinky and Perky. A *Pottery Gazette* representative who visited the pottery shortly after the move to Meir reported that Sooty pieces were being produced at the rate of about 100,000 dozen annually. This range consisted of eggcups, cups and saucers, fruit dishes and beakers, which were supplied mainly to companies which filled them with chocolates.

▲ **Advertisement, 1960**
Published in *The Pottery Gazette* in July 1960, this advertisement underlines Keele Street's links with the popular end of the market. It too made that old favourite the flying duck! 234

◀ **Children's television ware, 1950s**
Children's ware, decorated with popular TV characters such as Sooty and Andy Pandy, was made in huge quantities during the 1950s. Much of it was sold by confectionery companies. 235

KEY FACTS

Location: Keele Street, Tunstall, 1916–58; Meir Airport, Longton 1958–65, Staffordshire, UK.
Important dates: Founded 1916. Acquired other firms and renamed Keele Street Pottery Group late 1940s. Active until at least 1965.
Production: Earthenware.

MARKS

Early ware mainly unmarked. Marks include impressed initials 'KSP' or this round printed mark (sometimes in gold) with central pattern name.

KEELING & CO.

This pottery produced a full range of dinnerware, teaware, kitchen-ware, toilet ware and table fancies, as well as ornamental bowls and vases. In its high-quality body and brilliant glaze it developed a range of ware which was marketed under the Losol Ware trade name, in use from 1912.

However, the company specialized in hospital ware and badged ware suitable for use by hotels, shops and restaurants. In 1920 it brought out a range of toilet ware, with panels of solid ground colours, including blue, pink and yellow, lined off in black, as well as vases in strong Jacobean colourings. In the same year it launched extremely good replicas of birds and animals, and among these one of the chief novelties was a penguin lampstand.

Later the pottery introduced new lines in bowls and vases in a more colourful modern style, and in 1934 it added to its catalogue a range of ornamental leafage ware called Brantique. Production ceased two years later.

◀ **Losol vase, 1930s**
Keeling used its Losol trade mark extremely widely and over a long period. With its hand-painted floral decoration in typical 1930s style, this vase reveals the influence of market leaders such as Gray. [236]

KENSINGTON POTTERY

The pottery originally made inexpensive earthenware for everyday use, but from the 1930s it expanded its ornamental ranges. In 1934 it made many new shapes and modern patterns in teaware and ornamental useful ware, as well as ordinary domestic pottery, including chamber pots. Typical are the Eton flower jug and the Eton flower vase complete with flower holder. Animal figures, figures and statuettes, ornamental teapots and other novelties were added later. In 1954 Kensington brought out heavily decal-decorated chintz teaware in two distinct patterns, Summertime and Blossomtime. Shapes include teapot, sugar bowl, cream jug, cup, saucer and handled beaker, ashtray, honey jar, egg set, vase and a Cosy Set consisting of a rectangular teapot and a hot-water pot on a tray. The firm also made Huntsman Ware teapots and related items.

➡ **Chintz Ware advertisement, 1953**
Advertised in *The Pottery Gazette* in 1953, Kensington's chintz range is a blend of 1930s and 1950s styles. [237]

JAMES KENT

From the outset James Kent was mainly a producer of good-class, medium-priced printed earthenware for household use, but it also made more richly decorated table services and fancies. Production was concentrated on traditional ware, of which the firm always had good displays at trade shows although it rarely attracted the attention of critics. The pottery earned its reputation as a specialist in chintz and floral patterns. These it produced from the 1920s onwards, and many were still in production in the 1950s. Perhaps the best-known chintz is Du Barry, but throughout the 1960s the firm also heavily promoted its Rosalynde chintz-pattern dinner, tea and table fancies portraying the English moss rose. The demand for traditional floral patterns seems to have remained constant throughout that decade, and in order to meet it the company constantly added new shapes for existing patterns such as Davenport and Chinese Rose, a traditional *famille rose*-style pattern.

Occasionally the firm produced children's ware, such as a nursery set designed by Peter Fraser in the 1940s. It also made some more contemporary lines in the 1920s and 1930s, and even a 1960s contemporary modern range of tableware fancies in shades of red, yellow and green which it called Salad Days, although production of these seems to have been short-lived. In the 1950s the pottery reproduced a wide range of traditional Staffordshire figures, animal groups and Toby jugs.

Oven-to-table ware was introduced in the 1980s, and the tableware range was expanded. In this period the pottery also made gift items reproduced from 50–100-year-old originals. Since the mid-1980s James Kent Ltd and incorporated companies have introduced the Fleshpots Modern Art ornamental range of colourful and exotic forms, including a head-and-shoulders portrait figure of Marilyn Monroe, and, between 1985 and 1989, the limited-edition Next Collection by artists such as Gail Fox, Carol McNicoll, Janice Tchalenko, Hinchcliff and Barber, Karen Bunting, Sabina Teuteberg, Jane Willingale and Joanne and Andrew Young.

Decal-decorated chintzware, to a lesser degree, was still in production in 1989 when the firm was taken over by M. R. Hadida Ltd of Bletchley, Buckinghamshire, which immediately halted its production because it was

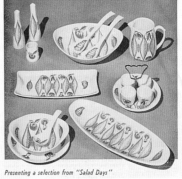

▲ Du Barry chintzware, 1940s
Kent was an important maker of chintzware. In 1998 the company reintroduced the Du Barry pattern on the Square Diamond shape, which has enjoyed renewed success. 238

Salad Days

Presenting a selection from "Salad Days"

▲ Salad Days advertisement, 1954
In this advertisement for its Salad Days range, from *The Pottery Gazette Reference Book*, Kent demonstrates an unmistakably contemporary look. 239

◀ Fleshpots Modern Art range, 1980s
An advertising leaflet shows a selection of colourful and exotic forms from Kent's Fleshpots Modern Art range, made at the Old Foley Pottery in the 1980s. Among other items in this range is a portrait bust of Marilyn Monroe. 240

too labour-intensive and not cost-effective. However, after years of lobbying from customers, in 1998 the new owner relaunched the 1920s designs. It used the old moulds saved from the scrapheap and the original Du Barry and Hydrangea artwork, and the Cobridge-based Old Chintz Company marketed the products. However, whereas the earlier chintzware was aimed at the cheaper end of the market, the produce became a premium item for collectors and the prestige sector.

KEY FACTS

Location: Old Foley Pottery, Longton, Staffordshire, UK.
Important dates: Founded 1897. Bought by Bayer (UK) 1981, Fleshpots (UK) Ltd 1986, and others subsequently. Closed 2003.
Production: China, earthenware.
Trade names: James Kent, Foley, Old Foley, Fleshpots, Next.

MARKS

Various globe or shield marks used, incorporating company name or initials; 'Ltd' added from 1913.

◀ **Next Collection series, 1980s**
Artist-potter Janice Tchalenko designed this decorative artware, made by Kent for the Next Collection series between 1985 and 1989. 241

KIRKHAMS

A manufacturer of ornamental ware and other items in terracotta and domestic earthenware, William Kirkham was succeeded by his sons, H. G. and D. Kirkham. In 1890 H. G. Kirkham bought the copper printing plates originally used by T. J. & J. Mayer and Bates, Elliott & Co. for decorating tableware, and these were used by the firm for decorating pot lids. The prints were reissued in the 1920s. During World War II production for Kirkham and Parrot & Co. was concentrated with that of Burgess & Leigh (*see* p.36), which made white ware for Kirkhams. All the companies continued to trade under their own names. Kirkham's production continued after the war, when its catalogue included ashtrays, advertising, scientific, chemical, hospital and laboratory ware, kitchenware, jugs, ointment jars, photographic trays, rolling pins and jelly moulds.

When the company's factory came on to the market in 1961, it was bought by Susan Williams-Ellis and her husband Euan Cooper-Willis, who modernized it. Kirkhams was one of several potteries that supplied white ware for decoration to A. E. Gray & Co. (*see* p.78), which the couple had bought the previous year. From 1 January 1962 the merged companies began operating under the new name of Portmeirion Potteries (*see* p.163).

KEY FACTS

Location: Kirkham Street, Stoke, Staffordshire, UK.
Important dates: Founded 1862. Merged with A. E. Gray & Co. 1961.
Production: Earthenware.

MARKS

This printed mark used c.1946–61. Company name usually included.

◀ **Kitchenware, 1950s**
After World War II decorative kitchenware enjoyed considerable popularity, prompting many lesser makers, such as Kirkhams, to enter the market. 242

EDWIN M. KNOWLES CHINA CO.

Plans for a new pottery company in Chester, West Virginia, were announced in 1900. Edwin M. Knowles, youngest son of Isaac W. Knowles (*see* Knowles, Taylor & Knowles, opposite), C. A. Smith and Albert G. Mason formed a corporation and built a factory in Chester to manufacture semi-vitreous tableware and toilet ware, spittoons and Ohio covered jugs. Chester is on the Ohio River opposite East Liverpool, Ohio, and throughout its history the Knowles China Company maintained offices in East Liverpool and used the address there in its advertising.

In 1913 the company built a new factory with 15 kilns in Newell. Factories were operated in Chester and Newell until 1931, when Harker (*see* p.89) bought the buildings in Chester and all Knowles's operations were concentrated in Newell. By 1940 Knowles was the third largest pottery in the USA, employing 900 workers. However, World War II and subsequent market changes caused severe business problems, and production of pottery ceased in 1962.

The company made tableware, including dinner services and serving pieces, and kitchenware. Toilet ware was also made in the early years. Moulded shapes and decal patterns were both traditional and modern. Favourites with collectors include Deanna (1938), a solid-colour ware with decal on the ivory version, and Yorktowne (1936), an Art Deco globular ware with colourful angular decals. Various fruits decorated the kitchenware. From 1956 to 1962 Knowles produced Russel Wright's Esquire pattern, which combined modern elegant coupe shapes and pastel glazes with delicate incised botanical decorations. Although popular with store buyers, Esquire never sold well to customers, who found it costly compared with foreign ware. A series of collectors' plates issued with the name of the Edwin M. Knowles China Company in the early 1980s is related to the original pottery in name only and not made by it.

▲ **Damask Rose dinnerware, mid-1950s**
Introduced in 1954, the Damask Rose decoration was used on the semi-vitreous Accent line. 243

▲ **Utility Ware, 1943**
Knowles Utility Ware, a semi-vitreous kitchenware, was introduced in 1939 and made through the late 1940s. It was decorated in solid colours as well as brightly coloured bands and decals, such as Valencia shown here. 244

◀ **Hostess platter, late 1930s**
One of many semi-vitreous dinnerware shapes made by Knowles, Hostess hollowware has angular handles and terraced finials. 245

KEY FACTS

Location: Chester and Newell, West Virginia; offices in East Liverpool, Ohio, USA.
Important dates: Founded 1900. Closed 1962.
Production: Semi-porcelain tableware and kitchenware.
Principal designer: Russel Wright.

MARKS

Trade mark 'K' used in backstamps from 1948, often with pattern name. Earlier devices included a bulbous vase and a masted ship.

KNOWLES, TAYLOR & KNOWLES

The Knowles family already had a long history as potters in East Liverpool, Ohio, in 1870 when Isaac W. Knowles, his son Homer S. Knowles and son-in-law John N. Taylor took over an earlier Knowles family pottery and started Knowles, Taylor & Knowles.

The new company eventually became the largest dinnerware manufacturer in the United States. At first Knowles, Taylor & Knowles continued making the Rockingham and yellow ware that were the staple products of the first generation of East Liverpool potters, who had begun production in the 1850s. But by 1872 the small Knowles, Taylor & Knowles pottery had begun to turn out white ware.

⬆ Trade catalogue, c.1893
Knowles, Taylor & Knowles's 'Souvenir' was actually a trade catalogue showcasing its achievements. Four separate potteries, having 31 ware kilns and four decorating kilns, were incorporated in one factory. 246

Demand for the company's goods grew quickly, and so it built a new eight-kiln factory in 1880 and, the following year, bought the old Buckeye Pottery to convert entirely to the production of white ironstone. The company's success in these years was certainly related to the expanding markets in the western USA. However, success could also be attributed to mechanical improvements in the manufacturing process. For example, Knowles's regulated pull-down helped standardize quality in the production of flatware in the factory.

In 1888 Knowles, Taylor & Knowles built a five-storey factory for making vitreous hotel ware and fine-art porcelain. Belleek ware was produced from 1889, under the guidance of Joshua Poole, who was brought in from the Belleek factory in County Fermanagh, Northern Ireland. The Knowles, Taylor & Knowles version matched, in quality of body and character of design, the best pieces coming from the original factory as well as the fine Belleek ware being made in Trenton, New Jersey, at the time. Manufacture of the East Liverpool version was short-lived, however. Knowles, Taylor & Knowles's china factory was destroyed by fire in 1890. It was rebuilt immediately, and production continued as Lotus Ware, a bone-china artware, rather than the earlier Belleek imitation. When Lotus

⬆ Lotus Ware dish, c.1895
Lotus Ware was a bone-china artware that developed from an earlier Belleek imitation. It was decorated in the factory and also by independent decorators, both professional and amateur. This dish is factory decorated. 247

◆ China coffee pot, c.1905
When the firm discontinued Lotus Ware in 1897, it began making china and semi-porcelain in the same works. This coffee pot with fine moulding was decorated with a pale yellow matt finish sprayed over the glossy glaze. 248

Ware production ceased in 1897, as a result of the declining market for exotic porcelains, the manufacture of semi-porcelain tableware was initiated in this factory.

When the company was incorporated in 1891, with capital of $1 million, it boasted of having 29 kilns in operation and declared itself to be the largest pottery in the USA. Promotional literature of the 1890s described the pottery in the following terms: 'The Decorating Department of the Knowles, Taylor & Knowles Co. is equipped for doing work of any kind to suit the fads and fancies of the most exacting. A speciality of this department has been the production of ware upon which is printed names, crests, borders, emblems and monograms. Some of the leading hotels, restaurants, clubs and steamers are using exclusively the ware made and decorated by the Knowles, Taylor & Knowles Co., while the United States Government and several state departments are using large quantities, rendering the goods made by this Company practically a Government standard.' By this time the company was operating 31 ware kilns and 13 decorating kilns. These were arranged in four separate factories within the large manufacturing complex.

About 1900 Knowles, Taylor & Knowles decided to manufacture hotel ware and specialities for hospitals and asylums. Electrical porcelain was made in a separate plant, and these products also met with a ready market. By the early 20th century the firm's manufacturing capacity was more than double what it had been ten years earlier.

Business declined in the mid-1920s as the US economy sank into a major depression. In 1929 Knowles, Taylor & Knowles merged with the American China Corporation, but the new firm was not able to recapture the previous successes. The American China Corporation went into receivership in 1931, and all manufacturing ceased permanently.

◆ Pitcher, c.1905
The pitcher was made for holding hot water in a toilet set. Like many others from this era, this pattern was given the name of a state – in this case, Virginia. It incorporates transfers of small blue rosebuds as an overall design pattern. 249

◆ Spittoon, c.1905
This Harvard-shape spittoon carries transfers of the passion flower. The pottery used the names of US colleges for other lines as well, including Yale, Cornell and Oberlin. 250

KEY FACTS

Location: East Liverpool, Ohio, USA.
Important dates: Founded 1870. Merged with American China Corporation 1929. American China Corporation went into receivership and all manufacturing ceased 1931.
Production: Tableware, artware, institutional ware and electrical porcelain.

MARKS

Initials 'K', 'T' and 'K' incorporated in marks, sometimes accompanied by pattern name.

LAMBERTON CHINA

Lamberton China was the product of two companies over a 60-year period. Established by the Maddock Pottery Company in 1893, the new product drew its name from the section of Trenton, New Jersey, where the pottery was located. The strong vitreous body developed for sanitary fixtures by Thomas Maddock formed the basis of the durable vitreous Lamberton China sold to homemakers, hotels and institutions. In 1923 the Scammell brothers bought the works from Maddock and continued to make Lamberton china under the name Scammell China Company.

Most of Scammell's work was for the USA's premier hotel, railway and steamship companies. Among hotels, Scammell supplied china for the Waldorf-Astoria, Plaza, Savoy-Plaza, Hotel Pierre and others in New York City; the New Willard, Mayflower, Raleigh and others in Washington, D.C.; and the Stephens and Drake hotels in Chicago. In railway china, Scammell's most outstanding commission was the service made in 1927 for the centenary of the Baltimore and Ohio Railroad. The elaborate designs, executed in blue transfer print, completely covered the exterior surfaces. Among other prominent rail companies using Maddock and Scammell china were the Boston and Maine Railroad, Chesapeake and Ohio Railroad, Chicago, Rock Island and Pacific Railroad, Pennsylvania Railroad and New York Central Railroad. Steamship companies ordering Lamberton China included the Norwegian America Line, Panama Pacific Steamship Line and United States Line.

The Lamberton service and commemorative plates are among the finest US institutional china with elaborate decal borders and pictorial devices. Service plates for the Hotel Baltimore in Kansas City, Maxim's in New York, the Hotel Bossert in Brooklyn and many other hotels, as well as commemorative series for institutions such as Lafayette College and Washington and Jefferson College, both in Pennsylvania, are among the many pieces produced at the Lamberton works. Special single commemoratives, for events such as the George Washington birth bicentennial in 1932, were also made.

In addition, the pottery produced dinnerware for domestic use from 1939 until its demise in 1954. Fischer, Bruce and Company of Philadelphia worked with Scammell to develop Lamberton Ivory China, which eventually embraced some 28 patterns.

◆ **Brass Rail service plate, c.1925**
The Brass Rail was a chain of taverns in New York City. The plate was made by Scammell China Company. 251

◆ **Daniel Boone hotel service plate, late 1920s**
This design was intended to show the 'development and colonization of the North American continent'. Motifs include the *Mayflower* and the Wright brothers' first flight. 252

◆ **Hotel Baltimore service plate, c.1915**
This plate was made by Maddock Pottery Company using the trade name Lamberton China. The small mark is composed of the word 'CHINA' with an 'M' above (for Maddock) and an 'L' below (for Lamberton). 253

KEY FACTS

Location: Trenton, New Jersey, USA.
Important dates: Founded 1893. Bought by Scammell China Company 1923. Closed 1954.
Production: China.
Principal designers: Charles May, George Ellis, Geza DeVegh, Jacques de Kort, Emil Schnepf, Anthony Dragonetti.

MARKS

Scammell backstamp used 1923–54. Similar mark, with 'M' instead of 'S', identifies earlier Maddock ownership.

LANCASTER & SONS

This company made general domestic earthenware, including a range of lettered grocery jars and fancies, for a wide market. In the 1920s it introduced many popular styles of decoration, such as printed patterns in useful and fancy earthenware, and specialized in sets of jugs, teapots, five-piece teapot sets and miscellaneous table extras designed to capture the middle-class market at home and abroad.

Continuing in full production throughout World War II, the pottery extended its ornamental range in the mid-1940s to win the export market. It also made cigarette boxes with Dickensian characters in low relief, character jugs, tankards, novelties and fancies, advertising ware, figures and statuettes, flower pots and garden pottery, ornamental useful ware, and tea and coffee pots. Also produced was nursery ware, notably Teddyware, designed by Elizabeth Sandland in 1961, and Playtime, launched two years later. The firm, which had become Lancaster & Sandland in 1944, used at various times the trade names British Crown Ware, Dresden Ware and Sandland Ware. It closed in 1970.

➤ **Sandland Ware advertisement, 1957**
Published in *The Pottery Gazette*, this unusually graphic advertisement shows typical Lancaster products. 254

KEY FACTS	MARKS
Location: Dresden Works, Hanley, Staffordshire, UK.	Variations of this mark used from 1920. Later marks give full name.
Important dates: Founded 1900. Closed 1970.	

HOMER LAUGHLIN CHINA COMPANY

Every collector of ceramics in North America has heard of Fiesta Ware, and many search for it. Its creator was the Homer Laughlin China Company. Founded by a china dealer and managed by astute businessmen, the company has been among the largest and most successful of the US potteries, and today it is one of the largest in the world, supplying tableware to significant sectors of the institutional market and Fiesta to the vital retail market.

Fiesta is undoubtedly the company's most famous pattern, both in the original form of the 1930s and in its current revived form. But even if it had never been created, millions of American homes would still have had Homer Laughlin's tableware or kitchenware. Distributed primarily through Woolworths, Penneys, Grants and other dime stores as well as mail-order catalogues and department stores, the company's products appealed to householders throughout the USA because of their price and design.

The brothers Homer and Shakespeare Laughlin were in business with their father, selling imported and domestic ceramics from a china warehouse in New York City, when they decided to set up a white-ware factory in East Liverpool, Ohio, in 1873, with the backing and blessing of the city. The pottery began production in the latter part of the following year. Recognition of its superior product came quickly: at the Centennial Exhibition in Philadelphia in 1876 the Laughlins won awards for their white ware. Despite this early success, Shakespeare decided to work elsewhere the next year, and Homer began to sign his goods with his

➤ **The China Book, 1912**
Homer Laughlin's Pattern H-135, shown here, is typical of the semi-vitreous ware made by the company in the style of French Limoges china, with fancy shapes and tiny flowers. The catalogue boasted of the firm's 110 kilns. 255

LANGLEY: see LOVATT & LOVATT p.118

Wells Art Glaze Ware, 1930s
The Wells shape was designed by
Frederick H. Rhead and introduced in
1930. Semi-matt art glazes developed
for the line were available in blue, leaf
green, peach, rust brown, vellum ivory
and melon yellow. Sometimes decals
were applied to the ivory glaze. 256

**Kitchen Kraft OvenServe
casserole, c.1940**
The Kitchen Kraft line, designed by
Frederick H. Rhead and launched
in 1937, was decorated with solid
Fiesta colours and decals on ivory.
Bowls, casseroles, pie bakers, covered
jars, a jug and a shaker are among the
limited forms in this line. 257

Century line, 1930s
Designed by Frederick H. Rhead
and introduced in 1931, Century
has a 'square' form. Decals included
Mexicana, Hacienda, Conchita and
English Garden. In the late 1930s
solid brightly coloured glazes
were applied, and the line was
called Riviera. 258

own name. He further identified them as American by use of a device
showing the American eagle conquering the British lion.

Homer Laughlin operated the pottery as a sole proprietorship until
1896, when it was incorporated as the Homer Laughlin China Company.
W. Edwin Wells, who had joined the company as a bookkeeper in 1889,
became a major shareholder in the corporation, while Laughlin himself
gradually withdrew, selling his interest to members of the Aaron family of
Pittsburgh. By 1900 Wells, company vice-president Charles Aaron and the
chief salesman, George W. Clarke, had established themselves as the company's design committee. Art director Arthur Mountford and Edward L.
Carson, head of the decorating department, gave advice to the committee,
but were not members.

The company's emphasis on market demands and Wells's superior abil-
ities at cost analysis were a successful combination for developing the
business rapidly. By 1902 the firm had three factories in East Liverpool; by
1905 it was investing huge sums of money to create its own village and factory complex across the Ohio River in Newell, West Virginia, and by 1910
it had constructed four factories in Newell, with 1400 workers. Two years
later it was supplying 10 per cent of the US ceramics market from its 110
kilns in East Liverpool and Newell. The East Liverpool facilities were
closed in 1929, and in 1930 Wells was succeeded by his son, Joseph M.
Wells. Today the company is still privately held by descendants of the
Wells and Aaron families.

Despite the company name, the Homer Laughlin China Company made
semi-porcelain dinnerware, kitchenware and novelties during most of its
first 75 years of business. Following the growing fashion for an ivory body
established by Lenox's (*see* p.114) ascendancy in fine china in the early
1920s, Homer Laughlin developed an ivory earthenware body called
Yellowstone in 1925-6. In 1959 the company introduced vitreous dinnerware and institutional china. Today it boasts of having a 100 per cent
alpha-alumina clay body and a product that is completely lead-free.

Throughout its history the company has made patterns in dinnerware
and kitchenware at modest prices and to suit every taste from traditional
to modern. Some modern lines, such as Riviera, Fiesta and Harlequin,
were presented in solid colours, but decal decorations predominate. Even
Riviera often had decals added on the ivory glaze. Many lines that are
nowadays collectable started as exclusive shapes or patterns for manufacturers, such as Quaker Oats, who used pattern pieces as premiums
(Harvest, Tudor Rose, Wild Rose, Pastoral, Carnival and Tea Rose).
Alternatively, they were patterns made for sale through single retailers.
Fiesta, for example, began as an exclusive for Gimbels. Harlequin, a less
expensive solid-colour ware, like Fiesta, for purchasers who were more

conscious of cost, was made exclusively for Woolworths. J. J. Newberry bought the White Flower pattern on the Rhythm shape. Dinnerware sets were also made for sale through retail catalogues such as those distributed by Sears and Montgomery Ward.

Although many designers and craftsmen worked in the company's design and modelling departments over the years, two in particular contributed lines which are much appreciated by collectors today: Frederick Hurten Rhead and Don Schreckengost. Rhead, an Englishman, started with Homer Laughlin in 1927 as art director. While Fiesta (1936-72, revived 1986) is his most enduring creation, the Century shape (1931) and particularly its Riviera colour range (1937), Wells (1930) and the Kitchen Kraft OvenServe line (1937) are also desirable. Don Schreckengost contributed Jubilee (1948), Epicure (1953) and Rhythm (1955). Jubilee found further life in 1952 with the introduction of Suntone (brown) and Skytone (blue), which had solid-colour bodies and contrasting white finials and handles. Rhythm was based on the coupe shape and issued in solid colours and with decals such as American Provincial (with a Pennsylvania Dutch theme also designed by Don Schreckengost), Golden Wheat, Rhythm Rose and White Flower.

Other noteworthy Homer Laughlin lines include Historical America; made from 1939 to 1958, this features transfer-printed American scenes based on the art of Joseph Boggs Beale. Eggshell, a lightweight ware, was introduced in 1937 and made in several shapes, including Nautilus, Swing (1938, with solid-colour handles), Theme and Georgian in 1940. Theme, which has a relief border of grapes and vines, was bought by many decorating companies as blanks and decorated on special order outside the Homer Laughlin factory. These are frequently found on the market. Yellowstone, introduced in the late 1920s, was the first yellow (cream-coloured) body; it had an octagonal shape with decoration.

Kitchen lines included OvenServe (1933) and Kitchen Kraft Ovenserve (1937). These ranges included covered canisters, covered casseroles, a covered jug, bowls, pie and cake plates, spoon, fork, cake server, salt and pepper shakers, a four-piece stacking refrigerator storage set and dinnerware.

Collectors of Homer Laughlin's dinnerware are fortunate to have date codes included in the backstamps since 1900 that identify the year each piece was made. From 1900 to 1909 a single-digit month and single-digit

◆ **Dinnerware, 1930s**
Tulips in a Basket is one of many decal patterns made in the 1920s and 1930s. Floral patterns were extremely popular in the American market. 259

◆ **Fiesta Ware, 1930s and 1940s**
Frederick Rhead designed Fiesta and it was introduced in 1936. Although it was not the first solid-colour casual dinnerware made in America, it was certainly the most popular. It is made today, but in different colours. 260

◆ **Jubilee Ware, late 1940s**
Designed by Don Schreckengost and issued in 1948 to celebrate the company's 75th anniversary, Jubilee was decorated in solid pastel colour glazes. In the 1950s the same shape was issued in brown with white handles (Suntone) and blue with white handles (Skytone). 261

year were followed by '1', '2' or '3' to designate the factory of origin. From 1910 to 1920 the first numeral identifies the month, the next two numerals the year, and the letter and/or digit cluster indicates the factory. From 1921 to 1929 a letter identifies the month, a single digit records the year, and the last figure designates the factory. From 1930 to 1960 the month is a letter and the years are two digits, while the factory is identified by a letter and number combination. Since 1960 the month and year have been identified by a discrete combination of two letters; for example, 'FE' is May 1965, 'RJ' is October 1977 and so on. A further aid to identification for the collector is the fact that Homer Laughlin's backstamps are specific to the ware and pattern.

KEY FACTS

Location: East Liverpool, Ohio, and Newell, West Virginia, USA.
Important dates: Founded 1877. Incorporated as Homer Laughlin China Company 1896. Still active.
Production: Dinnerware and hotel ware.

MARKS

Company name and/or 'HL' cipher included in every backstamp. See above for additional information.

◆ **Golden Wheat pattern plate, mid-1950s**
Rhythm, a slim coupe shape, was designed by Don Schreckengost. The wheat motif was used by most American potteries during the 1940s and 1950s. 262

THOMAS LAWRENCE

The output of the Falcon Works, Longton, the factory of the firm of Thomas Lawrence, was very similar to that of Shaw & Copestake (*see* p.198), who owned the premises. Lawrence did not make tableware but specialized in toilet ware, including children's toilet ware, trinket sets, vases, jugs, novelties and fancies for the home market and a strong export market which continued throughout World War II. In the early 1940s, when Shaw & Copestake's factory was relinquished by the Ministry of Defence, the firm moved into the Falcon Works. Thomas Lawrence and Shaw & Copestake continued with full production for export and their permitted quota for the home market.

After the war the two firms continued this arrangement, using each other's designs and marking them either Falcon Ware or SylvaC. Lawrence's designer, Reginald R. Thompson, created designs for both factories. He had joined Lawrence in 1917, at the age of 14. He was employed as a painter, but his creative talent soon became obvious, and after completing a course for potters, decorators and designers at the local school of art, in 1922, when he was only 19, he was promoted to the position of decorating manager. He worked for Lawrence until he was 75, creating, among many other lines, his Zooline nursery ware in the 1960s. Among other designers associated with the company was Jeanette Ruth, who also designed children's ware, namely Teddyware, launched in 1952.

Immediately after the war the pottery brought out a range of tableware accessories and the Cavalier range, which included jugs, bowls, plates and a Toby jug. By the early 1950s the company was widely advertising its Toby jugs, namely Beefeater, Cavalier, Henry VIII, Punch, Pickwick, John Bull and Dick

◆ **Falcon Ware advertisement, 1952**
This 1952 advertisement illustrates a Lawrence speciality: the character Toby jug. 263

Turpin. Also in this series are George Bernard Shaw and William Shakespeare. These jugs were modelled by the company, although some later models brought out by Shaw & Copestake in the 1960s were modelled by the Longton New Art Pottery Co. (*see* p.118). The Longton Art Pottery also produced the same models marked with its Kelsboro trade mark and the later Winsor backstamp.

In 1946 the Falcon Works was producing a wide range of animal figures, ashtrays, cigarette boxes, cruet sets, fancies, fruit sets, jugs, table lamps, wall vases or pockets, and other novelties, vases, ornamental bowls and teapots, as well as undecorated utility ware. By 1957 the firm was an associate of Shaw & Copestake at the Sylvan Works in Longton, and in 1961 they both moved to the new Sylvan works in the same town. The following year Thomas Lawrence ceased trading under its own name; in 1964 Shaw & Copestake and Thomas Lawrence were fully merged, and the Falcon trade mark was dropped.

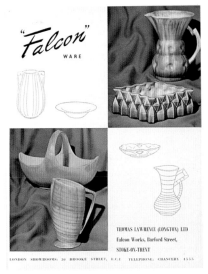

◆ Falcon Ware Fancies advertisement, 1954
Lawrence's Falcon Ware trade mark was much used in the 1950s. This 1954 *Pottery Gazette* advertisement reveals the overlap between 1930s and 1950s styles. 264

KEY FACTS

Location: Trent Bridge Pottery, Stoke c.1888–97; Falcon Works, Liverpool Street, Longton 1897–1957; Sylvan Works, Barford Street, Longton 1957–61; new Sylvan Works, Normacott Road, Longton 1961–2, Staffordshire, UK.

Important dates: Founded c.1888. Renamed Thomas Lawrence (Longton) Ltd 1938. Merged with Shaw & Copestake 1964.

MARKS

Early ware unmarked. T. Lawrence and/or Falcon Ware marks used from 1920s. Falcon Ware marks in various forms. Early example has 'LG' (Lawrence & Grundy) monogram.

LENOX

Lenox has been America's premier dinnerware maker since at least 1918, when the company began supplying china to the White House. Founded in 1889 in Trenton, New Jersey, as the Ceramic Art Company by American designer Walter Scott Lenox and Jonathan Coxon, a practical potter, the firm made hand-painted china artware and tea pieces. At the turn of the century Charles Fergus Binns, son of Royal Worcester's (*see* p.191) Richard W. Binns, developed a bone-china formula for dinnerware. By 1906 the new dinnerware line was so successful that the company changed its name and direction. Lenox's white bone china was replaced fully by its signature ivory-coloured china by 1920. Artware, or what is today called giftware, has continued to be made in fashionable as well as traditional styles, but the ivory-coloured dinnerware has long been the backbone of this company.

When Walter Lenox started the Ceramic Art Company he intended to make only artware, a finely crafted ivory china (similar in many ways to the body of Irish Belleek) that was exquisitely decorated by the leading decorators in the USA. Some of them, for example William and George Morley, Hans Nosek, Sigmund Wirkner and Lucien Boullemier, emigrated from England, Bohemia, Germany and France, while others, such as Kate Sears, were American. All specialized in a particular type of subject. The Morleys, uncle and nephew, were flower painters; Nosek painted putti and beautiful women, and Wirkner was a figure painter; but Sears's work was the most unusual. Trained in the Boston area, she was referred to in

◆ Orchid plate, 1926
William H. Morley's masterly flower, fruit, fish and game sets command high prices today. This plate is from a 1926 set of 12 decorated with orchids. The centre of each plate shows a different species. An Englishman by birth and training, Morley worked for Lenox from 1900 until his death in 1935. 265

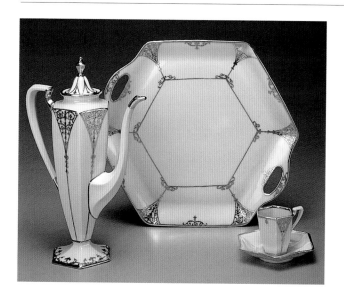

trade accounts as a 'Yankee carver' for her talent at carving greenware into elaborate figural scenes with a penknife. The earliest hand-painted artware and cabinet plates are the most expensive Lenox items in the current collectors' market. The Englishman William H. Morley is perhaps the company's most famous painter.

China blanks were also sold for decorating outside the factory. Early Ceramic Art Company and Lenox backstamps bearing a small artist's palette denote those pieces sold 'in the white'. While some of the blanks were embellished by leading independent decorators working in both New York City and Philadelphia, many others were decorated by amateurs and hobbyists. Lenox china blanks were also used by silver manufacturers for silver overlay, a process in which molecules of sterling silver were electro-deposited on the china in patterns previously applied to the ware in a substance that attracted the silver molecules. Both artware and tableware shapes decorated with silver overlay can be found today, especially vases and teasets.

◆ Silver-overlay dessert pieces, 1920
The Rockwell Silver Company, of Meriden, Connecticut, probably decorated this Lenox dessert service with a silver overlay pattern. A similar set, now in the Newark Museum, New Jersey, was given as a wedding present in 1920 by President and Mrs Woodrow Wilson. [266]

When the dinnerware line was first introduced just after 1900, each service was individually designed and decorated. The highly trained enamellers and gilders who had been brought together to decorate the artware were responsible for the exquisite borders and monograms that decorate services made to order in the early 20th century, rarely found in the antiques market-place today. As sales for this line increased, stock patterns were added to the repertoire from about 1910. These were often printed and filled patterns or decalcomania (lithographic colour printing) with enamelling added. Many of Lenox's contemporary patterns still have raised enamelling added to the pattern by hand.

◆ Cache pots and bird figure, c.1940
Lenox's ivory body could be stained several colours, including salmon-pink, yellow, sage-green and medium blue. The coloured bodies were used as contrasting elements on a variety of giftware and dinnerware during the 1930s, 1940s and early 1950s. These pieces show several ways in which the coloured clays were combined. [267]

The company's reputation for dinnerware was firmly established by the commission it received from President and Mrs Woodrow Wilson in 1917 to supply china to the White House for official use. Before this commission, china used in the White House had been made in other countries because no American firm could supply a high-quality service large

enough for elaborate state functions. After the company had fulfilled this commission, its china services were requested by heads of state around the world. The Wilson service continued to be used in the White House until President and Mrs Franklin D. Roosevelt requested a completely new service in 1934. New services were designed for President and Mrs Harry Truman in 1948 and President and Mrs Ronald Reagan in 1981. The Reagan service, with brilliant red and gold borders, is still in use. Throughout the 1920s, 1930s and 1940s Lenox china was made for America's first families.

However, about 1950 the company changed its marketing and production substantially to appeal to a broad cross-section of consumers who could not previously have purchased the ware. Bridal registries, which became common in the USA after World War II, allowed wedding guests to divide the purchase of a china set, and Lenox's clever advertising made the product irresistible.

After 1950 Lenox broadened its market, and stylish patterns such as Kingsley (1954–80) by Winslow Anderson have been judged among the company's most popular in terms of total sales.

Lenox's design during the 20th century has consistently been at the forefront of the ceramics industry. From 1906 until his death in 1954, Frank Graham Holmes was the company's chief designer. Educated at the Rhode Island School of Design, Holmes had a great facility with ornament and could design easily a broad range of patterns, from those based on historical styles to the latest Art Nouveau and Art Deco designs.

Some of Holmes's most traditional patterns, such as Autumn (1919–present) and Ming (1917–66), were made throughout most of the 20th century as generation after generation of homemakers found them appealing. By contrast, modish patterns such as Fountain (designed 1926) lasted hardly more than a decade in stock. Holmes also designed the White House services ordered by Presidents Wilson, Roosevelt and Truman.

Until 1954 all Ceramic Art Company and Lenox china was made in Trenton, New Jersey, at the workshop and factory on Prince and Mead Streets. After World War II, as production expanded, a new manufacturing site was located in Pomona, New Jersey, near Atlantic City, although the making of giftware continued in Trenton until 1964. Today two additional factories are working in North Carolina. Lenox's giftware is more collectable than the dinnerware. Art Deco figurines, streamlined vases and boudoir lamps are very popular with buyers who are decorating their homes in retro styles. Traditional shoppers prefer the delicate figurines by Patricia Eakin made in the 1940s and early 1950s, complete with frilly skirts and stylized poses. Mistress Mary, Floradora, Colonial Lady, Natchez Belle and others were meticulously assembled from slip-cast and handmade parts.

Lenox first produced a wide variety of lamps and lamp bases between 1925 and World War II. The earliest examples were in the form of shades and figural lamps lit from within to supply indirect lighting in rooms for entertaining and low light for boudoirs. However, by the mid-1930s lamp companies were

◆ **Ballerina, 1940s–early 1950s**
Patricia Eakin designed figures like this with ruffles, ribbons and bows that were moulded, rolled, folded and draped by hand. 268

◆ **Rutledge Ware advertisement, 1952**
Aggressive advertising was crucial to Lenox's success after World War II, when its biggest competitors were other US companies. 269

approaching Lenox for unique lamp-base designs. Most of these bases are stamped on the bottom of the china base with the Lenox mark, but the lamp has to be disassembled to reveal the mark. Lamp-makers who came to Lenox for bases included the leading companies of the day, such as Beaux Art Shade Company, Paul Hanson, Mutual Sunset Lamp Company, Lightolier Company and Levolite Company. More recently, Lenox itself has also made lamps.

Today's collectors of new issues are attracted in particular to Lenox's holiday ornaments and bridal accessories. Lenox Collections, which markets figurines and gifts, made in the USA and abroad, through direct sources, is a separate company, although it is part of the Lenox family. Lenox also owns Lenox Crystal, Dansk, a maker of casual china, and Gorham, a maker of sterling and stainless flatware.

▲ Kingsley plate, 1954–80
Kingsley featured stylized flowers with raised enamel centres and a solid border in a co-ordinating colour. The solid-colour rim was enclosed with platinum bands. Kingsley is among Lenox's most popular patterns. 270

KEY FACTS

Location: Trenton and Lawrenceville, New Jersey, USA.
Important dates: Founded as Ceramic Art Company 1889. Still active.
Production: Artware, fine-china dinnerware, lamps, souvenirs, giftware.
Principal designers: Walter Scott Lenox, Frank Holmes, Winslow Anderson,

MARKS

This backstamp used 1906–88. 'MADE IN U.S.A.' added below insignia from 1930. Mark green until 1953, gold until 1988; sage green and including full name 'LENOX' and wreath from 1988.

LIMOGES CHINA COMPANY

Established by Frank Sebring in 1902, the pottery was originally called Sterling China, but by 1903 its name had been changed to the Limoges China Company. Despite this name, inspired by the china-making town in France, the managers decided early on to use a semi-porcelain rather than a china body, so that the pottery could produce a larger volume for less money. Its products included calendar plates, teasets and children's dishes. In the 1930s kitchenware was added.

National Unit Distributors bought the pottery in 1943, and in 1949, under pressure from factories in Limoges, its name was formally changed to the American Limoges China Company. Operations ceased in 1955, bankruptcy was declared in 1956 and the firm dissolved in 1957.

Frank Sebring patented a moulded swirl design in 1928, which the firm called Ripple and issued in solid colours or decal decorations. Viktor Schreckengost designed for Limoges and American Limoges, creating Triumph in 1937 (with horizontal fluting); Casino about 1954 (a bridge set of triangular shape with figures from playing cards); Jiffy Ware, a refrigerator container line; and the Manhattan shape with many different decals.

KEY FACTS

Location: Sebring, Ohio, USA.
Important dates: Founded 1902. Renamed American Limoges 1949. Closed 1957.
Production: Semi-porcelain dinnerware.
Principal designers: Frank Sebring, Viktor Schreckengost.

MARKS

Incorporate 'Limoges' or, after 1949, 'American Limoges', usually in conjunction with details of shape, pattern or glaze name.

▼ Triumph plate, late 1940s
Viktor Schreckengost's Triumph line (1937) is similar to Victory, which he designed for Salem. The romantic decal and elaborate gold border have nothing in common with the modernist terraced rim. 271

LONGTON NEW ART POTTERY CO.

Founded in 1932, this firm specialized in animal figures and Toby jugs. In 1982 Shaw & Copestake's (*see* p.198) factory was bought by the United Cooperative Society and leased to Longton Ceramics. This workers' cooperative lasted 18 months until the UCS took it over and, as Crown Winsor, produced designs including those formerly modelled by the Longton New Art Pottery Co. under the trade name Kelsboro Art Ware.

LOVATT & LOVATT

This Nottinghamshire company traded as Lovatt & Lovatt from 1895, but used the Langley trade mark, making artware, domestic ware and industrial stoneware. From 1931, as Lovatt's Potteries, it concentrated on mass-produced domestic ware and giftware. After World War II it made all its products, useful and ornamental alike, from a vitreous stoneware body. Bourne's of Derby acquired the firm in 1959. Renamed the Langley Pottery in 1967, it made oven-to-table ware, dinnerware and tea and coffee ware for the domestic market and hotels and catering firms, as well as decorative vases and bowls. Production ceased in 1982.

◄ **Jug, 1961**
A hand-painted jug, typical of 1960s stonewares, designed by Glyn Colledge for the Sherwood giftware range. 272

▶ **Langley Stoneware, 1915**
This *Pottery Gazette* advertisement shows a typical selection of domestic and ornamental stoneware. 272b

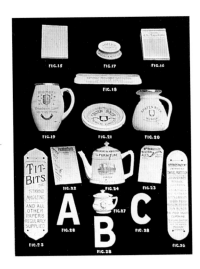

LOVATT & LOVATT LIMITED Works LANGLEY MILL, Near NOTTINGHAM.
London Showrooms: 26 & 27, HATTON GARDEN, Holborn Circus, E.C. LANGLEY STONEWARE. — LEADLESS GLAZED —
JOSEPH LOCKETT & SONS, Ltd., Agents.

JAMES MACINTYRE & CO.

In 1852 James Macintyre formed a partnership with his brother-in-law, William Sadler Kennedy, to produce, in the main, high-quality utilitarian ware. He became the sole proprietor shortly after the formation of the company, which was to become both influential and renowned for its technical innovations. These included patenting methods of turning non-circular forms on the lathe (1863) and the development of glazes such as black jet – which was later used throughout the Potteries by makers of inexpensive teapots – and decorative clay bodies, such as agates, malachites and imitation ivory. New glazes were also developed. By the end of the 19th century Macintyre production included pub and advertising ware, door furniture, ceramic letters, chemical ware and artist's palettes, along with more conventional ranges.

In 1893 production was expanded by developing ornamental artware, and the following year Harry Barnard was appointed director of a new art-pottery department. His main responsibility was to develop Macintyre's slipdecorating techniques, which included producing a form of *pâte-sur-pâte* in which hand-painted layers of slip were built up to create a relief decoration. This new product was called Gesso Faience. Despite some early promise, the art pottery was not a commercial success, and by the end of 1896 its future was uncertain. It was further threatened in March 1897 when Macintyre appointed the young William Moorcroft. Within months Moorcroft introduced Aurelian Ware, a new shape and decoration

▼ **Catalogue, 1890s**
James Macintyre was a major producer of domestic ware, commemoratives, novelties and advertising wares, as shown here. 273

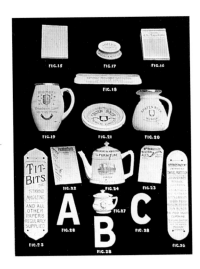

for Macintyre's printed and enamelled ware. The highly conventionalized floral motifs, frets and diapers reflected the decorative influence of William Morris. Three of these designs were registered in February 1898.

After Barnard left the firm in September 1897, Macintyre invited Moorcroft to develop a range using the technique of slip trailing and underglaze colour which Moorcroft had already begun to explore. The result was the successful Florian Ware, for which designs were first registered in 1898. Moorcroft also designed Dura tableware for the firm.

Until he left in 1913 to start his own pottery, Moorcroft's decorative slip-trailed goods were the backbone of Macintyre's reputation. Widely exhibited internationally, they were sold by major retailers in many parts of the world.

KEY FACTS

Location: Washington Works, Burslem, Staffordshire, UK.
Important dates: Founded 1852. Designer William Moorcroft left and firm concentrated on making electrical porcelain from 1913.
Production: Earthenware, china.

MARKS

This mark designed by Harry Barnard. Impressed or printed marks usually include Macintyre name and pattern range.

◀ **Catalogue, 1890s**
Macintyre made a large variety of domestic wares, often featuring novelty shapes, such as these bird's egg condiments. 274

NELSON McCOY POTTERY COMPANY

Organized as the Nelson McCoy Sanitary & Stoneware Company in 1910, the pottery was started by Nelson McCoy with financial backing from his father, James McCoy (who ran an art pottery in Roseville from 1899 to 1911). In 1933 the name was simplified to the Nelson McCoy Pottery Company. During the pottery's early years Walter Bauer designed most of the kitchenware. Englishman Sidney Cope was hired in 1934 to develop glazes and also created new shapes and lines. He ultimately replaced Bauer and continued as chief designer until his death in 1961.

Between 1961 and 1966 Cope's son Leslie was designer, and afterwards Billie McCoy was in charge of the design department. The pottery made only stoneware kitchen items until 1926, when it introduced a line of industrial artware. This included garden crockery, jardinières with stands, dog dishes, pitchers and decorated canisters.

Cookie jars were introduced about 1940 and were the firm's main product until it closed in 1990. These are what collectors of McCoy look for today, attracted by their originality, charm and

▲ **Loy-Nel-Art vase, 1910–15**
Originally developed by Nelson McCoy's father, James, the line was named for his sons Lloyd, Nelson and Arthur. Nelson also made the underglaze slip-decorated ware at his pottery. 275

◀ **Art Deco vase, 1930s**
Although made quickly, McCoy's moulded ware was very stylish and well suited to use by florists for flower arrangements. 276

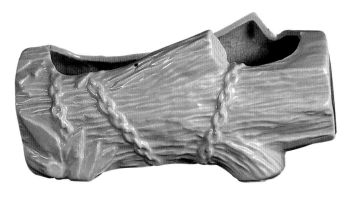

whimsy. Numerous price guides and collectors' books add to the jars' value by making them easy to identify and price. Among the most desirable of the firm's cookie jars in terms of market value are Baseball Boy, Teddy Bear, Dog House, Snoopy, Jack O' Lantern, Mammy (hands on stomach), Cookies and Mother Goose. However, there are hundreds of designs and colour variations to collect. Their manufacture over such a long period represents a virtual history of popular motif in the American market. The earliest examples are typical of pre-war kitchenware – basically geometric shapes with floral decoration – but interesting characters, including pigs, mammies, clowns and birds, are already evident. Fruits were popular in the late 1940s and 1950s. Early American, rustic, cowboy and Wild West themes appear in the 1960s, and a homage to the Apollo moon mission was issued in 1970. Note that fake Mammy cookie jars bearing McCoy marks are in circulation.

After a disastrous fire in 1950 McCoy built a new facility with all the latest equipment, and by the end of the decade the firm was the largest producer of pottery in the USA. A small variety of wares besides cookie jars was introduced after 1940. In 1954 a Cook and Serve Line was designed for outdoor and casual service. It eventually included pitchers, large bowls (for salad or spaghetti), individual salad bowls, covered casseroles, mugs and beanpots, teapots and a coffee server. In 1963 soup-and-sandwich sets were first offered in glossy green or brown. The firm's primary dinnerware line was Brown Drip, which included a few kitchenware items. El Rancho was a line of serving pieces that included coffee and iced-tea servers, food warmer, coffee mug and soup tureen. The iced-tea server is a barrel with a spigot, and the food warmer is in the shape of a covered wagon. McCoy made teasets, too; Pine Cone (1945), Ivy (1949), Daisy (1953) and Moderne (1954) are very collectable.

The company also produced a large line of imaginative figural and decorated flower pots, jardinières, planters, wall pockets, lamp bases and vases. These included Stretch Animals, Alligator, Banana Boat, Bathtub, various Ducks, Cowboy Boots, Frog with Lotus or Umbrella, Humpty Dumpty, Hillbilly, Pelican, Piano, Pig, Rhinoceros, Rodeo Cowboy, Stork, Uncle Sam and Scotties.

◄ Lamp, 1950s
McCoy's cowboy boots served as the basis not only for this lamp but also for a vase and a planter. This piece still retains its original shade. 278

◀ Chilly Willy cookie jar, 1950s
This character was issued in three variations: with a blue, red or yellow scarf; his hat forms the lid to the jar. Other figures produced included Hocus the Rabbit, Mr and Mrs Owl, Gray Rooster, Timmy Tortoise, Goodie Goose and many others. 279

Collectors should be careful not to confuse the Nelson McCoy Pottery with the J. W. McCoy Pottery (also known as the Brush-McCoy Pottery), which was owned and operated by Nelson McCoy's father James. Nelson McCoy ran the Nelson McCoy Pottery Company until 1954, when his son, Nelson McCoy Jr, took over its management. In 1967 Nelson McCoy Jr sold the pottery to the Mt Clemens Pottery (see p.140). The Lancaster Colony Corporation bought the company in 1974 and sold it to Designer Accents in 1985. Throughout these changes of ownership the Nelson McCoy Pottery's ware continued to carry the McCoy name until the factory closed in 1990.

KEY FACTS

Location: Roseville, Ohio, USA.
Important dates: Founded 1910. Closed 1990.
Production: Novelty cookie jars, dinnerware, figural florists' ware and vases.
Principal designers: Walter Bauer, Sidney Cope, Leslie Cope, Billie McCoy.

MARKS

Most marks moulded into bottom of ware. Alternatively, paper labels used. Some early ware shows 'NM' monogram.

⬥ **Teapot, 1970s**
Brown Drip dinnerware was made over a long period and included a wide variety of tableware, teaware and kitchenware. 280

JOHN MADDOCK & SONS

During the interwar years the pottery produced gently fashionable tableware shapes and patterns, notably the Earl and Venice shapes with teacup handles of open triangular and diamond form respectively. Launched in 1932, these were treated with simple, modern floral patterns. More adventurous was the Art Deco-style Sunset Ware, introduced about 1930. From the 1930s to the 1950s the company made children's ranges decorated in various styles, freehand-painted, transfer printed and enamelled as well as decal-decorated patterns such as Circus nursery ware, launched in the early 1930s.

In 1946 Maddock produced for Cunard's *Queen Elizabeth* a 30,000-piece earthenware table service in deep ivory colour, simply decorated with golden-brown, grey and black lines. The company also made the popular Thatched Cottage teaware, but it increasingly concentrated on producing tableware for hotels, restaurants, hospitals, canteens and the catering trade.

➡ **Sunset Ware jug, c.1930**
Introduced c.1930 as part of Maddock's Royal Ivory range, this Sunset Ware jug is decorated in a bold, freehand-painted Art Deco style, which makes it of interest to collectors today. 281

KEY FACTS

Location: Newcastle Street and Dale Hall, Burslem, Staffordshire, UK.
Important dates: Founded 1855. Closed c.1982.
Production: Earthenware and ironstone.
Trade names: Ivory, Royal Ivory.

MARKS

This mark introduced c.1945. Printed marks usually include crown and company's full name.

C. T. MALING & SONS

Christopher T. Maling succeeded his father at the Ouseburn Bridge Pottery, Newcastle upon Tyne, in 1853. Four years later, on a nearby site, he built the Ford A Pottery, where he produced large quantities – reputedly 800,000 articles a year – of pots, jars and bottles for the meat and dairy, ink and preserved-food trades. The Ford A Pottery dwarfed its predecessor and was said to produce more in a week than the old pottery had produced in a year. This increase is partly explained by the fact that some of the processes at the new factory had been adapted to steam machinery. Among such products were jars for marmalade for Keillers of Dundee, a connection which was to provide a solid source of income for Maling until the 1930s.

In 1878 Maling built the huge Ford B Pottery on a 14-acre (5.5-hectare) site in Walker, also in Newcastle upon Tyne. All the processes, from grinding and preparing the raw flints onwards, were done under one roof at this new factory. Ford B was the catalyst for moving into new areas of production, and by the time it was completed the company was already moving on to bottle production on an even bigger scale. However, soon production of jars outstripped demand, and the firm began to include such lines as sanitary ware, photographic and chemical apparatus, water filters, electrical ware, kitchen and dairy equipment as well as the full range of tableware and toilet ware with fashionable decoration which was made at both factories.

Maling took his sons into partnership in 1889, and when he retired ten years later he left what was claimed to be one of the largest earthenware factories in the world. John Ford Maling became manager of Ford A and his two brothers managed Ford B. The pottery traded as C. T. Maling and Sons, retaining this name until it closed in 1963.

During the 1890s the production of decorated tableware was further expanded with the introduction of many new shapes and ranges and the establishment of a new department to produce decals. Expansion continued after the death of C. T. Maling in 1901, and among other significant new lines in the first decade of the 20th century was Cetem Ware, launched in 1908. Aimed at the new middle-class markets, this was a new range of dinner, tea, breakfast and toilet services in the pottery's white, china-like semi-porcelain body, which it claimed to be superior, brilliant and durable. Decoration was largely the work of Harry Clifford Toft,

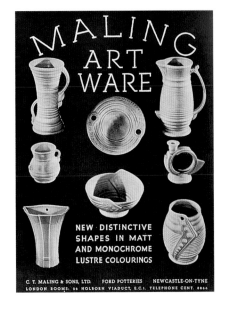

◆ **Maling Art Ware advertisement, 1937**
In this advertisement in *The Pottery Gazette*, Maling attempted to bring itself up to date with Art Deco shapes and matt and monochrome glazes. Commercial necessity encouraged diversity. 282

◆ **Windmill plate, c.1935**
Maling produced a series of large wall plates, distinguished by their bright colours and raised tube-lined outlines. The themes were extremely varied and included oriental designs as well as this image of a windmill and flowers. 283

Advertisement, 1934
Published in *The Pottery Gazette*, this advertisement shows Maling's lustre ware at the height of its success. Even in the most austere Art Deco years there was a great demand for this kind of decorative and escapist pottery. 284

Maling's new designer and pottery painter, who came originally from Staffordshire and was a nephew of the well-known Charles and Joseph Toft. As the production of Cetem Ware expanded, so did the pottery's decorating department, which now included paintresses, blowers – whose job it was to apply background colours to the ware with pressurized-air guns – and stencillers.

By 1921 the company was producing various striking new effects in ornamental ware, which included floating bowls, vases, footed bowls, lamp pillars and toilet ware. One of the newest effects was a powder-blue ground with fruit panels and a best gold finish. Black-ground ware with supplementary decorations was also popular, as were designs with contrasting colours such as purple, yellow, green and blue – all of these were deep tones. The firm also introduced its new Chinese Japonica in the early 1920s and new lines in toilet ware 'suitable for display *in situ* with Chinese lacquer furniture'. One of these innovations, a Chinese pagoda decoration, was carried out in bright colours on a black ground. Another was a stork pattern in best bronze gold, in conjunction with a wealth of rich enamelling.

Toft died in 1922 and was replaced as head designer by C. N. Wright, who had previously worked for Wedgwood (*see* p.230) and Doulton (*see* p.187). Wright was joined in 1926 by Lucien Boullemier, the son of the Minton (*see* p. 132) painter Antonin Boullemier, and a new chapter in the history of the firm began with the introduction of a new class of decorated ware and fancies marked with the Maling Ware castle.

The firm continued its modernization programme and introduced a small number of new lines for the Jazz Age, including patterns with its zig-zag Tango border design and, from 1931 and 1932 respectively, the more dramatic Anzac geometric pattern teaset and the Tulip stylized floral pattern. Other designs from this period are the Anemone pattern, the Doric fruit set and the Ritz-shape vase. The company also continued to make its unique range of fancies in addition to a comprehensive range of general domestic and hotel earthenware, sundries such as cigarette boxes, and various items of giftware, including specialist ornamental ware with lustre and pastel decoration.

Floral dish, c.1928
The contrast between the pink and yellow flowers and the deep-blue mottled ground is typical of Maling's decorative ware of the 1920s and 1930s. 285

Ginger jar and cover, c.1930
This popular floral design was widely used by Maling on a range of shapes, including the ginger jar. The jar was made in four sizes and was also produced as a lamp base. 286

However, like many other companies, Maling felt the effects of the general trade depression and the General Strike of 1926, during which the Ford A factory was forced to close. The situation was exacerbated by the outbreak of World War II in 1939 and the difficulty of resuming normal production after the war. The diversity that had once been one of the firm's major assets was now a handicap, and the need to rationalize became evident. The business was sold to Hoult's Estates in 1947 (C. T. Maling, the fourth Christopher Thompson Maling, entered the glass industry), and under Frederick Hoult it briefly enjoyed renewed development. Patterns such as Peony Rose were advertised in 1954 and the Two Tone range of lustre vases in 1961, but two years later the company ceased production.

KEY FACTS

Location: Ford A and B Potteries, Newcastle upon Tyne, Tyne and Wear, UK.
Important dates: Founded 1857. Closed 1963.
Production: Earthenware.
Trade name: Cetem Ware.

MARKS

Printed castle marks used as standard since 1890. Early examples include company initials. Cetem Ware mark first used c.1908. Variations of this mark incorporating company's name and 'Newcastle on Tyne' used from c.1949.

◆ **Cobblestone kitchenware, 1930s**
This popular overall-printed range was made in a variety of colourways. 287

MASON, CASH & CO.

This traditional manufacturer of a wide range of functional bowls and other yellow ware has remained in the same location in Derbyshire since its foundation, using only the natural clays which lie close to the surface under and around the site. In the 20th century the pottery's production included cooking ware, bulb bowls and grave or cemetery vases. The best-known products are the mixing bowls, natural cane outside and white on the inside, which have been made in at least nine sizes and in other colourways. The firm's utilitarian emphasis allowed it to continue working during World War II, when others suspended the production of ornamental ware. The catalogue includes pie dishes, casseroles, pets' feeding bowls, hot-water bottles, mortars and pestles, fancies and flower jugs. Among more recent additions are utensil jars with hand-turned banded slipware, hide rocks for reptiles and hanging bird feeders and bird tables.

KEY FACTS

Location: Pool Potteries, Church Gresley, Derbyshire, UK.
Important dates: Founded late 18th century. Merged with T.G. Green 2002, now run by Tabletop Company.
Production: Earthenware, yellow ware, vitrified stoneware.

MARKS

Early marks scratched into clay; later, impressed marks made in the mould. 'Mason Cash' logo mark introduced for coloured and hand-banded ranges 1970s.

Mason Cash

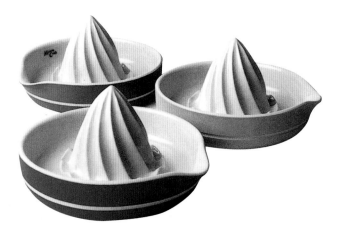

◆ **Citrus juicers, 1990s**
With its modern look combined with traditional techniques and styling, the juicer continues Mason Cash's long-established link with the kitchen. 288

MAYER CHINA COMPANY

The company was in business for more than a century, first as a maker of domestic table china and later as one of the USA's foremost manufacturers of china for hotels, restaurants and institutions. In 1881 the brothers Joseph and Earnest Mayer, who had emigrated from England, established Mayer Potteries Company in a small pottery that had been operated by the Economite Society in Beaver Falls, Pennsylvania, on the Ohio River north-west of Pittsburgh. Joseph and another brother, Arthur, had briefly been china importers in New York City, and from this experience Joseph could see the value of making dishes for the burgeoning western market. Beaver Falls' access to this market at the head of the Ohio River attracted the Mayer brothers to the location. Soon after the company opened, its name was changed to the Mayer China Company. It made white ironstone and was well known for its version of Lustre Band and Sprig, the pattern today called Tea Leaf.

In 1902 or 1903 the pottery, with about 150 employees, began making white granite and semi-porcelain dinner sets, toilet sets and odd sets. It brought in ball clay from Tennessee; feldspar from Canada, Connecticut and New York State; kaolin from England and Florida; and flint from Illinois. About 1915 the firm focused on hotel ware and gradually discontinued the production of china for home use. Mayer prospered for most of the 20th century with these sturdy goods as its product. Famous hotels, transportation companies and institutions were its clients, and collectors in all these areas can find examples with the pottery's backstamp. However, in recent years increased Asian competition in these products has seriously damaged the American china industry, which had dominated the hotel ware trade for most of the 20th century.

The Shenango China Company (*see* p.203) bought Mayer in 1964, but had little time or inclination to change its production. In 1968 both firms were taken over by Interpace. In 1984 Mayer was acquired by Syracuse China (*see* Onondaga Pottery Company, p.145), which provided technical assistance, made biscuit ware and invested in a specialized decorating operation. At first Mayer prospered, but increasing pressure for efficiency from Asian competitors, as well as Syracuse's other activities, had an enormous impact on Mayer's long-term success. In 1989 Susquehanna-Pfaltzgraff bought Syracuse China, including Mayer and Shenango, and the Mayer facility was closed.

▲ **Hotel plate, 1940s**
The Indian Tree pattern was made as a stock pattern for distribution to many customers. 289

▲ **Hotel plate, 1950s**
The Bayberry plate was made exclusively for the Chalfonte-Haddon Hall in Atlantic City, New Jersey. 290

◀ **Hotel plate, 1970s**
Made for the Hotel DuPont in Wilmington, Delaware, this plate was produced during Interpace's ownership of Mayer China. 291

KEY FACTS

Location: Beaver Falls, Pennsylvania, USA.
Important dates: Founded 1881. Closed 1989. After closure, some Mayer shapes and patterns continued to be made by other manufacturers, including Shenango and Libbey, but name later discontinued.
Production: Semi-porcelain dinnerware, toilet ware and hotel ware.

MARKS

Company name often used in conjunction with name of pattern and retailer.

ALFRED MEAKIN

The brother of James and George Meakin (*see* J. & G. Meakin below), Alfred Meakin ran a successful business making ordinary domestic ware and traditional tableware for the mass home market, and built up a healthy export market. The firm also made children's ware, such as Peter Pan, launched in 1932. A new Victoria & Highgate Works was built in 1957, from which time many new tableware shapes and patterns, both traditional and modern in style, were launched. Of special interest is the Princess range, a strikingly contemporary shape introduced in 1963. Decorations include underglaze and on-glaze decals, underglaze prints with hand enamelling, coloured glaze and coloured slip accessories.

KEY FACTS
Location: Royal Albert and Victoria & Highgate Works, Tunstall, Staffordshire, UK.
Important dates: Founded 1874. Merged with Myott, Son & Co. 1976. Bought by Churchill Group 1991.

MARKS
Usually 'Alfred Meakin Ltd.'

BLEU DE ROI
ALFRED MEAKIN
ENGLAND

◆ **Plate, 1930s**
This simple design, with its restrained florals, reveals the impact of Art Deco styling on Staffordshire potteries. 292

J. & G. MEAKIN

The pottery was founded by James Meakin. He was succeeded by two sons, James and George, in 1851, and the business remained under the control of the family, which enlarged the Eagle Pottery after selling the Eastwood Works in 1958. The firm became part of the Wedgwood Group (*see* p.230) in 1970, by which time it was mass-producing a prolific range of plain and fashionably decorated tableware and associated products.

Between the wars J. & G. Meakin brought out a number of Art Deco-influenced lines under the Sol Ware trade name. Among these was the late-1920s Moderne shape of elongated and streamlined form. In 1953 came the new Studio Ware shape with coupe plates, inspired by Russel Wright's late-1930s American Modern shapes. The new shape became a vehicle for a vast range of contemporary patterns, including Habitat,

← **Coronation mug, 1937**
Meakin was a major producer of commemorative ware. Typical is this coronation mug for George VI, which takes a familiar 1930s shape and uses stock decals. 293

◆ **Holiday Ware advertisement, 1954**
This *Pottery Gazette* advertisement illustrates Meakin's Holiday range of monochrome glazed ware with US-inspired, rounded Studio shapes. This shape appeared in many contemporary patterns. 294

Holiday and Peony. The Horizon shape was introduced in 1955, and the new Studio shape in the early 1960s. Shapes and patterns from this period were created by the firm's staff artists under the direction of Frank Trigger, with the assistance of its designer-consultant Tom Arnold, and include the Ascot pattern and the Crofter patterns Rockfern, Summertime, Flamenco and Boscobel. During the 1970s and 1980s J. & G. Meakin became well known for up-to-date fashionable ranges introduced under the Bull in a China Shop and Creative Tableware labels.

KEY FACTS

Location: Eagle Pottery and Eastwood Works, Hanley, Staffordshire, UK.
Important dates: Founded 1851. Part of Wedgwood Group from 1970. Renamed Creative Tableware 1980 and Johnson Bros 1991.
Production: Earthenware.
Trade names: Sol Ware, Bull in a China Shop.

MARKS

Crown mark c.1939. Sol trade mark registered 1912. Other stylized marks, 1930s–1950s.

◆ **Coffee ware, c.1968**
Tall shapes and semi-abstract patterns in rich colours place these pieces firmly in the late 1960s. 295

MEDALTA POTTERIES

Medalta specialized in the least expensive ware, such as stoneware crocks, pigeon nests, dog bowls, cream jugs, teapots and lamp bases, in addition to hotel ware and florists' crockery. In 1918 the plant was bought by Charles Pratt, W. A. Creer and Ulysses S. Grant, and by the 1920s it was enjoying international acclaim. Business continued to be good in the 1920s and into the 1930s. With the arrival of Englishman Tom Hulme a decorating department was added in 1927; this produced decorations with atomizers and applied decals. Ed Philipson, a ceramic engineer, joined the company in 1937 and developed a line of fireproof ovenware lined with white clay. Early in 1939 the pottery began making hotel ware with ball clay from beds it had owned for years but never used.

The company prospered during World War II, and hotel ware production expanded greatly after the war. Philipson's ingenuity in making dinnerware with a yellow edge and hard glaze for the Canadian National Railroad led to further accounts, including the Canadian Pacific Railroad and most of Alberta's restaurants and hospitals. However, a change of ownership and the ill-conceived idea of supplying earthenware free of charge to cinemas bankrupted the pottery in 1955.

KEY FACTS

Location: Medicine Hat, Alberta, Canada.
Important dates: Founded 1916. Closed 1955.
Production: Kitchenware, hotel ware, teapots, flower pots, lamp bases.

MARKS

One of many marks used. Many pieces unmarked.

◆ **Pitcher, c.1930**
Despite the fact that Medalta Potteries specialized in making the ordinary, serviceable pottery of everyday life, its ware was colourful and decorative. Medalta teapots were used throughout Canada. 296

DAVID METHVEN & SONS

David Methven founded a pottery in Kirkcaldy, Fife, before 1830. He died in 1827 and after it was taken over by two of his sons, George and John, in the 1830s, the factory was enlarged to make brown earthenware. John's nephew David Methven, formerly a maker of coarse earthenware at Kirkcaldy, later took over the pottery and founded David Methven & Sons, which continued to make every kind of earthenware.

The pottery's 1916 catalogue included ware in 'C.C.' (cream colour), sponged, printed, enamelled and gilded, for all home, colonial and other markets. In the early 1920s Methven pottery was used as a vehicle for work by decorators who bought blanks from the firm. Notable was Jessie M. King, who also experimented with underglaze colours in collaboration with the pottery. The fruits of this work were shown in *The Studio* in 1922. These highly collectable designs were derived from fairy tales such as *The Blue Bird* and *Sleeping Beauty*.

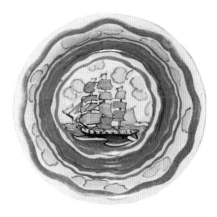

♠ **Galleon plate, late 1920s**
Painted by Jessie M. King with on-glaze enamels, this is one of her later pieces; her earlier work used underglaze painting. Methven supplied Jessie M. King with pottery blanks, some made to her own design. 297

♦ **Old Heather eggcup, c.1928**
The combination of traditional Scottish sponged decoration with hand-painting in three colours is typical of Methven's domestic ware. 298

KEY FACTS

Location: Kirkcaldy, Fife, UK.
Important dates: Founded before 1850. Closed c.1930.
Production: Earthenware.

MARKS

'D. M. & Sons', 'D. M. & SS' or 'David Methven', usually painted.

METLOX POTTERIES

Founded in 1927 to produce ceramic signs, the pottery began to make dinnerware in 1934 when it launched California Pottery, a casual, brightly coloured ware. Also in that year it introduced Poppytrail tableware and kitchenware. Mission Bell, a pastel-coloured line of tableware and kitchenware for Sears, Roebuck and Company, was made from 1935 to 1938. Metlox also produced in this period a line called Yorkshire, based on English Staffordshire ware. From 1934 Carl Romanelli created lines of small animal figurines and other novelties, as well as Modern Masterpieces, a line including figures, figural vases, busts, wall pockets, book-ends and vases with relief figures. After World War II the pottery introduced decorated lines. In 1958 it bought the Vernon Kilns name and moulds and made Vernonware in a separate division. From 1959 until it closed in 1989, Metlox designed and made an extensive line of cookie jars.

KEY FACTS

Location: Manhattan Beach, California, USA.
Important dates: Founded 1927. Closed 1989.
Production: Table and kitchenware, figurines, vases and novelties.
Principal designers: Carl Romanelli, Frank Irwin, Bob Allen and Mel Shaw, Harrison McIntosh, Helen Slater.

MARKS

'Poppytrail' used after 1934, with or without 'Metlox'.

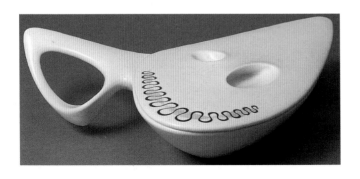

♦ **Aztec covered vegetable dish, 1950s**
'Bold' and 'primitive' were the words used to describe the Aztec decoration on Frank Irwin's exotic Free Form line for Metlox. Many forms in the line are extreme, including a boomerang-shaped relish dish and attenuated beverage servers. 299

W. R. MIDWINTER

William Robinson Midwinter, after working at Royal Doulton (*see* p.187) for 14 years, branched out on his own in 1910, making mainly Rockingham teapots. By 1914, despite the outbreak of World War I, he was able to move into larger premises; he acquired the adjoining pottery. This had been making sanitary ware in a small way, and he changed production to making mostly teaware and toilet ware. On his return to Burslem in 1918 after serving in the Royal Navy, Midwinter again increased production and bought another adjoining factory. After merging the three factories he responded to a rapid decrease in demand for toilet ware between the wars by expanding the production of teaware and dinnerware. In 1921 he marketed a series of fancies and ornamental, both in earthenware, with the firm's new stencilled decorations, a line of dinnerware, decorated for the most part with decal borders, some all-over silver lustred teapots with solid black handles (another new line) and 21-piece teasets with mazarine-blue band and neat decal-decorated borders. Stock lines during this period included gold-lined and coloured banded teaware. Also made were toilet sets, such as one decorated with a shaded ground in grey-and-helio, in combination with a large red-rose design with green leafage and edges and handles in black.

By 1928 the firm was well known for its popularly priced semi-porcelain dinnerware, teaware and suite ware in a variety of decorative styles. These ranged from traditional Blue Willow to mazarine-blue and gilt ware and the lighter-coloured patterns such as bright lithograph borders on a broad band of ivory and handcraft patterns. Advertisements for this period highlighted a range of Nursery Rhymes ware designed by W. Heath Robinson. The designs were reproduced lithographically and can be identified by the distinctive band of comic faces inside the hollowware and round the rim of plates. Among other nursery patterns is the delightful Peggy Gibbons Nursery Ware, which was advertised in trade papers from 1946 and remained in production until at least the early 1960s.

In 1953 a small experimental studio in Hanley developed into the Clayburn Pottery under the direction of William Lunt, a Midwinter director, in partnership with Harry Edgerton. The original idea was to create individual pieces, mainly vases and lamp bases, from true porcelain, their

◆ Grosvenor pattern advertisement, 1937
This advertisement in *The Pottery Gazette* shows Midwinter, at that time a very conventional company, coming to terms with Art Deco modernism. 300

Peggy Gibbons Nursery Ware

◆ Peggy Gibbons Nursery Ware advertisement, 1960
Midwinter's most successful nursery ware range featured Peggy Gibbons's drawings. Although rather dated, this was still selling in the Stylecraft era, as this advertisement from 1960 suggests. 301

◆ Jessie Tait flask, beakers and candlesticks, early 1950s
In the early 1950s Jessie Tait designed a limited range of tableware and ornaments in distinctly contemporary shapes and styles. The candlesticks feature the music-score pattern of the same period. 302

shapes and decorations both being inspired by ancient Chinese production. Early pieces were high-fired, but the firm soon reverted to producing a semi-porcelain body, using an easy-firing biscuit temperature. About this time W. R. Midwinter grew interested in the experiments and became the third partner, taking special responsibility for sales. Clayburn's ware was produced in a wide variety of shapes and decorations, although lamp bases were the main product.

⬥ Caribbean pattern, mid-1950s
Jessie Tait's colourful Caribbean pattern of the mid-1950s is seen here on the rounded Fashion shape. 303

Already a significant pottery before World War II, Midwinter was, by the 1950s, one of the leading dozen domestic earthenware manufacturers in Staffordshire, but was still essentially a family business. During this period the export market, largely Canada, was looking for ware in the new Contemporary style, and US potters were increasingly taking the initiative while British manufacturers hesitated. Roy Midwinter, son of the founder, began his own intensive market research, and followed this with a trip to Canada. On his return he set about designing industrial ceramics to match contemporary trends in interior design, furniture and architecture. Under his influence the firm became one of the most prolific and outstanding producers of stylish tableware of the 1950s and 1960s. An early example of Roy Midwinter's commitment to modern industrial design was technically advanced Stylecraft Coupe tableware range, launched around 1952 and backed by an extensive advertising campaign. Homeweave, like other patterns from a range of about three dozen, most of which were abstract or stylized in varying degrees, was hand-painted in underglaze acid-proof colours and available in over 50 different pieces which could be bought separately.

More extreme in style was Stylecraft Fashion tableware, designed by Roy Midwinter and William Lunt and introduced in 1955. For this remodelled range, consisting of over 50 pieces, the rim completely disappeared and the extremities, such as handles, spouts, lips and knobs, assumed graceful, free-flowing, curved shapes that harmonize with the main bodies of the ware. Pieces were also designed for more than one specific use – the oatmeal, for example, could serve for fruit, soup or cereal. The first six patterns in this series were Festival, Falling Leaves, Nature Study, Capri,

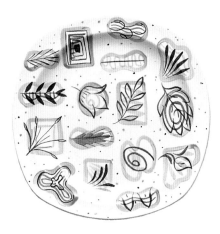

⬥ Primavera plate, c.1954
This Stylecraft plate dating from around 1954 carries Jessie Tait's famous Primavera pattern, which was inspired by contemporary fabrics. 304

⬥ Hugh Casson ware, late 1950s
Lively sketches of the South of France were used for the two Hugh Casson patterns Riviera and Cannes. The design is seen here on the Fashion shape. 305

Zambesi dish, c.1956
A covered vegetable dish in the flared Fashion shape is a good vehicle for Jessie Tait's dramatic Zambesi pattern. 306

Terence Conran dish, 1956
A Fashion-shape vegetable dish carries Terence Conran's popular Plantlife design. 307

Pierrot and Magnolia. These were variously abstract, naturalistic or symbolic in character and applied by transfer printing and enamelling, hand-painting and decals, some underglaze and others on-glaze. Among the abstract patterns in both ranges were some by Jessie Tait, the firm's own prolific designer. In addition, Midwinter commissioned well-known freelance designers such as Hugh Casson and Terence Conran.

The 1960s were no less innovative, and 1962 saw the launch of the new Fine-shape tableware range, designed by David Queensberry in collaboration with Roy Midwinter. This shape's straight sides allowed a larger area for pattern, making it a perfect vehicle for decoration. Patterns include Sienna, Whitehill, Evesham, Kingcup, Meadow, and Queensberry, the first of the stripe patterns that swamped the market in the 1960s.

After purchasing A. J. Wilkinson's (*see* p.239) Newport Works, formerly associated with Clarice Cliff (*see* p.43), in 1964, Midwinter seemed better able to compete with larger manufacturers. However, after the move and the failure of some of the new shapes, financial difficulties led to the company's takeover in 1968 by J. & G. Meakin (*see* p.126), which itself was taken over two years later by Wedgwood (*see* p.230). Around this time Eve Midwinter, Roy Midwinter's wife, became one of the innovative forces behind many of the new ranges. She was involved with the new Creative glaze patterns for Stonehenge, Midwinter's matt-finished range of 1972, for which she also produced the Sun, Moon and Earth patterns. Among her many other patterns were those for the Stoneware shape designed by Robin Welsh, namely Natural, Hopsack, Denim and Blueprint, introduced in 1979, and Petal and Province, which were added to the range soon afterwards. Eve Midwinter was the firm's last principal designer. The factory closed in April 1987, although some patterns were made at another group factory and bore the Midwinter name after this date.

Queensberry coffee ware, 1960s
With his Fine shape, David Queensberry brought Midwinter firmly into the 1960s. He also designed the first of the vertical stripes patterns that were to swamp the market. 308

KEY FACTS

Location: Albion Works, Navigation Road and Hadderidge Potteries, Burslem, Staffordshire, UK.
Important dates: Founded 1910. Took over A. J. Wilkinson's Newport Works 1964. Merged with J. & G. Meakin 1968. Taken over by Wedgwood Group 1970. Newport Works closed 1987.
Production: Earthenware.
Principal designers: Roy Midwinter, Terence Conran, Hugh Casson, Jessie Tait, David Queensberry.

MARKS

Variations of this printed mark used from 1959 with figures to indicate year and month of manufacture. Marks usually incorporate Midwinter name; some used after 1945 include crown.

Midwinter
Stylecraft
STAFFORDSHIRE ENGLAND
FASHION SHAPE

The pottery was established in 1793 by Thomas Minton, in partnership with the ceramicist Joseph Poulson and backed by the Liverpool businessman William Pownall. It made mainly transfer-printed tableware in earthenware, trading first as Minton & Poulson; later the name of Pownall was added. Bone china was made between about 1798 and 1816 and reintroduced in about 1822. From this period production increased and was further expanded in about 1826 with the introduction of figures and ornamental ware. The firm continued to grow in size and stature under Herbert Minton, who succeeded his father in 1836. In 1849 the distinguished potter Léon Arnoux became art director, and encouraged other French artists, painters and modellers to come to Stoke. He developed new coloured glazes which he called majolica. Introduced at the Great Exhibition of 1851, these were important in establishing Minton's reputation in the 19th century, although the firm's stability rested largely on its tableware.

Colin Minton Campbell, who became head of the firm in 1858, attracted many influential designers to work for the company as well as commissioning work from outside designers such as Christopher Dresser. Under Campbell's guidance important innovations in production introduced in the previous decade were expanded, and new decorative techniques, including acid gilding and *pâte-sur-pâte*, were developed. After his death, in 1885, the business remained under family control and consolidated its position as the 19th century's leading pottery manufacturer. Production was still diversified in the early years of the 20th century, and included artware such as Sèvres-type ornamental ware and services, majolica, glazed ware, earthenware, parian, cream-coloured ware, decorative tiles and *pâte-sur-pâte* pieces. The latter were created by, among others, Louis Solon, until his retirement in 1904.

Louis Solon's son, Léon, became the company's art director at the beginning of the 20th century, and John W. Wadsworth was appointed his assistant. Together they developed the Secessionist Ware range of ornamental tableware which was introduced in 1902. These slip-trailed and

◆ **Advertisement, 1934**
By the 1930s Minton had become a rather conventional and unadventurous company trying to keep in touch with popular taste. This stylish advertisement reveals the pottery's approach to Art Deco modernism. 309

◆ **Secessionist Ware vases, c.1904**
These vibrantly coloured slip-trailed Secessionist vases, designed by Léon Solon and John Wadsworth, were inspired by continental Art Nouveau styles. This short-lived but now highly collectable range represented the last attempt by the Minton factory to maintain the trendsetting position that it had enjoyed throughout the 19th century. 310

Service plate, c.1911
Minton maintained its reputation for high-quality tableware well into the 20th century. This plate has *pâte-sur-pâte* decoration by Birks and raised gilding of astonishing richness. 311

Delft plate, 1920s
Always a major manufacturer of tableware, Minton produced its share of blue-and-white ware. The Delft pattern was first produced in the 1870s, but its lasting popularity kept it alive at least until the 1930s. 312

Daisy tableware, early 1930s
This simple design, with a stylized floral motif in a restrained Art Deco style, was created by Reginald Haggar, Minton's art director from 1929 to 1934. 313

moulded ornamental pieces, which bear a special backstamp, were freely decorated with flowing coloured glazes and loosely based on Viennese Art Nouveau styles. Secessionist Ware has become very collectable.

By 1915 both Wadsworth and Solon had left the firm, which was slow to adopt the more extreme Art Deco styles. However, Art Deco ware appeared between the wars, particularly in the work of Reginald George Haggar, art director from 1929 to 1934. Among Haggar's first designs was a series of geometric vases, Les Vases Modernes, of 1929. In this period Minton produced a version of the Cube teapot, kitchenware with brightly coloured bands and lettering, stylish table lamps, a variety of stylized tableware patterns for earthenware, and china tea services, including one, pattern number B1242, enamelled in bright greens, coral and yellow, launched in 1934, as well as Art Deco-influenced figures by Doris Lindner, Richard Bradbury and Eric Owen.

Soon after rejoining the firm in 1934, replacing Haggar as art director, John Wadsworth introduced Solano Ware, a range of pastel-coloured glazed earthenware tableware, with stencilled designs of leaves, spots, stripes and geometric patterns. He also created a collection of bone-china vases with bold emerald, black and gold stylized decoration, as well as Byzantine, Rostique and Tulippa ware decorated in a variety of stippled ground colours with printed and enamel borders.

After the outbreak of World War II in 1939 the manufacture of earthenware was discontinued, but bone-china production for the home market continued throughout the 1940s. Minton's main lines during this period were breakfast sets, cigarette boxes, coffee pots, coffee sets, cruet sets, dinner sets, eggcups, fancies, fruit sets, hotel ware, jugs, table lamps, morning sets, ornamental bowls, pie dishes, sandwich sets, supper sets, teasets, toy teasets and vases. Once wartime restrictions on pottery manufacture were lifted in 1952, Minton's high-quality bone-china tableware was in considerable demand in both home and export markets. Traditional patterns dating back to the 1830s continued to be made alongside many new patterns, including one of the firm's most successful, Haddon Hall. Designed by John Wadsworth and first produced in 1949, this is still made today. Wadsworth also designed the vase presented to the Queen by the British Pottery Manufacturers' Federation to commemorate the

Coronation in 1953. In the same year Minton built a new factory in London Road, Stoke. Two years later Wadsworth died, and in 1957 Douglas Henson was appointed chief designer. He is known for the contemporary Monarch shape and the best-selling Bellemeade pattern. In 1968 Minton joined the Royal Doulton Tableware Group (*see* p.187). New designs from this era include Joseph Ledger's Grenville shape and St James's pattern, Monica Ford's Grasmere pattern and Walter Hayward's Consort pattern. Later tableware includes Barry Meeson's Birds of Paradise, Bobbie Clayton's Tapestry and Marilyn Hankinson's Caliph.

Throughout the 1970s Minton continued to produce a full range of bone-china domestic tableware as well as making fancies and presentation ware. The firm's figurative tradition was continued in 1979 with 11 cast-bronze and ivory china figures, designed by Eric Griffiths, which remained in production until 1984. Robert Jefferson's limited-edition figures based on classical sources, made in bisque and glazed white and gilt, were introduced in 1991. In 1987 the clothes designer Jean Muir created a collection of boxes, trays and vases based on textile designs. More recently the design manager, Kenneth Wright, used artwork and pattern books from the Minton Archives to produce the Contrasts coffee can collection, which was based on Pugin's designs, and Donovan Bird, an interpretation of number 51 from the company's first pattern book.

In 1992 production at the Minton Works ceased, and Minton bone china has since been made by other factories in the group. Minton continues to receive commissions for hand-painted plaques. For a while Minton continued to produce high quality prestige pieces using traditional skills and styles, but now the name exists only as a brand and production is outsourced in the Far East. The famous factory has been demolished, the site redeveloped and most of the contents of the Minton Museum have been sold.

▲ **Cube coffee pot, 1939**
Minton was one of a number of potters to make Cube Ware under licence; most used conventional patterns. 314

▲ **Sea Breeze figure, c.1980**
Minton introduced its short-lived bronze and ivory figure range, designed by Eric Griffiths, in 1979. 315

♦ **Haddon Hall tableware, 1970s**
Designed by John Wadsworth and first made in 1949, Minton's decal-decorated Haddon Hall design has become one of the best-selling tableware patterns of all time. 316

KEY FACTS

Location: Stoke, Staffordshire, UK.
Important dates: Founded 1793. Became member of Royal Doulton Tableware Group 1968. Production ceased at Minton Works and production of Minton pottery transferred to other factories in group 1992. All ware now made in the Far East.
Production: China dinnerware, earthenware, stoneware, majolica and parian.
Principal designers: Léon Solon, John W. Wadsworth, Reginald Haggar, Richard Bradbury, Eric Owen, Douglas Henson, Joseph Ledger, Monica Ford, Walter Hayward, Barry Meeson, Bobby Clayton, Marilyn Hankinson, Eric Griffiths, Robert Jefferson, Kenneth Wright.

MARKS

Versions of globe printed mark used before 1950. This revised standard mark introduced 1951. Secessionist Ware included special script backstamp.

MINTON, HOLLINS & CO.

This company earned a reputation in the 19th century for making high-quality artistic tiles for the better market. When, initially as a sideline, it began to produce decorated pottery, the most successful range was Astra Ware. This consisted largely of vases, including miniatures, with coloured glaze effects, and was in production from at least 1917. The striking colour combinations are predominantly within the art-colours range of blue, green, red and purple. Rarely are more than two glazes used, although firing often produces a third colour. The advertising of Astra Ware seems to have stopped in the mid-1930s, when the taste in ceramics was for more subdued colours.

◆ **Astra Ware vase, c.1925**
Produced mostly in the 1920s, Astra Ware represents Minton, Hollins & Co.'s best-known foray into decorative pottery. 317

KEY FACTS

Location: Patent Tile Works, Stoke, Staffordshire, UK.
Important dates: Founded 1868. Closed 1962.
Production: Tiles, architectural ceramics and decorative ceramics.
Principal designers: Reginald R. Thomlinson, Gordon Forsyth.

MARKS

This printed mark c.1920. Other versions include impressed 'M. H.' in crescent with star, and circular relief mark incorporating 'ASTRA WARE M.H. MADE IN ENGLAND'.

MOIRA POTTERY CO.

Founded in 1922 in Moira, Staffordshire, this manufacturer of domestic stoneware made animal figures, bottles, bulb bowls, casseroles, pharmacists' ware, sundries, figures and statuettes, flower pots and garden pottery, hot-water bottles, jamjars, jugs, novelties, ornamental bowls, pickling jars, pudding bowls and screw stoppers. By 1973 the catalogue included brownware oven dishes and oven-to-table ware in addition to stoneware oven and oven-to-table ware, jugs, bulb bowls, foot-warmers, pet dishes, hotel and catering items, bottles and jars. In 1993 the firm merged with Pearson & Co. at Chesterfield, Derbyshire.

MARKS

Various printed marks with 'Moira Handcrafted' or 'Moira Pottery' in capitals. Trade name or wholesaler's name impressed or stencilled on stoneware from c.1922. *Hillstonia*

WILLIAM MOORCROFT

In the mid-1890s William Moorcroft studied ancient and modern pottery and porcelain at the National Art Training School (later the Royal College of Art) and pursued further studies in Paris. By 1897 he was a qualified teacher, but he was offered the position of designer by the pottery manufacturers James Macintyre & Co., of Burslem, Staffordshire. Moorcroft made rapid progress within the company, rising to manager of ornamental ware early in 1898. During his period with Macintyre, he drew and controlled the design of every pattern executed in his department, thus establishing his own highly individual style. Appreciating the possibilities of slip-trailing, he had already turned his attention to slipware, and success in this field earned him a reputation as a designer.

◆ **Florian Ware vase, 1902**
Moorcroft's reputation in the early years at Macintyre was based on his Florian Ware, which exploited to the full his understanding of colour and the technique of slip-trailing. English Art Nouveau at its best, this Liberty peacock-feather design is typical. 318

Moorcroft won a gold medal at the St Louis World's Fair in 1904 and another at Brussels in 1910, and three years later received the Diploma of Honour at Ghent. He also built up many valuable trade connections, particularly with Liberty & Co., and when he left Macintyre to set up on his own, Liberty provided the finance.

On land he purchased at Cobridge, Staffordshire, Moorcroft had a factory built. He moved into the new works at the end of August 1913, with plant and equipment that he had acquired from Macintyre and a small team of craftsmen and craftswomen, many of whom had worked with him there. World War I had little impact on the factory, even though the introduction of conscription in 1916 reduced the workforce. Production continued throughout the war, and exports grew in line with government requirements. New designs appeared, including the Blue Porcelain range of speckled blue tableware, which was sold through Liberty as Powder Blue. This was a great success and remained in production until about 1963. Moorcroft also continued the development of designs he had launched successfully between 1910 and 1913, notably pomegranate, Spanish, brown Florian (chrysanthemum or revived cornflower), pansy, wisteria, Hazledene and Claremont. Landscape patterns featuring sinuous trees and hills, such as Hazledene, first produced in 1902, and others from the 1920s – Eventide, Moonlit Blue and Dawn – are particularly collectable, especially when they are combined with a rich flambé glaze.

Moorcroft's firm enjoyed enormous success in the 1920s, receiving Royal patronage and being granted the Royal Warrant in 1928. Contemporary reports were full of praise for the pottery. A report on the British Industries Fair of 1921 in *The Pottery Gazette* stated that Moorcroft's simple thrown pottery possessed a wealth of suggestiveness and made a powerful appeal to the imagination. At the fair, King George V is said to have greatly admired a pomegranate decoration, while Queen Mary appeared to be charmed by a lustre vase. Invoices from the early 1920s reveal some of the range of patterns in production: pomegranate, poppy,

▲ Teapot, c.1902
Moorcroft's first designs were for tableware. This often used his slip-trailed floral patterns on standard Macintyre shapes. 319

▲ Tulip vase, c.1904
With its Art Nouveau shape, stylized floral pattern and restrained decoration, this vase shows that Moorcroft's later Macintyre patterns reflect a greater awareness of European styles. 320

▲ Flambé Hazeldene vases, c.1932
Moorcroft used landscape designs from at least 1902, and the pattern that became known as Hazeldene was developed steadily through several variants and colourings. Most dramatic are the grand flambé versions of the early 1930s, with their exciting but unpredictable colours. 321

Claremont Ware, c.1935
The toadstool, or Claremont, pattern was first made for Liberty and then developed by Moorcroft at his own factory. 322

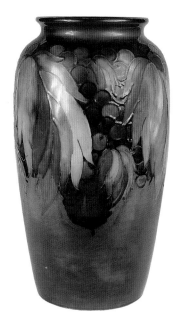

Flambé vase, c.1935
The leaf-and-grape pattern was particularly popular during the mid-to-late 1930s, and was much used by Moorcroft. This flambé version underlines his continual fascination with high-temperature reduction-fired glazes. 323

Walter Moorcroft ware, c.1970
Walter took over from his father in 1945, but didn't start producing his best-known patterns until the late 1950s. The Bermuda Lily range, shown here, dates from the 1970s. 324

moonlit blue tree, wisteria, heartsease, orchid, cornflower, toadstool, lemon, old gold and mauve lustre, blue porcelain and King's Blue, as well as rouge flambé and stoneware. This period also saw the expansion of items made to be mounted in silver, electroplate, pewter and brass.

The 1930s were difficult for Moorcroft, who, like most British potters, suffered directly from the effects of the Wall Street Crash of 1929. This decade saw Moorcroft make a dramatic change of style in which he returned to the use of pale grounds and the intensive application of matt glazes. In addition he withdrew some earlier styles. Even so, company records show that in 1935, when he was joined by his son Walter, the factory was still producing 55 patterns. This is an astonishing diversity, considering that some patterns were made in numerous colours and in both matt salt-glazed and conventional clear-glazed finishes.

Having survived World War II largely on the strength of its export business, the pottery was taken over by Walter Moorcroft in 1945 after his father's sudden death. As skilled a designer as William Moorcroft, Walter continued to maintain and build his company's reputation for decorative hand-made pottery. At the same time he introduced his own individual style with a series of patterns such as a few pieces of the early Columbine from flowers in his own garden, produced in 1947; his first Hibiscus pieces, based on pressed flowers sent from Jamaica; and, from the same source, Bougainvillaea.

In 1962 John Moorcroft, Walter's half-brother, joined the company and took over primary responsibility for sales and marketing, becoming a director in 1977. Then, in 1986, after several years of declining sales and a brief association with the Roper Brothers, a controlling share in Moorcroft was sold to Richard Dennis, Hugh Edwards and their wives, Sally (Tuffin) and Maureen. Soon afterwards Walter Moorcroft retired, and John Moorcroft became managing director. Sally Tuffin became principal designer, and by 1992, when the Dennises left, the fortunes of the ailing business had been restored. Tuffin produced a number of new patterns based on a bird-and-fruit theme; others were based on a William Morris fabric made for Sanderson, Tulips, introduced in 1989, peacock feathers, originally a Liberty exclusive, and many more. Sally also created special and limited-edition designs featuring polar bears, balloons, penguins, ships, owls, cats and elephants, all of which are highly collectable.

Since Rachel Bishop was appointed designer in 1993, Moorcroft has continued to expand. In 1997 the company acquired Okra Glass, of Brierley Hill, West Midlands, and founded a design studio for seven staff

designers and a complement of freelancers. Other designers have now followed in Rachel Bishop's footsteps, maintaining collector enthusiasm for the modern product. The company has recently launched Cobridge Stoneware plc., operating from the new Phoenix Works, Nile Street, Burslem, on land which was owned by James Macintyre & Co. at the end of the 19th century. Production includes high-fired flambé ware and sgraffito-decorated ware.

In November 1998 Moorcroft announced that it had bought Kingsley Enamels, a family business dating back to 1904, and it intends to produce enamel boxes created by members of its own design team. The method of production used since the time of William Moorcroft in 1897 is unchanged. Moorcroft pottery continues to sell, and even relatively recent designs are avidly sought after by collectors.

KEY FACTS

Location: Moorcroft Pottery, Burslem, Staffordshire, UK.
Important dates: Founded 1913. Still active.
Production: Earthenware and stoneware.
Principal designers: William Moorcroft, Walter Moorcroft, Sally Tuffin, Rachel Bishop.

MARKS

Various, including Moorcroft signature or initials, printed or impressed factory mark, retailer's mark, design registration number and pattern or shape mark. Paper labels with printed factory marks also used. Some important pieces marked with date.

▲ **Sally Tuffin fish vase, 1980s**
In the late 1980s Sally Tuffin took over design from Walter Moorcroft and produced a range of dramatic patterns. 325

BERNARD MOORE

When his father, a second-generation potter, died in 1867, Bernard Moore carried on the business in Longton, Staffordshire, with his brother, Samuel Vincent Moore. Moore Bros became noted for high-class decorative tableware, and from the 1880s Bernard researched the history of pottery, notably the early Chinese potters. His studies led to the reproduction of Chinese flambé on porcelain, the first pieces of which he presented to the British Museum in 1902. Moore was President of the Ceramic Society in 1902–3, and gave technical advice to many potteries in Britain, other European countries and the USA. In 1905 he sold the Longton firm to set up as a consultant potter at Wolfe Street, Stoke, and the following year was joined by his son, Bernard J. Moore, who took part in his experiments. Moore did not make his ware on his own premises but used blanks supplied by other factories, including Crown Staffordshire (see p.55), Minton (see p.132) and Wedgwood (see p.230), and had special pieces made by James Stephen Wilson in Longton.

At Wolfe Street, Moore, in addition to his consultancy concentrated on the development of oriental and Middle Eastern glazes, flambés and lustres, Persian blues, aventurine and crystalline and other glaze effects. He was one of the few European potters to discover how to produce glaze effects equal to those made by the old Chinese secret methods, and in addition to producing rich red *sang-de-boeuf* glazes, for which he became well known, he also achieved novel and wonderful effects by use of metals other than copper, treated in the same way. These glazes were often used over painted decoration. Productions included a wide range of vases, bowls, jardinières and ornamental ware such as tobacco jars, candlesticks

▲ **Longboat vase, c.1908**
This vase is decorated with the image of a longboat and its crew riding the waves; it is printed in gold and handpainted over a mustard-orange flambé ground. 326

and boxes in addition to large quantities of animal models and grotesques. In its heyday the firm employed many fine designer-decorators, including George Buttle, E. R. Wilkes, Annie Ollier, John Adams, E. Hope Beardmore, Dora Billington, Hilda Carter, Cecily H. Jackson, Hilda Lindop and Reginald R. Thomlinson.

Moore was awarded high honours for his work at many national and international exhibitions, and in 1915 King George V and Queen Mary visited his studio. However, the advent of World War I seems to have affected his output adversely, and, although the exact date is not known, it is generally accepted that he ceased manufacturing about 1915.

KEY FACTS

Location: Wolfe Street, Stoke, Staffordshire, UK.

Important dates: Founded 1905. Closed c.1915.

Production: Earthenware, porcelain.

MARKS

'BM' painted, or full name painted or printed, sometimes with date.

$\mathcal{B}$ERNARD $\mathcal{B}$MOORE

◆ **Exotic bird vase, c.1908**
The gold print, which is enriched by hand-painting, sits over a dramatic red-and-orange flambé ground. 327

MOORLAND POTTERY

The pottery was established in the mid-1980s by Jonathan Plant who took over the Chelsea Works, Burslem, Staffordshire, formerly the studio of Joseph Szeiler. He was joined by Adrian Plant six months later and they are now equal partners in the business. Early production included copies of Staffordshire wares of the 19th and early 20th centuries, such as figures and wall masks, along with wares decorated by the revived sponging technique, a popular late 18th century process for popular pottery. These include mugs, jugs and teawares sponge-decorated with pigs, hens, rabbits and other domestic animals. Also in the range is a series of fish designs commissioned from the artist-potter Kate Malone. In the late 1990s Moorland produced new ornamental ranges featuring unusual shapes and interesting glaze effects. Among these was N-Dangered, a collaboration between Jonathan Plant and Adrian Tinsley.

▲ **N-Dangered series teapot, 1990s**
This piece is from a series designed in the 1990s by Adrian Tinsley and Jonathan and Adrian Plant. 328

◆ **Animal Ware, c.1990**
Included in this range, for which 18th-century sponging techniques were revived, is a fish mug (left) designed by Kate Malone. 329

KEY FACTS

Location: Chelsea Works, Burslem, Staffordshire, UK.
Important dates: Founded c.1986. Still active.
Production: Earthenware.

MARKS

This mark also used without reference to Chelsea Works, Burslem.

Moorland
STAFFORDSHIRE
ENGLAND

STAFFORDSHIRE
CHELSEA
WORKS
BURSLEM

MT CLEMENS POTTERY COMPANY

The company was one of the many American potteries that supplied the dime-store and mail-order markets with inexpensive semi-porcelain dinnerware. Unlike most of the others, it was owned by the retailer that it supplied. In 1920 S. S. Kresge, K-Mart's predecessor, bought Mt Clemens and directed manufacturing for its own stores until 1965. The best known of the Kresge-era patterns was Petal, low-relief petal shapes on the wide rim made in solid colours of burgundy, blue, green and yellow. In 1965 K-Mart sold the pottery to David Chase, who hired out its operation to the Sabin China Company in McKeesport, Pennsylvania, a decorating company. After the McKeesport works were destroyed by fire in 1979, Sabin moved the operation to Mt Clemens. The pottery closed in 1987.

KEY FACTS

Location: Mt Clemens, Michigan, USA.
Important dates: Founded 1914. Closed 1987.
Production: Semi-porcelain dinnerware.

MARKS

Monogram 'MCPCo.' used on some ware, but most ware unmarked or with raised 'USA' only.

1132B

◆ **Serving dish, 1940s**
Mt Clemens's patterns were similar to many of the best-selling patterns of other potteries. Delicate flower patterns, such as those shown here, Old Mexico-type patterns, and patterns that look like petit point needlework were popular with Kresge buyers. 330

MUNCIE CLAY PRODUCTS COMPANY

The pottery was created as a division of Gill Clay Pot Company, owned by Charles Grafton, which made clay pots for the glass industry and crucibles for metal refining. Preliminary planning began about 1919, but production did not begin until late 1921 or early 1922 in a small factory built adjacent to the Gill facility. Boris Trifonoff, a designer from the American Encaustic Tile Company of Zanesville, Ohio, developed the clay body, the bright, colourful glazes and the two-colour style of their application. James Wilkins later introduced matt glazes and airbrush application of the two-colour glazes. The pottery produced lamp bases, book-ends, candlesticks, wall pockets, pitchers, bowls, vases and art novelties. Garden pottery was listed in the 1929 catalogue, but little is seen on the market today. In 1931 the company was reorganized as Muncie Potteries, Inc., and Charles C. Benham ran daily operations. But US economic conditions adversely affected the pottery's survival, and it ceased production in 1936.

KEY FACTS

Location: Muncie, Indiana, USA.
Important dates: Founded 1919. Production ceased 1936.
Production: Earthenware houseware, florists' crockery, garden pottery.
Principal designers: Boris Trifonoff, James Wilkins, Reuben Haley.

MARKS

Marked ware inscribed or die-stamped 'MUNCIE' in wet clay.

◆ **Ruba Rombic vase, early 1930s**
The Ruba Rombic line, designed in the Cubist style by Reuben Haley and similar to his glass pattern of the same name, is the most collectable of Muncie's output. 331

KEITH MURRAY

For over six years Keith Murray held a prominent place in the design of useful ornamental pottery and glass, as well as silver for Mappin & Webb. Born in New Zealand in 1892, he settled in England with his parents in 1906 or 1907. He studied in London to be an architect, but lack of opportunity in the field forced him to try other possibilities. His first, unsuccessful, design attempts, produced experimentally by Arthur Marriot Powell, a director of Whitefriars Glassworks, made him begin to realize the importance of understanding the material for which he was designing. Murray's first successful association was with Stevens & Williams, of Brierley Hill Glassworks, West Midlands, where he worked for three months a year from 1932. By 1933 he had a similar contract from Josiah Wedgwood & Sons (*see* p.230), of Etruria, and from that time combined glass designing with a very successful career as a ceramics designer.

As with his work for Stevens & Williams, Murray aimed to become thoroughly familiar with the medium. At first he had difficulty conforming to Wedgwood's requirements, but after frequent visits to the factory under the guidance of Tom Wedgwood he soon gained confidence. In addition to studying pottery at the Wedgwood Museum, he began to examine traditional methods of throwing and turning being used in the factory, and explored new ways to use them. He designed an enormous number of highly successful functional shapes for Wedgwood, concentrating on form rather than decoration.

Murray's arrival at Wedgwood coincided with the development of the white semi-matt Moonstone glaze, followed two years later by the matt-green and matt-straw ranges. His uncompromising architectural forms were the ideal vehicle for this new range of glazes, and his work for Wedgwood was highly praised from the outset. The new shapes that he designed for Wedgwood were shown at John Lewis & Co.'s department store in Oxford Street, London, in 1933. The range, which consisted of 147 pieces, included some fine earthenware pieces with matt glazes, black basalt vases and bowls, hand-turned pieces in Wedgwood Queensware with a deep ivory glaze, turned vases in owl's-egg white glaze, red stoneware, copper basalt, a newly invented stoneware, and a number of unique pieces, made under Murray's personal direction, of which at that time no copies were available. The latter were simple hand-thrown shapes in cream-coloured earthenware, covered with a clear champagne glaze,

◆ Ink-stand, 1930s
This ink-stand is part of a series of functional shapes conceived on architectural lines by the architect-designer Keith Murray in the 1930s. The series includes at least four ink-stands, of which the round version is the least common. 332

◆ Coffee can and saucer, c.1933
The coffee set from which these pieces come was among the first range of shapes that Murray designed for Wedgwood. In 1933 the set was offered in Moonstone (white) or green glaze. In the version seen here, lustre has been applied to the handle by hand-paintresses. 333

◆ Vases, 1933–5
Murray was able to build on the Wedgwood tradition to create an entirely new range of vases and other useful ware. Among the vases were this slender fluted trumpet vase and low vase with annular ribbing. Finishes included matt green (as here), Moonstone (matt white), matt straw, grey and clear champagne, the last two of which were phased out from c.1940. 334

finished with a black underglaze line; finger-finished earthenware vases; turned pieces in various coloured glazes; glazed stoneware pieces (the outcome of recent experiments in high-temperature glazes on Wedgwood stoneware); hand-thrown finger-finished pots in earthenware, with an opaque black semi-matt glaze; and, finally, finely turned stoneware in black or dark glazes.

Much of Murray's ware was made on a limited mass-produced scale until the 1950s. Among the wide variety of shapes are vases and bowls, book-ends, ink-stands, candlesticks, beer jugs and mugs. Also made were Coronation mugs, the shape by Murray and the ornamental relief modelled by Arnold Machin. Occasionally his ware was decorated with platinum or free-hand patterns designed by Millicent Taplin and executed by the hand-paintresses under her supervision. Among Murray's rare excursions into designing patterns for Wedgwood was the Lotus pattern for a range of teaware.

Around 1945 Murray produced some designs incorporating techniques such as sprigging, which were not produced in quantity, as well as the Commonwealth Service, which was shown in the Design at Work exhibition mounted by the Royal Society of Arts and the Council of Industrial Design. Murray's work was shown at many national and international exhibitions. These included British Industrial Art in Relation to the Home, Dorland Hall, 1933; the Fifth Triennale, Milan, 1933 (Gold Medal); British Art in Industry, Royal Academy, London, 1935; English Pottery Old and New, Victoria & Albert Museum, London, 1935; and a one-man show at the Medici Gallery, London, 1935. In 1936 Murray became one of Britain's first Royal Designers for Industry.

⬆ Slipware urn, c.1933
The range of which this piece forms a part was executed using the traditional methods of hand turning and combining different-coloured clays, usually celadon green with cream, and champagne with ivory. Shapes in this range were mainly vases and bowls used either for displaying flowers or fruit, or simply for decorative purposes. 335

◆ Basalt vase and grey vase, c.1935
A number of Murray shapes were made in black basalt and red stoneware, traditional Wedgwood materials. A new copper-coloured basalt, invented in 1933, was also used. Much of the ware was thrown and featured high-quality turning and finishing on the lathe. Such rare pieces bring together modern design and old handcraft techniques. Also relatively rare is the grey glaze, which had limited use on Murray's shapes until it was withdrawn in 1940. 336

MYOTT, SON & CO.

Between 1897 and 1976, when it merged with Alfred Meakin (see p.126), this Staffordshire firm exported earthenware and semi-porcelain domestic ware. Among its lines were mazarine-blue banded tableware and other traditional patterns, a wide range of toilet ware, 21- and 40-piece teasets with simple litho borders, ground-laid sets with shaded and gilt patterns in Derby style, and ornamental ranges such as vases in striking lustres with butterfly motifs printed in gold and hand-coloured. Between the wars the firm made stylized tableware shapes, decorated with modern wash-banded and transfer-printed and enamelled patterns, as well as Art Deco-inspired freehand-painted ornamental vases.

MARKS

This mark used from c.1936. Initials 'S M & Co.' incorporated in early printed marks. 'Stoke' indicates date before 1903. Myott name in full used from c.1907.

NEW CHELSEA PORCELAIN CO.

The company's early production at the Stanley Works was almost entirely limited to white-and-gold, blue-band and similar traditional lines. At the 1929 British Industries Fair it had a successful show which included several new tableware patterns applied to an ivory glaze as well as attractive new shapes in teaware, among them Devon and New Elite, and three new nursery ware patterns. The pottery gained in size and stature during the 1920s and 1930s until, during World War II, the Board of Trade Scheme appointed the parent firm, R. H. & S. L. Plant (see p.157), to take over production of teaware at its Tuscan Works. After the war the New Chelsea Porcelain Co. regained its factory and began modernization and re-equipment.

In 1951 the trade names New Chelsea and Royal Chelsea were bought by Susie Cooper China. One of the most collectable series from this period is Country Pleasures, the set of plates decal-decorated with pastoral scenes based on pen-and-ink drawings commissioned from Edward Ardizzone. The first six plates produced under the Royal Chelsea label, early in 1957, were Boating, Drinking, Bathing, Fishing, Courting and The Picnic. In 1961 the company became Grosvenor China Ltd, which itself was acquired by the Wedgwood Group (see p.230) in 1966.

◆ Noah's Ark nursery ware, 1930
First seen in *The Pottery Gazette* in 1930, this nursery ware range with its typical stylized motifs is indicative of the expanding market for children's china at this time. 337

◆ Country Pleasures plate, late 1950s
Designed by Edward Ardizzone, and first produced in 1957, this design is one of a set of six, now highly collectable. 338

KEY FACTS

Location: Stanley Works, Longton, Staffordshire, UK.
Important dates: Founded 1910. Bought and renamed New Chelsea China Co. by Susie Cooper 1951.
Production: China and porcelain.

MARKS

This printed anchor mark used from c.1913. Variations used from c.1919.

NEWPORT POTTERY CO.

In 1920 the Newport Pottery, in Burslem, was taken over by A. J. Wilkinson's (*see* p.239) Royal Staffordshire Pottery. The Newport Pottery Co. was set up mainly to mass-produce white and inexpensively decorated semi-porcelain dinner, tea and toilet ware, as well as special lines for hotels and restaurants. In 1926 Clarice Cliff (*see* p.43) was given her own studio at the pottery, where she developed a range of decorative patterns with the aid of a paintress. Art Deco sets were widely marketed by Wilkinson from 1928.

In 1941 production was concentrated with those of the Royal Staffordshire Pottery (*see* p.190) and Shorter & Son (*see* p.204). After the war its output consisted of advertising ware, animal figures, hotel ware, jugs, vases, ornamental ware and novelties. Newport and A. J. Wilkinson were taken over by W. R. Midwinter (*see* p.129) in 1964, and the former's factory was closed in 1987.

KEY FACTS

Location: Newport Lane, Burslem, Staffordshire, UK.
Important dates: Founded 1920. Taken over by W. R. Midwinter 1964.
Production: Earthenware and semi-porcelain.
Trade names: Newport, Clarice Cliff.

MARKS

Variations of this mark used from 1920. Clarice Cliff designs have facsimile signature.

← Fruit and Flowers range, 1921
This advertisement features a typical Newport range from the pre-Clarice Cliff years. 339

NILOAK POTTERY

Charles Hyten was making utilitarian stoneware in 1910 when he developed an unglazed agate ware from naturally coloured clays. The simple hand-thrown giftware that he marketed was called Mission Ware. In 1911 the Niloak Pottery Company was incorporated, with Hyten as director and general manager. By 1912 the ware was offered nationally through housekeeping magazines. Forms included bowls, candlesticks, steins, sets of pitcher and tankards, punchbowls with cups, smoking sets, fern dishes, clocks, and vases in many shapes and sizes. From 1931 to 1937 the firm offered a glazed version of the agate ware under the trade name Hywood Art Pottery. In 1947 it became the Winburn Tile Company.

KEY FACTS

Location: Benton, Arkansas, USA.
Important dates: Founded 1911. Became Winburn Tile Company 1947 and still active under this name.
Production: Agate giftware, mosaic tiles.

MARKS

This stamp impressed on all marked ware.

NILOAK

↑ Mission Ware vases, 1920s
The surface of every piece of Mission Ware is different because of the agate body, which gives rise to innumerable variations when thrown on the wheel. The naturally coloured clays were wedged together so that the colours remained distinct and made patterns as the clay twisted and turned during the manufacturing process. 340

OMEGA POTTERY

The Omega Workshops were opened in 1913 under the direction of the painter Roger Fry and his two fellow directors and artists, Duncan Grant and Vanessa Bell. In addition to designing and decorating ceramics, the Omega artists, who were at first self-taught in pottery design, worked with textiles, furniture, carpets, stained glass and interiors. Vanessa Bell painted ware, most of it thrown by Fry; some of her designs were figurative and depicted contemporary scenes, but her later designs were mainly colourful abstract patterns. Omega's pottery output was given a boost when the Poole Pottery (*see* p.159) offered the artists facilities for throwing and firing. From 1914 until 1917 pottery was produced for sale at the Omega Workshops from prototypes thrown by Fry. After struggling through the difficulties imposed by World War I and internal disagreements, the Omega Workshops went into voluntary liquidation in 1920.

KEY FACTS

Location: Fitzroy Square, London, UK.
Important dates: Founded 1913. Closed 1920.
Production: Earthenware.

MARKS

Incised or painted loosely drawn Omega.

◀ **Duncan Grant vase, c.1917 (far left)**
This vase – probably a Phyllis Keyes shape – exemplifies Duncan Grant's lively style. 341

◀ **Roger Fry vase, c.1914 (left)**
The hurried brushwork and semi-abstract design are typical of the rather amateur approach of the Omega decorators. 342

ONONDAGA POTTERY CO.

The pottery was organized in 1871 and in that year bought the facilities of the Empire Pottery in Syracuse, New York. White-granite tableware and toilet ware were the earliest products. The mark for this ware was an English lion-and-unicorn armorial with the words 'IRONSTONE CHINA' and 'O.P.Co.'. The firm also made coarse c.c. ware (cream-coloured, corn-coloured or common ware) for table and toilet services, which was unmarked. While these two bodies shared some forms, the ironstone ware was more clearly for table service and the c.c. ware for kitchen and barnyard use. Both the ironstone and c.c. ware met with ready markets, and by 1885 the company had increased its capacity from one to four kilns. In 1885 it introduced a high-fired semi-vitreous ware guaranteed against crazing. This was an improved earthenware, not truly porcelain, but its initial success was met with the introduction of several new shape designs over the next few years. A new mark distinguished the new ware: the initials 'O.P.Co.'

➤ **Juno toilet ware, late 1890s**
Onondaga's Juno line was designed for table and toilet ware. The toilet set seen here is decorated with the Orchid pattern. 343

over 'CHINA'. The company continued to make its earlier bodies for different goods and different markets. In 1895 c.c. ware was discontinued, but white granite was available until 1897. Decoration on the pottery's early output was generally limited to moulded ornament with some transfer printing for special pieces. From 1884 to 1886 much of the decorating was sent out to the newly established Boston China Decorating Company across the street, but after a fire there in 1886 the decision was made to incorporate a decorating department into the china factory.

The development of improved earthenware in 1885 was followed by the introduction in 1891 of Imperial Geddo, a fully vitreous fine china that was used for tableware designed in the French taste and artware decorated in the English taste. Onondaga made the ware available in table and ornamental shapes in the white for decoration. The same shapes could be ordered with decoration from samples.

In 1895 the name Syracuse China was first used in company backstamps as a trade name for the improved vitreous-china body that was the only clay body it used, beginning in 1897. The earliest mark featured a globe bisected by 'VITREOUS' and surrounded by 'SYRACUSE CHINA' and 'O.P.Co.'. By 1897 the firm had settled on a standard mark in three lines that was used until 1920: 'O.P.Co./SYRACUSE/CHINA'. Imperial Geddo became a tableware shape in the Syracuse China line, along with Iona and Marmora, while the Syracuse, Juno and Oneida shapes were designed for toilet sets. The company's modeller from 1891 to 1926 was Mark Haley, who was responsible for creating these shapes and many others, including Mayflower, which became a signature dinnerware shape for the pottery after it was introduced about 1910.

◆ Marathon pattern plate, 1926
Much of Syracuse China's work in the 20th century has been for institutional customers, who received stylish custom and stock patterns for use in their schools, restaurants, hospitals and railway dining-cars. 344

◆ Missouri-Pacific Railroad service plate, 1949–61
Mo-Pac's diesel 'Route of the Eagles' went through 11 central US states. The dining-car service plate pictures the capitals of Missouri, Kansas, Colorado, Mississippi, Nebraska, Illinois, Arkansas, Louisiana, Texas, Tennessee and Oklahoma. 345

◆ Syracuse China advertisement, 1920s
The Somerset pattern features in this advertisement placed in a popular women's magazine. The illustration by Edmund Davenport suggests that the product is suitable for a wealthy home, and the copy identifies it as the 'choice of the hostess who appreciates the importance of a beautiful, well-set table'. 346

◆ **Catalogue, 1937**
This page from Onondaga's trade catalogue shows a variety of the hand-painted and hand-lined, decal and print decorations available on Econo-Rim, designed by R. Guy Cowan. The tan body was called Adobe, and its decorations were usually more casual than on the white body. 347

◆ **Mayflower Hotel service plate, 1930**
Syracuse China's interwar service plates are exceptional examples of the technical achievements and design skills that characterized the US pottery industry at the time. 348

In 1897 the company introduced a rolled or round edge on its shapes that had been worked out by Haley for institutional ware. Round Edge immediately became popular, and the pottery continued to use this shape for many years. When R. Guy Cowan joined the company in 1932 (*see* Cowan Pottery, p.53) as the shape designer, he introduced a modern design sensibility to the pottery's product. His Econo-Rim changed the basic shape of hotel ware in the 1930s by combining a narrow moulded rim with a broader, deeper well. The new shape, which quickly became the industry standard, contained juices and gravies successfully while using a smaller diameter and saving overall tray and tabletop space. Syracuse continued to make china for both institutional and domestic use well into the 20th century. Indeed, domestic china was discontinued only in 1970, when the overall market in the USA for fine-china dinnerware declined in favour of casual tableware, most of which was made abroad. Cowan designed several of the popular shapes, including Shelledge (1937), Federal (1938), Berkeley (1950) and Paul Revere (1951).

Decalcomania, or lithographic colour printing, was introduced in 1897 when the company installed in-house equipment for this purpose. The decal section of the decorating department grew rapidly in response to increasing orders. Transfer printing, often combined with hand-filling of colour, continued to be used, depending on the desired effect. Designers of decorations included company employees, such as Harry Aitkin, who headed the decorating department from 1904, as well as consultant designers, like Adelaide Robineau, who is famous today as a 20th-century studio potter. Other in-house pattern designers who created successful patterns over the years included John Wigley, Augustus J. Koch, Henley Hennock, Charles McKaig, E. M. Otis and Douglas Bourne. Many of the institutional service plates for railway companies and hotels, designed by this group and decorated in the factory, are among the very best examples of the type made by the US industry.

In 1927 the firm began introducing new body colours. The first, Old Ivory, was a cream-coloured body mainly for domestic dinnerware. It was introduced on the Mayflower shape, but soon the new Winchester line, designed by Bertram Watkin, was the exclusive Old Ivory shape. Watkin had taken over Haley's position in 1926. The Old Ivory trade name was included in a new ribbon-shaped mark that was used on this ware until 1960. Adobe, a tan body, was introduced in 1932 and made until 1972.

In 1966 the name of the company, which had bought the Canadian hotel ware maker Vandesca China, of Joliette, Quebec, in 1959, was officially changed to the Syracuse China Company. In 1971 the Syracuse China Corporation was reorganized, and in 1978 it was bought by Canadian Pacific, Ltd, which owned an extensive chain of hotels in Canada. The Susquehanna-Pfaltzgraff Company (*see* Pfaltzgraff Pottery, p.152) bought the Syracuse company in 1989 from Canadian Pacific and in 1995 sold it to Libbey Inc. of Toledo, Ohio. Libbey has combined Syracuse China with its long-time commercial glass operation.

The renamed company was successful and was able to make a major contribution to the Everson Museum of Art in Syracuse, with which it had had close links since the late 1920s. With generous support from Syracuse China's then owner, Canadian Pacific, galleries for the Everson Museum's extensive collection of 20th-century American ceramics were expanded and opened in 1986 as the Syracuse China Center for the Study of American Ceramics. Many companies are represented here, along with examples of ware made by the Onondaga Pottery and Syracuse China, in what is the world's largest collection of 20th-century American ceramics.

Seventy per cent of the company's product line was eliminated in 1971–2, and since then it has made only hotel ware. The mark changed too: since 1971 it has included a small line-drawing of tableware set together with a candle inside a circle above the company's name.

♠ **Hotel Blackhawk service plate, 1913**
Onondaga/Syracuse hotel, restaurant and railway service plates are collectable for the wide variety of images that refer to people and events in American history and contemporary American life. 349

KEY FACTS

Location: Syracuse, New York, USA.
Important dates: Founded 1871. Still active.
Production: China dinnerware and hotel ware.
Principal designers: Harry Aitkin, Adelaide Robineau.
Trade name: Syracuse China.

MARKS

Many pieces can be dated specifically by using pottery's letter/number code. Trade, customer and pattern names also used, in conjunction with 'Syracuse China' and 'O.P.Co.'.

PADEN CITY

The Paden City pottery was one of many American potteries in the 20th century that produced semi-porcelain dinnerware for sale in dime stores and department stores across the country. Founded in 1914 for the manufacture of the standard dinnerware product, in 1931 it added kitchenware called Bak-Serv, which was distributed by the Great Northern Products Company of Chicago.

A few lines and products made by the pottery are popular with collectors today; among these are a souvenir salad bowl made for the 1938–39 New York World's Fair and several dinnerware patterns dating from the 1930s and 1940s. These patterns include Elite (1936), Manhattan (1933), Shellcrest (1937), Shenandoah (1944), Virginia (1939) and the solid colours of Caliente on Elite (1936) and Shellcrest (1938). The pottery's Blue Willow, introduced in 1937, is the familiar pattern rendered in intaglio and completely covered in a blue glaze. Russel Wright contributed Highlight to Paden City's lines. The pattern was made from 1948 to 1953 and received the Museum of Modern Art Home Furnishings Award and the Trail Blazer Award of the Home Furnishings League in 1951. The pottery closed in 1963.

KEY FACTS

Location: Paden City, West Virginia, USA.
Important dates: Founded 1914. Closed 1963.
Production: Semi-porcelain dinnerware.

MARKS

Often only pattern name used in mark.

▶ **Platter, 1930s**
Paden City's semi-porcelain dinnerware was decorated for every taste. In addition to conservative floral patterns, collectors can also find colourful casual decals, bright solid colours, and handy kitchenware servers, coffeepots and teapots, and casseroles. 350

PALISSY: see A. E. JONES p.99

PARAGON CHINA CO.

This pottery, which started trading about 1899 as the Star China Co., became the Paragon China Co. in 1919. During the interwar period Paragon became well known for its high-grade tea, coffee, breakfast and dessert ware in china, which it made alongside a full range of tableware sundries. By the early 1920s it specialized in new styles of decoration, including modern adaptations of traditional patterns, such as Bourbon Sprig, which it brought out as an inexpensive decal-decorated design.

Between the wars Paragon was also renowned for its nursery ware. Early named examples include the Mother Goose series by Chloë Preston, Louis Wain's Tinker Tailor and a range of Charlie Chaplin ware. New for 1928 were teaware designs by Beatrice Mallet. In 1926 the Duchess of York commissioned the pottery to create china for the nursery of the infant Princess Elizabeth. This ware, which was decorated by Paragon's paintresses, illustrates two magpies and was given the name Two for Joy. In 1930 the Duchess commissioned a tea service to commemorate the birth of Princess Margaret Rose. The Princess Margaret Rose pattern consisted of a rose and sprays of heather supporting two love-birds. In 1933, in recognition of its work for royalty, the firm received its first Royal Warrant of Appointment, an honour conferred on the company again in 1938 and 1953. Other royal commissions included a child's mug from the Eileen Soper nursery ware series, brought out in 1938 as a Christmas gift from Queen Mary, and Eileen Soper's Pixie Playtime mug, brought out in December 1940 as a gift from the Duchess of York, wife of King George VI.

Paragon made a series of exclusive designs but, in 1930, believed that these were bettered by its new Mickey Mouse series, which reproduced the famous drawings of Walt Disney and conveyed a story rather than a mere pattern. Children were already familiar with Mickey Mouse, largely through the newspapers and the cinema. The subject was faintly printed in outline and colour was added by hand. The factory requested latitude over the assortment of patterns, because the production process required a number of subjects to be engraved on a single copperplate and, as a result, the prints could not be selected at will.

The pottery continued in production throughout World War II, and in 1946 it made a range of animal figures, ashtrays, breakfast sets, coffee pots, coffee sets, cruet sets, dinner sets, eggcups, figures and statuettes, fruit sets, morning sets, novelties, sandwich sets, supper sets, teapots and teasets. Paragon was at this time in the hands of Hugh Irving and his sons Leslie and Guy, who continued their association with the firm until it was taken over by T. C. Wild & Sons in 1960. Although Paragon continued as a separate concern, many of the designs and shapes were withdrawn. In

◆ Royal Wedding loving cup, 1981
Paragon has long been known for its royal commemoratives; this is a modern example. 351

◆ Eileen Soper Children's China advertisement, 1936
This advertisement promoted one of a number of nursery ware ranges made by Paragon between the wars. 352

◆ Teaset group, late 1920s
Paragon's Fortune Telling series of nursery ware, based on traditional children's rhymes, was designed by J. A. Robinson c.1928. 353

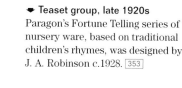

July 1964 T. C. Wild merged with the Lawley Group. Two years later Paragon's china production was substantially increased when the firm was given the use of a second factory, the Albert Works, which until then had been operated by another Wild subsidiary. Paragon continued to make traditional floral patterns, such as Belinda on the Corinth shape and Meadowvale on the Elizabeth shape, as well as fancies, limited editions, children's china and commemorative ware. Royal commemoratives were particularly popular with collectors, and some examples, such as the Queen's Silver Jubilee ware of 1977, were sold out before they were made.

◆ Traditional teaware, 1920s
During the 1920s and 1930s Paragon enjoyed a reputation for its high-quality blue china teaware, which was made for both use and display. This traditional design, with its dramatic colouring, is typical. [354]

◆ Art Deco teaware, 1930s
A stylish modern shape combined with a restrained floral pattern shows how well Paragon dealt with demand for contemporary designs. [355]

KEY FACTS

Location: Atlas Works (and other sites), Longton, Staffordshire, UK
Important dates: Founded as Star China Co. c.1899. Renamed Paragon China 1919. Part of Royal Doulton Group from 1968. Atlas Works closed 1987. Paragon name taken over by Royal Albert 1989.
Production: China, earthenware and stoneware.

MARKS

Backstamps incorporating royal coat of arms used from c.1935. This mark introduced c.1957.

PEARSON & CO.

The company is a typical Derbyshire manufacturer of stoneware, and is based at the Whittington Pottery near Chesterfield, where it makes mainly bottles. The pottery was acquired by Catherine Johnson (née Pearson) in 1810 and remained in family hands through various generations. James Pearson was running the firm in 1884 when the Oldfield Pottery, of Chesterfield, was purchased and merged with the London Pottery, which had been owned by F. Lipscombe & Co., the patentee of a type of stoneware water filter.

In 1928 Pearson & Co.'s catalogue included a wide range of practical stoneware, including jam, pickle, acid and wicker jars, patent-tap bottles, spirit kegs, bread pans, stew jars, foot-warmers and similar utilitarian articles. Also made was a new range of fireproof cookware, known as Kinstra, and a series of stoneware jugs and mugs, decorated with white embossed reliefs depicting traditional hunting scenes. By 1946 the firm was concen-

◆ Stoneware advertisement, 1915
A typical range of Pearson goods including salt-glazed, Chesterfield Brown and Bristol stoneware. [356]

trating on the production of bread crocks, bulb bowls, casseroles, chemical ware, coffee pots, hotel and catering ware, hot-water bottles, insulators, jam jars, jugs, kitchen ware, laboratory ware, ointment jars, oven ware, pickling jars, pie dishes, pudding bowls, screw stoppers, spirit jars, and vases.

In the 1960s Pearson & Co. introduced an interesting artware series, including vases and lamp bases, with incised decoration. Early in the following decade the company brought out a number of modern tableware ranges, such as Genesis, Snowdon, Delamere and Coniston. Many of the earlier stoneware lines had gone out of production, and the firm was producing a greater quantity of vitrified stoneware and earthenware for the hotel and catering trade. By the early 1970s it had also expanded its production of domestic cookware, oven-to-table ware, kitchenware and giftware.

In 1993 the Moira Pottery Co. (*see* p.135) closed its factory in Moira, Staffordshire, and merged with Pearson & Co. at Chesterfield.

◆ **Sgraffito artware vase, 1960s**
In the 1960s Pearson introduced a range of beautifully carved calligraphic sgraffito artware in a variety of colours. Short-lived at the time, this range is now very collectable. 357

PETERS & REED POTTERY

In 1898 John D. Peters and Adam Reed founded a series of companies that operated in succession in a pottery in Zanesville, Ohio. The first occupant of the site was the Peters & Reed Pottery, which was incorporated in 1901 to make flower pots. Later the company added spittoons, jardinières and cookware to its range, although the latter was made only between 1903 and 1906. Sometime between 1905 and 1912 the company introduced Moss Aztec, the line for which it is best known today. This ware, designed by Frank Ferrell, was made with a redware body moulded in relief and dipped in a mixture of paraffin and coal oil, which gave it a green cast. The company's 1921 catalogue noted the 'quiet effect of the rich red brown tones of the Historic Aztec Indians coupled with the apparent mossy deposit of nature'. After Moss Aztec had been successfully introduced the company offered additional lines, including Chromal, Landsun, Montene, Pereco and Persian.

◆ **Zane Ware vase, c.1920**
One of many varieties of artware made by Peters and Reed, and later by Zane Pottery, the red-clay vessel was decorated by dripping contrasting slip around the body. 358

◆ **Moss Aztec bowl, c.1915**
The Moss Aztec line was perfectly suited for use with plant materials. Glazed inside in order to make them impermeable, vessels had an unglazed exterior finish with an earthy appearance. 359

Peters retired in 1920, and the following year the firm's name was changed to the Zane Pottery by Reed and Harry S. McClelland, the company secretary, who had bought Peters' share. Reed died in 1922. Under McClelland the company continued to make garden flower pots, decorative garden pieces, jars, vases, birdbaths and art pottery, using a white clay after 1926. After McClelland died in 1931 his wife kept the pottery going, eventually selling it to Lawton Gonder in 1941. Gonder Ceramic Arts made vases and other speciality goods, also in white clay, including console sets and cookie jars. The pottery also made some dinnerware. Gonder developed commercial flambé and gold crackle glazes in addition to a standard repertoire of bright coral, yellow, blue, turquoise and celadon glazes. There was much demand for his products.

In 1946 Gonder enlarged the factory, and shortly afterwards set up an operation for making lamps in a lumber mill. (The latter company, the Elgee Pottery, was destroyed by fire in 1954.) When competition from foreign manufacturers threatened to erode business in the mid-1950s, Gonder switched to tiles as the firm's principal product.

KEY FACTS

Location: Zanesville, Ohio, USA.
Important dates: Traded as Peters & Reed 1898–1921; as Zane Pottery 1921–41; and as Gonder Ceramic Arts 1941–57.
Production: Flower containers, garden ware.
Principal designer: Frank Ferrell.

MARKS

'ZPCo' monogram used by Zane Pottery. No mark used by Peters & Reed. 'Gonder USA' and 'Gonder Original' are incised marks.

◆ **Gonder vase, c.1950**
Gonder's flower containers display a great variety of motif, from flowers, birds and animals to shells and fish. Variety and affordability together make Gonder an interesting collectable. 360

PFALTZGRAFF POTTERY

This pottery is considered the oldest family-owned pottery operating continuously in the USA. Indeed, the first generation of the Pfaltzgraff family in America began making redware in 1811. The name Pfaltzgraff Stoneware Company was used for the first time in 1894, but the company's product, utilitarian stoneware jugs and jars, had not changed for several generations. In 1906 the company was reorganized as the Pfaltzgraff Pottery Company, and its current site was established in West York, Pennsylvania, after a fire destroyed the plant on Belvidere Street. Seven years later the firm installed a machine for making redware flower pots, and by 1927 flower pots and florists' items made up more than 73 per cent of production. The balance included stoneware jugs and agricultural products, such as rabbit feeders and poultry fountains, as well as blue-mottled mugs, spittoons, salt boxes and butter jars. The blue mottling was applied with sponges cut in various shapes.

In 1931 the pottery began glazing the standard red flower pot, which became a large sales item with customers such as F. W. Woolworth. A line of flower containers was made between 1932 and 1937. The use of dark-green and bright rosy-pink glazes over a variety of decorative shapes is distinctive. During the late 1930s the company followed the lead of similar potteries by adding a line of cookware with

➤ **Utilitarian stoneware, 1870–89**
Marked by H. B. Pfaltzgraff, these jars are decorated with the brushed blue flower typically used in the mid-Atlantic region during the third quarter of the 19th century. 361

Country-Time tableware, c.1952
Ben Seibel initially designed the Country-Time line as table accessories, with dinnerware as an afterthought. At the time Pfaltzgraff was not making plates, cups and saucers to any great extent. Decoration consisted of stylized leaves, fruits and flowers. The snowflake design came from the earlier Gourmet Snowflake line. 362

bright, colourful glazes. At first this included casseroles, pitchers, teapots and bowls in a variety of colours over stoneware, white ware and coloured bodies. A line of bakeware called Gourmet was introduced about 1940. Gourmet was unglazed on the outside but had an opaque glossy brown glaze lining and covers. It was followed in the early 1940s by Ceramex Kitchenware, with rainbow-coloured glazes.

Although the Depression and World War II had a significant effect on production and product marketability, the subsequent years showed a steady improvement as existing product lines were broadened and new lines were added. The new Muggsy line was popular between 1950 and 1960. Designed by Dorothy and Norman Jessop, it included character mugs – Pickled Pete, Flirty Gertie, Diamond Dick (a baseball player), Muscles Moe and Fairway Freddie – a jar called Pretzel Pete and an ashtray called Burnie. The cookie jar in the line, Derby Dan, was one of several being made by Pfaltzgraff at the time. The Old Lady in the Shoe, the Cookie Time cookie clock and the Cookie Cop (a fat policeman) were popular cookie jars from the firm's small repertoire.

In the late 1940s the Gourmet line was expanded by the addition of many colours and a few new shapes: Gourmet Delight, Gourmet Copenhagen and Gourmet a la Française (this last came in Tangier Tan and Algerian Charcoal Brown). In 1950 Gourmet Royale, a line of giftware with solid glossy glazes (Glacier Brown and Stardust Pink) and a distinctive white dripped edge, was added to the line. From the Gourmet Royale line Pfaltzgraff developed its first dinnerware, packaged as four-piece place settings, as a result of introducing a dinner plate in 1951 to the shapes it had been making for several years. The success of this first try at dinnerware led the pottery to expand the concept, which eventually grew into its principal product during the second half of the century.

Ben Seibel designed Country-Time dinnerware and serving ware. Introduced in 1952, this line was promoted as America's most complete line of serving accessories, sold with its own place settings. It had a

Artware, 1932–37
Pfaltzgraff's artware line was moulded and attractively decorated in a variety of airbrushed, mottled and crystalline effects in blue, green, pink, mauve, pumpkin and yellow. 363

streamlined post-war shape that was decorated with stylized fruit motifs in several colours of textured glazes, including Saffron Yellow, Aztec Blue, Smoke Gray and Teal Blue. Additional lines were introduced during the 1960s, including Country Casual and Heritage. Heritage, from 1963, was designed by Georges Briard as a plain panelled shape with a prominent rim. Initially it came in four traditional colours – Bennington Brown, Williamsburg Green, Burnt Olive and York White; the last is still in the line. Thus Pfaltzgraff entered the dinnerware business gradually, but its early successes, such as Gourmet Royale and Heritage, convinced the company that it should continue the expansion of this area of production. By the mid-1960s Pfaltzgraff had an in-house design staff and an ambitious programme for upgrading equipment and processes in the factory.

Yorktowne, introduced in 1967, was the first in-house dinnerware pattern; its blue flower on a grey background is reminiscent of the company's early utilitarian stoneware. In the early 1970s Pfaltzgraff's marketing plan shifted the emphasis from giftware shops to department stores, which greatly expanded the markets for its ware. Village, introduced in 1975, took advantage of Yorktowne's popularity by using a similar stylized folk pattern in earth tones. The firm's growth was explosive during this period. Several new plants were added and processes greatly improved. Market testing led to the introduction of new modern patterns such as Aura and Sky, with pastel-coloured rim bands, in the late 1980s. At the same time an extensive line of fine bone china was introduced at affordable prices in patterns that would appeal to young brides. This line has since been discontinued, although Pfaltzgraff's stoneware tableware continues to be widely popular in the contemporary American dinnerware market.

During the late 1970s three dinnerware lines, Gourmet, Heritage and Yorktowne, accounted for almost three-quarters of the firm's total production. The balance was made up of mugs, ashtrays, commercial flower containers and contract work, such as crock pots for Rival and airline trays. New techniques developed for the contract work directly affected Pfaltzgraff's own production. The firm diversified into metal products and built a new factory in Dover, Pennsylvania, to make fondue pots and pewter and copper items to complement the Yorktowne and Village lines.

◆ **Yorktowne plate, late 1960s**
Pfaltzgraff's Yorktowne on a stoneware body may be its most recognizable dinnerware pattern. The design was based on familiar 19th-century utilitarian stoneware decoration. 364

◆ **Bone china, late 1980s**
Hampton was one of the first nine of Pfaltzgraff's bone-china patterns introduced to the trade in 1988. 365

The metal ware never became successful, but its introduction led Pfaltzgraff to develop licensing agreements for other tabletop products with its patterns. Also during the late 1970s, the company decided to take control of its own marketing, opening outlet stores from 1977 and establishing a direct-mail operation. At the same time new production systems were put in place. The construction of another new factory gave the firm the opportunity to introduce highly mechanized systems for taking in raw materials and processing them into finished goods. The USA's first dry-press tableware operation was installed there in the late 1980s. Items are formed, finished, decorated and glazed in one continuous process.

KEY FACTS

Location: York, Pennsylvania, USA.
Important dates: Founded 1894 by family active in pottery business since 1811. Still active.
Production: Utilitarian stoneware, cookware, novelties, dinnerware.
Principal designers: Ben Seibel, David Walsh.

MARKS

Ware usually marked with company name in association with 'USA', sometimes incorporating outline of a Bavarian castle. Recent marks often include line or pattern name as well. Outline of a keystone used in early marks.

THE
PFALTZGRAFF
POTTERY
© USA

◆ **Naturewood Ware, 1997**
Pfaltzgraff's latest entry in the casual china line features muted colours and motifs drawn from nature. 366

PICKARD CHINA COMPANY

Wilder Pickard established a studio for decorating china in Wisconsin in 1894, but by 1898 had moved to Chicago, Illinois. The decorators used mainly French and American china blanks, and many stock patterns were developed, including Aura Mosaic, Twin Lilies and Aura Argenta; all-over gold-etch patterns were sought after. Unique decorations and commissions were also executed. From 1930 to 1938 the firm experimented with making china under the direction of Wilder's son, Henry Austin Pickard, and in 1938 introduced a line of china dinnerware. In 1939 Wilder died, and Henry Austin took over the business; eventually china decoration was phased out. During World War II Pickard made gravy boats for the US Navy and in 1977 began making china for US embassies.

Edward Challinor is probably the company's most famous decorator. Brocade, designed by John Eustice, was its best-selling china pattern. The early studio-decorated china is very popular with collectors today, while the dinnerware is not yet seen as collectable.

KEY FACTS

Location: Chicago and Antioch, Illinois, USA.

Important dates: Founded 1894. Still active.

Production: China giftware, teaware and dinnerware.

MARKS

Decorating company's mark often used with maker's mark.

◆ **Hand-painted china, c.1910**
Pickard had many standard hand-painted patterns, including Aura Argenta Linear, seen here on a cream jug and covered sugar bowl. 367

PILKINGTON'S TILE & POTTERY CO.

The company was established by four Pilkington brothers after clay was discovered during a search for coal seams. Manufacture of decorative tiles began in 1893 under the guidance of William Burton, a young chemist who previously had been in charge of Josiah Wedgwood's (*see* p.230) mixing of clay, colours and glazes. He soon joined forces with his brother Joseph, and they were responsible for the artistic and technical development in the firm's formative years. They gathered about them a strong team of designers and craftsmen, the earliest of whom were the chief designer, John Chambers, and the modeller Joseph Kwiatowski.

Many of the new glazes developed for tile production were later used for decorating ornamental ware, made from about 1898 when the firm engaged Robert Tunnicliffe, an ex-Minton (*see* p.132) thrower. His duties included making moulded vases and small ornamental items such as buttons and hat-pin tops, probably to supplement income from pottery brought in for glazing and decoration by the Firth family of Kirkby Lonsdale. Edward Thomas Radford (*see* p.167) joined the firm as a thrower in 1903 for the start of full production of Lancastrian Pottery, the name given to the new range of decorative glazed ware.

Within two years William Burton's passion for research into the secrets of ancient glazes led to the development of a variety of glazes, including an opalescent effect (a glaze showing changing colours like opal) discovered by chance late in 1903. The following year the examples were shown at Graves Gallery, London, with other Lancastrian glazes. Early shapes were thrown and based on Greek, Persian and Chinese originals. By 1906 the first lustre pottery was being produced, and lustre ware became the firm's main output apart from tiles.

A new team of artists headed by Gordon Forsyth, who had worked for Minton, Hollins & Co. (*see* p.135), was engaged. Among artist-designers associated with the firm were Richard Joyce, William S. Mycock, Charles Cundall, Gladys Rodgers, Annie Burton, Jessie Jones and Dorothy Dacre. Richard Joyce worked for Moore Bros until Bernard Moore (*see* p.138) established his studio in Wolfe Street, Stoke. Pilkington's also commissioned work from leading designers such as Lewis F. Day, C. F. A. Voysey and Walter Crane, although only the latter is known to have designed for the pottery. As a rule, Pilkington artists were influenced in their designs by art of the past but were allowed to treat each piece of pottery as they

→ Royal Lancastrian vase, 1932
This vase is evidence of the exciting lustre effects achieved by Pilkington's chemists. The artists at the pottery drew on heraldic and Arts and Crafts imagery for their designs. This pattern, reminiscent of designs by the architect C. F. A. Voysey, was painted by W. S. Mycock. 368

→ Royal Lancastrian catalogue, 1930s
This page from an early-1930s factory catalogue features a range of Lapis Ware. The subdued colours and semi-abstract patterns express the spirit of the 1930s and reveal the adaptability of the Royal Lancastrian artists. 369

◀ **Royal Lancastrian catalogue, 1930s**
In its early years Royal Lancastrian was known for its rich monochrome glazed ware. The catalogue reveals the lasting popularity of some of these dramatic glazes. [370]

◀ **Vine vase, 1929**
Painted by William S. Mycock, this late Pilkington vase shows the move towards the hand-thrown look that was typical of the 1930s. [371]

wished, so that individual styles began to emerge. For example, Forsyth produced many heraldic designs, Cundall favoured mythological subjects and heraldic beasts, and Joyce's work reveals Japanese influences in his treatment of animal and fish subjects, while Mycock specialized in painted ships, birds and flowers as well as modelled animals.

The Lapis Ware range was introduced in 1929 and developed over the next year. The design was applied direct to the body in the biscuit state and covered with an eggshell glaze. A pearl-white version of this glaze was used to decorate a series of modernist stylized bowls and vases designed by Joseph Burton around 1934. Lustre effects are among the most desirable, but this was most difficult to produce, and very little was made after about 1930 or once the production of Lapis Ware was established. Other decorations from this period include sgraffito and incised designs.

Production ceased in 1938 but was restarted in 1948 under William Barnes, who designed most of the pieces. He left the pottery in 1957, and soon after the department closed. Production of Lancastrian Pottery was revived in December 1972 and continued until December 1975.

KEY FACTS

Location: Clifton Junction, Manchester, UK.
Important dates: Founded c.1891. Closed 1964. Ornamental earthenware made c.1896–1938 and 1948–57. Tile business merged with Carter, Stabler & Adams, 1964. Pottery revived 1972; closed 1975.
Production: Ornamental earthenware, tiles.
Principal designers: Gordon Forsyth, Richard Joyce, William S. Mycock, Charles Cundall, Gladys Rodgers, Annie Burton, Jessie Jones, Dorothy Dacre.
Trade names: Pilkington's, Lancastrian Pottery, Royal Lancastrian, Lapis Ware.

MARKS

Early mark 'P' incised. 'P and L' monogram with bees, printed 1904–5, impressed until 1914. Variations of this mark used until 1938. Artist's or designer's initials or monogram used on most pieces.

R. H. & S. L. PLANT

In 1881 R. H. Plant established the firm of R. H. Plant & Co. At the Carlisle Works, Longton, Staffordshire, he and his brother, S. L. Plant, made breakfast ware and teaware, trinket sets, souvenirs and giftware. In addition they opened a branch at the Stanley Works, Longton, which they operated as Plant Bros., producing household ware between 1889 and 1906. The brothers built a reputation for quality with their many new specialist lines in bone china and in 1898 moved from the Carlisle Works to the Tuscan Works, also in Longton, operating under their joint names. From this time production was substantially expanded.

The firm's Tuscan heraldic china was marketed from at least 1908 until the mid-1920s. Between the wars the catalogue listed a range of modernist-style ware, including dressing-table sets, bird and animal models, crinoline figures, novelties and high-class children's china. Perhaps the most collectable of the latter are the series designed by the children's book illustrator Gladys Peto, including Tinker, Tailor, Soldier, Sailor, and a later series called Kiddies-in-Wonderland, launched in 1947.

Under the government's Concentration Scheme the pottery continued in production throughout World War II, and after the war underwent extensive modernization. In 1946 it was making breakfast sets, coffee pots, coffee sets, eggcups, fancies, fruit sets, hotel ware, morning sets, novelties, sandwich sets, supper sets, teapots, teasets and toilet ware. It continues today as part of the Josiah Wedgwood & Sons Group (*see* p.230), producing a full range of bone china, hotel ware, fashionable tableware and ornamental ware.

▲ Advertisement, 1921
Models of birds and butterflies in Plant's Tuscan China with hand-painted decoration were marketed aggressively in the 1920s. 372

◆ Teaware advertisement, 1954
In the 1950s Plant's Tuscan range included a wide selection of bone-china teaware patterns, mostly traditional in inspiration. 373

POINTON & CO.

The pottery traded as R. G. Scrivener & Co. from 1870 to 1883. From 1883, at the Norfolk Street Works in Shelton, Pointon & Co. produced a range of good-quality decorated and plain ware, including tea, breakfast and dessert services and fancies in china as well as toilet sets and ordinary domestic articles in earthenware.

From 1917 the company traded as Ford & Pointon, producing a wide range of decorative items, tableware and crested china. Ford & Pointon became a branch of J. A. Robinson (*see* p.178) in 1919 and about two years later amalgamated with Cauldon (*see* p.40) and Coalport (*see* p.47).

POOLE POTTERY

The tradition of pottery-making in the Dorset town of Poole is centuries old, but the company now called the Poole Pottery was founded in 1873 when Jesse Carter bought and enlarged the pottery established by James Walker. In 1901, after Jesse Carter retired, his sons Owen and Charles formed Carter & Co. From this time the pottery produced an expanding range of work, and lustre-glazed vases, candlesticks, dishes, jardinières and other useful ware became an increasing part of its output. After World War I the demand for ranges of decorative pottery grew, and to satisfy this the firm expanded production and began to show examples from its new range at the British Industries Fairs. The first Handcraft Pottery catalogue was issued in 1920, featuring simple hand-painted ware designed by James Radley Young. About this time the decision was taken to set up an independent but wholly owned subsidiary company to expand production of ornamental and useful ware. Charles Carter and his son Cyril invited the artist, designer and goldsmith Harold Stabler to become a partner. Stabler encouraged the Potteries-born potter John Adams and his wife Truda, herself an artist and designer, to join them.

In 1921 Carter, Stabler & Adams was formed to produce pottery which was modern in style but made using the best traditional handcraft methods. In addition to its own progressive designers the pottery also employed outside designers such as Edward Bawden, and during the 1920s and 1930s its name became synonymous with elegant and decorative modernism. Other designers who worked for the pottery included Dora Batty, who created, among other lines, some charming children's ware, and Phoebe Stabler, Harold's wife, who developed a series of pottery figures which were later made at Poole with richly coloured glazes. Phoebe's sister, Minnie McLeish, also designed for the firm, but John Adams was the designer of most of the shapes and Truda Adams (later Truda Carter), designed most of the freely painted patterns, including the bright floral designs which were to become the pottery's hallmark.

Among the first productions were unglazed ware with hand-painted brown and terracotta decoration; grey semi-stoneware with designs painted on to the unfired glaze; and red-bodied earthenware with

⬥ Lustre vase, c.1906
Owen Carter's lustres were the first Poole art pottery; they were made from 1900 to 1918 in Art Nouveau-inspired forms. [374]

⬥ Covered jar, c.1922
Simple sprigged floral designs, freely painted on to rich opaque glazes, are characteristic of the first ware produced by Carter, Stabler & Adams. [375]

⬥ Truda Adams vase, c.1930
From 1921 Carter, Stabler & Adams made ranges of decorative pottery that were hand-painted with the dynamic contemporary designs of Truda Adams (later Truda Carter). This vase, with its French-inspired design, is an example of English Jazz Age modernism at its best. [376]

variations of the hand-painted 'Portuguese' stripe and geometric border designs as well as floral sprig patterns, some of which were produced before the new partnership. By the mid-1920s Truda Adams' more vibrant and colourful style of ware was being made. A number of her patterns were later adapted for brooches, in production from 1939. The ornamental range was expanded to include a wide variety of new models such as The Galleon, designed by Harold Stabler, animal models, book-ends and candlesticks, some of which were decorated with glazes by John Adams. Among other glazes were Chinese blues, powder and sapphire blues, and some streaked and mottled glazes based on wood ash. The Picotee range of aerographically sprayed colours applied in rings around the body of the ware was introduced in 1932; the orange-pink earthenware body was superseded by cream or white by 1930. Over the next decade production became fully standardized and consisted mainly of tableware and table accessories such as John Adams's Streamline tableware of the mid-1930s.

Post-war the company sold a large quantity of undecorated Utility tableware but the mainstay of the revived post-war production was painted ware, Poole's most characteristic product. Many pre-war shapes continued in production, including vases and ornaments, domestic ware, animal and bird figures, shells and book-ends. New additions to the range included turned banded ware and sgraffito or incised decoration, followed by Alfred Read's elegant and free-form 1950s ware with its textile-inspired abstract decoration.

John Adams's tableware shape Wimborne, with a two-colour finish, was made briefly before the war. This was followed by Sherborne, a slip-decorated tableware range designed by Adams before the war but not produced until 1949. However, Streamline became the standard such range and was very popular, decorated either with Truda Carter's and, later, Ruth Pavely's simplified designs or with a revised range of two-colour glazes marketed as Twintone. Under the inspiration of Robert Jefferson, post-war developments included the introduction of new domestic ware, including his own oven-to-table ware ranges from the 1960s, which were brought out in a variety of patterns and colourways.

The 1960s also saw the great expansion of the Poole studio under Jefferson. With Guy Sydenham he produced individual pieces which launched the studio when first shown to the public in 1961. From these

● **Truda Adams Persian Deer vase, 1930s**
One of Poole's best-known hand-painted patterns is Truda Adams's Persian Deer, seen here on a 1930s vase. 377

◀ **Streamline coffee set, c.1938**
Designed by John Adams, this fluid shape exemplifies Poole's modernist approach during the 1930s. Similarly contemporary in feel are the two-tone finish and the soft vellum glazes. This style of tableware was also closely associated with Poole in the 1950s and 1960s. 378

emerged a new series of shapes, and experimentation with glazes and colours led to the launch of a new range of decorative ware, Delphis. Tony Morris joined the design team in 1963, and over the next two years he and Jefferson, with selected paintresses, further developed this range and set its distinctive style, which is marked by exciting shapes, vibrant colour-ways and dramatic, mainly abstract designs.

Delphis remained in production until 1980. Among other notable ranges from the 1970s are the series of map plates by Robert Jefferson and Tony Morris's Cathedral and Calendar plates. In 1972 Barbara Linley Adams, an internationally recognized sculptor and ceramic modeller, joined Poole and produced a series of stoneware wildlife sculptures, plates and related ware designed for the emerging collectors' market. The first model was Wren on a Branch, and in the 11 years she worked with the firm she provided it with 100 models for production. Ros Summerfelt designed the Camelot series of plates in 1977 and developed the Beardsley Collection two years later. A selection of jewellery and other ranges includes Bow Bells, Country Lane, Kandy and Wild Garden, the latter designed by Elaine Williamson, who headed the design unit in the early 1980s. She was also the designer of Nursery Rhymes children's ware in 1979 and the Concert tableware shape in 1985.

Nursery ware has been an important part of production since the earliest days of Carter, Stabler & Adams and is increasingly collectable. Many artists have worked in this area, including Dora Batty and Truda Carter in the 1920s and 1930s, Alfred Read in the mid-1930s, and Eileen McGrath, who supplied Poole with stylish nursery ware designs around 1934. Robert Jefferson designed a three-piece children's set decorated with animal screenprints in 1963, and Elaine Williamson's Nursery Rhymes design was introduced in 1979, followed by her adaption of Hambro Industries' My Little Pony designs in 1985. The children's range of nine shapes introduced in 1994 and entitled The Mad Hatter's Tea Party was developed by Sarah Chalmers from an idea by Christopher Woodhead.

Throughout the 1980s Poole relied on both its own design team and outside artists and designers, including John Bromley and Robert Welsh. More important was the contribution made by the Queensberry Hunt Partnership and David Queensberry, who took over the role of design director for Poole. Their first commission resulted in the Flair tableware

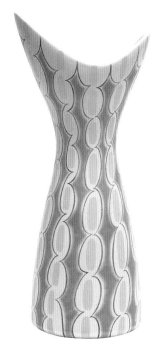

▲ **Free-form vase, c.1958**
Dramatic designs by Alfred Read and Guy Sydenham took Poole into the 1950s and reflected the contemporary enthusiasm for abstract textiles and Scandinavian style. 379

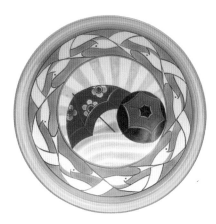

▲ **Sally Tuffin dish, c.1996**
During the 1990s Sally Tuffin designed a number of Poole art ranges, among which was this parasol dish. 380

▶ **Delphis vases, late 1960s**
With its strong shapes and exuberant colours, Poole's Delphis ware is entirely characteristic of the 1960s. The abstract patterns were individually created by the Poole paintresses. 381

also designed Astral tableware, introduced in 1989, and a group of modern decorative ware with new shapes and glaze effects. Notable among these are Calypso, introduced in 1984 and brought out in various colourways, and the fluted Corinthian range. These were followed in 1990 by the marbled finish known as Cello ware. After decades of ownership by Pilkington and the Thomas Tilling Group, Poole became independent again in 1992. After a brief period of closure in 2003, it is now in business again.

◄ Fresco tableware, 1997
Since the 1980s Poole has increasingly concentrated on tableware, producing a range of simple patterns in informal styles that are aimed at the casual dining market. 382

> **KEY FACTS**
>
> **Location:** Poole, Dorset, UK.
> **Important dates:** Founded 1873. Carter, Stabler & Adams founded 1921. Bought by Pilkington's Tiles and renamed Poole Pottery 1963. Independent from 1992.
> **Production:** Earthenware.
>
> **MARKS**
>
> Dolphin symbol, usually printed, used since 1960s. Earlier, impressed, marks used Poole name or 'Carter Stabler Adams Ltd'.
>
> POOLE ENGLAND

THOMAS POOLE

From 1880, in Longton, Staffordshire, this firm made mass-market china and earthenware. In 1946 its catalogue included tea, breakfast, coffee, dinner, morning, sandwich and supper sets, fancies and hotel ware. It merged with Gladstone China in 1948, and from 1952 the pottery traded as Royal Stafford China. John Maddock & Sons (*see* p.121) bought the Royal Stafford China trade mark in 1985, and in 1994 it merged with Barratt's (*see* p.20) as Royal Stafford Tableware (*see* p.190).

> **MARKS**
>
> Various printed marks used, often incorporating 'Royal Stafford China'.
>
> ROYAL STAFFORD
> BONE CHINA
> MADE IN ENGLAND

POPE-GOSSER CHINA COMPANY

Founded in 1902 by Charles F. Gosser and Bentley Pope, the Pope-Gosser China Company originally intended to specialize in china tableware, but switched to a semi-vitreous body. Pope, an Englishman, had long experience in the potteries of Trenton, New Jersey, in the 1870s and 1880s, and worked for Knowles, Taylor & Knowles (*see* p.109) from the early 1890s until 1902. Pope-Gosser's products received medals at the St Louis World's Fair in 1904, for superior semi-porcelain, and at the Jamestown Tercentennial Exposition in 1907, for plain and decorated china and semi-porcelain. From 1929 to 1932 Pope-Gosser was involved with the American China Corporation, a merger of several potteries formed to counter the effects of the Great Depression on the pottery industry. In 1932 Frank Judge reorganized the company to produce semi-porcelain. The factory closed in 1958.

Over the years, Pope-Gosser's shapes and decorations followed the popular styles in American tableware. Louvre and Edgemore are among the patterns that are most sought after by collectors today.

> **KEY FACTS**
>
> **Location:** Coshocton, Ohio, USA.
> **Important dates:** Founded 1902. Closed 1958.
> **Production:** Semi-porcelain and china tableware.
>
> **MARKS**
>
> Include company name, often with pattern name.
>
> POPE-GOSSER CHINA. MADE IN U.S.A ROSE POINT 40 WARRANTED COIN GOLD

◆ Rose Point demitasse, c.1940
A small rose moulded into the handle identifies the pattern as Pope-Gosser's Rose Point, introduced in white in 1934. Decals were added in the next year. The pattern was so popular that silver and glassware were made to match. 383

PORTMEIRION POTTERIES

In 1960 Susan Williams-Ellis and her husband, Euan Cooper-Willis, bought the small pottery-decorating business of A. E. Gray & Co. (*see* p.78). Sir Clough, Susan's father and the architect of the village of Portmeirion, North Wales, had long been a friend of A. E. Gray, who had produced tableware for the Portmeirion Hotel and small items for the Portmeirion shop. In 1953 Susan and her husband, invited to take over the shop, approached Gray for special items of stock. Early designs for the shop included copper-plate reproduction prints in plain black and white, finished with splattered lustre, and Portmeirion Dolphin storage jars with printed labels engraved from Susan's own drawing.

After buying Gray & Co., Susan used malachite decals to create a range of richly gilded ornamental pieces as well as Gray's Moss Agate range, which, like Malachite, was expensive to produce. More commercial was her Gold Diamond ware, launched in 1961 and consisting of cups and saucers, jugs, bowls and apothecary jars produced on shapes bought in by Gray and decorated with either hand-painted geometric diamonds in black, silver and gold lustre or six different black-and-white cross-hatched diamond patterns from a copper plate. This was Susan's first design for coffee ware, a line that was later to be very successful for Portmeirion.

In December 1961 Susan and Euan took over the Stoke firm of Kirkhams (*see* p.105) and from 1 January 1962 they started trading as Portmeirion Potteries. Susan started to design shapes rather than surface patterns alone. Totem, launched in 1963, was based on cylindrical moulds found at the Kirkhams factory. These tall, straight coffee sets were an immediate success. Botanic Garden was created in 1972 and Pomona on the Romantic shape was introduced ten years later.

Portmeirion has continued to diversify its range of products. New tableware designs have included Welsh Dresser and Blue Harvest in 1992

⬥ **Moss Agate beaker, c.1960**
An unusual process developed by Susan Williams-Ellis has been used to decorate this early beaker: the engraving has been overlaid with rich gilding. 384

⬥ **Magic City coffee pot, c.1966**
Tall Serif shapes, such as that seen here, helped to establish Portmeirion as a style leader. This was one of its most popular patterns. 385

⬥ **Botanic Garden teaware, c.1975**
With designs based on early-19th-century floral prints, Botanic Garden proved an instant success and has remained Portmeirion's flagship pattern. Today the range includes about 160 ceramic items. 386

and 1995 respectively, designed by Susan's youngest daughter, Angharad Menna. China was introduced in 1994, when a range of shapes and four new patterns were launched: Welsh Wild Flowers, Summer Garland, Ladies' Flower Garden and Ancestral Jewel, which was designed by Susan's daughter Anwyl.

The hinged-box collection in Botanic Garden and Pomona consists of enamelled copper and china hinged boxes. Launched in 1996, these miniature versions of classic Portmeirion shapes are proving popular with collectors.

◗ **Jupiter coffee pot, c.1964**
Portmeirion pioneered the embossed shapes that became universal in the late 1960s. 387

POUNTNEY & CO.

The firm specialized in decoration using decals, but such ware was a small part of its output, which included sanitary ware, dinnerware, toilet sets, advertising ware and badged ware. Hand-painting was also important, and Blue Scroll, designed in the 1930s and painted exclusively by Charlie Smith, formerly at Wemyss (*see* p.237), was one of its best-loved patterns. Pountney introduced Amberone creamy-coloured glaze in the 1920s and several modern shapes in the 1930s, including J. F. Price's Dorland and Academy tableware. Price also designed a series of kitchen-ware and the underglaze painted pattern Bellflower of 1940. During the 1950s and 1960s the design team was headed by Kenneth Clark, who probably designed the Mooncurve shape. From this period are contemporary-style patterns such as Seedcress (by Clark), Lilybell and Golden Days. In the early 1960s Honor Elliot designed oven-to-table ware with an on-glaze printed Old Bristol Delft pattern and a range of kitchenware with underglaze prints depicting cutlery. In 1962 Pountney acquired the name, goodwill, moulds and pattern books of Cauldon (*see* p.40). From the mid-1960s it increased production of decal-decorated advertising and souvenir goods. In 1969 it became Cauldon Bristol Potteries Ltd, and in 1971 was bought by A. G. Richardson & Co. The latter firm was later acquired by Enoch Wedgwood (*see* Josiah Wedgwood & Sons, p.230).

◄ **Cock and Hen vase, c.1910**
Pountney bought reproduction rights for this pattern from Wemyss c.1905. It was painted by George Stewart. 388

◗ **Dorland vegetable dish, c.1935**
Designed by J. F. Price, this shape takes its name from the Dorland Hall Exhibition of 1933. 389

164

PRICE BROTHERS

This well-established earthenware manufacturer is best known for its production of teapots for all markets. Although the firm has been a follower rather than an innovator of styles, in the 1930s it produced some interesting modern handcraft teapot patterns and a line of Mattona Art Ware. The pottery continued in production throughout World War II, making many of its usual lines in teapots, teapot sets, fancies, sets of jugs and chamber pots, although its priority was export orders.

Under wartime regulations the production of the Kensington Pottery (*see* p.103), another Burslem-based earthenware manufacturer, was concentrated at Price Brothers' Top Bridge Pottery. Here the firm continued to produce Kensington's main lines of matt-glazed and lustre fancies, novelty lines, mugs and beakers. Price Brothers' 1946 catalogue included animal figures, ashtrays, chamber pots, cruet sets, eggcups, fancies, figurines and statuettes, jugs, mugs, novelties, teapots and vases.

In 1962 Price Bros merged with the Kensington Pottery, and the new company began trading as Price & Kensington. From this time the firm operated from premises at Longport, Staffordshire.

Recent catalogues included tableware, kitchenware and children's gift sets decorated with patterns such as Cockerel, Gingham and Cactus. Also made are Walking Wares, based on Carlton Ware originals, and a Cottage Ware range. Popular collectables are teapots in the form of animals, cars, telephones and postboxes. The pottery closed in 2003 and the name was sold.

KEY FACTS

Location: Top Bridge Works and Albion Works, Burslem, Staffordshire, UK.
Important dates: Founded 1896. Merged with Kensington Pottery as Price & Kensington 1962. Joined Arthur Wood Group mid-1980s. Closed 2003.
Production: Earthenware.

● Storage jar c.1955
This jar with banded decoration is from the Kitchenware range; it was advertised in *The Pottery Gazette* as ideal for 'the modern housewife'. 390

◆ Price teapot, c.1960
The combination of a traditional shape with a contemporary floral pattern is characteristic of many Price Brothers products. 391

PRINKNASH ABBEY POTTERY

Before making their own pottery the Benedictine monks of Prinknash Abbey sold religious objects made for them by Royal Doulton (*see* p.187). The chance discovery of a seam of clay when foundations were being dug for the new Abbey resulted in their starting their own pottery, in 1942. At first they worked in a small hut in the grounds of the old Abbey, but in 1974 they transferred production to new premises.

In the early 1980s Prinknash produced a range of children's ware based on the television series *Moschops*. The range consisted of a plate, bowl, and two types of mug with a choice of five characters. Later there followed Bunnies and Teddy Bears, also based on children's television series.

By the late 1990s production included a significant range of tableware, cookware, fancies, buffet ware and giftware. Patterns include the decal-decorated Florabunda and Abbeyfruits, and Dickens, a white embossed design. Prinknash also has a small decorating studio where it makes

◆ Jug, 1960s
Metallic glazes on red earthenware bodies are typical of Prinknash. 392

hand-decorated items such as personalized commemoratives. Throughout its history the Prinknash Pottery has retained many traditional craft-making skills. Output includes some of the vases and tankards designed in the earliest days of the pottery, notably the Portway vase.

In 1997 Prinknash commissioned Clifford Richards, a leading graphic designer, to create new tableware sets. Plate sets include Green Fingers, Temptations and Bewick's Beasties. This last is a set of six coaster plates with centres featuring Thomas Bewick's original prints and a striking black printed border.

In the same year Prinknash Abbey offered the pottery, which was at that time employing 27, for sale. It was quickly acquired by the Welsh Porcelain Co. of Maesteg, Mid Glamorgan, a wholly owned subsidiary of Heredities Ltd of Kirkby Stephen, Cumbria. Production ceased in 2002.

◆ Greenfingers tableware, 1990s
Designed by Clifford Richards, these stylish items define the new Prinknash work. Related patterns feature equally realistic cherries and Bewick's animal engravings. [393]

KEY FACTS

Location: Prinknash Abbey, Granham, Gloucestershire, UK.
Important dates: Founded 1942. Closed 2002.
Production: Earthenware.

MARKS

Various printed or impressed marks with pottery's name or monk's head used from 1945.

PURBECK POTTERY

The pottery was established in 1966, and its early output was mainly tableware designed by Robert Jefferson. One of the first new shapes was Country Fare, available with two decorations: Pheasant, in stoneware glazes which are banded in greens and browns or which run into the flutes of hollowware, and a slip-sprayed white opaque glaze, which appears to be tinged with celadon green. This line was followed by a coffee set with a gold spot-decorated band on a black matt background or a brown matt glaze. The company continued to develop its ornamental stoneware ranges and to introduce new lines, including money boxes with decal decoration, tankards with hand-painted lustre, vases and a series of naturalistic birds and animal studies modelled by Jefferson in the late 1960s. In 1995 the pottery moved from Westbourne, Bournemouth, to Poole, also in Dorset.

◆ Toast tableware, c.1968
Designed by Robert Jefferson, who had previously worked for Poole, this popular range remained in production until the 1990s. The combination of modern shapes and a handcraft look is characteristic of the Purbeck style. [394]

◆ Stoneware vases, trays and ornaments, 1960s
Robert Jefferson's familiarity with studio-inspired ware informed this range. Deliberately roughly finished, with matt handcraft shades set off by pools of colour, these pieces echo the styles of contemporary Troika pottery. [395]

The pottery has earned its reputation for quality vitrified stoneware such as ovenproof dinnerware, teaware, coffee sets and decorated giftware. It uses traditional methods and extremely fine and strong clays from Dorset's Purbeck Hills. It also continues to use the same glazes, which are produced from natural materials completely free from lead. Today the firm concentrates on producing tableware.

◆ **Rondo tableware, 1990s**
Introduced in 1993, this design is Purbeck's best-selling tableware range. [396]

KEY FACTS

Location: Branksome China Works, Westbourne, Bournemouth 1966–95, Hamworthy 1995–, Dorset, UK.
Important dates: Founded 1966. Still active.
Production: Vitrified stoneware.

MARKS

This mark used from 1960s; other marks include double 'P' monogram.

QUEEN'S CHINA

Based in Longton, Staffordshire, Queen's China has its roots in two other Longton china establishments, George Warrilow & Sons and Taylor & Kent (*see* p.216), whose histories date back to 1875 and 1876 respectively. These two firms merged in 1989 to form Crownford China, which in 1994 became Queen's China, a division of Churchill (*see* p.41). Queen's continues the earlier tradition of making fine-quality china tea and dinner ware, children's ware and mugs, as well as giftware and collectables.

MARKS

Variations of this standard mark in use since c.1900.

RADFORD HANDCRAFT POTTERY

Edward Thomas Brown Radford was born into a well-known family of potters and had the benefit of studying the technique of throwing and modelling at Pilkington's (*see* p.156) Royal Lancastrian Pottery, Manchester, under his father, Edward Thomas Radford, who had moved to Pilkington's from Josiah Wedgwood & Sons (*see* p.230) in 1903.

The younger Edward lived in Burslem, Staffordshire, from at least 1907; from about 1920, following a distinguished career in the army , he worked for Wood & Sons (*see* p.241)and, under an arrangement with Harry J. Wood, set up an independent pottery in Amicable Street, Burslem, which operated as the Radford Handcraft Pottery. It was well established by 1930, making a wide range of largely hand-thrown ornamental useful ware in earthenware. Production included vases, jugs, mugs, teapots, bowls, posy baskets, cigarette boxes, ashtrays, fancies, wall pockets, candlesticks, cruet sets and cheese dishes. Shapes were both traditional and modern, the latter including some modernist Art Deco-inspired geometric forms.

The decoration of this ware was mostly painted under the glaze in soft colours with foliage and foliate designs, in particular the Michaelmas Daisies, Blossoms on Bough and Indian Tree patterns, although the most popular and recognizable is Anemones. The patterns were available in various colourways and in a variety of finishes, including matt and bright glaze. The firm also specialized in stippled backgrounds, applied by hand in either green (also called 'copper'), blue, pink or fawn. Artware from the 1930s, with this form of decoration combined with stylized floral patterns, is among the most highly sought-after of the firm's ware.

◆ **Vases, 1930–35**
Underglaze painted vases, including the first recorded design for the pottery (top right), a sgraffito peasant pot (front right) and a rare Deco design incorporating platinum in on-glaze enamels (front centre). [397]

Many of the designs were created by Radford himself, although in the early years paintresses who had received training at local art and design schools were also given a free hand and encouraged to design their own patterns, or given an idea to interpret as they wished. Later ware became more uniformly floral. Among key paintresses employed by Radford were May Keeling, who had worked for Clarice Cliff, Mabel Hadgkiss, Eleanor Buckley and Jessie Skelding. Paintresses usually marked their work with a painted symbol on the base.

During World War II, production was combined with that of Wood & Sons, although H. J. Wood continued to trade separately. During this period, handcraft pottery was made for export only, but, despite this restriction, Edward Radford continued to produce designs until about 1948, when he retired. He went on to become a pottery instructor.

After his departure, H. J. Wood went on to produce Radford's designs into the 1960s and to mark them with a printed E. Radford backstamp.

♦ **Art Deco landscape vase, c.1930**
Lively stylized trees set against a hand-stippled ground typify the very individual and now highly collectable early Radford style. 398

SAMUEL RADFORD

The pottery made fine bone-china teaware, breakfast ware and dinnerware, as well as tableware accessories, for all markets. Its 1934 catalogue included a wide variety of patterns in both traditional and mildly modern styles. The firm also made functional items and some interesting fancies and giftware such as a handled basket in poppy form (made in three sizes), an open-work (or wicker-threaded) sweet dish with applied modelled flowers, and a number of delicate flower groups, intended as cabinet pieces, with naturalistic flowers in assorted colours, including mauve, pink, yellow, orange and crimson. In 1936 the pottery brought out loving cups and a cigarette box in its Coronation Ware. Production ceased during World War II, when T. G. Green (*see* p.80) took over the firm's orders. Despite steady expansion after the war, Radford ceased trading in 1957.

♦ **Tableware, 1920s**
Across the British pottery industry Imari-inspired designs have proved unceasingly popular. Radford's rather minimalist version still retains the colours and spirit of the more elaborate versions of the past. 399

ERIC RAVILIOUS

Born in West London in 1903, Eric Ravilious was by far the most prolific and interesting of the freelance designers employed by Josiah Wedgwood & Sons (*see* p.230). After early training at Eastbourne School of Art, in 1922 he won a scholarship to the Royal College of Art's Design School, where he was taught by Paul Nash. Ravilious studied engraving, illustration, colour printing and mural painting, and between 1929 and 1938 was himself an instructor at the RCA.

After a visit to Italy in 1926 Ravilious held his first watercolour exhibition and received the first of the many commissions for book illustrations and wood engravings which were to become the prime activity of all but his final years. By 1928 he was working on murals at Morley College, London, a commission which he shared with Edward Bawden and which led to other commissions for such work. Ravilious was introduced to industrial design in 1933 when he took part in a tableware design scheme organized in the Potteries by E. Brain & Co. (*see* p.28) and A. J. Wilkinson Ltd (*see* p.239). Twenty-seven leading contemporary artists and designers were given a completely free hand, and the results were shown in a special exhibition of pottery and glass held in Harrods department store in London in 1934.

Ravilious was introduced to Tom Wedgwood around 1935 and appears to have worked steadily and with considerable success for the firm between 1936 and 1942. Victor Skellern, who had known Ravilious at the RCA, was, by the mid-1930s, head of design at Wedgwood, and would certainly have encouraged the collaboration. As an experienced artist and engraver, Ravilious was able at Wedgwood to demonstrate the possibilities of applying modern design to some of the finest traditions in tableware production. He is noted for his revival use of on-glaze printing and for moving the firm towards modern decal-decoration techniques. His first design, a commemorative mug, was originally produced for the coronation of Edward VIII, but was adapted for later coronations. This piece proved that he was a natural designer of ceramics, and his originality and craftsmanship, aided by his knowledge of colour lithography, extended his scope in this field, while his sense of humour added charm to his designs.

In addition to commemorative ware, Ravilious also designed for Wedgwood patterns for dinnerware, teaware, nursery ware and related items. Notable among his work for the company are Afternoon Tea

◆ **Nursery ware mug, late 1930s**
Introduced in 1937, this mug with its printed Alphabet pattern illustrates the sympathy between Ravilious and the craftsmen at Wedgwood. Samples were also made in black basalt with gold lettering. 400

◆ **Edward VIII coronation mug, 1936**
Ravilious's first commission for Wedgwood in 1936 was a mug to celebrate the coronation of Edward VIII. Not issued because of the abdication, the mug was later modified for the coronations of both George VI, in 1937, and Elizabeth II, in 1953. As with most of Ravilious's designs, the mug was produced in various colourways. 401

◆ **Lemonade set, 1939**
This Liverpool-shape jug and beakers with Ravilious's Garden Implements design in sepia print, painted with purple and pink lustre, were introduced in 1939 and are reminiscent of some of the finest 18th-century printed ware. 402

teaware, Alphabet nursery ware, Noël Christmas pudding set, Travel, Garden, Persephone and Golden Persephone tableware patterns, and a Boat Race Day bowl, cup and stand. Also designed by Ravilious was the Garden Implements lemonade set, a modern version of a traditional 18th-century gardening theme. This pattern was produced in the 1950s with matching textiles. Ravilious's last design for Wedgwood was the Barlaston Mug, commissioned to celebrate the firm's move from Etruria to Barlaston, also in Staffordshire. By April 1940 samples of the commemorative mug had been produced. It is appropriate that this pattern was produced with decal decoration at the new factory. The design was drawn by Ravilious for direct application to the ware and is significant as the finest ceramic decal decoration on the market at that time.

Ravilious died in 1942. Most of his designs for Wedgwood were put into production, although, because of restrictions imposed during World War II, many were not produced in quantity until the 1950s.

◀ **Travel plate, 1950s (far left)**
Ravilious's Travel pattern was drawn and engraved in 1938 but, because of World War II, was not produced until 1953. 403

◀ **Persephone, late 1930s (left)**
Introduced as Harvest Festival in 1936, this pattern was renamed in 1938 and reintroduced as Coronation Golden Persephone in 1952 (it was adapted for use at the coronation banquet given by Britain's Foreign Secretary for Elizabeth II). 404

RED WING POTTERIES, INC.

Starting with utilitarian stoneware and adapting production through many market changes to include artware and dinnerware, the pottery survived longer than most of the other stoneware manufacturers established in the 19th century. The Red Wing Stoneware Company began making crocks, jugs and utilitarian stoneware in 1878 in a steam-powered factory in Red Wing, Minnesota. Importing utilitarian ware from Ohio had been sufficient during early settlement of the area, but as such need grew, the feasibility of operating a pottery profitably improved. During the first year of business the company produced 270,000 US gallons (2 million litres) of wares.

Following Red Wing's success, the Minnesota Stoneware Company was incorporated in 1883 and the North Star Stoneware Company was organized in 1892. Supporting three potteries became more difficult as a result of the serious economic depression that swept the country in 1893. In 1894 the three potteries formed the Union Stoneware Company, a marketing arrangement in which each pottery maintained its own facilities and business organization. North Star closed in 1896; the prospects of the other two companies improved, and by 1900 both were profitable again.

In 1906 Red Wing and Minnesota merged to form the Red Wing Union Stoneware Company. The market for utilitarian stoneware was changing dramatically as lighter materials, such as glass and metal, were replacing the heavier stoneware storage vessels. Home canning in glass was much

◆ **Red Wing Union Stoneware crock, 1915–30**
Patented in 1915, the wire and wood handles were needed to lift this 10 US gallon (39 litres) crock. Ware such as this was used in certain rural areas well into the 20th century. 405

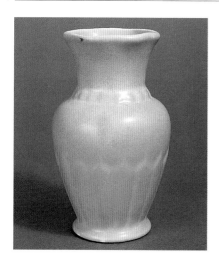

easier, and commercial canning in metal containers was increasing rapidly. New products needed to be developed in order for Red Wing to remain profitable. Improvements were made in utilitarian stoneware production over the years, but the pottery finally started making new ware in the early 1930s. In 1936 the company's name was changed to Red Wing Potteries, Inc. Stoneware was eliminated from Red Wing's line in 1947.

In 1933 Red Wing began making florists' crockery and artware for George Rumrill, a relationship that continued until 1938. RumRill pottery (in trade literature and in the mark, the name appears with two capital Rs) was made with a variety of pastel matt glazes. Shapes generally followed the styles of the 1930s, with softened contours and simplified design elements. Leaf forms, nudes, cornucopias, swans and other birds, fruits, shells and flowers are among the most common motifs. Vases, candlesticks, bowls, ashtrays, candy dishes, book-ends, planters and garden crockery are the typical shapes.

Red Wing introduced its first dinnerware line in 1935. In the wake of its success, Belle Kogan designed in 1939 the Gypsy Trail Hostess Ware, which included a collection of four lines, each styled differently: Chevron is plain, brightly coloured hostess ware with animal handles; Fondoso, in bright or pastel colours, has geometric patterns in low relief; Reed is characterized by vertical ribbing; and Plain. The Terrace Fruit Service Group, also designed by Kogan in 1939, includes casseroles, cookie jars, marmalade jars and salad bowls in a variety of fruit shapes – apple, pear, banana, grapes and pineapple – with bright colours.

Designer Charles Murphy began a long association with Red Wing in 1940, and many believe that the pottery's market success from the 1940s to the 1960s was largely based on his designs. Murphy grew up among the potteries of south-eastern Ohio, and worked briefly for Homer Laughlin (*see* p.110) and its main supplier of decals, Decalcomania. For Red Wing he first developed the Brittany and Orleans dinnerware, both with hand-painted designs. Figural cookie jars followed, including at first Chef Pierre, Katrina (a Dutch girl) and Friar Tuck, with Carousel, Jack Frost, King of Hearts and dancing Peasants coming later. In 1942 he tackled artware, developing a line of high-priced modelled figures, in grey or tan slip with turquoise, suitable for sale through jewellery stores.

♠ **RumRill vase, 1930s**
Pastel matt glazes were typical of the RumRill line made for George Rumrill. The shapes were stylish, though often based on traditional forms. 406

♠ **Gypsy Trail Hostess platter, late 1930s**
The Fondoso line of the Gypsy Trail Hostess Ware designed by Belle Kogan was stylishly modern in colour and shape. Colours included orange, light blue, turquoise and yellow as well as pastel shades of blue, green, pink and yellow. 407

♦ **Magnolia dinnerware, 1940s**
Magnolia on the Concord shape is one of the many patterns Charles Murphy designed to be painted freehand by the staff decorators. Patterns from this period are bold in execution but painted in the quiet colour palette typical of the era. 408

The figures were short-lived because only a small amount of art-ware was purchased in the USA during World War II.

Eva Zeisel designed Town and Country, an earthenware line, for Red Wing in 1946, and it was introduced in 1947. She had recently achieved some renown with her Museum design for Castleton (*see* Shenango China Company, p.203), but her Red Wing shape was quite different. Following the success of Russel Wright's Casual China for Iroquois (*see* p.96), informality had become the new keynote in dinnerware design. Rather than the elegant formality of Museum, Town and Country would be Zeisel's first biomorphic design in dinnerware, an informal concept that is slightly asymmetrical with glossy and half-matt glazes. Her famous salt and pepper shakers were designed for Town and Country. Red Wing, as the client, asked for something 'Greenwich Villagey', meaning that it should be modern and colourful, but sturdy and useful. The forms designed for this service followed these guidelines. A bean pot, various bowls, casseroles, jugs, plates, relishes and platters, as well as an ashtray, a cream jug and sugar bowl, teapot, sauce dish, cup and saucer, soup tureen, cruet, mustard jar, mug and Lazy Susan, were made. Glaze colours included Chalk White, Chartreuse, Dusk Blue, Forest Green, Metallic Brown, Peach, Rust and Sand.

After war service, Charles Murphy returned to Red Wing from 1946 to 1949. He designed a group of five ceramic clocks, including the polo player, Tik Tok (a clown), the chef, fat mammy and Gretel with yellow braids and a blue dress. He also reorganized the decorators into a mass-production operation. Instead of painting designs on pieces individually, decorators worked as an assembly line, each worker painting a part of the design rather than the whole. From 1949 Murphy served a brief stint with the Stetson China Company in Illinois, but returned to Red Wing as a design consultant in 1953. His period of greatest productivity followed, during which he designed 70 lines of hand-painted dinnerware. Capistrano and Tampico, two popular patterns introduced in 1955, were brightly painted and exotic; they won national awards. However, Murphy's biggest commercial success was the Bob White line on the Casual shape, also introduced in 1955. The wide variety of forms included a beverage

▲ **Eva Zeisel's Town and Country, mid-1940s**
These shapely marmites, or individual casseroles, were used for serving hot foods as an early course during dinner. The biomorphism characteristic of this line is evident in the handles. The colours were deeply saturated and very modern. 409

▲ **Tampico coffee server, 1955–65**
The Tampico pattern, another of the many designed by Charles Murphy, is shown here on the highly attenuated Futura shape. Tampico was described in a company sales brochure as having a 'South of the Border look'. 410

◀ **Charles Murphy's Bob White, late 1950s**
Introduced in 1955, Bob White is a casual rendering of the chirpy fowl. The casserole, with its asymmetrical finial, and hors d'oeuvre holder in the shape of the bird are special pieces in this line, although other items are more valuable on today's market. 411

server and butter warmer, cookie jar, gravy boat, cruet, pepper mill, relish dish, tray, Lazy Susan, various casters and a water jar, in addition to the usual plates, bowls, casseroles, cups and saucers and teapot. The hors d'oeuvre holder is a large Bob White figure with holes in its back for toothpicks. Murphy also designed art pottery for Red Wing, creating several hundred shapes during his tenure; Sgraffito, Hobnail, Decorator Line, Chromoline and Doric Ensemble are among the most popular today.

Manufacturing at Red Wing Potteries ceased in 1967. The company's continuing financial problems were exacerbated by a strike that began in June of that year; liquidation started in August and continued until 1969.

▲ Charles Murphy plate, 1950s
With this pattern Murphy has captured the quintessential elements of 1950s style, including the bright colours, asymmetry and overlapping free-form motifs. With so many of his patterns available on the market, the collector of Red Wing dinnerware has a large field in which to work. 412

KEY FACTS

Location: Red Wing, Minnesota, USA.
Important dates: Founded 1877. Closed 1967.
Production: Utilitarian stoneware, artware and tableware.
Principal designers: Charles Murphy, Belle Kogan, Eva Zeisel.
Trade name: RumRill.

MARKS

Except for RumRill, all Red Wing ware marked with company name. Pottery name frequently stamped in conjunction with image of red wing, or incorporated into shape of bird's wing. Other marks moulded and include 'USA'.

CHARLOTTE RHEAD

Born in Burslem, Staffordshire, in 1885, Charlotte Rhead was the daughter of Frederick Alfred and Adolphine Rhead. Coming from an illustrious family of designers, she was introduced to pottery at an early age, and learned many decorating techniques, including the art of slip-decorating, at her father's knee.

Frederick Rhead introduced tube-lining at a number of companies, including Wileman & Co., around the turn of the century, and had been a pupil of Louis Solon, the leading *pâte-sur-pâte* artist at Minton (*see* p.132). He had also been an art-school instructor, and used this experience to teach his children to paint and draw. Charlotte Rhead attended school at Longport and afterwards at Hanley before she and her sister

▲ Burleigh Ware bowl, c.1934
The unusual octagonal shape and the strongly geometric fan pattern (number 4908) make this a distinctive piece. 413

◀ Bursley Ware dish, c.1932
The overall pattern (TL5) and soft colour palette reflect Rhead's use of textiles and other flat-pattern sources for her designs. 414

Dollie enrolled at the Fenton Art School, which had been established by her grandfather, George Woolliscroft Rhead. There, among other subjects, she was taught enamelling.

In 1901 Rhead was taken on as a tube-liner at Wardle & Co. (*see* p.227), where her brother, Frederick Hurten Rhead, had become art director two years earlier. She was involved in the *pâte-sur-pâte* technique, introduced by the firm under the general supervision of her father. She then worked as a tube-liner and an enameller for other companies. Around 1908 Rhead and her brother joined their father at the Atlas Tile Works, Hanley, where Frederick Rhead had formed a partnership to produce tiles with F. H. Barker. After this venture failed, around 1910, she obtained her first job as a designer with T. & R. Boote, one of the leading Staffordshire manufacturers of tube-lined tiles. She moved to Wood & Sons (*see* p.241) shortly after 1912, when her father was appointed art director of that company. Later, with Frederick Rhead's encouragement, Wood established Bursley Ltd. This separate branch, based at Wood's nearby Crown Works, specialized in the production of ornamental artware such as jugs, vases, bowls, and plaques under the trade name Bursley Ware. Working alongside her father, Rhead was employed as a designer and decorator. In addition to helping to develop tube-lining and *pâte-sur-pâte*, she trained new tube-liners. She also designed for another Wood subsidiary, the Ellgreave Pottery (*see* p.63), and some of its pieces carry the 'Lottie Rhead' backstamp.

During this period Rhead's output was considerable, and with a growing reputation she moved to another Burslem company, Burgess & Leigh (*see* p.36), where she worked from 1926 to 1931. Again she produced many new patterns for ornamental and useful ranges, including some with tube-lined decoration, and trained tube-liners to carry out her designs. She designed under the firm's trade name, Burleigh, at first using shapes already in production, and later decorating specially designed ones. Patterns included fruit and flower designs sometimes set against dark-coloured grounds, very similar to her work for Wood, as well as some more abstract and geometric designs, such as Florentine. Other ranges, for example Sylvan and Garland, consisted of black tube-lining on white grounds with blue and gold patterns. In 1931 Rhead left Burgess & Leigh and began working as a designer for A. G. Richardson (*see* opposite), makers of Crown Ducal Ware. Over the next 11 years she produced a large

⬥ **Crown Ducal wall plaque, c.1936**
The well-balanced purple-and-blue palette and strongly drawn tube-lined pattern are typical of Richardson's Crown Ducal Ware by Charlotte Rhead. 415

⬥ **Crown Ducal vase, c.1936**
Decorated in soft tones with pattern 4794, this cylinder-shaped vase has the prominent throwing bands that were fashionable at the time. 416

⬥ **Crown Ducal Persian Rose vase, c.1936**
The Persian Rose pattern was made in a number of colourways. This version was shown at the British Industries Fair in 1936. The thick handles underline the Mediterranean sources for the pot's shape. 417

and varied amount of designs, some of which became best sellers. In addition to ornamental artware, such as tube-lined products marketed under the name of Rhodian Ware, she designed freehand-painted ware, tableware and children's ware. She also developed a range of new lustres and glazes, including a snow glaze introduced in the mid-1930s. Other designs for Richardson include Byzantine, with a stylized pattern of orange and yellow flowers within a border, and Wisteria and Foxglove, using the thick opaque white glaze developed in about 1934.

Throughout her career, most of Rhead's work was for the ornamental or fancies trade. Although such pieces had some functional purpose, as non-essential goods they were badly affected by World War II restrictions. In 1942 she left Richardson to work for H. J. Wood's Alexander Pottery, for which she produced many designs. However, because the war stopped all production, and austerity measures remained in force afterwards, she did not live to see these designs in production, dying in 1947.

A. G. RICHARDSON

The company was established in 1915 at the Gordon Pottery, Tunstall, Staffordshire, to make useful and ornamental lines and novelties under the Crown Ducal trade name. By 1920 four new ovens and seven new kilns had been erected at the Gordon site, and other enlargement was in progress. The firm specialized in vellum and decal-decorated ware such as the original vellum-grounded ware, black grounds with decal patterns and all-over decals; shapes include Victorian Silver in vases and teapots. During this period Richardson also produced a series of ornamental pieces decorated with tube-lined slip filled with coloured glazes. By 1921 transfer-printed ware and teaware decorated in plain colours applied by aerograph were being advertised, and by 1930 many new patterns and shapes in both utilitarian and decorative earthenware were in the catalogue. The newly modelled Gainsborough tableware shape, with an embossed design on the rim, was launched in 1930.

In the early 1930s Richardson needed more capacity to meet the growing demand for Crown Ducal products, and in 1933 the firm reopened the Britannia Pottery, Cobridge, mainly for the production of tableware such as Linden pattern, enamelled in green and yellow and touched up with

◆ Crown Ducal tableware advertisement, 1930
This advertisement features one range of items with the widely used Crown Ducal trade mark. This Gainsborough-shape tableware is decorated with embossed borders. 418

◆ Chintzware tray, c.1935
Richardson's Crown Ducal trade name was applied to a huge range of goods, reflecting the pottery's diverse production range and its willingness to take up fashionable styles such as chintzware. 419

red, and Pussy Willow, both introduced in 1934. Production of tube-lined ware was revived after the war. Some of the designs marketed during this period were earlier designs by Charlotte Rhead (*see* p.173) – who worked at the Gordon Pottery from 1931 until 1942 – and Richardson continued to produce these until at least 1955.

The Gordon Pottery closed during World War II, but the Britannia Pottery (*see* p.33) continued to make earthenware tableware, hotel ware and catering ware, teapots and oven-to-table ware in Berkeley and Norvic shapes until 1974, when it was sold to Enoch Wedgwood (*see* p.230).

◆ **Plant pot, c.1970**
This small plant pot, with simple banded decoration, is typical of Richardson's extensive range of competitively priced ware for the popular market in the late 1960s and early 1970s. [420]

KEY FACTS

Location: Gordon Pottery, Tunstall 1915–c.1942, Britannia Pottery, Cobridge 1933–74; Staffordshire, UK.
Important dates: Founded 1915. Bought by Enoch Wedgwood 1974.
Production: Earthenware.
Trade names: Crown Ducal, Old Hall Ivory.

MARKS

Printed marks with crown above oval, incorporating 'Crown Ducal Ware' with or without 'A. G. R. & Co.', from c.1916. This version used from c.1930. Some registration numbers or pattern names indicated. Impressed marks giving company name also used.

RIDGWAYS

The pottery's early output included a comprehensive range of domestic and ornamental earthenware, jet, stone, terracotta and jasper for the home and export markets. Ridgways was one of the pioneers of decoration with decals and made its own decals. Notable among the many new ranges introduced around 1900 were the Coaching Days and Coaching Ways Series on the Majestic shape, launched in 1898 and in production until the 1970s.

Developed in the early 20th century under John and Edward Ridgway, the Ridgways style continued through the 1930s, 1940s and beyond, and many original patterns, such as Windsor Festoon and Willow, were produced. Catalogues for the 1930s also include a range of hand-painted tableware such as the Somerset and Californian patterns. Some of the tea, morning and coffee sets were produced in semi-china with bold enamel

◆ **Widdicombe Fair mug, 1950s**
Well-known themes and images were often used by Ridgways with the aim of keeping in touch with popular taste. [421]

◆ **Tableware, 1930s**
A major producer of a wide range of popular tableware patterns, Ridgways did not develop a truly distinctive style until the 1950s. [422]

and silver decorations in Art Deco-style patterns. Among other lines were brightly decorated flower jugs and a series of pierced wall-bracket vases, and a seven-piece lemonade set with the Nile-shape jug.

Tom Arnold worked mainly for Ridgways in the 1950s. Among his many contributions, he designed the highly organic Metro-shape tableware for Ridgways and Adderley (*see* p.13) around the middle of the decade. This was made with decorations such as Park Lane, designed by Margaret Wagg, and the later Conference pattern created by Pat Albeck. The popular Homemaker pattern, designed in contemporary style by Enid Seeney, was also introduced in this period. Other shapes include Sapphire, launched with the Prelude and Bahamas patterns in 1957.

Hotel ware has featured strongly in the firm's 20th-century production. In 1968 it launched the Atlanta-shape stackable range in its new vitreous-china hotel ware body decorated with a new pattern by Julia Chandler. Decorations were available in underglaze prints, decals and bands, or on-glaze decals. Steelite T 10, the name given to the body, was chosen by David Queensberry.

Ridgways had three divisions in the 1970s: Ridgway Bone China, Longton, for domestic tableware, teapots and fancy tableware; Ridgway Fine Ceramic Tableware, Baddeley Green, Stoke, for similar items in earthenware; and Ridgway Steelite Hotelware, Hanley, for Steelite tableware for the hotel and catering trades. The trade name was dropped around 1983 but since then has been occasionally reused for special lines.

⬤ **Homemaker tableware, 1950s**
The best-known 1950s design – an icon of its period in fact – Homemaker is Ridgways' greatest claim to fame. Designed by Enid Seeney, and sold exclusively through Woolworths between 1955 and 1967, the pattern features a range of easily identifiable 1950s objects, including a Gordon Russell sideboard and a Robin Day chair. 423

⬩ **Indian Summer tableware, 1970s**
Introduced in 1973, this chunky tableware shape reflects the contemporary enthusiasm among potters for this type of pattern and colour range. Midwinter began the trend and many potteries followed it. This range stayed in production until 1979. 424

KEY FACTS

Location: Bedford Works, Shelton, Staffordshire, UK.
Important dates: Edward John Ridgway in partnership with father, William Ridgway, and Leonard Abington from 1838. Bedford Works built 1866. Firm traded as Ridgways from 1879. Renamed Ridgways (Bedford Works) 1920. Under family control until taken over by Cauldon Potteries 1929. Traded as Ridgway Potteries Ltd from 1955. Became part of Allied English Potteries 1964, and subsequently part of Royal Doulton Tableware Group.
Production: Earthenware.
Trade name: Ridgways.

MARKS

This backstamp used from c.1930. Marks from c.1905 often include a named body type. Mark showing crown above 'RIDGWAY IRONSTONE' used 1970s. 'Est. 1792' added c.1950 and used by later firms.

J. A. ROBINSON & SONS

From 1903 the ceramics manufacturer Harold Taylor Robinson acquired, alone or with others, various china and earthenware makers. In 1910 he formed a new company in Stoke, J. A. Robinson & Sons Ltd, in the name of his father. At the British Industries Fair in 1920 this firm had a huge success, which embraced the specialities of its many associated potteries and included an impressive range of toilet ware and rich majolica artware by Wardle Art Pottery. The company bought Cauldon and, under the name Cauldon Potteries Ltd, H. T. Robinson began to amalgamate most of the firms he owned or in which he had a controlling interest.

KEY FACTS

Location: Stoke, Staffordshire, UK.

Important dates: Founded 1910. Bought Cauldon 1920 and subsequently traded as Cauldon Potteries Ltd.

Production: China and earthenware.

ROBINSON-RANSBOTTOM

In 1900 four Ransbottom brothers acquired the Oval Ware and Brick Company in Beem City, near Roseville, Ohio. Early the next year, as the Ransbottom Brothers Pottery, they began producing stoneware jardinières, spittoons and red flower pots. By 1916 the company was the world's largest producer of stoneware jars.

The Ransbottom Brothers Pottery merged in 1920 with the Robinson Clay Products Company, of Akron, Ohio, a maker of tiles and bricks. The new Robinson-Ransbottom Pottery Company changed production to garden ware, including strawberry urns, large vases, bird baths and planting tubs, although stoneware containers are still made. Kitchenware was added to the product line in the 1930s, including bakers, bowls, casseroles, pitchers, refrigerator ware, cookie jars, jugs and pie plates in many bright and pastel colours. The hand-decorated Old Colony ornamental ware and Rustic kitchenware, which are identified by company marks and labels, were introduced in the mid-1930s. Old Colony was discontinued in 1940 and Rustic Ware in the 1960s. Both were marketed under the company's Crown brand name. The kitchenware and dinnerware ranges currently produced by the company are decorated with sponged blue or green glazes over traditional stoneware bodies.

EXTRA LARGE COVERED BREAD BOWL

Complete, $1.00 each.

◆ **Advertisement in The Broadside, c.1910**
Ransbottom Brothers Pottery offered this covered bowl for making bread at $1.00. The stoneware body kept the rising dough warm. 425

◆ **Covered bean pot, 1950s**
While other makers of sturdy goods have disappeared during the past half-century, Robinson-Ransbottom continues to make serviceable stoneware kitchenware vessels. An extensive line of garden ware is also available, including birdbaths, garden seats, decorative flower pots and other novelties. 426

KEY FACTS

Location: Roseville, Ohio, USA.

Important dates: Founded as Ransbottom Brothers Pottery 1901. Merged with Robinson Clay Products Company, Akron, Ohio, 1920. Still active.

Production: Stoneware, kitchenware and dinnerware.

MARKS

Crown used since mid-1930s; others feature 'R.R.P.Co.' and 'Roseville, Ohio'.

ROOKWOOD POTTERY COMPANY

Drawn to ceramics through china painting, Maria Longworth Nichols longed to have her own pottery. Potters in Cincinnati, Ohio, had developed a way to paint in coloured slip on a damp earthenware body to achieve effects similar to those of the Barbotine potters of France. In 1880, with backing from her father, Mrs Nichols established the Rookwood Pottery to produce Cincinnati faience, or what came to be called Rookwood's Standard Glaze. Ladies from the local pottery club who were also trained in china painting, decorated vases and teaware turned or moulded by Rookwood's professional potters. The early ware was decorated with flowers, animals, fish and sea creatures, American Indians and the like, rendered in various naturally coloured slips on backgrounds airbrushed to shade from ochre to dark mahogany and covered all over with a glossy yellow-tinted glaze. Eventually the ladies from the pottery club were replaced as decorators by graduates of the Cincinnati Art Academy.

In 1883 Mrs Nichols arranged for William Watts Taylor to take over the management of the pottery. Taylor developed a variety of marketing concepts to promote Rookwood's products. Each piece was clearly marked with the year of its production and the pottery's distinctive 'RP' cipher. All pieces were individually decorated and then signed by their decorators, and lists of decorators' initials were published periodically to encourage collecting. Colour palettes and subject matter were standardized to make the product recognizable, and distribution was limited to the best jewellery and department stores in order to keep its price high; for example, Rookwood's agent in New York City was Tiffany and in Chicago Marshall Field. Mrs Nichols noticed that when Taylor took charge, things began to assume a business air, and the pottery had, to a certain extent, to be harnessed to the commercial world. She was, however, recognized throughout her life as the founder of one of America's great art industries.

In 1889 Rookwood was awarded a Gold Medal at the Exposition Universelle in Paris, which brought the little pottery worldwide recognition. By 1892 the company was moving into the first of the distinctive half-timbered buildings on Mt Adams, above Cincinnati, that would become its long-term home, and which survive today as landmarks. During the 1890s Rookwood's chemist and superintendent, Stanley G. Burt, developed new colour treatments that lightened the palette and used cooler shades. Iris and Sea Green were introduced in 1894, but not prominently displayed until the Paris Exposition of 1900. Other new glazes followed soon after: Tiger Eye was the trade name that described an aventurine effect; Vellum was Rookwood's term for its matt glaze, introduced in 1904 at the St Louis World's Fair; Ombroso, tones of matt grey and brown with colour accents, came out in 1910. Also in this era, Rookwood began to design, make and sell unsigned pieces at lower prices in order to compete with the growing number of companies specializing in art pottery. These pieces had decorations moulded in low relief and covered with coloured matt glazes. Architectural tiles for domestic and public interiors were introduced in 1902.

Taylor died in 1913 and was succeeded by Joseph H. Gest, who retired in 1934 when financial problems plagued the company. John D. Wareham succeeded Gest. Harold F. Bopp replaced Burt as superintendent, working from 1929 to 1939.

◆ **Rookwood's Standard Glaze, 1905**
Decorated by Edith Noonan, this vase is typical of the skill of Rookwood's artists in composing and executing delicate painting with clay slips. 427

◆◆ **Catalogue, 1904**
Illustrations of the Iris glaze (above) and the Conventional and Incised Mat Glazes (below) from a Rookwood trade catalogue. 428

In 1941 Rookwood went bankrupt and was purchased by Walter E. Schott. Over the next 18 years the pottery passed through several owners, eventually being bought in 1959 by the Herschede Hall Clock Company. During this period wares were still made, but their quality declined. In 1960 Herschede moved the operation to Starkville, Mississippi, where a small amount of pottery was made before all production ceased in 1967.

In addition to prestigious shops, sales outlets for Rookwood pottery included a mail-order catalogue. The 1904 edition showed vases, ewers, teaware, low bowls, mugs, and coffee and chocolate pots that were artist-signed and hand-decorated with flowers, fruits, birds and pine cones. Prices ranged from $8 to $150, but most pieces were in the $10–$30 range. Since no two pieces were alike, buyers would receive their choice on approval. Also included were a few pieces moulded in designs derived from American Indian motifs; these could be bought for as little as $2.50.

One hundred and ten decorators have been identified as working for the Rookwood Pottery between 1880 and 1959. The work of a few stands out in its long history; among these are Lenox Asbury, Sallie Coyne, Matt Daly, Edward Diers, Lorinda Epply, William Hentschel, Edward Hurley, Jens Jensen, Sturgis Laurence, William P. McDonald, Clara Chipman Newton, Sara Sax, Charles Schmidt, Kataro Shirayamadani, Charles Todd, Sallie Toohey, Albert Valentien, Artus Van Briggle (*see* p.223), Grace Young and Maria Nichols. In addition to painting, Rookwood decorators also designed the moulded pieces that were made for stock.

For many years serious collectors of Rookwood concentrated on the early artist-signed work made before 1930, driving prices to very high levels. But in recent years, as the value of the early work has soared, unsigned ware has become more collectable. Moulded designs in the Arts and Crafts and Art Nouveau styles are attracting more interest.

◆ **Moulded vase, 1921**
Rookwood's moulded ware has become very collectable. This large example was sold as a vase and lamp base. Although moulded ware was not hand decorated, the level of design artistry was very high. 429

◆ **Vase, 1921**
Rookwood continued to produce artist-decorated vases well into the 20th century; this example was decorated by Loretta Holtkamp. The white body contrasts boldly with the blues and purples of the decoration. 430

KEY FACTS
Location: Cincinnati, Ohio, USA.
Important dates: Founded 1880. Bought by Herschede Hall Clock Company 1959. Closed 1967.
Production: Artware, tableware and hostess ware.
Principal designers: Matt Daly, Jens Jensen, Sara Sax, Charles Schmidt, Kataro Shirayamadani, Charles Todd, Grace Young, Albert Valentien (all decorators).

MARKS
'RP' monogram adopted 1886 with one flame added for each year until 1900; then year of production impressed below 'RP'.

ROSEVILLE POTTERY

Founded in 1890 by George F. Young and associates to make stoneware jars, flower pots and spittoons, the company began production in Roseville, Ohio. In 1898 it bought a second plant in Roseville, to make more stoneware, and a third, in Zanesville, to produce painted ware. From 1900, Rozane Ware was made in the latter plant. This line, developed by Ross C. Purdy, was similar to the Standard line created earlier by Rookwood (*see* p.179), consisting of decorations painted in slip on a damp clay body that was already turned or moulded into the final shape. Although the work of Rozane's decorators never approached the high quality of the finest Rookwood pieces, the early Rozane work was creditable, popular and less expensive than Rookwood's ware. Like Rookwood's, Rozane's subjects included flowers, animals and portraits on a dark brown blended background. Other potteries also mimicked these goods, among them Lonhuda, Stockton, Owens and Weller (*see* p.234).

In 1902 Roseville bought the Muskingum Stoneware plant in Zanesville. Through consolidation efforts all production was concentrated in Zanesville by 1910, and the Roseville plants were shut down. However, the Roseville name was retained and the Rozane line continued to be made. Artware was never actually made in Roseville, as the facilities there were used to produce only utilitarian stoneware.

Between 1900 and 1920 a number of hand-decorated artware lines were developed and introduced. John Herold became art director of Roseville in 1900 and created the Rozane Mongol line, with an excellent ox-blood glaze, as well as a number of other decorative glaze effects to compete with the variety of wares being produced at the Weller and Rookwood potteries. Mara was meant to compete with Weller's Sicard; Egypto was meant to remind the consumer of Egyptian antiques; Woodland, designed by the Japanese artist Gazo Fudji (or Fujiyama), had floral designs incised on a stippled bisque background; and Della Robbia was a laborious decorative method that involved incising the design, removing clay and inlaying contrasting clay and glazes. Della Robbia was developed by Frederick Rhead, who was Roseville's art director from 1904 to 1908. When Rhead left, his brother Harry took over the decorating department, and artware production was greatly simplified and stream-lined. Donatello, introduced in 1915, is typical of the firm's new direction.

◄ Persian flower bowl, 1916
This hand-painted earthenware bowl has three loop handles for attaching hanging chains. Alternatively, it could have been used as a centre bowl with a flower frog. 431

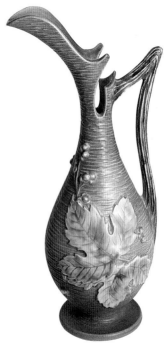

◄ Bushberry ewer, late 1940s
Roseville's floral lines, made from 1920 to 1950, are extremely popular with collectors today, and rare pieces command high prices. Designer Frank Ferrell combined stylish shapes with fashionable colours and natural motifs that were recognized and appreciated by the pottery's many customers. 432

◗ Trade sign, 1940s, Carnelian vase, c.1915
The vase, with one solid colour dripping over the ground, was the first line in Carnelian, designed by Harry Rhead in 1910. Another Carnelian line was introduced in 1916 and had a textured glaze with blended colours. The Roseville trade sign was used in shops and department stores. 433

This line was completely moulded and then covered in a contrasting glaze that was wiped off the high spots to emphasize the frieze of putti and decorative fluting.

Frank Ferrell replaced Harry Rhead in 1918 and introduced the floral artware that distinguished the pottery's work at the time and remains today as its distinctive contribution to industrial artware production in the 20th century. The Pinecone pattern was perhaps the most financially successful of Ferrell's designs for Roseville, but there were many others. Apple Blossom, Bittersweet, Blackberry, Bleeding Heart, Cherry Blossom, Clematis, Columbine, Cosmos, Dahlrose, Dogwood, Forget-Me-Not, Foxglove, Freesia, Fuchsia, Gardenia, Iris, Jonquil, Landscape, Laurel, Lotus, Magnolia, Morning Glory, Peony, Poppy, Primrose, Sunflower, Thorn Apple, Wisteria and Zephyr Lily are some of the many floral lines that were designed and introduced between 1920 and 1950. Also popular were lines with stylish decorative motifs, including Corinthian, Cameo, Donatello, Florentine, Medallion, Ming Tree, Olympic, Persian, Silhouette, Tuscany, Victorian and Windsor. Some were matt glazed, some glossy; some were conceived as very simple effects, and others were more elaborate. This variety made the ware extremely popular and contributes greatly to its current collectability. Mostique, in the Arts and Crafts style, and Futura, an Art Deco line, are among the most collectable patterns.

In 1952 Roseville introduced Raymor oven-to-table ware, designed by Ben Seibel. The line was offered in several plain matt and glossy mottled glazes in various greens, brown, terracotta and grey. Roseville hoped that this new direction for its product line would improve sales, but the company was already too far behind its competitors. Manufacturing was halted in 1954. Roseville was sold in the same year to the New England Ceramics Company, and then to Franklin Potteries of Franklin, West Virginia, but the plant never reopened.

▲ **Pinecone vase, early 1930s**
Pinecone is thought to be the most profitable of Frank Ferrell's many floral designs for Roseville. 434

▲ **Wincraft vase, late 1940s**
Wincraft is characterized by modern shapes that move from apricot, blue or chartreuse at the top to brown at the bottom and carry relief floral or animal motifs. 435

◀ **Foxglove ewer, mid-1940s**
This ewer is among the many floral designs on exaggerated shapes that were invented by Frank Ferrell. 436

KEY FACTS

Location: Roseville and Zanesville, Ohio, USA.
Important dates: Founded 1890. Closed 1954.
Production: Artware and flower containers.
Principal designers: Ross Purdy, John Herold, Frederick Rhead, Harry Rhead, Frank Ferrell.

MARKS

Moulded mark
1930s and 1940s;
also 'Rozane' on
early, and conjoined
'Rv' on later, ware.

Roseville
U.S.A.

ROYAL ALBERT

After the death of his father Thomas Wild in 1898, Thomas Clarke Wild became sole proprietor of Thomas Wild & Co., a rapidly expanding china manufacturer. Production of Royal Albert China was moved from the Albert Works to St Mary's Works, also in Longton, in 1905, when the latter factory was purchased. Wild's sons, Thomas E. and Frederick J. Wild, joined him in 1906 and 1908 respectively, and became directors in 1914. By 1910 the company was well established, and built up a large export trade in the foreign and colonial markets, mainly with high-class tea and breakfast sets produced in Royal Albert Crown China. Also made were dinner and dessert services and other tableware in the same body, as well as badged ware and fancies. Decorations included gold on dark blue, acid-etched border designs, and richly enamelled and gilt tea and breakfast services, fish sets and game sets for the North American markets. The firm made a feature of Queen's white fluted ware.

Between the wars the company continued to produce a wide range and variety of its renowned traditional shapes and designs, although it also brought out mildly modernist ranges of teaware and tableware, such as the Apex registered shape launched in 1934. Decorations included freehand-painted or decal patterns. From the 1930s children's ware with colourful decals was also made. A later children's range was Teddy's Playtime, registered about 1953. The shapes for this range were by Harold Holdcroft, and the pattern was by the children's book illustrator A. E. Kennedy. Holdcroft, who was appointed works designer in 1934, was responsible for many of the new designs from that era. He also designed Royal Albert's best-known pattern, Old Country Roses, introduced in 1962. Almost every Royal Albert pattern had been a variation on a floral theme, and yet when Old Country Roses was first produced it received a lukewarm reception from shopkeepers. Since then it has become one of Britain's most successful patterns and is still in production.

The firm was bought by Pearson & Co. in 1964, becoming part of Allied English Potteries, which later merged with the Royal Doulton Group. In 1975 Royal Albert extended its range from dinner, tea, coffee and breakfast services to include ornamental pieces such as trinket sets, boxes, candlesticks, vases and sweet dishes. Later Old Country Roses florals were introduced, along with related lines such as models of Cottage Garden Year Window Boxes. Beatrix Potter figures and fancies are among Royal Albert's more recent collectable products.

After the closure of St Mary's Works, production was transferred to other Doulton factories. All ware is now outsourced in the Far East.

◆ **Royal Albert teaware, c.1968**
The Nova Scotia Tartan pattern was used on the Montrose shape between 1967 and 1973. It was one of a series of patterns featuring tartans with Canadian connections. [437]

◆ **Old Country Roses miniatures, 1990s**
Royal Albert's Old Country Roses is one of Britain's best-selling tableware patterns, and this success has been exploited by the company for both tableware and collectors' markets. These miniatures are typical of goods produced for the latter. [438]

KEY FACTS

Location: Albert Works and St Mary's Works, Longton, Staffordshire, UK.
Important dates: Founded as Thomas Wild & Co. 1896. Bought by Pearson & Co. and became part of Allied English Potteries 1964. Merged with Royal Doulton 1972.
Production: China.
Trade names: Royal Albert Crown China, Royal Albert Bone China.

MARKS

This mark, sometimes incorporating pattern name, used from c.1945.

ROYAL ALLER VALE AND WATCOMBE ART POTTERY: see ALLER VALE ART POTTERY p.14
ROYAL ART POTTERY: see ALFRED CLOUGH p.46

The pottery was established in 1876 by a limited company whose principal directors were Edward Phillips, a practical potter, and William Litherland, head of a family china and glass retail business in Liverpool. The two men built a new factory in Osmaston Road, Derby, and began production in 1877. Between 1882 and 1889, under Richard Lunn's direction, Crown Derby rose to great heights as a result of its highly decorative ornamental pieces. Talented modellers, painters, gilders and fine craftsmen were drawn to the new factory, among them the artists James Rouse (senior) and Count George Holtzendorf, who was for a time the company's chief painter. In 1890, the year that Désiré Leroy, a noted ceramic artist, arrived at the works, the company received Queen Victoria's permission to style itself the Royal Crown Derby Porcelain Company. Leroy was given his own department, where, assisted by his two pupils John Dale and George Darlington, he designed and painted his celebrated bird, flower, musical trophy, fruit and nut subjects with elaborate raised paste gilding and jewelling. The porcelain included an eggshell body developed by the firm in this era and used for delicate teaware. Also noted for their delicacy are the finely finished perforated baskets. Printed decoration was carried out in a purpose-built department added to the factory in 1891. The Derby tradition of fine painting was carried into the 20th century by Leroy and other artists, notably Charles Harris, Albert Gregory, Cuthbert Gresley and W. E. J. Dean; the last three were responsible for much of the firm's hand-painted ware in the 1930s.

After World War I the company developed a collection of decorative goods and table services in Early English and Louis Seize styles, as well as Derby-style vases with exquisite painted decoration on grounds of the richest blue or green, set off with a moderate amount of gilding. Late-19th-century Derby patterns are still in production, as are the 'hat men' of the old Chelsea factory, known as 'the Derby dwarfs'. In 1935 Royal Crown Derby acquired the King Street Works, whose small, gifted group was merged with the parent company. Figure production was increased from the 1930s and included reissued models from the 1880s, such as Don

Sèvres-style tray, 1912
Derby's reputation for fine flower-printing and rich gilding was maintained into the 20th century. This French-inspired pierced tray was painted by Albert Gregory, a leading exponent of this traditional style. 439

Rose-painted ware, 1900–1930
Various artists were involved in the production of this traditional Derby ware. Notable is the heart-shaped dish painted by H. S. Hancock, which dates from c.1930. The Silver-shape coffee cup has the pottery's famous eggshell body. 440

Advertisement, 1954
This advertisement is for Derby's traditionally styled boxed fancies. 441

Imari Honey Bear, 1990s
Derby has always been associated with Japanese-inspired Imari patterns. The first tableware designs date from the 1760s, and Imari has been a bestseller ever since. The pattern is now used on a range of other wares, including bear paperweights. 442

Royal Antoinette teaware, 1990s
Introduced in its present form in 1959, this pattern draws on designs dating from the 18th century. The traditional garland pattern complements the classic Royal shape, creating a look that is popular as far away as Japan. 443

Quixote, Robin Hood and characters from Dickens and Shakespeare. Royal Crown Derby continued to produce its traditional Japan tableware patterns into the 1940s, and the same rich red, blue and gold oriental-style patterns were popular in miniature lines.

During World War II output was largely restricted to useful ware, although by 1946 animal figures, fancies, figures and statuettes were included in the catalogue. Later ware included prestigious services for export to the Middle East, specially commissioned presentation ware as well as tableware and fancies, and animals and birds modelled by Arnold Mikelson. Decorations included traditional Derby designs such as the ever-popular Imari pattern, number 1128. Among later Royal Crown Derby commissions is the new bone-china shape Queen's Gadroon, commissioned by the Queen Mother when she visited the factory in 1971.

In 1964 Royal Crown Derby was acquired by the Lawley Group (renamed Allied English Potteries) and subsequently formed part of the Royal Doulton Tableware Group (*see* p.187) when Doulton and Allied English Potteries amalgamated. During this era Robert Jefferson was retained by Royal Doulton as a sculptor. After joining the firm in 1972 he worked closely with the art director, Jo Ledger, on projects for Royal Doulton, Royal Crown Derby and Minton (*see* p.132). His first commission for Royal Crown Derby was the Quail service, whose teapot, sugar and cream were shaped as quail and decorated in Imari style with details such as feathers picked out in the traditional Derby red, blue and gold. Jefferson later modelled a series of animal and bird paperweights, six of which were launched in 1981. The decoration of these and later editions has continued the tradition of adapting the old oriental colours and motifs, and gold is used lavishly. This range has continued to expand, with new editions by John Ablitt, and some of Jefferson's earlier models, such as Cat, Rabbit, Duck, Badger and Hedgehog, have recently been remodelled. Royal Crown Derby paperweights are among the greatest successes in the firm's recent history and are avidly collected.

Other models by Jefferson which have been popular with collectors include Les Saisons (The Seasons), a group of figures inspired by Alphonse Mucha, and The Great Lovers, depicting Antony and Cleopatra,

185

Romeo and Juliet, Lancelot and Guinevere and Robin Hood and Maid Marian. In this period the company launched its Classic Collection, created by Jo Ledger in 1986 and modelled by Jefferson. The first figures represented Persephone, Dione, Penelope and Athena. Among later models are the aristocratic cats, brought out in 1987. These, each wearing royal headgear, symbolize the crowned heads of Abyssinia, Siam, Persia, Egypt, Russia and Burma. In addition to bone-china tableware, current products include miniature clocks, kettles, a watering can, an iron and stand, a wheelbarrow and garden roller, a wide range of giftware and presentation ware, limited-edition plates, plaques, vases and bowls and other collectables.

◆ Old Imari teaware, 1990s
Traditional Imari can here be seen applied to a new oval shape that harks back to the Regency period. The ram's head (below the spout of the teapot) and horn handles add a modern touch that at the same time echoes 18th-century animal modelling. 444

KEY FACTS

Location: Derby, Derbyshire, UK.
Important dates: Founded as the Derby Crown Porcelain Co. 1877. Bought by Lawley Group (later Allied English Potteries) 1964. Part of Royal Doulton Tableware Group from 1973. Independent since 2001 after a management buy-out. Still active.
Production: Porcelain.

MARKS

Printed Royal Crown Derby mark with crown above monogram introduced c.1890. Variations of this mark include 'Made in England' c.1921 and 'Bone China' on marks after World War II. Year cipher marks also used 1882–1958.

ROYAL DEVON ART POTTERY

The Devon Art Pottery – the royal prefix was added before World War I – was founded in Exeter in 1894 by Alfred Moist and William Hart, who were later joined by Alfred's brother, Joseph. Output was mainly earthenware utility ware finished with a white slip interior and a coloured slip motif combined with a scratched motto or verse. Early patterns were mostly blue-grey and terracotta, together with a little white. Later the firm concentrated on traditional Aller Vale imitations, making a feature of Devon mottoed slip and sgraffito ware with ships, birds and cottages. By this time output included jugs, flower pots, teapots and teasets, and candlesticks, in various designs and colourways. All the pottery has a speckled brown or reddish-brown body made from local clays. Moist died in 1910, and after Hart's retirement in 1921 Joseph Moist became sole proprietor of the pottery until it closed in the mid-1930s.

◆ Advertisement, 1914
This *Pottery Gazette* advertisement shows typical South Devon ware; aimed at the tourist market, it features typical mottoes and cottage and ship designs. 445

MARKS
Impressed or printed, and always incorporating company name.

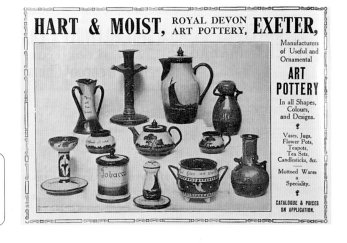

ROYAL DOULTON

By 1900 the production of Doulton, which became Royal Doulton in 1902, spanned the whole world of pottery and porcelain. The original factory in Lambeth, London, was still producing large quantities of domestic and industrial stoneware, architectural and garden ware, advertising ware and art pottery. At the factory in Burslem, Staffordshire, the staple earthenware tableware and ornaments were increasingly important, particularly after the appointment of Charles J. Noke as art director. The manufacture of richly decorated and experimental bone china was also becoming steadily more significant as a result of successes at international exhibitions. By now the firm was established as a major Staffordshire manufacturer, and the Burslem works was starting to eclipse Lambeth in reputation, as well as in scale and diversity of production.

However, the Lambeth studio was still influential. Early in the 20th century it was advertising 'New Style' artware in contemporary Art Nouveau forms, and the individual creations of artists such as Mark Marshall, John McLennan and F. C. Pope also echoed European trends. Traditional associations between Lambeth and art production were underlined by new ranges of figures modelled in contemporary styles by Leslie Harradine and John Broad. These were to be the prototypes of the extensive figure ranges made in Burslem from 1913. As an artistic centre Lambeth continued to flourish at least until the 1920s and early 1930s, thanks in part to tiles and architectural ceramics. It was the development of a new polychrome stoneware building material, with its strong colours and all-weather surface, that brought the sculptor Gilbert Bayes into the Royal Doulton orbit. From 1924 he designed a striking series of garden figures and panels, architectural components and friezes that combined the fluid forms of modern sculpture with the exciting colours of polychrome stoneware. His masterpiece was a 50ft (15m) long low-relief frieze depicting sculpture through the ages, made for the façade of Doulton House in 1939. When the building was demolished in the late 1970s the frieze was rescued, and is now in the Victoria & Albert Museum, London. Individual studio pottery continued to be made at Lambeth in the 1930s, by artists such as Vera Huggins, and between 1952 and 1956, when production in Lambeth finally ceased, the studio was under the control of the Danish potter Agnete Hoy.

◆ Dessert plate, 1916
This piece, *The Close of a Summer Day*, was painted by J. H. Plant, the artist of many seascapes, landscapes of historical interest and studies of animals, game birds and fish. [446]

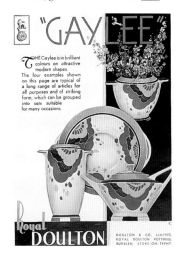

◆ Gaylee advertisement, 1934
This smart tableware design and the modernist shapes of the items exemplify the response of a major company to the success of Clarice Cliff's Bizarre Ware. In the 1930s Doulton was known for elegant and modern tableware. [447]

◆ Flambé ware, 1920s
Royal Doulton's exploration of high-temperature flambé glazes started with Sung and veined Sung ware, and was developed for the far more experimental Chang ware. [448]

Although the Lambeth works was sufficiently important for Royal Doulton to retain a traditional London base until 1956, the major developments during the first half of the 20th century all occurred at Burslem. From the early years of the century the company was a major producer of tableware and popular domestic ware in both earthenware and bone china. Patterns reflected contemporary styles. Typical was the blue-printed Norfolk range, first made in 1906 and in production until 1961. Commemoratives were also important, as when Doulton received the commission for 100,000 beakers to celebrate the coronation of Edward VII and Queen Alexandra in 1902.

Also inspired by the demands of the popular market was Series ware, introduced in 1901. These goods were groups of thematically and stylistically linked printed images that reflected aspects of history, literature and popular culture and were presented on a wide range of shapes. Best known was the extensive Dickens range, which was introduced in 1908 and survived until the 1960s. However, of greater appeal to collectors are Series ware ranges that feature designs by famous contemporary artists and illustrators, including Will Bradley, Charles Dana Gibson, H. M. Bateman, Cecil Aldin and John Hassall. From the early part of the century a considerable variety of wares was aimed specifically at the children's market. One early series featured Alice in Wonderland, but the best known is Bunnykins, a huge range of rabbit designs – originally by Barbara Vernon – that has proved continuously popular since its introduction in 1934.

It was Charles J. Noke's consummate design skill and marketing ability that drove the company ever upwards at the start of the 20th century. Under his direction it achieved a new reputation as a maker of high-class painted and gilded porcelain. There were dessert ware and ornaments, painted by artists such as Raby, Dewsberry, Plant, Birkbeck and Curnock, that could match in quality similar goods made by Minton (see p.132), Derby (see p.184), Worcester (see p.191) and other traditional leaders in this field. At the same time Noke encouraged the matching of fine painting with unusual or experimental glaze effects, such as the blue-green Titanian finish, or the deliberately rough-cast Rembrandt Ware and the deep-toned Kingsware. Glaze experimentation during this period centred on high-temperature reduction-fired flambés, first produced about 1904 with the help of Bernard Moore (see p.138) and a Doulton favourite for many decades. The flambés led directly to the colourful Sung ware and the richly glazed and dramatically coloured Chang ware, both popular during the 1920s. Noke's enthusiasm for experimentation also inspired the short-lived crystalline glazes of c.1910 which, in their styles and finishes, matched similar developments at Copenhagen, Berlin, Sèvres and elsewhere in Europe and the USA.

The company's history during the 20th century was marked by its skill in reconciling art and design with the demands of the popular market-place. Probably the best example of this is the famous figure range, a cast of elegant ladies, characters and children that has grown year by year since the series was introduced in 1913.

▲ Lily Maid, c.1930
The sculptor Gilbert Bayes modelled a series of large garden and fountain figures for Royal Doulton in the 1920s and 1930s. They were made at Lambeth in polychrome stoneware. 449

▲ Bunnykins plate, 1950s
The pottery's Bunnykins range, which was created in the early 1930s by Barbara Vernon, has proved perennially popular. 450

◀ The Bather, 1920s
Designed by Leslie Harradine, this stylish Art Deco figure was produced in a number of colourways, and was issued with or without a painted bathing costume. 451

⬥ **Captain Hook character jug, 1960s**
Royal Doulton's character jugs have
been collected since the 1930s. 452

⬥ **Elizabeth Bennet figure, 1998**
The heroine of *Pride and Prejudice*
joins a host of Royal Doulton
lady figures. 453

⬥ **Darjeeling teaware, 1997**
This delicate pattern underlines the
company's long association with the
bridal market. 454

Initially models were by leading sculptors such as Albert Toft, Phoebe Stabler and Charles Vyse, but from the early 1920s modelling was in the hands of Leslie Harradine, who was in turn succeeded by Peggy Davies, and other modellers directly associated with the ceramics industry. To date thousands of different figures have been produced, and new models are added in most years, while others are deleted, thus encouraging the collector. The figures have always had a broad appeal, reflecting as they do the styles and attitudes of the periods that produced them.

Also made with collectors in mind were ranges of character and Toby jugs, popular since the 1930s, and a large collection of finely detailed animal models, especially champion dogs. In some ways Royal Doulton reached a high point of artistic achievement during the 1930s. At this time the company produced tableware in elegant Art Deco patterns, including Tango, Gaylee, Athlone, De Luxe and Syren, on stylish modern shapes such as Envoy. Many of the figures had a distinctly contemporary look, designed to match the tableware. Leading artists such as Richard Garbe and Sir Frank Brangwyn designed, respectively, figures and other wares.

Since World War II Royal Doulton has maintained a balance between the production of tableware and the needs of the collectors' market. Contemporary styles featured again in the 1950s, but since then the emphasis has often been on the more conventional designs that satisfy the North American and bridal markets. From the 1960s a series of mergers gave the company a commanding position in the market, helped by famous names such as Minton, Royal Crown Derby, Beswick, Royal Albert and Paragon. However, the last few years have witnessed the progressive closure of all the Group's potteries, and now Royal Doulton exists only as a management company for the brands, with all production outsourced in the Far East.

KEY FACTS

Location: Lambeth, London, UK, 1815–1956.
Important dates: Founded 1815. Bought Pinder, Bourne & Co., Burslem, Staffordshire, 1882. Merged with Allied English Potteries to form Royal Doulton Tableware Group, incorporating Minton, Royal Crown Derby, Royal Albert, Ridgways and Paragon 1968. Production now in the Far East.
Production: Earthenware, china and stoneware.
Principal designers: Charles J. Noke, Leslie Harradine, Peggy Davies, Gilbert Bayes, Barbara Vernon.
Trade names: Doulton & Co., Royal Doulton.

MARKS

Most 20th-century marks
incorporate four Ds symbol
surmounted by crown
and lion. Signature
and pattern name
may also appear.
Impressed date
codes often used
up to c.1950.

ROYAL GRAFTON: see A. B. JONES & SONS p.99
ROYAL LANCASTRIAN: see PILKINGTON'S TILE & POTTERY CO. p.156

ROYAL STAFFORD TABLEWARE

The company was formed in June 1994 as a result of the merger of two well-known pottery manufacturers, Royal Stafford China and Barratt's of Staffordshire (*see* p.20). The former name, the established trade name of Thomas Poole (*see* p.159) of Longton, founded in 1845, had been adopted by Thomas Poole and Gladstone China (*see* p.75) after their merger in 1952. Under the Royal Stafford China name the Burslem company's output included many popular tea and dinner services, often with traditional-style decal decoration, for which they were well known.

Royal Stafford Tableware has been successful in changing emphasis to become designer-led and in doing so has built up a successful business in own-brand wares for High Street chain stores as well as for individual designer-name companies such as Ralph Lauren. The appointment of Eve Midwinter (*see* p.129), an acknowledged pioneer of modern ceramic design, as design consultant from 1987 to 1998 proved extremely successful for Royal Stafford. Her expertise helped to develop the Lincoln range of tableware into one of the company's best-selling lines. She also designed print patterns such as Songbirds, Trellis and Samarkand, and her styling of such ranges as Geo Floral, Seville and Naturelle were a turning point for the company.

In recent years, bold colours and textures have continued Royal Stafford's success in casual dinnerware and domestic ware. Notable patterns are Riviera, Strata, Hopsack, Fresco and Spongata, while new directions in development include pastel florals and bold geometric designs.

At present the company produces mainly tableware and has a growing market for its hotel, restaurant and corporate ware in both fine bone china and earthenware. Tableware shapes include the Devon and Gadroon bone-china range and Regal, Lincoln and Portsmouth earthenware. The pottery also produces a number of earthenware shapes with a relief-moulded border design, such as Strawberry, Lincoln and Trellis. Patterns include Apple, Daisy and Bluebell, several blue-and-white ranges, such as Bordeaux, Spring Garden and Blue Clover, and Chequers.

◆ Advertisement, 1954
While many companies were following a modern route during the 1950s, Royal Stafford was aiming at a more traditional market, drawing inspiration from revived Rococo styles. 455

◆ Fresco tableware, c.1998
This Fresco cup and saucer on the Classique shape is part of Royal Stafford's modern range. Fresco was introduced in 1988 and is still in production. 456

◀ Tableware, 1960s
Soft colours and restrained floral patterns are typical of the late 1950s and early 1960s. With this tableware Royal Stafford followed the lead of Royal Doulton. 457

KEY FACTS

Location: Royal Overhouse Works, Navigation Road, Burslem, Staffordshire, UK
Important dates: Founded from merger of Royal Stafford China and Barratt's of Staffordshire 1994. Still active.
Production: Earthenware and china.
Principal designers: Eve Midwinter.

MARKS

Standard mark for current production. Early marks include some used by Thomas Poole.

ROYAL WORCESTER

The story of Royal Worcester, one of the greatest names in British ceramics history, falls conveniently into three parts. In the 18th century Worcester was one of the great pioneers of English porcelain, able to achieve greater quality, and thus greater success, than many of its rivals. Many new technologies were developed, not least the extensive use of transfer printing. The 19th century brought further technical improvements and stylistic advances, but at the same time it witnessed the fragmentation of the Worcester name into a number of different companies – Flight, Barr & Barr, Chamberlain, Kerr & Binns and Grainger & Co. – before it emerged again as the Worcester Royal Porcelain Company. The main productions were fine and extravagant porcelains, in French and Renaissance styles, but there was an increasing emphasis on figure-making, in bone china, parian and majolica. From the late 1860s Worcester was associated with fashionable and avant-garde Japanese and Persian styles, the former best expressed by the work of James Hadley, one of the most important modellers of the 19th and early 20th centuries.

The company's reputation was further advanced by a succession of high-quality porcelain painters, by the extensive use of jewelled porcelain, and by the extraordinary technical complexity of George Owen's reticulated ware. At the end of the 19th century Worcester became known for the colour of its porcelain: soft tints of ivory, pink and other tones that echoed the contemporary art glass being made in England by Webb and others, and in the USA by Tiffany. A particularly decorative multicoloured glaze effect was a feature of Worcester's Sabrina Ware, made from 1894 until about 1930. On a more basic level, the pottery was also known for its tableware, domestic ranges and commemorative items, as well as for its pioneering use of decal decoration.

The third part of the story takes place in the 20th century. In the early years there was a simplification of both forms and decorative styles, following the appointment in 1901 of the collector and benefactor Charles William Dyson Perrins as chairman. Under his direction, Worcester took control of its main rivals, Grainger & Co., in 1902, and James Hadley in 1905. There was a greater output of everyday ware, but grand and ambitious painted porcelains were still made, and these were decorated by a new generation of famous painters such as Harry Davis, the Austins, Sedgeley and the various members of the Stinton family, best known for

◆ **Hadley figure, 1910**
The modeller James Hadley had a long association with Royal Worcester, and established a distinct style. Many of his models came in contemporary dress but were given ivory finishes. The girl seen here is one of a pair of typical candlestick figures. 458

◆ **George Owen cup and saucer, c.1900**
The cup and saucer seen here were hand-pierced by Owen at the beginning of the 20th century. Pieces such as these are among the most sought-after examples of Royal Worcester, not least because the secret of such fine pierced work died with Owen in 1916. 459

their cattle scenes. One of the most typical Worcester products of the early 20th century is a vase or plate painted by Stinton with a view of Highland cattle gathered beneath a lofty peak and a lowering sky. By this time, all major Worcester artists were signing their work.

In 1915 John Wadsworth became art director, and this important but underrated designer was to stay with Worcester until 1934, when he returned to Minton (*see* p.132), his former employer. He introduced both a more modern look and the use of lustre effects, but he was never able to change fundamentally the company's traditional dependence on high-quality decorative ware and lavishly painted and gilded porcelains. In 1934 Dyson Perrins purchased the company and established a new sense of financial stability. However, the greatest achievement of the 1930s was the production of a series of magnificently modelled and naturalistically painted ceramic sculptures, often issued as limited editions. A number of artists were involved, each with a special subject area. F. Gertner concentrated on historical military and naval themes, but far more famous were the bird and flower models produced by Dorothy Doughty and her sister Freda. In terms of pure modelling skill and a sense of detailed naturalism, porcelain has probably never been bettered, and the creations of the Doughtys have also been highly collectable. Their position in terms of 20th-century creative art is more debatable, for the precise and extraordinary accuracy of their naturalistic detail reflects more the attitudes of the 19th century. Another modeller, Antonio Vassalo, specialized in detailed flower models.

A far more significant contribution was made by Doris Lindner, who over a long period linked the Worcester name with fine animal models, mainly horses. An established independent sculptor, who had worked for both Minton and Worcester in the 1930s, Lindner became well known internationally for her equestrian portrait of Princess Elizabeth taking the salute at the Trooping of the Colour on the horse Tommy. This was modelled at sittings at Buckingham Palace and the Royal Mews. There followed an equally famous portrait of the Duke of Edinburgh playing polo on his pony Inez. Lindner has modelled a range of thoroughbred and individual horses for Worcester, including the famous steeplechaser Arkle, along with some fine examples of pedigree cattle. Such highly detailed

◆ **American Saddle Horse, 1970**
Modelled by Doris Lindner in 1970, this is one of a number of horses created for Royal Worcester. This example is one of a limited edition of 500. 460

◆ **Traditional tableware, 1960s**
Classic tableware patterns have been part of the Royal Worcester tradition throughout the 20th century. 461

and meticulously finished models, always made in limited editions, have long been popular with collectors, particularly in the USA. Other Lindner models, for example children, were made for large-scale production.

The early years of the 20th century were also marked by extensive experiments at Worcester to improve the porcelain body. These resulted in the development of a European-type hard paste material which proved to be ideal for both tableware and oven-to-table ware, important areas of Worcester production throughout the century. In 1954 Worcester became a public company, and expansion followed with the takeover of various Staffordshire brand names, including Palissy (*see* A. E. Jones, p.99).

In the latter part of the 20th century Royal Worcester, which merged with Spode (*see* p.208) in 1978, established a reputation as a maker of high-quality tableware, drawing patterns from both its historical past and more contemporary sources. One of the best known is Evesham, a fruit pattern used for a wide range of kitchenware and oven-to-table ware. Another long-time favourite is the traditional Worcester egg coddler. Worcester has also continued the tradition of figure modelling, with services and collections in historical and contemporary styles. Elegant ladies and children, aimed at a broad-based collectors' market, are particularly popular. Today the company has a wide product range, marked by a distinctive style that echoes the long history of the Worcester name.

◆ Egg coddler, 1990s
First made in 1890, the egg coddler is a favourite Royal Worcester product. A wide range of designs is still used; Hanbury, seen here, is based on 18th-century blue-and-white ware. 463

◗ Herbs oven-to-table ware, 1990s
Inspired by botanical drawings, the Worcester Herbs pattern is used on tableware, oven-to-table ware, giftware and accessories. 464

◗ Days of the Week, 1990s
Royal Worcester makes two versions of Days of the Week: boys and girls. Although they are still in production, the models date back to the 1920s and retain a distinctive period look. 462

KEY FACTS

Location: Severn Street, Worcester, Worcestershire, UK.
Important dates: Began production in 18th century. Worcester name fragmented into separate companies of Flight, Barr & Barr, Chamberlain, Kerr & Binns and Grainger & Co. in 19th century. Worcester Royal Porcelain Company founded later in century. Became a public company and took over several Staffordshire brand names 1954. Merged with Spode 1978.
Production: Bone china and porcelain.
Principal designers: James Hadley, Harry Davis, Stinton family, Austin family, F. Gertner, Dorothy and Freda Doughty, Doris Lindner.

MARKS

Variations of this standard mark used from 1891. Year dots appear either side of crown until 1915; then, until 1963, year symbols appear below mark. 'FINE BONE CHINA' included from 1959.

RUBIAN ART POTTERY

The pottery was established in 1906 to make ornamental and useful decorative ware in earthenware. In 1923 its output consisted of a wide range of vases, flower pots, rose bowls, toilet sets and trinket sets, and miscellaneous items for the table. The pottery's ornamental ware ranged from fairly standard majolica-glazed ware to elaborately modelled and decorated mantel vases with shaded and decal decoration. In addition to the more elaborate useful ware, the company produced heavy-duty domestic and toilet ware.

About 1913 the Rubian Art Pottery became a branch of Grimwade Bros (*see* p.83), but continued to operate under its own name, producing artware under the Rubay Art Ware trade name. From 1933 to about 1950 Grimwade continued some of the ranges, using 'Rubian Art' in its mark.

KEY FACTS

Location: Park Road, Fenton, Staffordshire, UK.
Important dates: Founded 1906. Bought by Grimwade Bros 1933.
Production: Earthenware.

MARKS

'L. S. & G.' mark 1906–30; 'RUBAY ART WARE' used c.1926–33.

RUSKIN POTTERY

Towards the end of 1897, encouraged by experiments in a kiln in his garden, Edward Richard Taylor purchased land and buildings at Oldbury Road, Smethwick, Birmingham, and established a pottery workshop. Meanwhile his son, William Howson Taylor, was gaining valuable experience at the pottery of relatives in nearby Hanley, Staffordshire. By December 1898 the two men had begun recruiting staff for their projected business, which was first styled the Birmingham Tile and Pottery Works.

Their work was on show at the Arts & Crafts Exhibition in London by 1903, and E. R. Taylor had resigned his position as principal of Birmingham School of Art to promote the Ruskin Pottery, as it was now known.

Early output consisted of ornamental and useful ware such as vases, bowls, tableware and other domestic ware as well as a range of enamels for mounting as jewellery, buttons, cuff-links and hat pins. The goods were normally made from local clay, but Howson Taylor also developed a white body which he used for high-fired pieces inspired by early Chinese pottery. Many of the early shapes were created on the potter's wheel, and some bowls were almost as light as eggshell porcelain. Howson Taylor's primary interest, however, was in glaze effects. Colourings ranged from slightly broken colours, through gradations of two colours, to textures and patternings rivalling cloisonné enamels. The glazes and colours were leadless, and the decoration all hand-painted. Inspiration for some of the glaze effects came from Taylor's observing rich hues in rock pools at low tide and other natural sources.

Unlike many small potteries, the firm managed to survive World War I and in the 1920s regained its pre-war standing. It was a major exhibitor at the Wembley Exhibition in 1924 and in Paris in 1925. Interviewed for *The Studio* that year, Howson Taylor reaffirmed that his chief aim was to produce fine shapes, combined with delicate workmanship, rich and infinitely varied colouring, and

Flambé vase, c.1920
The large mallet- or bottle-shaped vase was regularly used by William Howson Taylor for his experimental high-fired glazes. 465

Flambé vase and stand, c.1925
With its rich colour, large dimensions and original stand, this display vase represents William Howson Taylor's complete mastery of the demanding high-temperature reduction firing necessary to achieve orientally inspired flambé effects. 466

Brooch, c.1910
Professional and amateur jewellers mounted large numbers of Ruskin plaques and jewels in silver, pewter and other metals to form brooches and pendants. 467

Vase, 1920s
The colours produced by high-fired flambé glazes could vary from bright reds, blues and greens to a range of subtle pink-greys. 468

Glaze-effect ware, c.1910
The scent bottle on stand, baluster-shaped covered vase and covered ginger jar were favourite Ruskin shapes, seen here with rare dove-grey and snakeskin glaze effects. 469

a quality of surface which made the ware as delightful to handle as to see. His work included soufflé ware, with or without hand-painted patterns adapted from plants. Colours were either plain or varied slightly by mottlings, cloudy or shaded effects using a combination of colour tones ranging from dark blues and greens to turquoise and apple green, from purple to mauve and warm pink, and including greys and celadons. Lustres were produced in many colours, including lemon-yellow and orange, sometimes with a green or bronze underglaze painted pattern. Pearly blister lustres were also made, the Kingfisher blue lustre being the most highly prized.

Also much admired then, as now, were the pottery's extraordinarily rich and brilliant red flambé glazes, obtained by the use of an oxide of copper fired to 1400°C (2550°F). The Real Flambé Ware, the name given to this range, was noted for its variety of colour, texture and pattern. These unique and unrepeatable pieces included peach bloom, crushed strawberry, deep ruby, rouge Flambé with green flecks, ivory with pigeon's blood cloudings and many other glazes.

Throughout the 1920s the Ruskin Pottery continued to develop its ranges of shapes and glazes. Lustre ware was introduced on more delicate, lighter forms, and by the middle of the decade, as the Art Deco fashion emerged, bolder, heavier forms were put into production. By the end of the 1920s the company had developed new ranges of matt and crystalline glazes and moulded ware, particularly lamp bases.

However, in the early 1930s, in common with other manufacturers, the pottery faced increasingly difficult trading conditions. The firm's position was exacerbated by the ill health of Howson Taylor, who closed the factory in 1933 and retired in July 1935, two months before his death.

KEY FACTS

Location: Oldbury Road, Smethwick, Birmingham, West Midlands, UK.
Important dates: Founded as Birmingham Tile and Pottery Works 1898. Became Ruskin Pottery by 1903. Factory closed and production ceased 1933. Firing and glazing of stock continued until 1935.
Production: Earthenware.
Principal designers: Edward Richard Taylor, William Howson Taylor.

MARKS

Early pieces marked 'TAYLOR', with two crossed 'R's, or use 'W H T' monogram. Ruskin name incorporated c.1904.

RUSKIN
POTTERY
WEST SMETHWICK

RYE POTTERY

In 1947 the brothers John C. Cole and Walter Vivian Cole, having worked in London as studio potters and teachers, reopened the Bellevue Pottery in Rye (founded in 1869), which had closed at the start of World War II. Trading as the Rye Pottery, they kept many traditional shapes and produced them with a new style of on-glaze freehand-painted decoration which produced a soft range of colourings in which no two pieces were identical. By the early 1960s there were some 250 designs and colour combinations.

The pottery has produced a wide range of items, including tableware, presentation sets, bowls and ornamental pottery. Walter Cole's son Tarquin took over its day-to-day running in 1978 and started producing a wide range of ceramic figures. Today the pottery is renowned for its hand-painted figures such as American Folk Heroes, modelled by Neal French, and The Canterbury Tales, 24 Chaucer figures modelled by Tony Bennett.

KEY FACTS

Location: Ferry Road, Rye, East Sussex, UK.
Important dates: Founded as Rye Pottery 1947. Still active.
Production: Earthenware.
Trade name: Sussex Ware.

MARKS

Early ware marked with impressed or incised 'RYE', with initials. Printed Rye marks introduced 1947. Variations of this round mark used mid-1950s.

◆ **The Manciple, 1998**
Best known for its hand-painted items in typical 1950s styles, the Rye Pottery today produces a wide range of items. This Staffordshire-style slip-cast figure is part of its series inspired by Chaucer's *Canterbury Tales*. 470

JAMES SADLER & SONS

The pottery established an early reputation for the quality and variety of its teapots, available in traditional Rockingham, Samian, Russett and coloured bodies. It specialized in five-piece decorated sets consisting of teapot, stand, hot-water jug, sugar bowl and cream jug. Cottage ornaments, figures, standing and sitting lions, spaniels, cats and cow creamers were also made by the associated firm of John Sadler.

One of the leading lines in the interwar period was the Handy Hexagon spoutless teapot, introduced in 1923 and made in six sizes and all decorations. In the 1930s the firm produced a huge range of goods, including spectacular modernist teapot decorations and artware. New teapot patterns were launched in 1936, including some with a matt glaze, both plain and hand-decorated. Production continued throughout World War II, and afterwards the company developed other earthenware ranges, notably Sadler's Café Rough

▲ **Coffee pot, 1960s**
The tall shape and stylized floral pattern are indicative of Sadler's desire to keep in touch with the contemporary market. 471

◆ **Racing Car teapot, 1940s**
An example of popular Art Deco, the Racing Car teapot is probably the most famous 20th-century teapot. It was made in several colourways, some of them with silver detailing. There is a sugar bowl in the form of a small caravan, but these are rarely found today. 472

Russett teapots. In the 1970s the range grew to include giftware, vases and jardinières, kitchen sets, mixing bowls, fancies and souvenirs. Among recent collectables are ornamental and character teapots, mugs, tankards, trinket boxes and trays, and tea caddies. The ornamental teapots include the Three Kings and Historical Series on the Minster shape, Camelot Castles, the London Heritage Collection and English Country Cottages. Also made is the Heirloom Collection of reproduction teapots featuring archive designs.

▲ Teapot, 1990s
This coloured version of Sadler's original 1930s Clifton-shape teapot, introduced in the mid-1990s, was designed to co-ordinate with casual tableware made by other firms. 473

> **KEY FACTS**
>
> **Location:** Market Street, Burslem, Staffordshire, UK
> **Important dates:** Founded 1882. Taken over by Churchill Group 2000. Still active.
>
> **MARKS**
>
> Printed or impressed Sadler name from c.1937; earlier, impressed, mark with 'J. S. S. B' and 'ENGLAND'. This mark from c.1947.
>
>

SALEM CHINA COMPANY

The company was founded in 1898 by Pat and John McNichol, Dan Cronin and William Smith to make white granite and semi-porcelain tableware. It produced decorative tableware until 1960, when manufacturing ceased, and now it distributes ware made abroad. Chief among the designers who worked for Salem was Viktor Schreckengost, who created a number of the pottery's distinctive shapes and decal decorations. Victory (1938) and Tricorne (1934) are among his most distinctive shapes, although he also designed Free-Form (1940s), Lotus Bud, Symphony (1940) and others. Decal decorations were used interchangeably with shapes. This allows collectors to concentrate on shapes only, collecting all decorations in a particular shape, or decals only, hunting the uses of a single decal on many shapes. Petitpoint (also known as Basket Petitpoint), Godey Prints, Indian Tree, Sailing (designed by Margaret Blumenthal) and Bird of Paradise are popular decals with collectors.

> **KEY FACTS**
>
> **Location:** Salem, Ohio, USA.
> **Important dates:** Founded 1898. Manufacturing ceased 1960.
> **Production:** White-granite and semi-porcelain tableware.
> **Principal designers:** Viktor Schreckengost, J. Palin Thorley, Margaret Blumenthal.
>
> **MARKS**
>
> Wreaths and shields with company name, and often incorporating shape name.
>
>

◆ Victory dinnerware, c.1940
Viktor Schreckengost's Victory shape for Salem was available with a wide variety of decals. With the plainest of decoration, Victory is a very modern shape, but many of the patterns used on it were so traditional that they only contradicted that modernity. 474

SANDLANDS & COLLEY

In 1907 Alfred Colley took over Sandlands Ltd, which made china and earthenware for all markets and special lines for the colonial and foreign trade. Production at the Lichfield Pottery, in Hanley, Staffordshire, included toilet ware, dinnerware, and china tea and breakfast ware, vases, flower pots and pedestals. Among the firm's lines were Waldorf hotel and restaurant ware, and plates ornamented with subjects – Whist, Tennis and Golf – treated humorously in colour and designed by Victor Venner.

> **MARKS**
>
> Standard mark, probably continued by W. Sandland after company renamed c.1913.
>
>

SCAMMELL CHINA COMPANY: see LAMBERTON CHINA p.109

Founded by William Shaw in 1894 as the Sheaf Art Pottery Co., the firm initially made mainly ornamental useful ware such as decorated vases, jugs, flower pots, cheese stands, trinkets, toilet ware and fancy earthenware. William Copestake formed a partnership with Shaw in 1901, and although he did not stay for long, the company retained his name.

During World War I Shaw & Copestake made a number of cheaper lines and novelties, including a range of painted cellulose ware in attractive colourways which did not require glazing. (Even though the cellulose finish did not wear well, the novelties remained in production, and new models continued to be added to the range until the early 1950s.) Clock sets and clocks were among the most important products made during the 1920s and 1930s. These items were available with a variety of decoration – painted, printed, and an embossed design with a cellulose finish. The first animal models appeared in the late 1920s, starting with a range of elephants in black cellulose finish as well as a swan and gnomes for the garden.

From around this time Richard Hull, who had formed a partnership with William Shaw in 1903, was responsible for many of the firm's developments. He worked closely with a local glaze manufacturer to produce the range of low-fired matt glazes associated with Shaw & Copestake products. Many fresh novelties in animal figures and ornamental useful ware and fancies from this period were decorated with matt glazes and, from 1936, marked with the SylvaC name.

After the death of Thomas Lawrence (*see* p.113) in 1932, the Falcon Pottery was run by his nephew, John Grundy, and when Grundy died in 1938 Shaw & Copestake took over the pottery and ran it as well as its own. Shaw & Copestake vacated its Sylvan Works during World War II, and from 1941 it concentrated production with Lawrence's at the Falcon Pottery. The two firms continued to make their own standard lines, each using its own backstamp. Shaw & Copestake reopened the Sylvan Works in 1945, and over the next few years both factories worked to full capacity, using each other's designs and marking them either SylvaC or Falcon. Thomas Lawrence already had its own designer and modeller, Reginald Thompson, who produced new designs for both factories.

In 1946 Shaw & Copestake was making animal figures, animal troughs, drinking fountains, ashtrays, cruet sets, fancies, figures and statuettes, jugs, table lamps, mugs, novelties, teapots and vases. In the 1950s and 1960s its catalogue included a wide range of animal models – for example,

◆ **Diamond flower vase, 1930s**
Dramatic geometric shapes and soft colours are typical SylvaC features. However, collectors tend to prefer ware with more dramatic modelling and naturalistic elements. 475

◆ **SylvaC novelty rabbit, 1930s**
The most familiar of all the SylvaC animals, the rabbit was made in various sizes and colours. Other animals include several breeds of dog, cats, lambs, frogs and hares. 476

◆ **SylvaC tableware, 1950s**
In typically 1950s style, this cheese dish, butter dish and toast rack reflect Shaw & Copestake's attempts to pursue a more contemporary look. There are echoes here of Poole and other 1950s style leaders. 477

a series by Arnold Machin – and novelties such as garden gnomes, floral ware, money boxes, bowls, book-ends, flower and posy holders, wall vases, trinket boxes, jewellery and ashtrays, many decorated with models of animals. Also made were Tudor Cottage and other cottage teaware, tableware fancies and some interesting lines in children's ware. In 1957 the firm opened a new factory on land opposite the Sylvan Works, and combined the production of the two sites.

After Shaw & Copestake went into voluntary liquidation in 1982, it was bought by the North Midland Cooperative Society and leased to Longton Ceramics, a workers' cooperative. This failed, and from 1984 the Cooperative Society took over the pottery and ran it as Crown Winsor, producing SylvaC and Falcon Ware designs. Subsequently bought by Frank Heath, the pottery soon went into receivership and closed.

> KEY FACTS
>
> **Location:** Normacott Road, Longton, Staffordshire, UK.
> **Important dates:** Founded as Sheaf Art Pottery Co. 1894. Closed 1982.
> **Production:** Earthenware.
>
> MARKS
>
> Various SylvaC Ware marks used from 1930s. This mark, used in 1960s and 1970s, is a variation of a 1930s backstamp with 'MADE IN ENGLAND' added.

◆ **Pineapple vase, 1930s**
The widely used naturalistic forms in the SylvaC range blend Art Deco styling with a rather literal and old-fashioned approach to the natural forms themselves. 478

SHAWNEE POTTERY COMPANY

The pottery began operations in 1937 in old buildings associated with the American Encaustic Tiling Company. It made art pottery, brightly coloured dinnerware and kitchenware in an earthenware body, to designs supplied by S. S. Kresge, Kress, Woolworths and McCrory stores. Later Sears had its kitchen and dinnerware produced by Shawnee. The name Kenwood Ceramics was used by Shawnee for ware made for sale through department stores, gift shops and florists.

Shawnee is probably best known among collectors for the whimsical characters designed by Rudy Ganz, such as Smiley Pig, Puss 'n Boots and Muggsy, of the 1940s, as well as the Corn-King and Corn-Queen corn-shaped dinnerware and table novelties made from 1945 to 1961. However, the company also made a wide range of other items, including cookie jars, lobster tableware novelties, figurines, flower pots, jugs and pitchers, novelty shakers, lamps, teapots, novelty planters and kitchenware.

The company's figural cream jugs and sugar bowls, especially Smiley Pig, Puss 'n Boots and Elephant, and figural jugs, especially Chanticleer, Little Bo Peep, and Smiley Pig, have a ready market among today's collectors. The pottery closed in 1961.

> KEY FACTS
>
> **Location:** Zanesville, Ohio, USA.
> **Important dates:** Founded 1937. Closed 1961.
> **Production:** Earthenware kitchenware, dinnerware and flower containers.
> **Principal designers:** Rudy Ganz, Robert Heckman, Louise Bauer.
>
> MARKS
>
> 'Shawnee' found as incised script, but paper labels used on most ware. On corn-shaped ware only 'Oven Proof' used. American Indian appears within an arrowhead, as seen in this mark.

◆ **Vase, c.1940**
Pouter pigeons flank this trumpet-shaped vase. Figural vases and planters were a large part of Shawnee's production. Highly collectable subjects on planters include Cat and Sax, Circus Waggon, Canopy Bed, Gazelle, and High Chair with Kitten. 479

SHELLEY POTTERIES

In 1872 Joseph Shelley entered into partnership with James Wileman, whose family had been in ceramics since the 1850s. Wileman retired in 1892, and when Shelley died in 1896, Percy Shelley took control. The Shelley family continued to operate the china-making part of the company as Wileman & Co. until 1925.

Frederick A. Rhead became the firm's art director in 1896, and worked closely with Percy Shelley until he left to become a freelance designer around 1905. New shapes from this period were commissioned from important modellers such as Rowland Morris. Among Morris's works for Shelleys was the well-known Dainty White, a fine-body teaware range with fluted panels and scalloped edges which was registered in 1896 and remained in production until 1966. Originally made in white, this shape was later decorated with coats of arms, and from 1932 produced with a painted flower in high relief on the handles under the name Floral Dainty.

The factory was extended to accommodate earthenware production in 1898, and Frederick Rhead created a number of hand-painted earthenware art lines such as the commercially successful Intarsio range, in which the brilliant coloured decoration was painted directly on to the unfired earthenware body before glazing. Many of these designs were registered, the first 40 in December 1898. Teapots were added to this range around 1900 and featured well-known politicians. Rhead also modelled a series of miniature grotesques, animals and Toby jugs which were deliberately made to look ugly.

Walter Slater, who had specialized in painting floral subjects for Royal Doulton (*see* p.187), took over as art director from Rhead. By this time the demand for art pottery had lessened, and production was now aimed at the expanding popular market. The range included toilet sets, which were sold in large quantities, earthenware dinner services and related ware, advertising and ordinary domestic items, children's ware and bone-china tea, breakfast and dessert services, for which the firm became noted. Slater is best known for his traditional Japan, or rich oriental-style, patterns in red, blue and gold, such as Ashbourne (1913) for bone-china tea, breakfast ware and dinnerware and simple floral designs which were in vogue in the early years of the century. He expanded the firm's artware production with a new range of Intarsio in 1911, and Flamboyant Ware

★ Our Pets, 1920s
The pottery produced a range of figures and groups inspired by Mabel Lucie Attwell's drawings of tubby and humorous 1920s children. 480

★ Baby's plate, c.1916
The thick-walled baby's plate was made by many potters from the early 20th century onwards. This version draws on the nursery rhyme 'Ride a Cock Horse to Banbury Cross'. 481

◆ Cloisonné-pattern teaware, c.1930
This overall pattern, seen here on the Queen Anne shape, is closer to contemporary chintzware than to the Japanese enamel from which it takes its name. 482

Well known for its modern designs
and advanced marketing techniques,
Shelley Potteries produced its own
magazine, *The Shelley Standard*, and
used the stylish image of the Shelley
Girl in advertising and window
displays. The Shelley Girl became
almost a trade mark and is celebrated
by this porcelain figure. 483

with its striking glaze effects. Roself, a series of ornamental earthenware
vases and bowls with a rose motif stencilled on to a self-coloured background of green, blue, grey, pink, mauve, brown or, most commonly, black,
was launched in 1915. Later variations included violets and carnations. A
related series of vases was brightly hand-painted with parrots, kingfishers
and bluebirds. Moiré Antique, a watered-silk effect printed in fine lines,
was used on earthenware and porcelain from 1914, mainly in pink, blue or
green varieties. During World War I and the following years arms or
heraldic miniatures were marketed in large numbers and by 1922 over 400
models had been produced.

In 1919 Walter Slater's son Eric joined the firm. Slater senior continued
his experimental work and in 1920 produced a new line of ornamental lustres, using a technique of laying a ground of gradually changing colour
such as a deep crimson changing to a deep blue, which was painted in gold
and other colours and finally covered with an iridescent glaze.
Decorations included oriental-style patterns, especially Japanese scenes,
galleons, fish, butterflies, water-lilies and Celtic geometric patterns, as
well as the Vinta series featuring vines and a bird on an off-white ground.

After changing its name to Shelleys in 1925 and to Shelley Potteries in
1928, the company became more up-to-date, with a well-defined house
style, and was one of the first Staffordshire firms to adopt aggressive marketing. It produced some of the finest bone-china teaware of the interwar
years, much of it influenced by Art Deco modernism. Eric Slater designed
many of the new teaware ranges, including the ultra-modern Vogue and
Mode shapes launched in 1930. He also designed one of the best-known
shapes from this period, Queen Anne, with delicate octagonal hollowware
and square plates. This design was registered in 1926 and launched with
over 170 different patterns, some of which were also used on matching
earthenware dinner services. Other patterns ranged from simple designs
for ordinary ware to the most ornate and ostentatious service plates,
intended primarily for table ornamentation, for the American market.
Slater also supervised the development of Harmony Art Ware, introduced
in 1932, a hard earthenware body hand-decorated on-glaze with simple
bands in graduated shades of one or more running colours. The same decoration was used on bone-porcelain teasets and other tableware.

⬥ Sunrise and Tall Trees
teaware, c.1929
The octagonal Queen Anne shape,
first registered in 1926, was used for a
wide range of patterns; this example, a
subtle interpretation of the landscape
designs used by many potters during
the 1920s, is very characteristic. 484

At this time the firm was particularly noted for its range of nursery ware, which had been introduced in 1902 with a range of nursery-rhyme designs and was later expanded to include other series, such as Peter Pan and Boy Scouts. The much-collected children at play series, by the illustrator Hilda Cowham, was registered in 1924, while the Linda Edgerton series was made from around 1925 and the equally popular Mabel Lucie Attwell designs, featuring her well-known Boo Boos, from 1926. Teasets by Mabel Lucie Attwell included pieces modelled in the shapes of animals and toadstools. Around 1937 a series of her figures was introduced.

Production continued throughout World War II on the strength of the extensive export trade, and was combined with that of Jackson & Gosling (*see* p.97), then part of Copeland. Thus Shelley became involved in producing china dinnerware, using Copeland's moulds and patterns. Indeed, after the war the firm stopped making earthenware and devoted its whole production to china. During this period many of the high-quality printing and hand-finishing processes on which Shelley's reputation rested in the 1920s and 1930s were being replaced by modern printing techniques. Surprisingly, however, the firm was unaffected by the 1950s contemporary-design movement, although it did reintroduce some earlier patterns and a sgraffito range, launched in the 1930s, which fitted the new fashion for hand-crafted studio ware. Patterns from the 1950s include Forest Glade by Eric Slater, Wild Flower and Chantilly Rose.

In 1953 the company acquired the adjoining Jackson & Gosling site and formed a subsidiary, Shelley Electrical Furnaces Ltd, which produced, from 1956, electrical kilns developed by Donald Shelley, Percy Shelley's nephew. After the death of Norman Shelley, in 1966, both Shelley China Ltd (the name was changed from Shelley Potteries in 1965) and the subsidiary kiln-making company were acquired by Allied English Potteries. The Shelley name became the property of the Royal Doulton Tableware Group (*see* p.187) in 1972.

◄ **Mode teaware, c.1930**
The avant-garde Mode shape, with its solid triangular handle, was generally used with contemporary Art Deco patterns. This powerful abstract design in red and black is typical. 485

◆ **Tea and coffee ware, c.1930**
Most of these typical Shelley patterns are on the Queen Anne shape. Of these, the most desirable is the green and gold trio (bottom left), which uses the geometric Vogue shape, made only between 1930 and 1933. 486

KEY FACTS

Location: Foley China Works, Longton, Staffordshire, UK.
Important dates: Formerly Wileman & Co. 1853–1925. Renamed Shelleys 1925 and Shelley Potteries 1928, Became part of Royal Doulton Tableware Group 1972.
Production: China.

MARKS

Name in script from 1925. Early ware has 'W & C' monogram.

SHENANGO CHINA COMPANY

In 1901 two manufacturers of pottery were established in New Castle, Pennsylvania: the New Castle Pottery Company and the Shenango China Company. For the second the early years were difficult, but the company became financially successful after introducing hotel ware in 1909. Three years later Shenango bought the plant of the New Castle Pottery and moved its operations there. A fine-china dinnerware line was developed in 1928, but the difficult economic conditions imposed by the Depression led to the project's being abandoned.

From 1936 to 1958 Shenango manufactured American Haviland for the Theodore Haviland Company. In 1939 Louis Hellman of Germany's Rosenthal China arranged for Shenango to make Rosenthal's shapes and patterns, and in 1940 Castleton China Inc. was created to produce the Rosenthal china. With all of these projects in house during the 1940s, Shenango had 1200 employees. China made for Haviland and Rosenthal was in patterns typical of these European potteries, but adapted for American buyers. Flowers, solid-colour borders and lavish use of gold characterized the work.

Shenango China, Inc. was created in 1954. The "Fast-Fire" kiln developed by the company revolutionized the vitrified-china industry. In 1968 Shenango was chosen by President and Mrs Lyndon Johnson to make a set of china for official entertaining at the White House. The pattern features wild flowers of the USA. That same year Shenango was sold to Interpace Corporation. By 1977 the highly mechanized plant covered 17 acres (7 hectares), and 1000 workers were employed. Syracuse China (*see* Onondaga Pottery, p.145) purchased the plant in 1988, but closed it only two years later after finding that its inefficiencies made profitability difficult.

Besides the White House china, Castleton China's most famous table service was that designed by Hungarian-born Eva Zeisel in 1943 but not produced until after World War II. Museum, the first free-form modern shape made in fine china, was introduced through an exhibit at the Museum of Modern Art in New York City in 1946. It is avidly sought by collectors of Modernism.

◆ **Custard cup, 1955**
Hotel ware patterns are often quite conservative, seeming far removed from their time of production. 487

◆ **Cowboy diner plate, c.1950**
The tan body colour and brown print decoration give this plate a rustic character suitable for service in a Western-style chuckwagon diner. 488

◆ **Eva Zeisel's Museum dinnerware for Castleton China, late 1940s**
Zeisel's Museum line for Castleton was elegant and modern, an unusual combination of elements in American fine china, which tended to follow traditional models. The fanfare that accompanied the appearance of the design in the Museum of Modern Art brought recognition for Castleton and for Zeisel's talents. 489

KEY FACTS
Location: New Castle, Pennsylvania, USA.
Important dates: Founded 1901. Closed 1990.
Production: Fine china dinnerware and hotel ware.
Trade names: Theodore Haviland, New York; Rosenthal, Castleton China Company.

MARKS
Include an American Indian decorating a pot, and give trade name and line.

SHORE & COGGINS

etween the wars the pottery made medium-priced china teaware in a wide variety of styles, from simple floral designs to traditional Derby-style patterns and the noted Chelsea Willow pattern. During the 1930s it also introduced some mildly Art Deco patterns. At this time all decoration was of either the banded or the printed-and-enamel style; examples are Crocus, Tulip and Nasturtium. Throughout the 1940s output consisted of breakfast, coffee, morning, sandwich, supper and tea sets. In the 1950s the firm introduced further traditional-style patterns such as Shangri-la and Royal Kew Gardens, but it also made the modern Eden shape. Among the more interesting lines in the 1960s were Crown Ware coffee sets with larger coffee pots and teacup-sized coffee cups. These were launched with floral and geometric-style patterns.

KEY FACTS

Location: Queen Anne China and Edensor Works, Longton, Staffordshire, UK.
Important dates: Traded as Shore & Coggins from 1911. Bought by T. C. Wild & Sons 1918. Taken over by Lawley Group 1964. Merged with Royal Doulton 1972.
Production: China.

Bell China
MADE IN
ENGLAND

SHORER & SON

ntil about 1927 this pottery made almost exclusively majolica and associated products. Output consisted mainly of ornamental useful ware, fancies and novelty items with low-relief moulded or embossed decoration and one-colour or blended majolica glazes. In 1910 the catalogue included tableware, flower pots and stands, fern pots, bulb bowls, vases and jugs. Some of the majolica tableware shapes remained popular throughout the firm's existence, notably Strawberry & Bow (later renamed Pompadour) and Cherry Ripe. Toby jugs were made from at least 1917, and Toby teapots and character jugs were also produced.

At the British Industries Fair in 1921 Shorter had a notable show of art pottery, mostly vases, flower pots and fancies in self-coloured glazes. The firm's traditional majolica jugs, as well as new, highly stylized modernist and Art Deco shapes, were later brought out with the same treatment. Among the most important developments between the wars were the matt-glaze ranges in contemporary pastel shades. Harry Steele, who arrived in 1932, pursued diversity, and the company became well known for its many ranges of decorative fancies and ornaments, in both traditional and contemporary styles, aimed at the popular market. In 1933 Steele recruited a new designer, Mabel Leigh. Although she stayed for only a short time, Leigh helped to revolutionize the pottery's output. Her

Stag Ware vase, mid-1930s
Shorter introduced a series of new soft-matt glazes in pastel shades in 1936. The glazes were used to decorate, among other pieces, some of the pottery's more traditional designs such as the Stag Ware vases, which look back in style to Victorian majolica, and Syringa, with its embossed floral pattern. 490

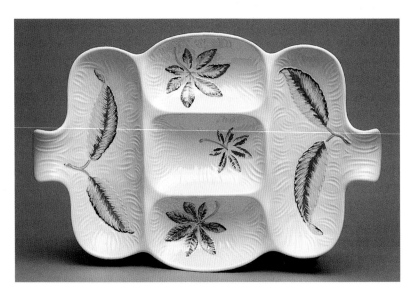

Hors d'oeuvre dish, 1950s
With this embossed and hand-painted hors d'oeuvre dish, Shorter demonstrated its versatility in adapting its ornamental range to include shapes and patterns in keeping with the contemporary taste for less formal dinnerware. 491

◆ **Gilbert and Sullivan figurines, c.1940**
Shorter obtained permission from the D'Oyly Carte Opera Company to model jugs from five Gilbert and Sullivan operettas, and the concept was extended with the issue of figurines. This series based on *The Mikado* was designed around 1940, although not marketed until after the end of World War II. 492

◆ **Thisbe vase, early 1930s**
This is one of a series of five vases influenced by modernism which are quite different from Shorter's other production. Other shapes in this series include Pyramus, Rhomboid, Noni and Olwen. 493

main creation was Period Pottery, colourful and decorative ranges with painted and sgraffito decoration that looked modern but drew inspiration from traditional European, Middle Eastern, African and other exotic sources. Leigh also designed hundreds of shapes and her own interpretation of traditional cottage ware, the Shantee and Pagoda ranges. Throughout this period of diversity the firm's best-known product was its fish range, which was produced at least until the early 1970s.

A range of figurines based on D'Oyly Carte actors in the Gilbert and Sullivan operettas entered production in 1949, designed by Clarice Cliff (*see* p.43) in close collaboration with Shorter's designer and modeller Betty Silvester. In the 1950s Shorter again followed contemporary trends, introducing a range of white matt-glazed vases and bringing back many of the earlier embossed fruit and flower designs in new colourways. At the same time two new series in this style, Harmony and Petal, gave these traditional goods a modern look. This trend continued into the early 1960s, by which time the pottery's products looked tired and dated, although they were still selling well. By 1964 Shorter was struggling, and moved into Fielding's (*see* p.66) Devon factory. Although the firm maintained a degree of independence and produced new tableware patterns, soon Shorter patterns and shapes were appearing with Crown Devon backstamps.

◆ **Period Pottery, c.1933**
This range of Period Pottery shows the Khimara pattern. All the shapes and patterns for Period Pottery were designed by Mabel Leigh, who trained a small team to decorate the ware with sgraffito and freehand painting. 494

KEY FACTS

Location: Batavia Works, Copeland Street 1878–1964 and, as part of S. Fielding & Co., Crown Devon Works, Sutherland Street 1964–; Stoke, Staffordshire, UK.
Important dates: Formerly Shorter & Boulton. Traded as Shorter & Son from 1878. Taken over by S. Fielding & Co. and moved to that company's Devon Works 1964.
Production: Earthenware.
Principal designers: Arthur Shorter, Colley Shorter, Joan Shorter, Clarice Cliff, Mabel Leigh.
Trade names: Batavia, Sunray, Aura, Period Ware.

MARKS

Usually incorporate Shorter & Son name. This 'GENUINE STAFFORDSHIRE' printed mark introduced 1940s.

WOODLAND
GENUINE
STAFFORDSHIRE
HAND PAINTED
SHORTER & SON LTD
ENGLAND

SIMPSONS (POTTERS)

Founded as the Soho Pottery, (*see* opposite), this firm specialized in toilet ware, dinner, tea, coffee, breakfast, supper, sandwich and morning sets, cruets, eggcups and mugs, concentrating on traditional patterns for the popular market. These included the Hampton Court pattern on the Beaded shape and Queen's Green and Green Banded ware. The Thistledown pattern on the Vogue shape, a new contemporary-style dinnerware range designed by Colin Haxby, was launched in the mid-1950s. The firm stopped making tableware in the mid-1970s, but continued to produce oven-to-table ware and fancies. Later on it introduced contract ware, including Ovenstone cookware, slow-cooker bodies and storage jars.

KEY FACTS

Location: Elder Works, Cobridge, Staffordshire, UK.
Important dates: Formerly Soho Pottery. Traded as Simpsons from 1944. Closed 2003.
Production: Earthenware.

JOHN SKEAPING

In 1926 the 25-year-old sculptor, artist and designer John Rattenbury Skeaping sent Wedgwood (*see* Josiah Wedgwood & Sons, p.230) samples of animal carvings he had carried out at London Zoological Gardens. The firm made trials of at least 14 models, and ten were put into production in 1927: the Bison, Buffalo, Duiker (seated), Duiker (standing), Fallow Deer, Kangaroo, Monkeys, Polar Bear, Tiger and Buck and Sea Lion. Many different glazes have been recorded in these models, including Ivory, Cream Colour, Satin Grey, Turquoise Blue, Celadon, Honey Buff, Terracotta and Black Basalt. The last two glazes required a higher firing, and as a result the models are visibly smaller but benefit from sharper detail. Norman Wilson, Wedgwood's works manager, was responsible for many of the new bodies and glazes, and among the most highly prized are the Skeaping models in Wilson's Grey and Tan, comprising a terracotta body with grey glaze, which when fired created a most unusual mottled effect.

Skeaping's only other involvement with Wedgwood was as an entrant in the international competition held in 1930 to design a vase celebrating the bicentenary of the birth of Josiah Wedgwood. He and his wife Barbara Hepworth both submitted designs, and Skeaping won two of the prizes.

▲ **Monkeys group, late 1920s**
Introduced in 1927, this was one of the most popular of all the Skeaping animal models. It is shown here in Celadon, an effect intended to suggest old Chinese jade. 495

◀ **Seated Duiker, late 1920s**
The Seated Duiker was the least expensive of the ten Skeaping models introduced in 1927. This one is shown in Honey Buff, a warm buff-coloured body with a transparent glaze. Black wooden stands were available for each of the models. 496

KEY FACTS

Important dates: Sent samples of animal carvings he had done at London Zoo to Wedgwood 1926. Trials carried out on 14 models by Wedgwood and ten models put into production 1927. Awarded two prizes in international competition organized by Wedgwood to celebrate centenary of birth of Josiah Wedgwood 1930.
Production: Models in earthenware and fine stoneware (black basalt).

MARKS

'J SKEAPING' impressed into side of base, in addition to usual Wedgwood backstamp. Artist's name omitted in some later editions.

J SKEAPING

SAMPSON SMITH

During the second half of the 19th century the firm was a leading maker of Staffordshire flatback figures. By the 1920s its most prominent lines included traditional tea and breakfast ware with patterns including white ware, fluted or embossed, edge line and sprig, three gold lines, turquoise and pink with gold lines, as well as some good decal border patterns and the popular enamelled floral sprays panel design. During World War II the firm's production was concentrated with that of its owner, Barker Bros (*see* p.19), but a few stock patterns came out under its own name. About 60 original moulds were found in the 1940s, and in 1946 the firm was listed as making figures, fancies and novelties as well as its usual lines.

KEY FACTS

Location: Sutherland Works, Barker Street, and other sites, Longton, Staffordshire, UK
Important dates: Founded 1846. Closed 1960.
Production: Earthenware. China in 20th century.

SOHO POTTERY

Between the wars the pottery became well known for its tableware and toilet ware, and for ornamental and ordinary domestic goods made under its Solian Ware and, later, Ambassador Ware labels. Among the many new shapes and patterns were the Verdun dinner service, of 1921, which had a square cover dish with off-set handles that made it appear diagonal, and toilet ware decorated with ground-laid treatments with prints and enamel patterns. By the early 1930s traditional patterns on fairly traditional shapes were gradually augmented with more angular shapes and stylized, hand-painted enamel patterns, such as the Palm pattern on the Princess-shape coffee set and Sunray on the Burlington-shape teaware launched in the middle of the decade. In this period Soho extended its ornamental range to include figure-modelled book-ends, powder bowls, cigarette lighters, smokers' sets and birds-in-flight wall-ornament sets. Queen's Green tableware, a range of underglaze banded ware, introduced about 1933, was one of its most successful lines. A series of matt-glazed pieces was launched in 1937, as well as a new range of banded ware in pastel shades of green and mauve on the Burlington shape. The firm became Simpsons (Potters) (*see* opposite) in 1944.

◆ **Jubilee beaker, 1935**
The jubilee of George V was much exploited by potters great and small. Soho contributed this beaker, which is decorated with stock decals. 497

◆ **Coffee cup, c.1935**
The impact of Clarice Cliff's success could not be ignored, even – perhaps especially – by small companies. Soho's response was this geometric shape and bold abstract pattern. 498

KEY FACTS

Location: Soho Pottery, Tunstall 1901–6, Elder Works, Cobridge 1906–44; Staffordshire, UK.
Important dates: Founded 1901. Became Simpsons (Potters) 1944, operating from the Elder Works. Still active.
Production: Earthenware.
Trade names: Solian Ware, Ambassador Ware.

MARKS

Usually include company name. This mark used from 1930s. After c.1944 Simpsons name used.

SOUTHERN POTTERIES, INC.

The company's earliest goods were decal-decorated semi-vitreous dinnerware and hotel ware. Plates, bowls and ashtrays are the most collectable items made during the early years. Underglaze hand-painting gradually replaced decals, and by the mid-1930s the name Blue Ridge was being used to designate the new ware. More than 4100 patterns were produced under this name. With no investment in decal stocks, the company could change patterns quickly. Most patterns probably never had names and would have been sold by pattern number. A line of speciality ware was added in 1942. By the early 1950s annual production averaged 24 million pieces, but escalating labour costs and cheap imported goods conspired to close the factory in 1957.

KEY FACTS

Location: Erwin, Tennessee, USA.
Important dates: Founded 1917. Traded as Southern Potteries, Inc. from 1920. Closed 1957.
Production: Semi-vitreous dinnerware and hotel ware.
Trade name: Blue Ridge.

MARKS

Incorporate Blue Ridge trade name. This trade name generally used by collectors to identify the company's ware.

◆ **Blue Ridge dinnerware patterns, 1940–55**
The Palisades-shape cake plate with Anjou pattern, the Colonial cup and saucer with Rugosa pattern, and the Skyline teapot with Rustic Plaid pattern are typical of hand-painted Blue Ridge ware, which is still popular with collectors. 499

SPODE

Like Royal Worcester (*see* p.191), with which it merged in 1978, Spode is one of the most renowned names in British ceramics. Josiah Spode pioneered the development of bone china at the end of the 18th century, making possible a huge expansion of the English porcelain industry. From that date the company was associated with fine-quality porcelain tableware and ornaments, initially in Regency styles and then in all those of the early Victorian period. It was also a major manufacturer of transfer-printed blue-and-white tableware and domestic pottery. Many patterns were introduced which have remained perennially popular, the best-known example being the Blue Italian pattern, first made in 1816 and produced ever since.

Major changes occurred after W. T. Copeland bought the company in 1833. Not only did the Spode name largely disappear, but the new company also became far more ambitious and innovative. Copeland made lavish painted and gilded ornaments in porcelain, reflecting the influence of France; it was one of the first to develop the new parian, or statuary porcelain, and introduced styles, ranges and techniques as diverse as majolica, tiles, *pâte-sur-pâte* and commemorative ware. Nevertheless, tableware remained the backbone of production at the ever-expanding Church Street pottery, and in the 20th century this pattern became steadily more dominant. Having restricted production to one site since the factory's foundation, Spode enjoys the advantage of an enormous archive

▲ **Sèvres-style plate, 1906–1907**
This copy of a Sèvres porcelain plate was produced by Spode as part of a set ordered by Tsar Nicholas II to match a service commissioned by Catherine the Great in 1776. Once complete, the order was never shipped to Russia because of the assassination of the Tsar in 1917. 500

◆ Cup and saucer, from c.1850,
teapot, 1920s
The cup and saucer are decorated with
the Lyre pattern, a 19th-century gilding
technique also used on this Temple-
pattern teapot. Spode's reputation
for underglaze blue-printed ware
continued into the 20th century, and
it still produces some of its original
Chinese-influenced patterns from
hand-engraved copper plates. 501

◆ Blue Italian jug, 1990s
The Blue Italian pattern, shown here
on a Windsor-shape jug, was instantly
popular on its launch in 1816; it has
remained in production ever since and
is Spode's best-seller today. The design
is now believed to be based on a
drawing dating from 1690. 502

◆ Two-tone tableware, 1950s
The fashion for two-tone tableware
in soft colours, often using tinted slips
on a white body, was started by Poole
and further developed by Wedgwood.
Spode's version is seen here. 503

and pattern library where 70,000 tableware patterns are held. The result
has been a tendency to rely on the styles of the past for design inspiration.
This historicism has been accompanied by a more frequent use of the
original Spode name, a process that led in 1970 to the decision to revert
totally to this name and cease using the Copeland name, even though the
two had been used jointly for some time.

Despite the overpowering dominance of its past, Spode has always
managed to keep in touch with the popular market-place, and to produce
wares that at least acknowledge or reflect contemporary styles and fashions. Art Deco certainly affected Copeland, albeit in a rather restrained
and derivative way, but even in its advertisements for modern designs the
factory tended to stress traditional virtues. Copeland's flirtation with
modernism took a more positive form in the late 1930s with the arrival of
the designer and modeller Eric Olsen. He created a range of vases, bowls,
jugs and other wares whose contemporary fluid forms and matt glazes in
pastel colours echoed the work of market leaders such as Wedgwood (*see*
Josiah Wedgwood & Sons p.230). Olsen's wares are not unlike those of
Keith Murray (*see* p.141), and there was a range of animals that seemed
inspired by the work of Skeaping (*see* p.206), also designed for Wedgwood.

Modernism crept into the company's output in the 1950s. That decade
saw the launch of the typical coupe-style Barbecue shape, decorated with
a range of contemporary images, and in 1960 the award-winning Royal
College tableware shape, designed by Neal French and David White, went
into production. Another feature of the 1960s was figure production,
paving the way for the famous series of children's figures modelled by
Pauline Stone in the early 1970s.

Around the time of the merger with Royal Worcester in 1978, a new emphasis on the kitchen in consumer and women's magazines revitalized the Blue Italian pattern. This trend also prompted further raids on the archive for other old blue-and-white patterns that could be adapted for modern techniques of decoration; examples are Primula, Geranium and Country Scenes. The influence of Spode's famous Blue Room, which has over 300 classic patterns on show, has led to the issue of various archive collections. Bone-china tableware patterns are also closely inspired by the past, particularly the Regency and Victorian periods.

◆ Cutie Kitten plate, c.1958
The Cutie Kitten children's ware series featured a cat in numerous sporting poses, and was designed by Christopher Boulton. The same shape was used for a series of plates given the name Barbecue, introduced in 1957, which were designed for informal entertaining. [504]

KEY FACTS

Location: Church Street, Stoke, Staffordshire, UK.

Important dates: Founded 1770. Bought by W. T. Copeland 1833. Reverted to Spode name after using Copeland 1970. Merged with Royal Worcester 1978.
Production: Porcelain, earthenware, stone china and parian.
Principal designers: Harold Holdway, Chris J. Boulton, Holmes Gray.

MARKS

This mark currently used for company's best-selling Blue Italian pattern. Other printed marks include version of Copeland Spode mark used in early 19th century with 'Fine Stone' added in 1962.

STAFFORDSHIRE POTTERIES

The Keele Street Pottery Co. (*see* p.102) was one of the many Staffordshire potteries to close down as part of the government's Concentration Scheme during World War II, and in 1945 Charles Griffith Bowers, son of the founder, Charles Hall Bowers, acquired a controlling interest in the company. During the next three years the firm took over a number of potteries, and in 1950 the whole group adopted the name Staffordshire Potteries Ltd.

Production was concentrated at Meir Airport, near Longton, in 1955, and by 1963 the sales and administration departments had also moved to this site. In 1979 the firm took over Taunton Vale Industries, a Somerset-based manufacturer of tableware accessories which owned the Howard Pottery (*see* p.94) and was trading as Royal Winton. Staffordshire Potteries itself was taken over by Coloroll in a hostile bid in 1986, and over the next few years there were various takeovers and name changes. In 1990 Biltons (*see* p.25) and Staffordshire Potteries merged in a management buyout and adopted the name Staffordshire Tableware. Biltons was sold in a management buyout five years later.

Early production consisted mainly of teaware and beakers, but Staffs Potts (as the company was affectionately known) began to invest heavily in modern automatic manufacturing and decorating machines and in 1967 launched dinnerware on to the market. In addition, it appointed a consultant designer, Valentine Chewter, and two full-time designers, John Evans and Jack Dadd. New machinery and new techniques, including silkscreen printing, enabled the firm to adapt and respond successfully to rapidly changing styles and fashions in ceramics. The dinnerware was made in such vast quantities that it could

Sets that set the pace

for fast-moving sales

Six Superb tea-sets. Yet we mass-produce them in such vast quantities that the price to you is fantastically low. Supplied in either mail order or hand-out cartons.

STAFFORDSHIRE POTTERIES LTD
MEIR, STOKE-ON-TRENT, ENGLAND

SUBSIDIARY COMPANIES O

◆ Teaware advertisement, 1960
In the mid-1950s Staffordshire Potteries began to market its tableware strongly. This *Pottery and Glass* advertisement features teaware in contemporary styles. [505]

● **Avanti tableware, 1990s**
The Avanti mix-and-match tableware comes in a range of three colours and is intended for casual dining. 506

● **Tom and Jerry mug, 1970s**
This children's mug featuring the ever-popular cartoon duo was introduced on this shape in the 1970s. 507

◗ **Indigo-pattern teaware, mid-1980s**
Produced from 1985 to 1986, the Indigo pattern was brought out under the Kilncraft trade name, which catered for the more modern taste in tableware. 508

be sold cheaply through mail order and other retail outlets, and a quick turn-over was achieved through aggressive marketing tactics, including television commercials. Sets were normally marketed in convenient take-away packages.

The company was also in close touch with changes in the lifestyles of the under-25s. Much of its output, for example ranges such as Pop, introduced in 1971, and mugs designed by Mary Quant in 1973, was aimed at this age group with its taste for casual tableware and mugs. By the early 1970s the company had cornered the market with its Kilncraft mugs; it was able to offer boxed sets of three mugs for less than £1, and by 1977 it was producing the widest range of mugs in Europe.

During the same period young designers created some amusing mugs for children and the young at heart. Among these were Whacky Stackers and Double Deckers by Cherille Mayhew, which were series of stacking mugs in which the design, extended over four mugs, made interesting and amusing combinations when the mugs were turned around. The pottery's children's mugs and nursery sets are now collectable. Particularly sought after are copyright designs and items featuring characters from children's films, comics, books and television. These include Disney's Mickey Mouse, Donald Duck and Tom and Jerry, Sooty, My Little Pony, Bob Godfrey's Henry's Cat, and Roger Hargreaves's Mr. Men, Little Miss and Timbuctoo, to name just a few.

As competition increased during the 1980s the company began to attach more importance to the production of dinnerware, and a programme of modernization helped it to survive the recessionary pressures of that decade. It continued to supply the popular market with a range of tableware, advertising wares and mugs with patterns such as Blueberry, Savona, Harvest Festival and Brighton Rock, until the company went out of business in 2001.

KEY FACTS

Location: Meir Airport, Longton, Staffordshire, UK.
Important dates: Founded from an amalgamation of companies 1950. Merged with Biltons to form Staffordshire Tableware 1990. Closed 2001.
Production: Earthenware and china.
Trade names : Kilncraft, Coloroll, Kingbury.

MARKS

Variations of this mark used 1986–90; then a Coloroll and later a Staffordshire Tableware mark.

STANGL POTTERY

In 1926 John Martin Stangl became president of the Fulper Pottery Company (*see* p.171) and bought a share of the company, which in 1928 purchased the old Anchor Pottery in Trenton, New Jersey. Stangl used the Trenton factory to make tableware. He bought the Fulper company in 1930, and the Stangl name came into use in association with the Trenton ware during the 1930s, although it was not officially adopted until 1955.

Cheery sgraffito-decorated redware tableware patterns characterized the pottery's early work. The sgraffito was embellished with painted decoration, introduced in the early 1940s. Fruits and flowers were favoured motifs, often depicted with strong, colourful borders. In 1940 Stangl introduced bird figurines designed by Auguste Jacob. Its market was established during World War II, when figurines from Europe and Asia were not entering the USA because of shipping problems. The Stangl birds were made until 1978, although their quality declined in later years. They were slip-cast in moulds and hand-painted, and because their colouring varied greatly, no two are exactly alike. The huge range of birds includes ducks, love-birds, orioles, roosters, blue jays and cardinals.

Kiddie Ware, or Kiddie Sets, were made with two and three pieces by Stangl from about 1942 until the 1970s. The two-piece sets included a cup and compartment dish, while the three-piece sets were made up of a plate, cup and bowl. The motifs were mostly taken from children's rhymes and stories, such as Mother Goose, Humpty-Dumpty and Little Boy Blue

The earliest Stangl dinnerware lines were decorated in solid colours in an informal style. Colonial was introduced in 1932, and Americana followed. Stoby Mugs, designed by Tony Sarg, were introduced in 1936. These character mugs were made in moulds and their features hand-painted. Popular at the time, they command relatively high prices today.

When John Stangl died in 1972 the pottery was operated by his estate until it was bought in 1973 by Wheaton Industries. Much of the historical collection and a large number of moulds were moved to New Jersey. Manufacturing ceased in 1978, when the property was sold by Wheaton.

▲ **Orchard Song coffee pot, 1950s**
Most of Stangl's dinnerware patterns were created using the sgraffito technique – a redware body was covered with a coloured slip, and the pattern cut through the slip to reveal the contrasting red below. Additional slips were added to the surface, and the whole was covered with a clear glaze. 509

▲ **Starflower dish, 1950s**
Stangl produced a large repertoire of cheerful fruit and flower patterns that used neutral background colours and limited colour ranges. 510

◆ **Pitcher and mug, 1950s**
The American market has long had the capacity to absorb traditional utilitarian pottery. These patterns, the blue-sponge decoration and mug in the shape of an ear of corn, have been made by many potteries since the mid-1800s. 511

KEY FACTS

Location: Trenton, New Jersey, USA.
Important dates: Founded in association with Fulper Pottery Company 1926. Stangl name adopted officially 1955. Manufacturing ceased 1978.
Production: Hand-decorated redware tableware.

MARKS

Usually an oval backstamp, often above pattern name.

STERLING CHINA COMPANY

The pottery was created in 1917 to make vitreous hotel china. During World War II it was a major supplier of china to the US armed forces, especially the Navy. By 1948, when Sterling asked Russel Wright to design a line, the company was a leading maker of hotel ware. Wright was careful to design the set to meet institutional expectations, and the result was forms that are both pleasing and useful. The plate, for example, is shaped to roll gently upwards from the bottom and curl under at the outer rim to provide greater strength and a form suitable for careful gripping by the waiter or waitress. Wright approved the solid colours – Ivy Green, Straw Yellow, Suede Grey, Cedar Brown, Shell Pink and White – while individual patterns were designed by Sterling.

In 1954 Sterling bought the Scammell China Company (*see* Lamberton China, p.109), but had discontinued all manufacturing in Wellsville and Trenton by 1975. Today Sterling is still in business in East Liverpool, Ohio. It sells china, but does not manufacture in the USA. Collectors should not confuse this company with Sterling China of Sebring, Ohio (*see* Limoges China Company, p.117).

KEY FACTS

Location: Wellsville, Ohio, USA.
Important dates: Founded 1917. Production ceased 1975.
Production: Hotel ware.
Principal designer: Russel Wright.

MARKS

Also used 'Caribe China', Lamberton Wreath with 'S' and customer's trade name.

◆ **Russel Wright hotel ware, c.1950**
The leaf pattern seen here was airbrushed through a stencil. Solid colours and decal patterns were also available. Collectors should note that much of this ware is not marked, and that familiarity with the range of shapes and colours in the line is essential. 512

STEUBENVILLE POTTERY COMPANY

American Modern by Russel Wright, made between 1939 and 1959, is the best known of Steubenville's many patterns. The firm reported having sold more than 125 million pieces by the mid-1950s, and it may be the most popular dinnerware ever made in the USA. This streamlined, functional, solid-colour casual ware could be bought in Chartreuse, Granite Grey, Seafoam, Cantaloupe, Cedar Green, Coral, White, Bean Brown, Glacier Blue, Black Chutney and Steubenville Blue. The many accessories included a covered butter dish, salad bowl, round relish tray, covered pitcher, salt and pepper shakers. After Steubenville went out of business in 1959, Canonsburg Pottery (*see* p.37) continued to produce some pieces of American Modern. Other Steubenville lines popular with collectors are Woodfield (1941), Adam Antique (1932), Betty Pepper (1936), Contempora by Ben Seibel, Shalimar (1938) and Olivia (1926).

KEY FACTS

Location: Steubenville, Ohio, USA.
Important dates: Founded 1879. Closed 1959.
Production: White-granite and semi-vitreous tableware and toilet ware.
Principal designer: Russel Wright.

MARKS

In addition to company name, marks incorporate 'SPCo' monogram and/or line name, for example 'Empire China' and 'Canton China'.

◆ **Russel Wright's American Modern, 1939–1959**
Wright's American Modern was promoted through active advertising, while Wright's marketing company also used tie-ins to gain widespread recognition for the ware. 513

STUDIO SZEILER

The Hungarian Joseph Szeiler settled in England in 1948, worked in the pottery industry and three years later set up a pottery in Hanley, Staffordshire. He began to produce a few small animals and figures, making his own models and moulds and doing his own casting, glazing and decorating. A local tilery fired the ware. The business grew, and in 1955 Szeiler established his Burslem studio. He employed at the two sites a total of six workers, including two compatriots, Laszlo Farkas and Joseph Ferenczy. Szeiler later moved into the Chelsea Works, next to the studio, where he continued to make animal figures, giftware and fancies. After his death in 1980 the pottery was run by his widow, before being taken over and renamed the Moorland Pottery (*see* p.139) in the mid-1980s.

➡ **Advertisement, 1960**
This *Pottery Gazette* advertisement features typical pieces from the range of Szeiler novelty animal models. 514

KEY FACTS

Location: Hanley, later at Burslem, Staffordshire, UK.
Important dates: Founded 1951. Taken over mid-1980s.
Production: Earthenware.

MARKS

Early ware printed or impressed with 'SZEILER ENGLAND'. Oval marks introduced c.1954; vase incorporated c.1956. This mark used from c.1962.

Studio Szeiler, 74 MOORLAND ROAD, BURSLEM, STOKE-ON-TRENT

Makers of Animal Pottery, Figurines, Caricatures and Contemporary Ware

TELEPHONE: STOKE-ON-TRENT 84631   CABLES, TELEGRAMS: SZEILER, STOKE-ON-TRENT

SWINNERTONS

The company was one of several large makers of earthenware dinner sets and teasets operating during the first half of the 20th century. During World War II the number of factories it operated was reduced under the Board of Trade's Concentration Scheme. However, throughout the 1940s Swinnertons produced a limited number of shapes and patterns, and it emerged from post-war reconstruction with four modern tableware factories and a healthy export market. In 1954 it was offering wares in three different coloured bodies, light ivory, dark ivory and Chelsea blue, with decoration in a variety of conventional and more contemporary designs such as Pink Champagne, a stylized floral design in charcoal, pink and platinum. Nursery ware from the late 1950s includes Funny Bunny, a three-piece set with an amusing decal design.

In 1959 the firm was taken over by the Lawley Group and subsequently merged with Royal Doulton (*see* p.187).

➡ **Pottery and Glass cover, 1953**
This front cover for *Pottery and Glass* magazine shows one of Swinnerton's traditional print-and-enamel patterns produced for the popular market. 515

KEY FACTS

Location: Hanley, Cobridge and Baddeley Green, Staffordshire, UK.
Important dates: Founded 1906. Taken over by Lawley 1959.
Production: Earthenware.
Trade names: Royal Wessex, Swinnertons, Hampton Ivory, Vitrion.

MARKS

This mark introduced c.1946. Other marks usually include company name or initials; some include brand names.

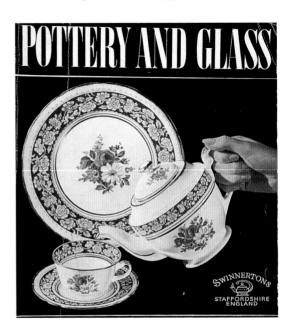

POTTERY AND GLASS

SWINNERTONS
STAFFORDSHIRE
ENGLAND

SYLVAC: see THOMAS LAWRENCE p.113 and SHAW & COPESTAKE p.198
SYRACUSE CHINA COMPANY: see ONONDAGA POTTERY CO. p.145

JOHN TAMS

The company established an early reputation for high-quality kitchenware, tankards, Imperial-measure ware and hospital and medical ware. By 1909 it had built up an extensive trade in ornamental ware in addition to a full range of useful domestic earthenware. At this time the catalogue included a new range of ornamental lustres marketed as Celestene Ware and comprising toilet ware, dessert ware, fruit trays and dishes, cake stands and plates, salad bowls and teapots. Outré Ware, an artistic range of vases and flower pots, was launched in the same period.

From the start of the 20th century the firm made tableware, and by the 1920s Willow Ware was one of its most popular lines. In 1927 it launched a coloured Willow pattern with bright enamelled colours and a classical range, with silhouette decoration in brown and white against a black ground, featuring subjects from Greek mythology. Among other notable wares from the interwar period was a range of popularly priced dinnerware, mainly with decal border patterns. Tams continued to produce many of its popular shapes throughout the 1940s, and maintained both its home and its export markets. After the war it continued as a family-owned business, specializing in competitively priced tea services, coffee sets, soup sets, cups and beakers supplied in attractive boxes through wholesalers.

In 1982 Tams bought Barker Brothers' (*see* p.19) works in Longton, and later built on this site the Sutherland Works, which opened in 1990. The firm became known as one of the largest makers of earthenware mugs and tableware and the leading supplier of plain mugs to the international decorator market. In 1989 it bought A. T. Finney and Sons Ltd, maker of Duchess China, and soon afterwards acquired the Nanrich Pottery, of Longton. These two firms were merged to form the foundation for Tams' bone-china operations. In 1992 the Bone China Division was expanded by the acquisition of Royal Grafton China. In 2000 there was a management buy-in and the Fine China Division was sold. The Earthenware Division continues to make tableware, including Dinner Party, Manuscript, Funky Fruit and Saturn Daisy, as well as coffee and designer mugs, notably Farmyard Friends, Head Chef, Cherry Tree and Pet Shop.

▲ Advertisement, 1915
Early in the 20th century Tams was an ambitious manufacturer of a wide variety of products, including the elaborate Nankin Ware seen here. 516

▲ Summertime Fruits, from 1996
Tams introduced this bone-china ware, made under the Royal Grafton trade name and decorated with the Summertime Fruits pattern on the Stirling shape, in 1996. The ceramic cafetière is in the Prunus Ovium pattern. 517

▼ Elevenses mug, 1998
Mugs continue to be an important part of the pottery's production. This example is one of a set of three called Elevenses, made in the Balmoral shape and colourfully decorated. 518

KEY FACTS

Location: Crown Pottery, Longton, Staffordshire, UK, and other sites in Longton, including Sutherland Works from 1990.
Important dates: Founded 1874. Still active.
Production: Earthenware. China from 1989–2000.
Trade names: John Tams (& Son) (Ltd), Tams Ware, Tams.

MARKS

Printed or impressed, including company name, monogram or initials; some show brand name.

TAYLOR & KENT

In the first quarter of the 20th century the pottery built up a large and interesting catalogue of Florentine-brand china with quiet, traditional patterns which was sold at competitive prices in the home and colonial markets. By the late 1920s it was moving towards a freer type of decorative treatments and more intense, Art Deco-influenced colourings. One of the best-selling patterns in Florentine china teaware during the 1930s was the Sundial print-and-enamel pattern on the Ascot shape.

Production ceased during World War II, but resumed soon afterwards, and in 1947 the Shufflebotham family bought the pottery. Throughout the 1950s the firm continued to produce mainly traditional teaware such as the popular Tartan series, launched in the mid-1950s. This depicts six famous Scottish scenes matched with the Royal Stewart, Gordon, Macdonald, Buchanan, Cameron and Campbell tartans. The Elizabethan trade name was introduced in 1962, and in 1983 the firm was renamed Elizabethan Fine Bone China. After a merger with Rosina both companies had success with bone-china tableware, giftware, collectors' tea cups and saucers and coffee mugs. Queens became the dominant brand name, but small ranges of Elizabethan products were still being made in the early 1990s. The company was taken over by the Churchill Group in 1995.

◆ **Advertisement, 1987**
Published in *Tableware International*, this advertisement features Taylor & Kent's Elizabethan range of bone-china mugs, teaware and fancies. 519

KEY FACTS

Location: Florence Works, Longton, Staffordshire, UK.
Important dates: Founded 1867. Renamed Elizabethan Fine Bone China 1983.
Production: Porcelain.
Trade names: Florentine, Kent China, Elizabethan.

MARKS

This mark introduced c.1939. Other standard marks incorporate crown and company name or monogram; some include Kent China trade name.

TAYLOR, SMITH & TAYLOR COMPANY

In 1899 John Taylor and Charles Smith founded a pottery and began the construction of a factory in Chester, West Virginia, which was in production by 1900. The company produced semi-porcelain toilet ware, dinnerware, kitchenware and specialities, as well as short sets of dishes, some decorated. Beginning in 1905, the pottery was closed for a year. In 1906 the Taylor family's interests were purchased by William L. Smith and his son and the plant was reopened. The firm's name was retained.

Taylor, Smith & Taylor made a wide variety of shapes and patterns over the years, including traditional transfer-printed scenic and ornamental patterns and patterns that mimicked European porcelain (decal-decorated rather than hand-painted), French Haviland-type pastel flowery patterns and French provincial ceramics like the ware made at Quimper. Popular decal patterns were frequently used on more than one shape line, perhaps because the company's wares were sold primarily through dime stores and mail-order catalogues (such as Sears and Montgomery Ward) and as proprietary premiums. For example, Taylor, Smith & Taylor's silhouette pattern, called Taverne, can be found today on Laurel as well as St Denis and Vogue. In all this variety, three lines stand out as the most significant for collectors today: Vistosa, Lu-Ray and Pebbleford.

Vistosa, introduced in 1938, was the pottery's contribution to solid-colour, Californian-type casual dinnerware, although it was a little late coming to the market. Bauer (*see* p.20), Homer Laughlin (*see* p.110),

◆ **Silhouette bowl, 1930s**
Known as Silhouette or Taverne, Taylor, Smith & Taylor's pattern was based on Hall China's popular Taverne line and is considered somewhat easier to find in today's market than Hall's version. Silhouette was used on both Laurel and Vogue shapes. 520

Lu-Ray dinnerware, 1940s
Lu-Ray is probably the most popular among collectors of Taylor, Smith & Taylor's dinnerware lines. The pastel colours, which are identified with the 1940s, provided a welcome alternative to the brightly coloured casual ware that had characterized the 1930s. 521

Dime-store dinnerware, 1940s
Floral decals were a staple for the dime-store trade during the 1930s and 1940s. Most patterns were unnamed, and many had gold filigree borders. Collectors concentrate on the shape lines, which are easier to identify. The plate seen here is from the Laurel shape line. 522

Walter Dorwin Teague Conversation plates, 1950s
Teague gave Conversation, issued in at least 16 patterns, a very modern post-war look. King O'Dell, which features a jack-in-the-pulpit flower, is found most commonly today. Day Lily and an unnamed pattern are seen here. 523

Paden City (*see* p.148) and other firms had introduced their versions earlier. Unlike the simple Californian-style ware, however, Vistosa featured a pie-crust rim and a more refined overall shape. Standard forms were available, including plates, soups, small dishes, cream jugs and sugars, cups and saucers, teapots, a water jug, salt and pepper shakers, eggcups and after-dinner cups and saucers. A sauceboat was added later. Vistosa came in brilliant green, blue, yellow and red. Dishes in red were priced 20 per cent higher than the other colours, although today's market makes no colour distinction in value. Sales literature encouraged homemakers to mix and match the colours. Vistosa continued to be made into the early 1940s.

Lu-Ray's pastel palette proved to be more popular. Introduced in 1938, the line was made until 1955. The first trade advertisement for Lu-Ray noted that the new line's 'delightfully delicate pastels [completed] the color cycle in modern dinnerware'. The colours were Windsor Blue, Surf Green, Persian Cream (yellow) and Sharon Pink. These colours are glossier on ware produced at the beginning of the pattern's period, and they become more matt through the 1940s. The palette was augmented by Chatham Grey in 1948. The simple, refined shape, organic finials and soft pastel colouring give the ware a very pleasing aspect. The shape, however, was not entirely new; rather it was newly assembled from the earlier flat-ware shapes of the 1933 Laurel line and the hollowware shapes of the 1936 Empire line, including the bud-like finial on the covers.

Pebbleford was the most popular line on the Versatile shape designed by John Gilkes, who became staff designer for Taylor, Smith & Taylor in 1950. Versatile is characterized by a plain round coupe shape, while the Pebbleford line is significant for its speckled, single-colour glazes. The Versatile shape remained in Taylor, Smith & Taylor's repertoire until the mid-1960s with a variety of decorative treatments, including solid uniform pastel colours, bright decals with airbrushed edges and stylish decals with formal gold- and platinum-lined rims. Pebbleford's palette, described as a 'smart, textured pattern', which could be colour-mixed in use, included Burnt Orange, Granite Gray, Honey, Mint Green, Pink, Sand, Teal, Turquoise, Sunburst Yellow and Marble White.

Also of interest to collectors are the patterns designed by J. Palin Thorley and Walter Dorwin Teague. Thorley's Vogue (1934–41), with moulded rims and handles having small relief flowers, and Laurel (1933), a globular Moderne shape with big circular handles, are popular. Teague, a consultant designer, contributed Conversation in 1950. This square and streamlined shape was very popular in its day (and is relatively common in today's collectable market) but was discontinued in 1954.

In 1972 the Anchor Hocking Glass Company purchased Taylor, Smith & Taylor and gradually phased out the original name in favour of the parent company's name. Production continued until 1981.

◀ **Pebbleford, 1953-1960**
On the Versatile shape, Pebbleford's textured glaze was popular. Mint Green, Honey and Burnt Orange are the rarest colourways. 524

TORQUAY TERRACOTTA CO.

Among the pottery's output were statuettes, single figures and groups, busts and animal and bird models, as well as a wide range of ornamental and useful ware such as vases, ewers, bottles, butter coolers, jugs, tobacco jars, candlesticks and platters. Vases in classical shapes with painted mythological scenes on a light slip were among early popular lines, but when the enthusiasm for classical terracotta waned the firm drew inspiration from Japan and other areas. Vases with underglaze painted birds, and flower studies by Alexander Fisher, were produced, some on a yellow ground. The pottery is believed to have closed in around 1905; it was reopened as the Torquay Pottery Co in 1908. Until its final closure in around 1939 the firm made glazed ware with printed landscapes and colourful birds, notably kingfishers, as well as Toby jugs, blue-ground ware with painted decoration, and souvenir and novelty items.

▲ **Cottage ware teapot, c.1955**
This cottage-and-motto teapot represents the style of slip decoration practised by most Torquay firms in the first half of the 20th century. 525

◀ **Money box, c.1925**
Made in the form of Cockington Forge, this is one of a range of novelties and souvenirs by Torquay Pottery. 526

TOOTH & CO.: see BRETBY ART POTTERY p.31

TROIKA POTTERY

In 1963 a partnership of three young men, Leslie Illsley, Benny Sirota and Jan Thompson, took over the Wells Pottery in St Ives, Cornwall, renaming it the Troika Pottery. The Wells Pottery had made mainly bedroom name-tiles, and the new owners continued to make these. In addition they developed new ranges of art tiles and small bottles and, after buying a larger kiln at the end of 1963, began to make wall-hangings from tiles mounted on board.

Quite early the partners decided to concentrate on distinctive moulded shapes, and developed lines in both textured and smooth white surfaces which reflected Illsley's background as a sculptor. Sirota set about perfecting the glazes and establishing the style of surface decoration, taking inspiration from the landscape of St Ives and the work of the Swiss artist Paul Klee in the use of tones, textures and motifs. The three men were not afraid to experiment with new materials, and among the more unconventional ones they used were slurry from local tin mines, emulsion paint and melted broken glass. Most of the output was decorative art pottery, but the firm also made a limited amount of tea and coffee ware, mugs and bowls. Jan Thompson left the partnership in April 1966.

A shop was fitted out in the pottery in the first year, and by 1967 business had expanded enough to require four trainees. The same year Heal's exhibited Troika ware in its shop in London's West End, the first of many exhibitions in places such as Stockholm, New York and Australia. The pottery was still prospering in 1970 when the local council terminated the lease on its premises. The business moved to Fradgan, Newlyn, which, like St Ives, has an avant-garde art tradition as well as a handful of potteries. For the first few years the firm continued to do well, employing eight decorators, but from the mid-1970s the Habitat style was in vogue and sales of Troika pottery were declining. Sirota, who had been developing his own pottery interests during the 1970s, left in 1980. A small band of workers stayed on, but this finally diminished to three, who were employed for between three and five days a week.

In December 1983 the pottery closed. The moulds and stock were put into storage, but they were sold after the building housing them collapsed as a result of subsidence. The name Troika still exists and is owned by Judith, Illsley's widow.

▲ **Urn, late 1960s**
Troika's unconventional methods of production resulted in some interesting tones and textures. The ware attracted critical approval soon after the pottery opened, and by 1967 business was good enough to justify employing four young trainees, who carried out designs such as this one, made at at St Ives between 1964 and 1970. 527

◆ **Spice jar, late 1960s**
In its first year Troika developed its now-familiar textured surfaces, which seem to echo the local landscape around St Ives. Contemporary reviewers often also noted the influence of the artist Paul Klee in the use of various textures, tones and motifs in this range of pieces. 528

KEY FACTS

Location: Wheal Dream, St Ives; later at Fradgan, Newlyn, Cornwall, UK.
Important dates: Founded 1963. Closed 1983.
Production: Earthenware.
Principal designers: Leslie Illsey, Benny Sirota, Stella Benjamin, Kristin Roth, Jan Thompson.

MARKS

Painted, incised or printed marks, usually including 'Troika' and 'St Ives'.

TROIKA
CORNWALL
ENGLAND

TUSCAN: see R. H. & S. L. PLANT p.157

UNIVERSAL POTTERIES, INC.

The pottery was created in 1934 by reorganizing the short-lived Oxford Pottery Company, which had operated from 1932 until that year. Despite its unsettled ancestry, Universal proved successful as a maker of semi-vitreous dinnerware, kitchenware and speciality ware. For a time it had three plants, two in Cambridge and a third in Niles, which was eventually dismantled. In 1947 a third plant was built in Cambridge.

The Ballerina dinnerware line was the company's most popular. The flatware has a slightly-flattened coupe shape, while the hollowware is globular with ring-shaped handles. Introduced about 1945, Ballerina had four original colours: Periwinkle Blue, Jade Green, Jonquil Yellow and Dove Grey. Sets could be made up of mixed colours, such as grey and yellow. In 1950 the colours Forest Green and Chartreuse, plus five patterns designed by Charles Cobelle, were added; Pink and Charcoal followed in 1955. Speciality sets were also available, including a barbecue set with small casseroles and mugs; a beverage set with pitcher, tumblers and coasters; an after-dinner coffee set with coffee pot and small cups and saucers; and a teaset with teapot and regular cups and saucers.

Collectors today look for Universal's cat-tail decal, which was used on the Ballerina, Camwood, Old Holland and Laurella shapes. Dinnerware, kitchenware and refrigerator jugs were decorated with this decal, and the same pattern can be seen in other media as retailers ordered it on textiles, painted kitchen furniture, and glass and metal kitchen items. Some of the more unusual Universal shapes with the decal include the tumbler, salad spoon and fork, salt and pepper, flat refrigerator jug and syrup jug. Universal was only one of several potteries that used the cat-tail decal.

The Woodvine decal was the pottery's most popular booster pattern, available as a shopping premium through grocery stores. Woodvine survives on table and kitchenware. Bittersweet (1949), which features clusters of red bittersweet berries on the vine, is popular with collectors of Jewel Tea Company premiums. It comes on a small range of table shapes. Upico, designed in 1937 by Walter Karl Titze, is a modern terraced globular shape with a wide variety of decals. These are placed on the smooth upper half of the hollowware, while solid colours usually cover the terraced bottom half.

In 1954 Universal discontinued making household ware and went into the tile business using its old Oxford trade mark. The plant closed in 1960.

◆ **Cat-tail plate, 1940s**
Sears, Roebuck and Company mail-order catalogues of the 1940s offered cat-tail ceramic kitchenware, metal pantry ware, painted-wood kitchen furniture and coordinated linens. 529

◆ **Woodvine kitchen bowl, late 1940s**
The Woodvine decal was used on many Universal shapes, including Ballerina, as well as its kitchenware. Grocery-store shoppers collected the pattern week by week, buying the various shapes in turn. 530

◆ **Ballerina teaware, late 1940s**
Trade advertisements described the Ballerina shape as 'smart, practical – moderately priced ... hot sellers from the moment you put them on display'. In addition to solid colours, Ballerina was also decal-decorated. Collectors can choose a particular colour or pattern to collect, or mix and match their sets. 531

KEY FACTS

Location: Cambridge, Ohio, USA.
Important dates: Founded 1934. Ceased manufacture of household ware 1954. Closed 1960.
Production: Semi-vitreous dinnerware and kitchenware.
Principal designers: Charles Cobelle, Walter Karl Titze.

MARKS

One of many marks including company name, shape line and sometimes pattern name.

UPCHURCH POTTERY

The company was founded by S. Wakeley in 1913 to manufacture artistic pottery, and much of the early work was designed by Edward Spencer, co-founder in 1903 of the Artificers' Guild. Upchurch pottery was sold through the Guild's retail outlets as well as at exhibitions such as the Decorative Arts Exhibition in Paris in 1914.

Production consisted mainly of artistic decorative bowls and vases in simple forms, with silk-like glazes in mauve, green and copper. In 1917 *The Pottery Gazette* reported: 'Owing to the nature of the glaze, the colour being largely dependent of the caprice of the fire, no two pieces of this ware can possibly be alike, and each, therefore, is a unique article worthy of the attention of the collector.' At the time of the British Industries Fair, four years later, a range of Upchurch salt-glazed art pottery was making its impact. Most pieces had severe antique shapes and were decorated with dull or matt glazes, the decorative effect being an integral part of the ware. By this time the pottery had moved beyond the experimental stage, and pieces were being bought by collectors and connoisseurs. The pottery continued in production until 1961.

◆ **Vase, c.1920 (far left); dish, c.1935 (left)**
Mottled monochrome glazes were a characteristic feature of Upchurch, and their use ensured that no two pieces were the same. 532

UTILITY WARE

Two years into World War II, the Board of Trade Order, 1941, led to a substantial reorganization of the British pottery industry, especially in north Staffordshire. This measure was followed by the Domestic Pottery (Manufacture and Supply) Order of 1942, prohibiting the manufacture for the home market of all but specified relatively essential types of decorated china and earthenware. The order also controlled manufacturers' prices and distributors' profits as well as retailers' maximum selling prices for plain white earthenware or light ivory earthenware cups, saucers, plates, dishes, jugs, mugs, beakers, pudding bowls, pie dishes and vegetable dishes. These so-called utility goods were put into price grades A, B and C, and stamped with the appropriate letter. Utility china was placed under similar controls and the decoration of china and earthenware was banned in the home market and permitted only on export goods, in order to liberate decorators either for other work in the industry or for other national service. The 1942 Order also prohibited the manufacture of domestic pottery without a licence and quota from the Board of Trade. More fortunate firms were allocated a nucleus certificate which enabled them to continue in production, some by taking over the production of firms forced to close to release their premises for the war effort. Others closed for the duration.

➥ **Utility advertisement, 1947**
Some potters were prepared to advertise lack of decoration as a selling point. 533

No Frills . . .

Government restrictions limited the number of pieces of different shapes and sizes that manufacturers of utility ware could make. However, firms could use the same materials as before, the same manufacturing processes and the same designers. In response to the challenge several manufacturers introduced exciting new ranges which followed government guidelines. Wedgwood (*see* Josiah Wedgwood & Sons, p.230), Spode (*see* p.208), Moorcroft (*see* p.135) and the Bovey Pottery (*see* p.28) designed their notable ranges to be as flexible as possible, and to emphasize shape and design in the absence of decoration.

Wedgwood's undecorated white ware was designed by Victor Skellern and had several inventive features. The lid of the vegetable dish could be reversed to become a bowl; the eggcup doubled as an individual butter dish; and unhandled cups could be used as sugar bowl and slop basin. The teapot lid fitted beakers and jugs in the same range. The whole range was limited to items considered essential for the needs of the table. There were 18 pieces: meat plate, pudding plate, tea plate, coupe soup, cup and saucer, beaker, two-purpose bowl, sugar bowl, jugs (three sizes), teapots (two sizes), eggcup, oval dishes (two sizes) and sauceboat. Victory Ware was the name given to this pottery.

Spode registered the design of its Utility Ware teapot, which, made in high-grade cream earthenware, had a non-drip pourer, self-locking lid and built-in strainer. The Bovey Pottery produced Bovey War Ware, a small but well-designed range to meet the real needs of wartime. Some existing shapes that were clearly suitable for their purpose were included, while the rest of the pieces were newly designed. New features included non-slip handles and multi-purpose shapes. For example, the teapot was also a good coffee pot, the cereal bowl could be used for fruit, soup and other purposes, while the utility bowl, without cover, could be a salad bowl, and its cover, when reversed, was suitable for vegetables, soup and stew.

As early as 1944 manufacturers and retailers were tired of bleak utility ware, but only in 1951 did the Festival of Britain give a hint of things to come; the following year all restrictions on manufacturing were lifted.

▲ **Spode Utility Ware advertisement, 1950**
Simple shapes without decoration were still being advertised towards the end of the Utility restrictions. 534

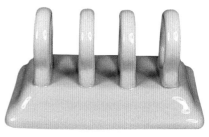

▲ **Spode Utility toast rack, c.1948**
This pre-war shape was one of many reintroduced by potters who were struggling to get production under way in the 1940s. 535

◄ **Ford Utility dish and cover, 1940s**
This stylish dish, whose shape is emphasized by the lack of decoration, is typical of the work of lesser makers who reintroduced 1930s forms after the World War II. 536

KEY FACTS

Prices: Utility pottery prices were controlled by the Board of Trade in consultation with nucleus manufacturers, with an upper price limit being given for all stages of manufacture right through to price charged to customer. Ware was priced as A, B or C. Group A included white- or cream-body ware; Group B glazed stoneware; and Group C natural clay-bodied ware with a brown or colourless glaze.

MARKS

Board of Trade regulations dictated that each ware must be marked under glaze to indicate which of set price bands it fell into: either A, B or C.

VAN BRIGGLE POTTERY

Artus Van Briggle joined Rookwood (*see* p.179) as a decorator in 1889. His early work was remarkably good, and in 1893 he was sent to Paris for three years' study. There he was enthralled by the matt glazes being developed by the Art Nouveau studio potters. When his enthusiasm for this new work was thwarted at Rookwood, and his health declined at the same time, he left Ohio. He continued his experiments in Colorado, and in 1901 created the Van Briggle Pottery in Colorado Springs. Working in ill health, with few assistants, he aimed to make high-grade moulded artware from his designs, using native flora as the primary design source and the dead-matt glaze that had intrigued him in France. He was accompanied in this venture by Anne Gregory, who became his wife in 1902.

Van Briggle sent 24 pieces to the Paris Salon of 1903 and received 15 gold, silver and bronze medals. At the St Louis World's Fair in 1904 his work received five gold, silver and bronze medals. He died as the fair was in progress. Anne Van Briggle, an artist and a designer, took over the creative and practical management of the pottery. Although most of the pre-1905 designs are by Artus, most of those done between 1905 and 1912 are by Anne. The Art Nouveau style of their low-relief designs is distinctive in the work of American art potteries. In several examples human figures are wrapped around the pieces. In others, motifs taken from local flora are rhythmically entwined on the forms.

In 1908 a new plant was built, and two years later a new company was organized: the Van Briggle Pottery and Tile Company. In 1913 the business was sold at a sheriff's sale. Although the company has changed hands several more times over the years, the Van Briggle Art Pottery (as it was renamed in 1931) is still active, working in the same style as and even producing some of the designs originally conceived by Artus Van Briggle.

Vases, before 1920
Lorelei (right) has been made more or less continuously since its original design in 1901. The smaller vase, which features a spiderwort, was also designed by Artus Van Briggle. [537]

Van Briggle ware, after 1920
Although the pottery continued to produce the early designs for many years, the colour palette and glaze application became more standardized. [538]

Iris vase, 1907
Additional carving in low relief accentuates the iris design of this pattern covered in a distinctive blue flowing matt glaze. [539]

KEY FACTS

Location: Colorado Springs, Colorado, USA.
Important dates: Founded 1901. Still active.
Production: Artware and giftware.
Principal designers: Artus Van Briggle, Anne Van Briggle, Emma Kinkead, Fred Willis, Craig Stevenson, Nellie Walker.

MARKS

Conjoined 'A's are for first names of Artus Van Briggle and his wife, Anne. Early ware dated.

VERNON KILNS

When Faye Bennison created Vernon Kilns in 1931 from Vernon China, the latter firm was making tiles, dishes and hotel ware. A number of designers were brought in to develop new shapes, including Gale Turnbull, who was art director from 1936 to the early 1940s, and the sisters May and Genevieve Hamilton, from 1936 to 1937. The Hamilton sisters designed modern shapes with low-relief patterns covered in pastel glazes, as well as Rhythmic and Rippled dinnerware patterns. The best-known designs from this era are those by Rockwell Kent. The Salamina series (1939) was based on Kent's 1929 books by the same name about his life in Greenland. The Moby Dick series (1939) was based on Herman Melville's classic, and Our America (1938–40) had 30 different designs illustrating regional scenes and activities. Don Blanding's Hawaiian-inspired designs, introduced in 1939, were popular until the early 1950s.

Janice Pettee designed figures of Gary Cooper, Dorothy Lamour, Bette Davis, Wallace Beery and many more movie stars. In 1941–2 a large series of figures from the cartoons *Fantasia*, *Dumbo* and *The Reluctant Dragon* was produced under licence from Walt Disney Productions.

After a fire in 1947 the factory was rebuilt with better machinery and much-increased capacity. The products were largely speciality wares, such as children's dishes, ashtrays, spoon holders, miniatures and souvenir series plates, cups and saucers. Dinnerware was also made, much of it designed by Harry Bird (tropical flowers, fish and birds), Gale Turnbull (plaids and California themes) and Royal Hickman (Melinda Shape).

Popular shapes and patterns included Montecito, Coronado, San Fernando, Early California, Modern California, Brown-Eyed Susan, Desert Poppy and Chinese Lantern. Increased competition after World War II was difficult to meet, and the factory closed in 1958. There are more than 1000 different Vernon designs, giving Vernon Kilns the distinction of offering the largest variety of collectable lines of any Californian pottery.

◆ **Rockwell Kent plate, 1939**
The transfer-printed patterns of Moby Dick are based on Kent's illustrations for Herman Melville's classic sea adventure. The designs were issued in Dark Blue, Maroon, Light Orange and Walnut Brown. 540

◆ **Tickled Pink casserole, late 1950s**
Anytime, the shape designed by Elliott House c.1955, carried several patterns that are popular today, including Tickled Pink, Heavenly Days and Imperial, an abstract sgraffito pattern on black. 541

◆ **Hey Day dinnerware, late 1940s**
The San Marino shape line was designed in 1947 and decorated in a variety of solid colours and decals. Hey Day combined two colours with the decal diaper pattern used on the plates. 542

WADE

The Wade group of potteries dates from the 19th century. Until the mid-1920s Wade & Co. made mainly earthenware jugs and teapots, and Albert J. Wade made glazed tiles for walls and fireplaces. George Wade & Son, established to mass-produce industrial items for the textile industry, was making articles such as gas burners for domestic lighting. Between 1926 and 1927 George Wade & Son established a small art department and Albert Wade incorporated his business into a private limited company as A. J. Wade Ltd. Albert Wade also had interests in Wade & Co., which became Wade, Heath & Co. at the same time. From 1935, A. J. Wade Ltd and Wade, Heath & Co. traded as Wade Potteries. In 1958 Wade Potteries and George Wade & Son merged as Wade Potteries.

During the 1930s both George Wade & Son and Wade, Heath & Co. expanded their production to include many new decorative goods. Following the establishment of an art studio, the former produced a range of moderately priced pottery figures with a patented finish known as Scintillite, and in 1934 its show at the British Industries Fair consisted almost entirely of pottery 'sculpturesque figures'. Models varied from those with restrained, Victorian-style poses, such as Dolly Varden in a crinoline dress, to Art Deco-influenced models such as Sunshine. At the same time George Wade & Son also produced a range of small to large animals. Many of the larger animals and birds were made from wood carvings by Faust Lang, while some of the figurines were modelled by Jessie van Hallen.

In the 1930s Wade, Heath & Co. also increased its range of ornamental ware and novelties with the introduction of children's ware for the King and Queen's Silver Jubilee, teasets, boxed giftware and novelty items, including musical ornamental jugs such as the new Little Pig jug. The Flaxman shape and other flower jugs with painted decoration date from this period, and over the next two years Flaxman Ware, which included a range of modernist matt-glazed vases, jugs and other useful items, some decorated, as well as embossed ornamental useful ware, including the Wadeheath and Gothic ranges, was widely advertised. In 1934 the firm secured the rights to reproduce in earthenware the Mickey Mouse subjects. Mickey, Minnie, Pluto and Horsecollar were brought out as a boxed set of children's ware with an attractive Mickey Mouse label. Mickey Mouse toy teasets of 8, 10 and 16 pieces were in production by 1935. Walt Disney figures were soon included in the Wade, Heath & Co. catalogue; Snow White and the Seven Dwarfs were early examples. In 1938 the firm took over the Royal Victoria Pottery in Burslem and concentrated on

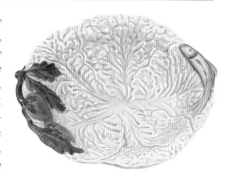

← Dish, 1930s
This Wade, Heath & Co. embossed and painted dish is similar to Carlton Ware designs, although the fish is a new feature. Among other designs from the period is a dish with hollyhocks and lupins, and another with cobnuts. 543

← Animal models and figures, 1950s
Many of the porcelain miniatures shown here are based on characters from Disney films, including *Lady and the Tramp* and *Bambi*. Some were produced for the Hat Box series, widely marketed in the 1950s and 1960s. 544

◆ Harmony Ware vases, late 1950s
Harmony Ware, which included bowls, jugs and vases, was introduced by Wade, Heath & Co in 1956 and made until the early 1960s. The pieces were either decorated with decals or came in two-tone grey and pink or green and peach colourways. 545

making earthenware tableware, decorative jugs, vases and urns, bowls and dishes, table lamps, platters and flower pots, plaques and wall decorations, nursery ware, figurines and ornamental fancies such as posy bowls, and tankards such as Cranky Tankards, advertised in 1939.

Wade, Heath & Co's giftware production was interrupted by World War II, and the firm concentrated on essential ceramics and then, from the later 1940s, on a reduced range of ornamental useful lines for export, notably Peony Ware. Some figurines were advertised in 1948, including Wynken, Blinken and Nod, and Curtsey, the first in a range of costume figures on which appliqué handmade flowers formed an important decorative feature. These too would only be available for the export market.

After wartime restrictions were lifted in the early 1950s, the Wade companies' output included many ornamental and novelty lines, some of which had only been available for the export market. In 1953 its range of 21 Nursery Rhyme figures was heavily promoted, and the first boxed set of George Wade Whimsies, consisting of a fawn, a horse, a poodle, a squirrel and a spaniel, was first advertised in 1954. These porcelain miniatures were an immediate success, and by February 1956 set number five had been brought out. This was quickly followed by the Hat Box series, featuring characters from Walt Disney's film *Lady and the Tramp,* and Wade Minikins, a series of 48 miniature models for sale in retail shops.

In the 1950s and early 1960s the Wade companies produced colourful tableware such as the Mode hand-painted range, with an olive-green band crossed with red, yellow and black lines, and richly coloured Rubytone teaware, with an embossed vine pattern. Responding to the demand for modern ware, in 1956 Wade, Heath & Co. introduced Harmony Ware vases and bowls in organic forms with two-tone colouring in pastel shades; these were later brought out with patterns in sympathetic styles such as Carnival, Parasols and Shooting Stars. Other notable lines of this period were Emett dishes with patterns by the Rowland Emett (1958); Zamba, a series of vases, bowls and jugs with dancers in silhouette (c.1957); Flair

♠ Shaving mug, 1950s
With shaving mugs still in regular use, many potters made them as giftware items. This Wade version is indicative of the popularity of veteran and vintage car motifs after the success of the film *Genevieve.* 546

♠ Cottage ware plate, c.1954
This plate features Wade's version of the broadly painted cottage-style patterns that were extensively revived in the 1950s. 547

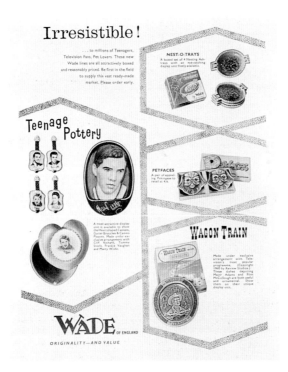

♦ Advertisement, 1960
This *Pottery and Glass* advertisement for Wade novelties features products designed to appeal to 'teenagers, television fans and pet lovers'. They may not have been irresistible at the time, but cameo plaques and guitar brooches featuring Marty Wilde and Tommy Steele would certainly appeal to collectors today. 548

tableware, with decorations such as Galaxy, Plantain, Red Polka and Cockerel designed by Georgina Lawton and Robert Barlow; the well-loved Clarence and Clara bud vases; and the Teenage Pottery series (1960).

When the demand for decorative items slumped in 1965, most giftware production was stopped, although George Wade & Son carried on making a small range of such items. Wade, Heath & Co had its own design and modelling team, and in 1969 it formed its own product, design and marketing company, Wade PDM. This, taken over by Beauford plc and named Wade Ceramics in 1989, still operates.

♦ **Nat West pigs, 1980s**
The famous pig family, given to young savers with the National Westminster Bank, are now very collectable, particularly as sets. 549

WARDLE & CO.

In the early 20th century, under the artistic direction of Frederick Hurten Rhead, in addition to its important majolica decorated ware, the pottery introduced Rockingham tea and breakfast sets as well as ivory-coloured toilet sets with striking decoration. Other developments included tube-lining decoration in the Art Nouveau style and *pâte-sur-pâte* decorated artware. In 1909 the firm produced a series called Night on the Sea, painted with views of ships at sea. Other ranges include Foxland, and Daffodil, which was applied to vases, pedestals and pots. In the same period Wardle was taken over by J. A. Robinson (*see* p.178) and renamed Wardle Art Pottery Co. It became a branch of Cauldon Potteries (*see* p.40) in around 1924, and continued to produce ornamental ware until 1935.

♦ **Advertisement, 1905**
Decorated with scenes from 18th-century, Elizabethan and farmyard life, this Wardle range was described at the time as being possessed of 'striking effects in artistic ware'. 550

WASHINGTON POTTERY

Teaware ranges advertised in 1953 include Regent, a lithographic pattern, and Autumn Flame, with three sprays and a matching border in autumn colours. Indian Tree dinnerware, printed in brown and hand-painted in five underglaze colours, was introduced in the same period. These were followed by Gainsborough tea and coffee sets, richly decorated with heavy gold stamping and wash bands, and the Windsor pattern dinner service, with heavy gold filigree border and colourful floral centres.

Tim Trouble nursery ware was heavily promoted at this time. In the 1960s the firm expanded its mug production and made a now collectable set of four candy dishes, each depicting a Beatle.

KEY FACTS

Location: Shelton and Stoke, Staffordshire, UK.
Important dates: Founded 1946. Renamed English Ironstone Ltd c.1970. Still active as Just Mugs.
Production: Earthenware.

MARKS

This mark used from 1946. Others give company name in full.

◆ Tableware, 1970s
Strong floral patterns in typical 1970s styles and colours were a staple of the Staffordshire industry as a whole. 551

HENRY WATSON POTTERIES

Founded by Thomas Watson around 1800, this pottery has been in unbroken family ownership ever since, trading from 1941 as Henry Watson Potteries. From the outset it specialized in making kitchenware in the local style by traditional methods. Included in the firm's 1946 catalogue were bread crocks, bulb bowls, casseroles, flower pots and garden pottery, kitchenware and seed pans. By the 1950s the pottery was also producing ornamental ware, including a wide variety of jugs, beakers, vases and bowls. In this period it employed Doreen Penfold and Peter O'Malley, graduates of the Royal College of Art, who designed a series of earthenware bowls with combed cream and brown slip decoration; they also produced other handmade studio pottery lines such as jugs, beakers, vases and bowls with simple decorations.

Throughout the 1950s and 1960s, and into the 1970s, Watson made a wide range of studio ware in addition to tableware. The firm has enjoyed a long association with the Queensberry Hunt design company, with which

◆ Advertisement, 1953
This Wattisfield Ware advertisement emphasizes the handcraft techniques and traditional slipware styles that were then being used by Watson. Although handmade, these decorative pieces were often heatproof and could therefore be used for serving direct from the oven. 552

◆ Original Suffolk Collection, 1990s
Designed by the Queensberry Hunt Partnership, the Original Suffolk Collection combines traditional terracotta with a unified style of graphic branding that brings to mind country life in Victorian England. It emphasizes the pottery's connection with the county where it has operated since its foundation around the beginning of the 19th century. 553

it has collaborated on several new ranges, the most recent being the Suffolk Tableware Collection. Also in production is Charlotte Watson's Country Collection, a fine cream earthenware range inspired by 18th-century rural pottery and finished with black-lacquer lettered decoration. The firm continues to develop and refine its terracotta ware, and many of its original lines are made and marketed as the Suffolk Original Collection. Included in Suffolk's present range are storage jars and canisters, bread crocks, utensil jars, mushroom, onion and salt keepers, butter and wine coolers, jugs, bowls, tea and coffee pots, cookware and many more domestic kitchenware items, as well as miscellaneous items such as candlesticks, a clock and a pestle and mortar.

KEY FACTS

Location: Wattisfield, Suffolk, UK.
Important dates: Founded c.1800. Still active.
Production: Earthenware and stoneware.
Trade names: Wattisfield Ware, Suffolk Ware, Suffolk Studio Style.

MARKS
Impressed 'WATTISFIELD WARE' mark used from c.1947. Printed and impressed marks from c.1948 include Wattisfield Ware trade name.

◆ **Suffolk Tableware Collection, 1990s**
The most recent product of Watson's collaboration with Queensberry Hunt is the Suffolk Tableware Collection. This studio ware in traditional Suffolk style was introduced during the 1990s. A choice of two glazes is available: Ocean and Forest. 554

J. H. WEATHERBY & SONS

This family-run firm began production in 1891. Its early output was plain and printed toilet sets, trinket sets, vases, teapots, tableware and tableware fancies, jugs, fern pots and lidded chamber pots. Soon after World War I Weatherby began to supply badged and advertising ware to hotels and caterers, and later to hospitals and institutions. In the 1920s and 1930s it experimented with modernist matt glazes and introduced Art Deco-style vases, tableware and fancies. In 1934 it launched Woodpecker Ware tableware, which is highly sought after today, as is its Harvest Time tableware. After World War II the pottery introduced many new lines in giftware and fancies which are now collectable. These include figures and statuettes, toy ware, animal models such as Zookies, dwarfs, Toby jugs and offbeat series such as Gonks and Dalek patterns. Brownie Downing nursery and giftware was launched in the early 1960s, as were Chucklehead cups and saucers for children.

➡ **Advertisement, 1957**
Published in *Pottery and Glass*, this advertisement is for the freely drawn Regency Rake pattern, which was aimed at the contemporary market. Much of Weatherby's output was far more conventional in style. 555

KEY FACTS

Location: Falcon Works, Hanley, Staffordshire, UK.
Important dates: Founded 1891. Closed 1999.

MARKS
This Union Jack design, introduced 1891, used as standard mark. Falcon Ware included from 1925.

WEDGWOOD & CO

Although best known for general domestic earthenware, notably dinner and teaware in traditional styles, including mazarine-blue patterns, Wedgwood & Co. has introduced many collectable ranges. In 1932 the firm launched Farnol, a new Art Deco-style shape for teaware which it later used for almost all its tableware. Decorations included banded, stylized floral print and enamel patterns. Other modern lines included ornamental vases and bowls decorated with matt white, glossy and matt marble glazes. After World War II restrictions were lifted, the firm responded well to contemporary trends. Patio, launched in 1954, was a complete range of dinner, tea, coffee, early-morning and fruit sets decorated with silkscreen-printed patterns. Innovations include oval coupe-shaped plates as well as streamlined teapots, coffee pots and covered sugar bowls and serving dishes. Named patterns include Tanglewood, Cadenza, Bobo, Fernbrake, Gingham, Frolic and Man Friday, the last showing Friday's black footprints across the plate. In similar graphic style is Bois de Boulogne, designed by Albert Wagg around 1956.

KEY FACTS

Location: Unicorn and Pinnox Pottery, Tunstall, Staffordshire, UK.
Important dates: Founded c.1860. Renamed Enoch Wedgwood (Tunstall) Ltd 1965. Taken over by Wedgwood Group and renamed Unicorn Pottery 1980.
Production: Earthenware and ironstone china.
Trade names: Unicorn Pottery, Wedgwood, Wedgwood & Co.

MARKS

This Unicorn mark used in various forms since 19th century.

◆ **Unicorn Pottery ware, 1960s**
Since the 1950s potteries of all sizes have employed David Queensberry or the Queensberry Hunt Partnership to give their ware a modern look. This Wedgwood & Co coffee pot is Queensberry's work. 556

JOSIAH WEDGWOOD & SONS

This highly respected company, established by Josiah Wedgwood in the 18th century, had lost some of its artistic direction in the closing years of the 19th century, a situation made more serious by the poor economic climate. John Goodwin, who was promoted to art director in 1904, immediately began an overhaul of the pottery's product range, and soon much of the elaborate Victorian ware was replaced by relatively simple shapes and patterns. Goodwin's brief was both to improve Wedgwood's commercial ranges and to target some bone-china lines for the expanding middle-class domestic market; for this latter area of production he built up a staff of painters and gilders working in traditional techniques. Heading these was James Hodgkiss, who was involved in the development of a Chinese-inspired powder-blue glaze which was used for a decorative range with printing, gilding and lustre decoration. Daisy Makeig-Jones started to design tableware under Hodgkiss before the introduction of her Fairyland Lustre.

Makeig-Jones was fascinated with the notion of Fairyland, and designing for Fairyland Lustre allowed her imagination to run wild with glimpses of elves, fairies, pixies, gnomes and bats, in fantastic landscapes containing toadstools, stars, spiders' webs and bubbles. Initially her lustre colours – purple, ruby, pink, blue, green, yellow and orange, mother-of-pearl and copper-bronze – were soft and harmonious. Later, after the introduction of Flame Fairyland, she used strong primary colours. Among other designs by Makeig-Jones were the Celtic range, based on decorative motifs from *The Book of Kells*, and nursery and toy ware. All of her work

➤ **Fairyland Lustre ginger jar, 1920s**
This piece features a design by Daisy Makeig-Jones: Ghostly Wood, several inhabitants of which were based on Gustave Doré's drawings for *The Legend of Croquemitaine*, first published in 1863. 557

◄ **Alfred Powell wall plaque, 1926**
To adorn this wall plaque Powell executed a finely painted view of Bisham Abbey, Berkshire. ⬜558

◄ **Millicent Taplin Cane Ware vase, c.1928**
Designed and painted by Taplin and signed with her monogram, this vase was probably a prototype for Wedgwood's Sun-lit pattern and other Art Deco-inspired patterns that were to be produced by the new handcraft department. ⬜559

▶ **Victor Skellern china coffee set, 1935**
This coffee set features one of a series of handcraft china patterns from the 1930s – in this case Persian Ponies – a number of which were shown at the Grafton Galleries, London, in 1936, helping to establish Skellern as Wedgwood's art director. ⬜560

is now sought after but most highly prized is her Fairyland Lustre, which, although expensive, was very popular from 1915 to 1929.

While John Goodwin's priority was to improve Wedgwood's mass-produced ranges, Alfred Powell and his wife Louise were brought in to create an artware range in earthenware. The couple's association with the pottery, which began in 1903 when Wedgwood accepted Alfred's designs, lasted until the early 1940s. They worked together as designers from 1906, and some of their work is jointly signed. The success of the early designs produced by Alfred Powell at Wedgwood led to a more formal arrangement between the Powells and the company. Included in their range are jugs, vases, chargers, bowls, plaques, ginger jars and small containers; these were decorated with landscapes, seascapes and animals, or bold stylized patterns derived from nature but with a strong graphic element.

At the time of the Powells' first visits to the factory, some of Josiah Wedgwood's first patterns were being produced using a printing and hand-colouring technique which they saw as a particularly dull occupation. Alfred persuaded Frank Wedgwood to allow him to establish a studio where the Powells could train some of the girls to paint the entire pattern freehand. Millicent Taplin was one of several designers trained as a freehand paintress. From the start her working relationship with the couple went beyond hand-painting their designs, for she was often asked to adapt their complex patterns, such as the Persian and Rhodian freehand-painted series of large vases and bowls launched in 1920. Wedgwood's success at the 1925 Paris Exhibition and the Powells' increased commitment to freehand painting led to the establishment of a small handcraft studio at Etruria in 1926. When it opened, Taplin was put in charge and was assisted by girls from the Burslem School of Art.

The effects of the Wall Street Crash of 1929 were felt strongly by Wedgwood, which depended on the North American market for sales of its expensive luxury lines. Fairyland Lustre was among the first casualties. New handcraft ware, such as the distinctive range in a cane body painted with the Art Deco-inspired Sun-lit pattern, offered a cheaper alternative. A new management team took over the running of the company in 1930. The works manager was Norman Wilson, who played a large part in turning the theory of modernism into practice. He was concerned

with developing many of the matt and stain glazes and coloured slips and celadons used by John Skeaping (*see* p.206) and Keith Murray (*see* p.141) in the early 1930s. He also perfected a series of monochrome glazes used for Veronese Ware, a handcraft range with metal-lustre decoration, and invented Alpine Pink, a translucent bone china. In addition he had a great flair for shapes. Throughout his time at Wedgwood he continued experimental work and produced many unique pieces with special glazes, often oriental in inspiration, now highly prized by collectors. For two years Sir Charles Holmes was art consultant to the firm; among his contributions was the striking Art Deco Sunbirds tableware range.

Victor Skellern joined the management team in 1934, when he took over as art director from Goodwin, having earlier completed an apprenticeship under him. Skellern, who was the first fully trained professional designer to be employed by Wedgwood and the first art director in the true sense, had a profound influence on Wedgwood design over the next 30 years. Among many other contributions, he instituted technical developments such as silkscreen and lithographic printing, collaborated with Norman Wilson on designs for new bodies and glazes, and created many patterns and shapes in Queen's Ware and bone china. The contacts Skellern made with artists and designers during his time at the Royal College of Art enabled him to attract fine freelance designers to Wedgwood, including Eric Ravilious, Edward Bawden, Rex and Laurence Whistler, Clare Leighton, Robert Grodden and Richard Guyatt. His continued association with the RCA later enabled him to choose skilled designers for his department, among them Peter Wall and Robert Minkin, who at different times from the 1960s to 1980s headed Wedgwood design teams.

Figures, which at the start of the 20th century had not been a prominent part of the firm's recent history, took on greater importance with the issue of animal and bird models by Ernest Light, and more so with the introduction in the late 1920s of stylized animal figures by John Skeaping. Models were generally provided by freelance artists such as the animal sculptor Alan Best and Doris Lindner, who was later to enjoy a long association with Royal Worcester (*see* p.191). Production was interrupted by the outbreak of World War II, but figure-making was resumed at Barlaston

▲ **Arnold Machin's The Country Lovers, c.1940**
This Queen's Ware version of traditional flatback figures modelled by Machin was painted by Millicent Taplin's handcraft paintresses. 561

▲ **Queen's Ware commemorative mug, 1953**
This mug celebrating Queen Elizabeth II's coronation was designed in 1953 by Richard Guyatt, one of a number of freelance designers who worked for Wedgwood during the 1950s. 562

◀ **Robert Minkin coffee set, 1963**
Minkin's black-basalt fine stoneware coffee set reflects the influence of Denmark and Finland. He was designer at Barlaston between 1955 and 1986, and his influence can be found on tableware patterns during that period. 563

Unique Ware vase, 1930s
This slip-decorated vase is part of
Norman Wilson's Unique Ware range.
The term 'Unique' refers to the glaze
effects, many of which were Wilson's
own invention. He also designed
shapes, some of which were used
exclusively for this range. 564

David Gentleman plate, 1977
Gentleman's bone-china plate is one of
a series featuring views of British
castles and country houses. Depicting
Windsor Castle, it was one of the first
two to be issued in 1977. 565

Peter Rabbit clock plate, c.1990
This clock is decorated with one
of Beatrix Potter's ever-popular
characters. These first appeared on
a series of children's ware in 1949,
when Wedgwood acquired the sole
reproduction rights from Frederick
Warne & Co. The range includes many
items, including money boxes, soap
dishes, eggcups and lamp bases. 566

shortly after the firm moved there in 1940. The sculptor-modeller Arnold
Machin was given a studio at the new factory. Throughout the war he produced over 20 delightful figures and groups for Wedgwood, mostly in the
traditional Staffordshire flatback style, as well as other designs, such as
chess pieces and relief decoration for earthenware fancies and jasper
ware. As freelancers, Richard Garbe and Herbert W. Palliser also provided
Wedgwood with some interesting models in the early 1940s. Shortly after
the war Eric Owen was employed as Wedgwood's full-time modeller.

The return of peace saw the introduction of lithography, and the new
technique took precedence at Barlaston during the late 1940s and the
1950s. Millicent Taplin, who after the war became a member of
Wedgwood's design team, proved to be an equally accomplished designer
for lithographic work. One of her first designs was Kingcup, while one of
the most successful was the Strawberry Hill lithograph, designed jointly
with Victor Skellern and honoured by a Design of the Year award by the
Council of Industrial Design in 1957.

Post-war successes include Peter Rabbit nursery ware, which was
introduced in 1949 when Wedgwood secured exclusive rights to reproduce Beatrix Potter's paintings. Continuing the established practice of
working with outside designers, the firm commissioned Laurence
Whistler, whose brother Rex Whistler designed a series of views of
Clovelly for Wedgwood in the 1930s. Laurence Whistler designed the
Dolphin tableware pattern and Outlines of Grandeur, a set of six plates
with views of Stonehenge, Tintern Abbey, Holyrood House, St Paul's
Cathedral, Clifton Suspension Bridge and the Viceroy's House, New Delhi,
made in limited editions around 1955. In 1977 David Gentleman was commissioned to design a series of views of British castles and country houses
for Wedgwood bone china. These were issued in limited editions of 5000.
More recent is the 1993 series of limited-edition plates which Wedgwood,
in association with the National Art Collections Fund, commissioned six
British painters and sculptors to design: Peter Blake, Patrick Caulfield,
Patrick Heron, Bruce McLean, Eduardo Paolozzi and John Piper. The last
of these designed for the company in 1971 a set of six plates with
silkscreen designs entitled Variations on a Geometric Theme.

Wedgwood also extended its policy of encouraging young talent by collaborating with, among others, Glenys Barton, some 20 pieces of whose work were exhibited in London in 1977. Also of interest to the collector is its collaboration in 1982 with the artist-jeweller Wendy Ramshaw, who produced more than 100 designs for necklaces, pins, brooches and ear-rings making use of Wedgwood bodies, notably jasper and black basalt.

The range of commemoratives, special commissions and limited editions has grown greatly since 1940, when Ravilious designed a mug commemorating the move to Barlaston. For example, the series of annual 'year' plates now includes a Calendar Plate, Peter Rabbit Calendar Plate, Jasper Year Plate and Peter Rabbit Birthday Plate. Historical Year Plates and a Jasper Mother Plate were introduced in 1998.

By the mid-1980s Wedgwood had acquired 11 pottery and porcelain firms, but itself became the target of several takeover bids. In 1986 the Wedgwood Group accepted an offer from Waterford Glass, the two companies merged, and in 1989 the Waterford-Wedgwood Group was created.

➤ Jasper Christmas plate, 1998
Wedgwood introduced this popular series of plates in 1969. 567

KEY FACTS

Location: Burslem 1759–69, Etruria 1769–1940, Barlaston 1940–; Staffordshire, UK. Still active.
Important dates: Founded 1759. Merged with Waterford as Waterford Wedgwood Group 1989. Only four brand names now in use: Wedgwood, Mason, Johnson and Coalport. Others, such as Clarice Cliff, may be used for special issues.
Production: Earthenware, basalts, jaspers and china.
Principal designers: Alfred and Louise Powell, Victor Skellern, Millicent Taplin, Norman Wilson, Peter Wall, Robert Minkin, John Skeaping, Eric Ravilious, Keith Murray.
Trade names: Wedgwood, Josiah Wedgwood & Sons.

MARKS

Portland vase used on porcelain ware from c.1878. This version standard from 1962, with or without pattern name. Creamware usually marked with round printed mark incorporating company name.

WEDGWOOD
Bone China
MADE IN ENGLAND

MEDINA

WELLER POTTERY

Samuel A. Weller opened his first pottery in Fultonham, Ohio, in 1872. He made plain flower pots and some stoneware. Business improved, and he built a new pottery about 1890 and bought an existing plant the following year. By this time he was making jardinières, hanging baskets and umbrella stands, in addition to flower pots and stoneware jars. Many American potteries were making the same products in the 1890s, so competition was spirited. Instead of continuing to serve the same dwindling market, however, Weller looked elsewhere. His new product line was successful and his pottery survived for many years, turning out mid-range artware for florists and gift shops across the USA.

Inspired by the slip-decorated ware of the Lonhuda Pottery of Steubenville, Ohio, that were shown at the 1893 World's Columbian Exhibition in Chicago, Weller acquired an interest in Lonhuda's operation and the services of William Long, one of its directors. Lonhuda ware was made in imitation of Rookwood's (see p.179) Standard line. However, while Lonhuda used the same palette of slip colours as Rookwood, it employed commercial, rather than fine, artists to execute the decorations. Weller and Long began making Lonhuda ware in the Zanesville plant in 1895, but after a year Weller released Long, kept the process and renamed the product Louwelsa.

Many lines of art pottery were introduced after the success of Lonhuda and Louwelsa. In 1900 Charles Babcock Upjohn, who became Weller's art director and designer after Long's departure, introduced Dickensware,

➤ Dickensware mug, c.1900
Despite the reference to Charles Dickens, not all of the themes came from his stories. The Dickensware line included American Indians, animals, golfers, and monks as well as characters from Dickens's novels. 568

which featured characters and scenes from Dickens's stories as well as figures from other genres. In 1902 Weller hired the French potter Jacques Sicard, who had worked in the studio of Clément Massier and learned the secret of iridescent glaze. In 1907 Sicard and his assistant left with the formula. Other lines from this era include Aurelian, Auroral, Turado, Eocean, Etna, Floretta, Jap-Birdimal, Dresden, Etched Matt, Hunter and L'Art Nouveau. All of these lines depended on the same technology of applying coloured slips to earthenware. An article about the pottery in a 1906 issue of *The Sketch Book* suggested that Weller's successful introduction of so many lines was the result of his employing artists of various nationalities, including French, Japanese, Austrian, German and American craftsmen.

Despite Weller's ascendancy in the competition for hand-decorated artware among the Zanesville potteries during the early 20th century, he decided to move towards a more industrial product after World War I. His decision was prompted by the same reasons that persuaded the Roseville Pottery (*see* p.181) to make a similar transition: changes in market demand and the need to streamline operations.

In 1920 Weller bought the Zanesville Art Pottery. As his art director he hired John Lessell, who designed several art lines before he left in 1924, including Lamar (dark trees on a red ground) and LaSa (black landscapes on a lustre ground). These were the last labour-intensive artware lines that the pottery produced. Lessell also developed red glazes for moulded forms, including Chengtu, a matt red-orange glaze, and Chinese Red.

Despite the change in product focus after World War I, Weller produced a veritable dictionary of motifs during the next three decades, rendered in vases, jardinières, teaware, planters, lamp bases and flower bowls. Most forms were moulded in low relief and then glazed to bring out the featured motif. Ardsley (1928) is made of cat-tails and water lilies. Arcola (1920s) has grapes, vines or roses in relief with matt glaze. Atlantic (1920s) has moulded fruits, flowers and leaves. Barcelona (1920s), shaded pink to yellow, has ridges in the mould which imitate hand-turning marks. Bedford (1920s) has a dark glossy glaze over moulded flowers on stems. Blossom (about 1940) features pink flowers and green leaves on a blue or green matt glaze. Blue Drapery (about 1920) is moulded as dark-blue matt vertical drapery with red roses. Bouquet (1930s) has blossoms of dogwood and lily of the valley. Breton (1920s) has a band of stylized flowers and leaves around the middle. Burnt Wood (1909) looks like wood ornamented with a burning tool. Chase (about 1940) mimics Wedgwood's (*see* Josiah Wedgwood & Sons, p.230) jasper ware, with relief hunt scenes

◆ Sicardo vase, c.1905
The secret of creating iridescent glazes was known to only a few potters. 569

◆ Hudson vase, c.1915
The Hudson line was hand-painted in coloured slips and covered with a matt on-glaze. 570

◆ Souevo vase, 1909
Souevo, a line inspired by American Indian pottery, used redware bodies boldly decorated with cream-coloured and black slips. The range may have been created to compete with the Clifton Pottery's Indian Ware. 571

◆ Ivory jardinière, late 1920s
The name of this line refers to the colour rather than the subject. Most of the ornament in Ivory was derived from the English Arts and Crafts style. The same design in another colourway was called Rosemont. 572

in white on a dark-blue matt ground. Coppertone (1920s) features a mottled green-and-brown glaze on flower frogs (holders) and vases moulded with fish, frogs and water plants. Forest (about 1920) is moulded and hand-coloured to look like a forest scene. Graystone (about 1910) is a garden-crockery line made to look like granite. Hobart (1928) has a vellum finish over green and white figures of humans and animals.

Matte Green (1905) has low-relief leaves and other natural forms under a green matt glaze. Mirror Black (1920s) has a black glaze over classic shapes. Morocco (1920s) features tree and fruit in carved relief on a ground of black or red. Ollas water bottles (late 1930s), designed by Dorothy England Laughead, are shaped like gourds. Pinecone (1920s) has pine cones in panels under a matt glaze. Racene (1930s) features deer and leaves in modern style. Silvertone (1920s) describes the pink, blue, green and lavender matt glaze used over moulded fruits, flowers or butterflies. Ting (about 1940) looks like teakwood. Sydonia (1920s) is shell-shaped with leaves at the base. Velvetone (1928) has blended green, pink, yellow, brown and green in a matt glaze. Zona (1920), designed by Rudolf Lorber, mimics the apple pattern of Gladding-McBean's (*see* p.73) Franciscan. And there were many more.

In 1922 Weller reorganized his sole proprietorship into a corporation, the S.A. Weller Company, which on his death in 1925 passed to his nephew, Harry Weller. After Harry's death in 1932, two of Sam's sons-in-law, Frederick Grant and Irvin Smith, took control. Despite much streamlining of design and manufacturing, business declined during the Depression. Two plants were closed in 1936. There was some improvement during World War II, when overseas manufacturers were otherwise occupied, but business could not be sustained after the war, and in 1948 the Weller Pottery ceased manufacturing.

➤ Lasa vase, early 1920s
The Lasa range, designed by John Lessell, has an iridescent background that gives the impression of a glowing sunset through the black outlines of trees. Lasa was the last artist-decorated line produced by Weller. 573

KEY FACTS

Location: Zanesville, Ohio, USA.
Important dates: Founded 1872. Closed 1948.
Production: Artware, flower containers.
Principal designers: W. A. Long, Charles Babcock Upjohn, Jacques Sicard, John Lessell, Fred Rhead, Frank Ferrell.
Trade names: Louwelsa, Sicardo, Eocean, Turado, Etna, Aurelian and others.

MARKS

Various marks used, some with line name; all incorporate 'Weller' or 'Weller Pottery'.

WELLSVILLE POTTERY COMPANY

In 1902 a group headed by Monroe Patterson purchased the old Pioneer Pottery in Wellsville, Ohio, which produced white-granite ware. The new company made semi-porcelain and white-granite dinnerware, toilet sets and specialities. Much of its early work mimicked French Haviland's flowery patterns or the standard popular patterns, such as Blue Willow. During the 1920s and early 1930s Wellsville made kitchenware, including bowls, covered casseroles, plates, custard cups and refrigerator jugs. Today its kitchenware is perhaps the most collectable of its goods. In 1933 the pottery began making vitrified hotel ware. Its neighbour, the Sterling China Company (*see* p.213), bought the business in 1959, but closed the factory a decade later.

Olive Shape 4158

KEY FACTS

Location: Wellsville, Ohio, USA.
Important dates: Founded 1902. Taken over by Sterling China Company 1959. Closed 1969.
Production: Semi-porcelain dinnerware, toilet ware, hotel ware.

MARKS

Various marks include company's full name. 'W.C.Co.' also used.

◆ **Olive ewer and basin, 1911**
The Olive shape seen here has been decorated with a red-rose decal and gold. A 10-piece toilet set in Wellsville's 1911 trade catalogue was priced at $3.50. 574

WEMYSS

The pottery was founded as the Fife Pottery in the early 19th century, and was making creamware within its first few years. Wemyss Ware was named in honour of Lady Grosvenor of Wemyss Castle, Scotland, who produced many of the designs. The range consisted of large pieces painted against a white ground with flowers or fruit; among subjects recorded are Canterbury bells, irises, carnations, violets, sweet peas, roses and shamrock, apples, citrus fruit, cherries, plums, strawberries and redcurrants. Also made in Wemyss Ware were models of pigs and cats, now highly collectable, and a cock-and-hen range that included a morning set with a black-cock pattern and 'Bonjour' on the rim of the flatware. Pieces were often finished with painted red or green lines. Wemyss Ware became increasingly well known and was later sold exclusively through Thomas Goode & Co. Commemorative items were also made in Wemyss Ware for Queen Victoria's Diamond Jubilee, the coronations of Edward VII and George V and other special occasions.

From 1916 the pottery was managed by Eric Sandland, who evolved a more impressionistic style of decoration. It closed in 1930 and production was subsequently transferred to the Bovey Pottery (*see* p.28) in Devon.

◆ **Jam pot, before 1928**
This jam pot shows the influence of the Nikola school of painting, which specialized in natural subjects with deep colours. Other designs include violets, sweet peas and plums. 575

◆ **Wemyss Ware pig, before 1930**
Pigs are among the most collectable items of Wemyss Ware, whether in this white crackle glaze or with the more traditional floral patterns. 576

KEY FACTS

Location: Fife or Gallatoun Pottery, Kirkcaldy, Fife, UK.
Important dates: Founded c.1820. Called Robert Heron (& Son) c.1837–1930. Wemyss name used by Bovey Pottery 1930–57.
Production: Earthenware and stoneware.

MARKS

This mark used c.1920–29.

WESTERN STONEWARE COMPANY

The success of this company is due in large part to the high quality of the clay available near its Monmouth, Illinois, factory. The pottery is well known for making premiums bearing the head of the Sioux chief Sleepy Eyes for the Sleepy Eye Milling Company. For the Chicago distributor Marshall Burns the company made the Marcrest line, an old-fashioned brown-glazed ovenproof ware sold at service stations and grocery stores in the 1950s. Marcrest was made into many kitchen and table shapes, such as casseroles, mugs, pitchers, dinner and luncheon plates, bowls, creams and sugars, salts and peppers, cookie jars, bean pots, ramekins, carafes and jugs. In 1954 the pottery commissioned Eva Zeisel to design a line of blue spongeware. Fifty new shapes and 15 new patterns were created, including solid-colour and hand-decorated patterns in blue on white bodies. Of particular interest are the bird-shaped casserole, sauce boat and teapot. Mojavi dinnerware, with solid-colour glazes in the Californian style, was made from the 1950s until 1975.

KEY FACTS

Location: Monmouth, Illinois, USA.
Important dates: Founded 1906. Still active.
Production: Utilitarian stoneware, flower containers, kitchenware, some dinnerware.
Principal designer: Eva Zeisel.

MARKS

Wide variety of marks used, some versions printed in maple-leaf outline or oval shape. Mark for Eva Zeisel's line includes her name, but incorporates 'Monmouth' rather than the usual 'Western Stoneware'.

◆ **Marcrest cookie jar, 1950s (far left); florists' ware vase, 1920s (left)**
Although a manufacturer of utilitarian stoneware for most of the 20th century, Western has survived by developing decorative products that could be made in large quantities. The cookie jar is from the extensive Marcrest line for Marshall Burns developed in the 1950s; the moulded vase on the right is florists' ware from the 1920s. 577

WILDBLOOD, HEATH & SONS

The pottery was producing tea and breakfast sets at the start of the 20th century, and during World War I it added novelty ware and fancies to counter the cessation of German and other imports. These were decorated with printed patterns and marketed vigorously into the 1920s. In 1921 the firm's output was tea and breakfast ware, and fancies, including view ware, fancy vases, crested china and souvenir ware. Among other specialist lines were toy teaware and children's china teasets, the latter first advertised in 1917 in 16-piece boxed sets with a choice of patterns.

➡ **Advertisement, 1916**
Published in *The Pottery Gazette*, this Wildblood advertisement shows the wide range of ornaments and teaware conventionally associated with minor, but nonetheless ambitious, potters in Staffordshire. 578

KEY FACTS

Location: Peel Works, Longton, Staffordshire, UK.
Important dates: Founded as Wildblood & Heath 1889. Renamed Wildblood, Heath & Sons 1899. Closed 1927.
Production: China.

MARKS

This mark used as standard 1899–1927.

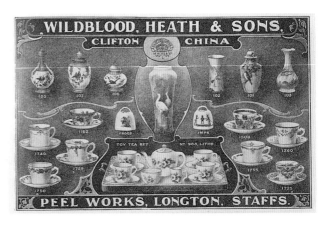

THOMAS C. WILD: see ROYAL ALBERT p.183
WILEMAN & CO.: see SHELLEY POTTERIES p.200

A. J. WILKINSON

The firm was taken over by the Shorter family (*see* p.204) in 1891, but under its own name continued to make table services, toilet and trinket sets, as well as ornamental ware, vases and bowls. Ornamental ware became an important part of its output in the interwar years. The firm had long produced models of birds and figures, and statuesque caricatures, but expanded its catalogue of general novelties and fancies between the wars with character Toby jugs and, notably, nursery ware by Joan Shorter and some children's lines modelled by Clarice Cliff. It also developed new ranges of hotel ware, toilet ware and medium-priced earthenware, a number of which were finished in Honey, an ivory glaze first introduced in the early 1920s.

In the early 1930s the firm collaborated with E. Brain (*see* p.28) on the experimental production of tableware and other stock pieces, with patterns which were carried out on earthenware. The tableware patterns had been commissioned from 27 leading contemporary artists and were issued in limited editions of 12. Wilkinson's pieces were marked with the artist's signature; for instance, 'Produced in Bizarre by Clarice Cliff'.

From the early 1950s and into the 1960s, apart from making a small quantity of Clarice Cliff ware, Wilkinson concentrated on traditional printed decorations, commemoratives and coronation ware.

KEY FACTS

Location: Royal Staffordshire Pottery, Burslem, UK.
Important dates: Founded 1885. Taken over by Shorter family 1891. Bought Newport Pottery 1920. Taken over by W. R. Midwinter 1964. Became part of Wedgwood Group 1970.
Production: Earthenware and ironstone china.
Trade names: Royal Staffordshire Pottery, Clarice Cliff, Bizarre.

MARKS

This mark introduced c.1930. Other marks incorporate artist or designer's signature, date, copyright and usual company backstamp of the time. Among backstamps used was 'Bizarre by Clarice Cliff' in script.

♦ **Carruthers-Gould George V Toby jug, c.1918**
The artist F. Carruthers-Gould designed a set of caricature Toby jugs for Wilkinson which depict the military and political leaders of World War I. 579

H. M. WILLIAMSON & SONS

Founded c.1879 in Longton, Staffordshire, the pottery made fine bone-china teaware under the Heathcote China trade name. It also became well known for children's china with patterns such as the Willebeek series of nursery rhymes. Other popular children's ranges depicted rabbits and cats as well as teddy bears playing ball games. Highly collectable is the Wireless series, launched in 1925, which shows young children listening to the radio. In 1941 the business was absorbed by E. Brain (*see* p.28).

MARKS

Variations of this mark used c.1928–41. Others include monogram or full company name.

WINTERTON POTTERY (LONGTON)

This versatile Staffordshire pottery made earthenware for both the home and a strong export market. Its output included tea, dinner and toilet ware, tableware accessories, ordinary domestic and general utility lines, including its patented Utility Hygiene Butter. Also made were ornamental ware, vases, art pots and fancies, often with cheaper finishes such as cellulose spraying. The factory was closed during World War II, but the firm continued to trade under its own name, with the Avon Art Pottery (*see* p.17) making its cellulose lines. However, Winterton never recovered from wartime restrictions and ceased trading around 1954.

MARKS

Variations of this standard mark used c.1927–54. Others used c.1939–41 incorporate trade name 'Bluestone Ware',

ARTHUR WOOD & SON (LONGPORT)

The pottery-making origins of the Wood family of Staffordshire go back over 250 years, but the present company dates from around 1884 and remains on the original site. Arthur Wood made his name with teapots. In the early 1920s the firm added decorated fancies to its catalogue: mainly rose bowls and vases, notably the Longport shape, a modernist octagonal tube-shaped vase, available in various self-colours as well as floral and other decal decoration. The fancies range was expanded in the 1920s and 1930s and included ornamental jugs such as Dick Whittington and Jack and the Beanstalk, modelled in relief and with figurative handles, and freely painted Art Deco-style useful ornaments. In response to its strong export market the firm worked at full capacity during World War II, making its usual lines in teaware, jug sets and other fancies.

Highly promoted throughout the 1950s was a contemporary range of white matt, matt and giltware bowls, flower jugs, wall vases, teapots, vases and miniature jugs, bowls and shoes. Tankards, some musical, were also made in large quantities; popular subjects were London Sights, Sports, English Inns, Hunting and South African Scenes. In the 1960s and 1970s the firm developed its range of hollowware: not only teapots but also cottage ware, cups, mugs, jars, containers mugs, piggy banks, plant pots, jugs, vases and ornamental chamber pots. After acquiring Carlton Ware (*see* p.38) in 1967, Arthur Wood continued Carlton's line in Rouge Royale gold-printed raised and hand-enamelled vases and covered jars, Walking Ware and other novelties. Later products included teaware and associated ware, lettered storage jars, jugs and giftware. One item in the range of teapots and mugs is Jolly/Sad, with a smiling face on one side and a sad face on the other. This was designed by Francis Wood, the son of the director, Anthony Wood, in 1990, when he was eight years old.

▲ Teaware, 1950s
Typical banded shapes and stylized patterns reflect Wood's place in the popular market. 580

▲ Cat model, 1950s
This stylish original model underlines the impact of contemporary designs in the 1950s. 581

◆ Traditional Teas teaset, 1990s
Teapots have always been an important part of Arthur Wood's production. The Traditional Teas teapot shown here is one of five Tea for One teasets and gift-boxed sets in current production. Others in the series are Herbal Teas, Afternoon Teas, Cream Teas and Garden Teas. 582

KEY FACTS

Location: Bradwell Works, Longport, Staffordshire, UK.
Important dates: Founded as Capper & Wood c.1884. Traded as Arthur Wood from 1904. Became limited company and renamed Arthur Wood & Son (Longport Ltd) 1928. Bought Carlton Ware Ltd 1967 and sold it 1987. Closed 2003.
Production: Earthenware.
Trade names: Arthur Wood, Royal Bradwell.

MARKS

This mark introduced c.1945. Other versions omit trade name. Before 1928, impressed or printed 'A W', above 'L', with or without 'England'.

WOOD & SONS

By the early 20th century Wood & Sons was one of the largest and most progressive businesses in the Burslem area, producing mainly dinner, tea, toilet, hotel and badged ware and fancies for the middle and mass markets. Harry J. Wood was a shrewd businessman, and in 1912 appointed the talented artist and designer Frederick Rhead as art director. Rhead's early designs were mostly for domestic tableware, but he also developed new ornamental artware, including some highly collectable early tube-lined designs and an inexpensive *pâte-sur-pâte* decorated range. The firm had a good show at the British Industries Fair in 1919, where it introduced tube-lined pieces under the name Rhodian Ware. In 1920 Harry Wood acquired the Crown Pottery, mainly for the production of good-class ornamental artware, and set up Bursley Ltd to run it.

The ware made by Wood & Sons was generally of a high standard. Its deep honey-coloured glaze was favoured by outside decorators, including Susie Cooper (*see* p.49), who bought blanks and had shapes made. She collaborated with Wood & Sons, and in 1931 the Crown Works became the new home of the Susie Cooper Pottery. Tableware from the 1920s followed fashion trends, and the firm's catalogues included some stylish Art Deco and handcraft patterns. During World War II the pottery remained in production and continued to market the goods of the Susie Cooper Pottery and H. J. Wood. Charlotte Rhead (*see* p.173) worked briefly for Wood & Sons in the 1940s. One of her tableware designs was a thin white tubed leaf pattern produced on Wood's standard green Beryl body; introduced just before World War II, it is still produced today.

Wood & Sons and its associated companies prospered through the 1950s, and a number of contemporary giftware lines, including Piazza Ware, were created by H. J. Wood, which it had taken over in the 1930s.

Piazza Ware, 1956
This advertisement shows a series of patterns from the popular Piazza range of stylish contemporary giftware, created in 1956. 583

Beryl Ware, early 1940s
Made from Wood's standard green body, this range of tableware was first introduced in the late 1930s and was available during World War II. It still forms part of the company's range of fine tableware. 584

Holly Cottage dinnerware, 1990s
The Holly Cottage pattern on the Continental shape illustrates Wood's contemporary style in tableware. 585

KEY FACTS

Location: Trent, New Wharf and other factories, Burslem, Staffordshire, UK.
Important dates: Founded 1865. Traded as Wood & Sons from 1910. Founded H. J. Wood as an independent company c.1884 (merged 1930s). Bought Crown Pottery 1920. Bought Ellgreave Pottery 1921. Bought by Yorke family 1982. In receivership 2002, now run by Strathay Green Wellies. Still active.
Production: Earthenware, redware, ironstone and semi-porcelain.
Trade names: Wood, Sons & Co., Wood & Son(s), Wood's Ware, Bursley Ltd.

MARKS

This mark and similar versions with different names used from c.1940. Others usually incorporate 'WOOD'S' or 'WOOD & SONS'.

WORCESTER: see ROYAL WORCESTER p.191
ZANE POTTERY: see PETERS & REED POTTERY p.151

In the five years since this book was first published the British ceramics industry has experienced radical changes. Staffordshire, once famous throughout the world for the design and manufacture of ceramics, and since the 18th century a name synonymous with British pottery and porcelain, no longer has these associations.

The reason for this change is that, over the last decade, the large conglomerates that had dominated the industry since the 1960s have been broken up by a steady process of merger and de-merger, take-overs and management buy-outs, closures and consolidation. Most significant has been the break up of the once powerful Royal Doulton Group. Their factories have been closed, and famous names that had belonged to them like Minton, Beswick, Adderley and Paragon have virtually vanished. Once started, the process of contraction seemed unstoppable, and now Royal Doulton has to all intents and purposes ceased to be a pottery manufacturer; all that remains is a small administration centre.

The main reason for this is outsourcing. Today, much of the pottery and porcelain marketed under famous and familiar names is actually made thousands of miles away, in Indonesia, Malaysia, Korea and China. The tableware market, once the backbone of the British industry, is, in effect, dead. It is an irony that the Far East, which introduced porcelain to Europe in the 17th century, has now taken it away again.

This process of change has been universal. Wedgwood have contracted their production to four brand names, one of which is entirely outsourced. Many smaller manufacturers have simply vanished, in some cases after centuries of production. About 20 names included in the first edition of this book have since closed down. However, a few names have escaped, for the time being, the process of attrition. Poole, Burgess & Leigh and T. G. Green have been closed, and reopened under new ownership. While a number of smaller companies have come and gone, their brief production span being, as a result, largely unrecorded, others have flourished, managing to keep the Staffordshire name on the map.

It is interesting to note that there have been some great successes, notched up by newer companies concentrating on niche and collector markets. This pattern was started by Moorcroft when it was revived in the mid 1980s. Moorcroft itself has spawned Cobridge, a factory dedicated to the interests of collectors. Others have followed successfully, notably Lorna Bailey, Highland Stoneware, Moorland Pottery and Dennis Chinaworks. The rise of these, and other specialist manufacturers working on a small scale, suggests a different future for the British ceramic industry, almost a reversion to the cottage industry structure of the 18th century.

Another route to survival has been the adherence by potteries to a well-defined product with a clear market position. Companies like Portmeirion, Bridgewater, and Burgess Dorling & Leigh are in this category: they are market aware, and adapt their production accordingly, something the traditional large companies cannot do.

The British ceramics industry is at a point of change. The next few years may see it disappear completely, or flourish and develop in new ways to suit the demands of emerging collector and niche markets. However, what is certain is that the age of the big companies and the dominance of famous names is coming to an end.

◆ **Dennis Chinaworks vase, 2004**
The Beetle vase was inspired by Christopher Dresser and made in a limited edition of 25. ⌐586⌐

◆ **Lorna Bailey charger, 2003**
This Art Deco Lady charger with its colourful tropical backdrop was introduced in April 2003 and is a limited edition of 50. ⌐587⌐

ALDERMASTON POTTERY

Founded in 1955 by Alan Caiger-Smith Aldermaston quickly became known for a type of ware different from the then dominant Leach style. Using a red earthenware body with a tin glaze, and local willow to fire the kiln, Caiger-Smith drew his inspiration from historical sources, notably the painted tin-glazed pottery of the Middle East, the Hispano-Moresque period in Spain, the Italian Renaissance and the European Delftwares of the 17th and 18th centuries. He developed a calligraphic style of painting that blended a modern approach with traditional handcraft techniques, including the extensive use of reduction-fired lustre. Many potters trained and worked with Caiger-Smith, including Geoffrey Eastop and Laurence McGowan, but the pottery was run as a co-operative, with everyone involved in all aspects of pottery making. Domestic- and table-wares were produced alongside one-off pieces, giving Aldermaston a reputation and a stature beyond the conventional studio pottery. Caiger-Smith, a brilliant potter, and a notable ceramic historian, closed the pottery in 1993. It has been reopened by his son, Nick, and Caiger-Smith himself has continued to work there on an individual basis.

◆ **Lustre painted pottery, 1960s**
A group of Aldermaston pottery by Alan Caiger-Smith showing a variety of hand-painted ornamental domestic ware in a typical range of shapes. 588

KEY FACTS
Location: Aldermaston, Berkshire, UK.
Important dates: 1955–93. Reopened c.1998.
Production: Tin-glazed earthenware with painted decoration, domestic wares.

MARKS
Incised or painted personal mark of Alan Caiger-Smith from 1955. Other monogram marks of potters working at Aldermaston also occur.

LORNA BAILEY ARTWARE

Set up as LBJ Ceramics in 1983 by Lionel Bailey in the former Ellgreave Pottery in Burslem, Lorna Bailey is now one of the best known of the new generation of small-scale Staffordshire potteries producing wares aimed at the collectors' market. Lorna, Lionel's daughter, started as an enthusiastic collector of Clarice Cliff and other Art Deco wares. After college, in the mid-1990s, she joined the business as its primary designer and quickly turned a pottery making Toby jugs and other Shorter-type wares into a highly successful producer of colourful and zany collector-orientated decorative wares with an international reputation. At first the designs were clearly Art Deco inspired, but now they reflect the extraordinary fertility of Lorna's imagination. Many are produced in limited editions. In 1998 the pottery moved into the Crownford Works in Burslem, and in 2003 expanded into the famous Price & Kensington factory at Trubshaw Cross. Lorna Bailey has won many awards, including Young Businesswoman of the Year.

KEY FACTS
Location: Burslem, Staffordshire, UK.
Important Dates: Founded 1983, still active.
Production: Hand-painted decorative earthenwares.
Principal designer: Lorna Bailey,

MARKS
Printed and painted marks with Lorna Bailey signature

◆ **Highfield shape jug, 2004**
Issued in May 2004, this design wittily combines Art Deco with space rockets, and bridges the gap between functional and craft ceramics. 589

◆ **Ziggy teapot, 2004**
A dynamic example of the Lorna Bailey style, issued in 2004, shows an understanding of the contemporary movement towards non-functional, sculptural ceramics. 590

BOURNE & LEIGH

Established in the Albion and Leighton Potteries in Burslem in 1891 as general manufacturers of earthenware tablewares and fancies, the company made its name in the 1920s and 1930s for producing domestic wares characterised by 'a strong and reliable body, potted in very practical style, and decorated with patterns designed to meet with a good reception by those folk who are on the lookout for something that is calculated to do them good service, and give them lasting enjoyment, and come within the limits of a moderate purse.' They also made hotel ware and children's wares, including the Fairyland and Gnomes ranges designed by Renée Pemberton.

The factory re-formed at the Leighton Pottery in 1940, then closed during World War II, with production concentrated at the Elijah Cotton pottery in Hanley. It reopened in Burslem in 1948, where they made all kinds of tablewares including sandwich sets and supper sets. The pottery closed in 1954.

◀ **Gnomes Playtime nursery ware, 1930s**
This *Pottery Gazette* advertisement from 1933 shows one of a series of patterns designed by Renée Pemberton. 591

BRANKSOME CERAMICS

Established in Bournemouth in 1945, Branksome was initially inspired by the nearby Poole Pottery, and made similar wares under the direction of Ernest Baggaley. The pottery was at its peak in the 1950s when it was known for its finely made tablewares, oven-to-table ware, animal and bird studies and ornamental ware. When the Purbeck Pottery was set up in 1966, it absorbed part of Branksome. However the name continued to be used by Baggaley who moved production to Fordingbridge, Hampshire in 1966. Baggaley died in 1987 and his family now run the business.

➡ **Branksome China dinnerware, 1953**
Available in 10 colour harmonies, the dinnerware was advertised in *Pottery Gazette*, 1953. 592

➡ **Branksome animal studies, 1954**
Elephants, polar bears and dogs made in Branksome fine felspathic china, *Pottery Gazette*, 1954. 593

BRIGLIN POTTERY

Started in 1948 in Baker Street, London, by Brigitte Appleby and Eileen Lewenstein, Briglin quickly became known for its studio-style wares with painted tin glaze and oxide decoration. Initially Scandinavian in style, the wares were sold by shops such as Selfridges and Heal's. After a fire in 1952 the premises were rebuilt with a much expanded showroom, in which were displayed tablewares, ornaments and animal and bird models. In 1959 the partnership ended and Brigitte moved to larger premises in nearby Crawford Street. The 1960s and 1970s represented the pottery's greatest period, with 3,000 pieces being made every week and sent all over the world. The pottery was also a successful training ground for many potters, and managed to bridge the gulf between studio and industrial production. By 1977 it was the only pottery of substance operating in central London. A large and distinctive range of standard lines and special pieces continued to be made until 1990, when Briglin finally closed.

▶ Piggy banks, 1950s
An example of the wide range of ornamental novelties produced by Briglin Pottery. 594

▶ Coffee set, 1960s
This scroll-design coffee set was Briglin's longest selling tableware design. 595

BURGESS DORLING & LEIGH

In the late 1990s Burgess & Leigh went into receivership and the future of the Middleport Pottery, where they were based, seemed insecure. However, William and Rosemary Dorling, owners of the China Box Company, an independent Burgess & Leigh outlet, were able to buy the business. Renamed Burgess Dorling & Leigh, the company is now a major producer of transfer-printed tablewares and kitchen wares, using the old Middleport Pottery patterns, such as Calico and Asiatic Pheasant, along with others bought from the Blakeney Pottery when it closed in 2001. The company is committed to maintaining traditional production processes and preserving the listed Middleport Pottery buildings, probably the best example of a Victorian pottery factory still in commercial use.

◀ Victorian Chintz teaware, 2002
Traditional transfer-printed ranges using designs such as this dark blue damask roses and primroses pattern fill the current catalogue. 597

▲ Tableware, 2002
From original 19th-century printed patterns. 596

CANDY & CO.

Founded in the 1870s as the Great Western Potteries Brick, Tile and Clay Works, the business was incorporated as Candy & Co. in 1882 by Frank Candy and Jeffrey Ludham. Rapid expansion and financial difficulties followed and in 1887 the company was taken over by the Fox family, who owned it until 1991. Using clay from their own extensive pits, production centred on architectural ceramics, fireplaces, sanitary wares, bricks and tiles. Art wares were introduced in 1922, under the name Westcontree Ware. In 1936 a new art range was launched under the title Candy Ware and remained in production until the early 1950s. The business went into receivership in 1991, was rescued, and was sold in 1997 to a Swiss Company, only to collapse a year later.

♦ Westcontree Ware vase, c.1925
This posy vase, in Prussian-blue matt glaze, shows the influence of the prevailing Art Deco style. 598

♦ Ornamental domestic items, c.1938
These items decorated with brown and beige streaked glazes are from Candy Ware's art range. 599

KEY FACTS
Location: Heathfield, Newton Abbot, Devon, UK.
Important dates: Founded 1887, closed 1991.
Reopened by Laufen UK Ltd and then again by BCT Ltd.
Art pottery made between 1922 and the early 1950s.
Production: Bricks, tiles, architectural ceramics, fireplaces, sanitary ware, artwares.

Trade names: Westcontree Ware, Candy Ware, Devon Fire.

MARKS
Range of printed marks incorporating trade names.

CANNING POTTERY

Famous for its teapots in jet, Samian and Rockingham glazes, the Canning Pottery was founded in Fenton, Stoke-on-Trent, in 1907. It also made flower vases, bulb pots, candlesticks, cruets and toast racks. At its most inventive in the Art Deco period, the pottery produced art and handcraft wares and fancies, using the Decoro trade mark. It closed in 1935.

MARKS
Incorporating the name Decoro from 1923–35.

♦ Redbody vase, c.1930
Decorated with exotic birds and flowers, this is from a series of artistic wares in Art Deco style. 600

CHELSEA POTTERY

In 1952 David and Mary Rawnsley set up the Chelsea Pottery in Radnor Walk, London, taking the name from its Chelsea location, not from the famous 18th-century porcelain factory.

All the pottery was hand made and characteristically pieces were decorated with incised patterns of naturalistic subjects which were then hand coloured. The pottery employed students and specialist artists such as Joyce Morgan, and in its wide range of wares managed to combine studio attitudes with semi-industrial production. In 1973 the pottery was making figures and animal models, flower and fruit bowls, lamp bases, tiles and domestic wares. The pottery later moved to Ebury Mews, Belgravia and was closed at the end of the 1990s.

MARKS
Incised, used with or without circular seal.

◆ Ornamental ware, 1990s
A range of decorative pieces made in the company's typical sgraffito floral style. 601

CLOKIE & CO.

The pottery was established in 1888 in Castleford, Yorkshire, as Clokie & Masterson, makers of tablewares, toilet wares, jugs, mugs, nursery wares, kitchen and hospital wares. Later, they claimed to be the largest makers of pudding bowls, offering at least ten sizes of bowls in their advertisements. By the 1950s they were making colourful litho-printed tablewares but were best known for their Ideal kitchenwares and Cornish-ware style blue-hooped range. The pottery closed in 1961.

MARKS
Printed marks with name of company or initials C. & Co. occur from 1888–1961.

▶ **Advertisement, 1954**
Clokie & Co. were one of a number of companies to produce blue-hooped kitchenware to meet an increasing demand in the 1950s, as shown in this *Pottery Gazette* advertisement. 602

COBRIDGE STONEWARE

In 1997, Hugh Edwards, the owner of Moorcroft, set up the Cobridge Pottery in a new custom-built factory with the aim of developing new ways of painting onto stoneware. At that time, the pottery was taking direct historical inspiration from the Martin Brothers and from the Ruskin Pottery, notably the high-fired and reduction-fired flambé glazes associated with William Howson Taylor in the early decades of the 20th century. Today, Cobridge production is a blend of pieces with historical inspiration, such as the high-fired flambés and the Martin Brothers-inspired grotesque creatures of Andrew Hull, and painted and decorated stonewares. A series of freehand-painted designs featuring local landscapes, industrial and architectural scenes, and naturalistic imagery, has been characteristic and achieved a popular following among collectors in many parts of the world. Production at Cobridge has concentrated on decorative wares and lamp bases.

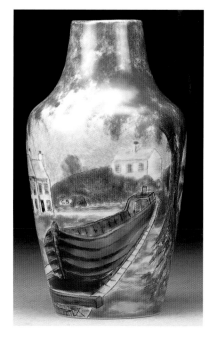

◆ **Philip Gibson vase, 1998**
This freehand painted design, depicting a view of Cauldon Lock, Stoke-on-Trent, is an early example of Philip Gibson's interest in Staffordshire's industrial heritage, and is a limited edition of 100. 604

◆ **Philip Gibson plate, 2000**
Painted with a view of Sneyd Colliery, Stoke-on-Trent, this is one of a series of designs by Philip Gibson depicting industrial Staffordshire. 603

KEY FACTS
Location: Cobridge, Burslem, Staffordshire, UK.
Important dates: Founded 1997. Still active.
Production: Painted and reduction-fired stonewares, modelled stonewares.

MARKS
Impressed and signed marks, date codes.

247

COLLINGWOOD BROTHERS

Established in 1887 as Collingwood and Greatbatch, the pottery operated originally from the Crown Works, Longton, Stoke-on-Trent. In 1919, as Collingwood Brothers, they moved to St. George's Works, Longton, and established a good reputation as makers of bone china tablewares, nursery wares, commemorative wares, hotel and restaurant wares and trinket sets, aimed primarily at the the middle-class market. Among the nursery wares were series decorated with Kate Greenaway designs and a Happy and Japhet range based on James Horrabin's newspaper cartoon characters. The best known commemorative was the Beatty jug, made to celebrate the surrender of the German High Seas fleet in 1918. Subsequently part of the Keele Street Group, the pottery changed its name in 1958 to Clayton Bone China. It closed in 1962.

KEY FACTS

Location: Longton, Staffordshire, UK.
Important dates: Founded 1887, closed 1962 after various restructurings.
Production: Bone china domestic wares, nursery wares and commemoratives.
Trade name: Collingwood China.

MARKS
Printed marks with company name or initials from c.1900.

➤ **Nursery china, c.1920**
Plate and mug with North Western Railways design, and 'Mamma's darling' plate. |605|

COMPTON POTTERY

In 1902 Mary Seton Watts, the wife of the artist G. F. Watts, set up a small studio pottery at her home in Compton, near Guildford, Surrey. Early productions include garden wares, figures, jardinières and stands made in terracotta and earthenware. Initially wares were moulded but from 1920 large-scale thrown wares were made, including chimney pots. The figures, unglazed, were painted in tempera colours. In 1938 the Potters' Art Guild took over the pottery and continued to operate it until 1956.

MARKS
Printed or impressed mark.   **COMPTON POTTERY**

◗ **Saint Michael panel, c.1908**
A typical example of a Compton panel, with Medieval and Art Nouveau details. |606|

CO-OPERATIVE WHOLESALE SOCIETY

The Co-operative Wholesale Society began to make tablewares for the shops of the Co-operative movement in 1922 at the Windsor Pottery, Longton, Staffordshire. In 1940, the company took over the lease of the Crown Clarence Works, also in Longton. Under the Co-op name, the pottery produced a wide range of middle-market tablewares, using more adventurous designs during the 1950s.

DARTINGTON POTTERY

Dartington has been a creative centre since the 1920s, with the origins of the pottery dating from the 1930s when Bernard Leach and his son David started working at Skinner's Bridge. The next phase, from 1947, featured Sam Haile and his wife Marianne de Trey, and led to the establishment of a pottery producing a range of decorative studio-type wares and a lively apprenticeship scheme which was the basis of subsequent training schemes and workshops.

In the early 1980s the pottery was taken over by Stephen Course and Sue Cook, marking the start of a design renaissance. Janice Tchalenko began her long association with the pottery in 1983, and other designers and artists were also drawn there, including Roger Law, Petra Tilly and Alexandra Copeland. Famous today for its use of complex glazes, Dartington produces a variety of standard designs, limited editions and one-off pieces that marry the philosophy of studio pottery with the demands of quantity production.

◆ **Petra Tilly platter, 2004**
Tilly approaches each piece as a 3-D painting. Surface and glaze textures are as important as colour. This dog appears both in her dreams and her work. [607]

DENNIS CHINAWORKS

In 1993 Sally Tuffin and her husband Richard Dennis set up a pottery in the former stables of their Somerset home. Well known as a fashion designer, Sally Tuffin was design director of Moorcroft from 1986 to 1993, and also designed for the Poole Pottery. Dennis Chinaworks, which now has over 12 employees, produces ranges of colourful, hand thrown and hand-decorated wares, using sgraffito, incising and slip-trailing techniques. The designs draw their inspiration from the Arts and Crafts movement, from exotic cultures and from the world of nature, and each design is carefully planned to suit the varied shapes of vases, bowls and dishes. There are now collectors of Dennis Chinaworks products in many parts of the world, and the pottery has its own collectors' club.

▲ **Mr T vase, late 1990s**
Tiger vase from a series of animal designs developed at the pottery in the late 1990s, shown in the 'Animals Under Glaze' exhibition at the Richard Dennis Gallery, London, 1998. [608]

◆ **Flute shaped vase, 1993**
Inspired by the capitals at Luxor, this is a striking geometric design from the pottery's Egyptian range, which also included a Papyrus design. [609]

DOLL POTTERY

Established in about 1915, the pottery was set up to fill the gap caused by the disappearance of the German import market during World War I. It was geared towards the novelty trade, specifically doll's parts, rather than to large-scale tableware production. In the early 1920s, it expanded its range to include novelties, comic figurines and jam pots based on fruit forms, Germany and France having become the centre of ceramic doll production.

DUNN, BENNETT & CO.

The company was formed in 1875, following the marriage of Mary Dunn, a daughter of William Dunn, an established potter, and Thomas Wood-Bennett. In 1887 the pottery moved into the Royal Victoria Works, Burslem, Staffordshire. From the start Thomas Wood-Bennett concentrated on hotel wares, and developed new, harder bodies to strengthen the wares and make them more chip-resistant. He also developed sunken knobs, stacking cups and no-drip tea- and coffee pots. As a result, the pottery concentrated on wares for hotels and restaurants, hospitals and schools, industrial canteens, shipping lines and railway companies, a pattern of production that has always been maintained. In 1939 the pottery moved to a new factory built on the site of the Dalehall Works, formerly operated by Keeling & Co. In 1966 Dunn, Bennett & Co. was absorbed into the Royal Doulton Group, subsequently becoming part of the independent Steelite Group.

KEY FACTS
Location: Burslem, Staffordshire, UK.
Important dates: Founded 1875, moved to Dalehall Works in 1939, taken over by Royal Doulton 1966, now part of Steelite Group.
Production: Hotel and institutional tablewares in earthenware and ironstone

MARKS
This mark in use in 1970s. Most printed marks have name in full.

◀ **Soup bowl, c.1972**
This classic style has become the trademark of their range of domestic and commercial tablewares. 610

THOMAS GOODE

A famous name from the 19th century, Thomas Goode was known as one of the world's leading and most adventurous china retailers. From the 1850s there were close links with the Minton factory and family, and in many ways Goode's were Minton's London showroom. Minton's entire stand of wares made for the Paris exhibition of 1889 was bought by Thomas Goode, including the famous elephants on stands, still on show today in the Thomas Goode shop on South Audley Street, London. Throughout the 19th and 20th centuries the Goode name appeared on wares specially commissioned from a wide range of British manufacturers, including tablewares, limited editions and commemoratives. In recent years, the business has changed hands a few times, and in 1994 Goode bought Caverswall China, their first direct involvement in manufacturing. Today, the name Thomas Goode is still associated with high quality ceramics and glass in both traditional and avant-garde styles.

KEY FACTS
Location: London, UK.
Important dates: Founded 1827, moved to South Audley Street site in 1844. Controlled by W. J. Goode from 1867, present premises completed 1876. Remained in family until latter part of 20th century, subsequently several changes in ownership. Still active.

MARKS
First appeared in 1860s, often incorporating company names.

◀ **Harlequin plate, 1990s**
Available in six colours. Prestige pieces can still be personalised. 611

HARTLEY'S (CASTLEFORD)

The pottery was set up in about 1898 at the Phillips Pottery, Castleford, Yorkshire, making utilitarian stonewares and earthenwares. In 1946 they were recorded as makers of acid containers, animal troughs, drinking fountains, bottles, bread crocks, bulb bowls, casseroles, chemical wares, hot water bottles, jugs, kitchen wares, mixing bowls, ointment jars, oven ware, pie dishes, poultry fountains, screw stoppers and teapots. The Hartrox trade name was used from 1953. In the same year an individually decorated artware range was introduced. The pottery closed in 1960.

MARKS
Trade name 'Hartrox' on art wares from 1953.

HARTROX

◆ **Advertisement, 1954**
These artwares were a new venture for the company, *Pottery Gazette*, 1954. [612]

Introducing . . . SOMETHING UNIQUE! ✶

HARTROX
Individual Pottery

Under the Direction of LEONARD P. LUKE

Six Classical vases, selected to display flowers in single sprays, bunches or sheaves in three beautiful shades of Eau-de-nil, Turquoise and Shell Sand.

These pieces are thrown on the wheel and hand-painted so that no two designs are alike. This is

Commercial Pottery with the Studio Touch

The designs are gay and colourful under a clear glaze and the line is so reasonably priced that the tax becomes merely incidental.

For prices etc. contact your wholesaler or write direct to

HARTLEY'S (CASTLEFORD) LTD
ESTD. 1845 · CASTLEFORD · YORKS · TEL. 2851

The Flowers help the Furnishings and PLEASANT POTTERY helps the Flowers

510

POTTERY GAZETTE AND GLASS TRADE REVIEW, APRIL, 1954

HIGHLAND STONEWARE

Founded in 1974 in Lochinver, Scotland, by David Grant and Graham Clarke, the pottery had two aims. Firstly, to make tablewares with the quality of studio pottery using industrial processes, and secondly, to bring employment to the Highlands. Despite the remoteness of the location, the pottery was soon underway, producing tablewares and cookwares made distinctive by hand decoration on the stoneware body. Since then the range has increased, and a number of artists have contributed designs, drawing inspiration from the landscape, and the flora and fauna of northern Scotland. The production process makes each piece an individual statement by the decorator which has attracted collectors all over the world.

➤ **Ginger jar, c.1998**
Painted landscape showing a view of Suilven. [613]

➤ **Tablewares, 1990s**
Seascape, c.1999, Wildberry, 1994, Landscape c.1999. [614]

KEY FACTS
Location: Lochinver, Scottish Highlands.
Important dates: Founded 1974. Still active.
Production: Hand-decorated stoneware tablewares.

Principal designers: Graham Clarke, David Grant, David Queensberry.

MARKS
Oval form, printed or stamped mark

HIGHLAND free hand STONEWARE painted SCOTLAND

HOLKHAM POTTERY

The pottery was set up in 1951 on the Holkham Hall estate in Norfolk by the Countess of Leicester and Keith Corrigan to make a range of tableware and children's ware using traditional applied slip decoration. In 1953 Wilton Elston joined as principal designer. Since then, the range has increased to include lamp bases, florist wares and gift wares, including a Shakespearian series. Throughout its life Holkham has bridged the gap between the individual studio potter and the industrial manufacturer. Recently the pottery has produced a range of mugs that celebrate Norfolk heroes and Norfolk life, designed by Matthew Rice of the Bridgewater Pottery.

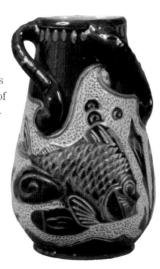

♦ **Cocking mug, c.2003**
From the Norfolk Seaside Pursuits range. 615

KEY FACTS
Location: Holkham, Norfolk, UK.
Important dates: Founded 1951. Still active.
Production: Studio-type domestic wares, also table-wares and decorative wares.
Principal designers: Keith Corrigan, Wilton Elston, Matthew Rice.

MARKS
Printed or impressed mark introduced 1961.

ALEXANDER LAUDER

In 1876 Alexander Lauder, in partnership with a Mr Smith, started a pottery near Barnstaple, Devon, making bricks, tiles, architectural wares and drain pipes. In about 1880, when the partnership was dissolved, Lauder began the production of art pottery, using local clays and decoration based on coloured slips and glazes, carving and sgraffito work. The wares, marketed under the name of Devon Art Pottery, were quite similar to those of his main rival, the nearby Brannam Pottery. The pottery closed in 1914.

MARKS
'Lauder Barum' in script, either incised or painted, was used between 1876 and 1914.

♦ **Ornamental fish vase, c.1905**
A typical example of Lauder carved slipware technique executed in the Brannam style. 616

LAWLEYS

In 1908 a retail china business was started in Birmingham by Tom and Edgar Lawley. The company was soon involved in the wholesale distribution of china and glass, and developed an export and import business. It was renamed Lawleys Ltd in 1929, by which time the Lawley name was already appearing on tablewares made for the company. In the 1940s Lawleys entered the manufacturing business by acquiring a number of Staffordshire potteries. Some of these, notably Ridgways, continued to trade under their own name. In 1952 Lawleys was taken over by the Pearson Group, an industrial conglomerate. In 1964 the various Lawley pottery interests were brought together by Pearsons under the Allied English Potteries banner, later becoming part of the Royal Doulton Tableware Group. However, the Lawley name still survives as a china and glass retailer.

LEACH POTTERY

When Bernard Leach returned to Britain in 1920, following a long stay in Japan, he set up a pottery at St Ives, Cornwall, in conjunction with the Japanese potter, Shoji Hamada. Strongly influenced by Oriental ceramics, Leach aimed to combine an Oriental approach to design and manufacture while maintaining certain local British traditions of the pre-industrial era, notably slip decoration. Soon successful, the pottery expanded and established the tradition of employing students and assistants who later became famous in their own right, such as Michael Cardew and Leach's son, David. The other aim was to produce hand made pottery that could be used as a viable alternative to mass-produced industrial ceramics. In 1939 Leach published *A Potter's Book*, a statement about the importance of the Oriental traditions and the handcraft ethic. This personal credo was to influence generations of ceramic students. In about 1946, while Leach continued to make his individual pieces, he launched a standard ware range aimed at the domestic and tourist market. This included ash trays, bulb bowls, casseroles, coffee pots, cruet sets, egg cups, jam jars, jugs, kitchenwares, mugs, mixing bowls, oven-ware, pudding bowls, teapots and vases. This set a pattern of production that is maintained today, with a clear division between individual studio pieces and production-line ranges designed by major potters and manufactured in quantity.

KEY FACTS
Location: St Ives, Cornwall, UK.
Important dates: Pottery founded 1921. Still active. Bernard Leach died in 1979.
Production: Slipwares, earthenwares, stonewares, porcelain.
Principal designers: Bernard Leach, Shoji Hamada, Michael Cardew, Norah Braden, David Leach, Janet Leach, Bill Marshall, Katherine Pleydell-Bouverie.

MARKS
Impressed seal mark from c.1921. A circular version also occurs. Some pieces have Leach's personal marks or initials.

↞ **Set of ramekins, 1940s**
Contemporary style emerging in the Leach standard ware range. 618

↞ **Leach charger, 1930s**
Slip decorated with freely painted shadow puppet. 617

LONGPARK POTTERY CO.

The pottery was set up in Torquay in 1883 to make primarily architectural terracotta. In about 1903 the business was taken over by potters who had formerly worked at Aller Vale, and from that point the pottery began to make decorative wares in the Aller Vale style, using painted slip and incised techniques. In 1905 it was launched as a limited company, as the Longpark Pottery Co. A number of decorative ranges were issued under the Tormohun trade mark, while other popular ranges were Sunset Scene and Alexandra Rose. Among the best known artists were Charles Collard, later the founder of the Honiton Pottery, and William Howard, famous for his painted kingfishers. The pottery had difficulties during the 1930s, and closed in 1957.

MARKS
Wide range of printed and stamped marks incorporating the Longpark name in full.

◀ **Motto ware jug, c.1920**
Many Devon potteries were producing incised and slip-decorated ware for the novelty and souvenir market. 619

MORLEY, FOX & CO.

Set up in the Salopian Works, Fenton, Staffordshire in about 1903, the company made tablewares, toilet wares, utility and kitchenwares and novelty items, a pattern of production that continued through the 1920s and 1930s. Imari and other Orientally-inspired patterns were always popular and in 1936 Coronation Ware for children was launched. In 1944 the pottery was renamed William Morley & Co. and in the 1950s the range was widened to include cottage wares, table lamps, cigarette boxes and other novelties and fancies. The pottery closed in 1957.

KEY FACTS
Location: Fenton, Staffordshire, UK.
Important Dates: Founded c.1903, closed 1957.
Production: Table-, kitchen-, novelty- and commemorative wares.

MARKS
Incorporating initials or name of range.

◆ Coronation nursery ware, 1936
Pieces were available individually. 620

RICHARD PARKINSON

The Parkinson Pottery was set up in 1952 by Richard and Sue Parkinson and quickly became known for its slip-cast figures, animals and domestic wares that reflected the look of the 1950s. Decoration, in a notably graphic style, was usually in black on a white body, and the models often echoed the sculpture of the period. The pottery was located at Bradbourne Lees, near Ashford in Kent. After the pottery's closure in 1963, some of the moulds were acquired by George Gray for use at the Cinque Ports Pottery.

MARKS
Trademark and/or company name.

1952-

◆ Theatrical figures, 1959
Paul Robeson as Othello and Laurence Olivier as Henry V, slipcast in hard porcelain by R. Parkinson. 621

PARROTT & CO.

A small family pottery established in Burslem, Stoke-on-Trent, Staffordshire, in about 1921, this company produced domestic and tablewares in popular Art Deco and traditional styles. During World War II the pottery was closed by the concentration scheme, but it reopened in about 1946, when many popular lines were advertised, including breakfast, tea, fruit and sandwich sets, cruets, egg cups, teapots, toilet seats, cigarette boxes, ashtrays, fancies and novelties. The pottery closed in about 1962.

MARKS
Trademark first registered 1921, reworked c.1935. 'Coronet Ware' may also occur with mark.

◆ Earthenware, c.1935
Jug and lidded jam pot with a cat finial. Low-relief moulded body with hand-painted decoration. 622

PORT DUNDAS POTTERY CO.

Initially established in 1815 at Port Dundas, north of Glasgow, by W. Johnson and John Forsyth, the pottery made stoneware bottles, chemical wares and domestic wares. The pottery enjoyed a chequered history during the rest of the 19th century, changing owners several times, but retaining the Port Dundas name. By the 1880s it was well known for domestic and industrial stonewares, water filters and brown-glazed teapots and jugs. Filters were made specially for ship-board use and for exporting to colonial markets. At the same time, decoration in raised slip and painting in impasto style became commonplace, and this was continued into the 20th century, particularly for domestic wares. The pottery closed in 1930.

KEY FACTS
Location: near Glasgow, Scotland.
Important dates: Founded 1815. Closed 1930.
Production: Domestic and utilitarian stonewares, water filters, impasto-decorated wares.

MARKS
Impressed or painted marks.

◀ **Domestic bottles, 1900–10**
Containers bearing the supplier's name were the mainstay of the stoneware industry. 623

RADFORD AND H. J. WOOD

The principles and styles of the Radford Handcraft Pottery were maintained until the late 1930s. By this time there had been considerable rationalisation and simplification of designs by Mabel Hadgkiss and others, and by about 1940 hand throwing had been given up. After the period of consolidation during the war, when Radford was absorbed into H. J. Wood, some Radford designs reappeared, marketed under the Radford name by H. J. Wood. Some new designs were added by Eddie Sambrook, Wood's chief designer from 1947, and by subsequent Wood designers until the early 1950s. By this time, the only real links with the original Radford Handcraft Pottery were some of the shapes (now cast but not thrown) and the general style of the patterns which were still hand painted under glaze.

MARKS
Facsimile signature of G. Radford and Burslem occur on wares 1933–48.

◀ **Printed catalogue issued by H. J. Wood, 1948**
The initials below these typical Radford pieces relate to patterns: 'J. N.', for example, is Anenome, 'W. G.' is Spring Collection. 624

SANDYGATE POTTERY

Established in about 1950 at Kingsteignton, Sandygate was a typical Devon pottery making wares aimed primarily at the visitor and souvenir market. Raised slip patterns and polka dots were popular, along with children's wares decorated with teddy bears.

♦ **Earthenware, 1971**
This child's named dish with alphabet border is from a range of commemorative wares. 625

SUTHERLAND CHINA

Sutherland is the best known trade mark of Hudson & Middleton, a company originally established in the Alma Works, Longton, Staffordshire, in 1889. In about 1892 the company moved into the Sutherland pottery nearby and, from that date, the Sutherland trademark was widely aplied to bone china tablewares, badged wares, fancies and ornaments. It was in use throughout the 20th century.

☛ **China teaware, c.1920**
Wares for hotels, ships and other institutions were the main-stay of many Staffordshire china companies at this time. 626

MICHAEL SUTTY

In 1961 Michael Sutty began to manufacture porcelain figures whose complexity was far greater than anything that could then be made by the main names of British ceramics. From this came a small studio devoted to the production of figures whose fame spread throughout the world. The emphasis was on military figures, usually made in limited editions. Later, he made figures inspired by the paintings of Russell Flint and Impressionist busts. In the 1980s and 1990s he faced business and financial difficulties, and ownership of the pottery changed several times. In 1993 it became part of Caverswall China. In 2001 Sutty celebrated 40 years of figure production, and in the process established himself as one of Britain's greatest ever porcelain figure modellers. After his death in 2003 the business closed.

♦ **Medieval figure, 1980s**
A typically finely-modelled historical figure in porcelain, in this case, of Matilda, Marquess of Salisbury. 627

CHARLES VYSE

Charles Vyse was an independent modeller and sculptor whose training started at Doulton in 1896. From 1905 to 1910 he studied at the Royal College of Art, London, and won a travelling scholarship in 1909 which took him to Italy. Later, he designed figures for Doulton and then in 1919 set up a studio and pottery in Chelsea, London, in partnership with his wife, Nell. Their first series figures, Balloon Woman and Lavender Girl, were a great success and many similar character figures followed through the 1920s and 1930s, in a range that eventually totalled 50. He also made experimental and one-off vases, dishes and decorative wares decorated with Chinese and Japanese glazes. The Vyses exhibited regularly, the last time in 1963 before their retirement to Kent.

◀ **Mei-ping shaped vase, c.1930**
Many of his vases were influenced in style and decoration by the work of early Chinese potters. [628]

◆ **Barnet Fair figures, 1933**
Also known as 'Jacky and Mother', this is one of a series of popular figure groups. 40–70 moulds were required for his more elaborate groups. [629]

KEY FACTS
Location: Chelsea, London, UK.
Important dates: Founded 1919. Closed 1963.
Production: Individually modelled figures and animals, decorative wares.

MARKS
Impressed or incised name or monogram.

WETHERIGGS COUNTRY POTTERY

Established in Clifton Dykes, Penrith, Cumbria, in about 1855 as a manufacturer of bricks, tiles and drain pipes, Wetheriggs was run for many years by John Schofield, who came from a Yorkshire pottery family. During the 19th and early 20th centuries, the pottery became well known for its wide range of country-style earthenwares, often with slipware decoration. In 1916 it was taken over by Harold Thorburn, who remained in control until the 1970s. By then the largely unaltered pottery, with its beehive kiln and steam engine, had been listed as an Ancient Monument. Despite a brief break in the mid 1990s, production has been continuous since the 1850s in what is now acknowledged to be one of the few remaining genuine country potteries in Britain.

◆ **Whinfell dinner service, 2004**
Traditional slipware such as this has been at Wetheriggs for 150 years and continues to be an identifying feature of their production. [630]

KEY FACTS
Location: Penrith, Cumbria, UK.
Important dates: Founded c.1855, studio-type pottery from 1916. Still active.
Production: Domestic and utilitarian wares, slipware and other types of traditional country pottery.
Principal designers: Harold Thorburn, Mary Chappelhow.

MARKS
Incised mark incorporating the name of the pottery.

GLOSSARY

acid etching technique involving treatment of glass with hydro-fluoric acid, giving a matt or frosted finish.

agate ware type of pottery resembling agate as a result of the partial blending of different-coloured clays.

applied decoration surface ornament made separately and applied to the body of an object.

Art Deco style characterized by geometric forms and bright, bold colours, popular from c.1918 to 1940. The name is taken from the 1925 Exposition des Arts Décoratifs et Industriels Modernes in Paris.

Art Nouveau movement and style of decoration characterized by sinuous curves and flowing lines, asymmetry, and flower and leaf motifs, prevalent from the 1890s to c.1910.

Arts and Crafts Movement 19th-century artistic movement, led by William Morris, which advocated a return to quality craftsmanship and simplicity of design in the face of mass production.

backstamp mark applied to the base of commercially made ceramic ware giving details of manufacturer.

basalt unglazed, very hard, fine-grained stoneware stained with cobalt and manganese oxides, developed by Wedgwood c.1768.

basketwork decorative relief pattern resembling woven willow or cane; applied to the borders of plates and dishes.

biscuit (bisque) unglazed porcelain or earthenware fired once only. Popular for neoclassical porcelain figures because it suggests classical marble sculptures. Also used for making dolls' heads.

blank undecorated ceramic ware.

blue-and-white white ceramics with painted or printed cobalt-blue decoration.

body the material from which a piece of pottery or porcelain is produced.

bone china a soft-paste porcelain consisting of petuntse (china stone), kaolin (china clay) and dried bone.

brownware salt-glazed brown stoneware, especially that made in Nottingham, Derby and elsewhere in England.

cachepot ornamental container for flower pots. A smaller form of jardinière.

caneware pale, straw-coloured, unglazed stoneware made by Wedgwood from 1770.

caster vessel for sprinkling salt, pepper or sugar.

celadon semi-opaque, green-tinted glaze used first on ware made during the Chinese Sung Dynasty (960–1280).

china originally an alternative term for Chinese porcelain. Since the early 19th century the term has been used to refer to bone china.

china clay see kaolin.

chinoiserie decoration consisting of Oriental-style figures and motifs, such as pagodas, pavilions, birds and lotus flowers, that permeated Europe from the Far East; prevalent from the late 17th century.

chintzware ware decorated with an all-over, usually dense, floral pattern.

cloisonné enamel fired into compartments (*cloisons*) formed by metal wires.

crackle glaze (craquelure) deliberate cracked effect achieved by firing ceramics to a precise temperature.

crazing tiny, undesirable surface cracks caused by shrinking or other technical defects in a glaze.

creamware cream-coloured earthenware with a transparent lead glaze, developed by Wedgwood c.1760.

decal multicoloured image, printed from a copper plate on to tissue paper and used to decorate ceramics. The decal is soaked with water and slipped from the backing sheet on to the surface of the unglazed ware, which is then glazed and fired. *See also* transfer printing.

Delftware tin-glazed earthenware from Delft, in the Netherlands. Refers to British ware when it does not have a capital letter.

earthenware type of pottery which is porous and requires a glaze.

eggshell porcelain type of slip-cast, razor-thin porcelain made in 19th-century Japan and Europe.

enamel form of decoration involving the application of metallic oxides to metal, ceramics, or glass in paste form or in an oil-based mixture, which is then usually fired for decorative effect.

faience French term for tin-glazed earthenware.

famille rose palette used on 18th-century Chinese porcelain, which includes a dominant opaque pink. Much copied in Europe.

famille verte palette used from the 17th century on Chinese porcelain, distinguished by a dominant bright apple green.

firing process of baking ceramics in a kiln. Temperatures range from 800–1100°C (1500–2000°F) for earthenware to 1400°C (2550°F) for the second firing of hard-paste porcelain.

flambé glaze made from copper, usually deep crimson, flecked with blue or purple, and often faintly crackled.

flatware term embracing all flat objects, such as plates and salvers, but more specifically applied to cutlery.

gadrooning decorative edging consisting of a series of convex, vertical or spiralling curves.

gilding method of applying a gold finish to a silver or electroplated item, ceramics, or glass.

glaze glassy coating that gives a smooth, shiny surface to ceramics and seals porous ceramic bodies.

hard-paste porcelain also known as true porcelain. It was first made in China using the combination of kaolin (china clay: 50%), petuntse (china stone: 25%) and quartz (25%).

hollowware any hollow items such as bowls, teapots, jugs; distinct from flatware.

Imari Japanese porcelain with dense decoration, based on brocade patterns, in a palette that is dominated by underglaze blue, iron red, green, manganese, yellow and gold.

incised decoration decoration that is cut into the body of an object with a sharp metal point.

intaglio carving type of carving whereby forms are sunken into, as opposed to moulded on to, a surface.

jardinière plant container made from a variety of materials, including glass, silver or pottery.

jasper ware hard, fine-grained, coloured stoneware developed by Wedgwood in the 1770s.

kaolin (china clay) fine, white-granite clay used to make hard-paste porcelain.

lead glaze clear glaze generally composed of silicaceous sand, salt, soda and potash mixed with a lead component.

lustre ware pottery with an iridescent surface produced using metallic pigments, usually silver or copper.

majolica corruption of the term maiolica, which refers to a type of 19th-century earthenware in elaborate forms with thick, brightly coloured glazes.

Ming porcelain ware produced during the Ming Dynasty, which ruled China from 1368 to 1644.

on-glaze any porcelain decoration painted in enamels or transfer-printed on top of a fired glaze.

parian semi-matt porcelain made with feldspar and therefore not requiring a separate glaze. Also called statuary porcelain, it became known as parian because of its similarity to the white marble from the Greek island of Paros.

pâte-sur-pâte type of ceramic decoration involving low-relief designs carved in layers of slip and resembling cameos.

piercing intricate cut decoration, originally done with a sharp chisel, later with a fretsaw, and finally with mechanical punches.

porcelain *see* soft-paste porcelain and hard-paste porcelain.

Queensware alternative name given by Wedgwood to its creamware made in honour of Queen Charlotte, who commissioned a creamware tea service from the company in 1765.

redware stoneware, generally unglazed and often decorated with applied motifs in relief.

relief decoration decoration that stands out from the surface of any object and is usually described, according to its depth, as low-relief or high-relief.

reticulation intricate pierced decoration on thin-walled porcelain.

salt glaze thin, glassy glaze applied to some stoneware and produced by throwing salt into the kiln at the height of firing. The glaze may show a pitted surface, known as 'orange peel'.

sang-de-boeuf brilliant red ceramic glaze developed in China in the early 18th century.

sgraffito form of ceramic decoration incised through a coloured slip, revealing the ground beneath.

slip smooth dilution of clay and water used in the making and decoration of pottery.

slip casting manufacture of thin-bodied ceramic ware and figures by pouring slip into a mould.

slip trailing application of slip to a ceramic form to decorate the surface.

slipware type of red-bodied earthenware decorated largely with slip in contrasting colours.

soft-paste porcelain (artificial porcelain) porcelain formula made from a range of ingredients, which may include soapstone or bone ash, but without the kaolin used in hard-paste porcelain.

sponging application, with a sponge, of colour or a glaze to a ceramic piece after firing, to produce a mottled appearance.

stippling technique of creating intricate painted designs on ceramics by applying dots of colour with the point of a brush. Characteristic of the Capodimonte porcelain factory in Italy.

stoneware type of pottery fired at a higher temperature than earthenware, making it durable and non-porous. May be covered in a salt glaze.

studio pottery pottery that has been individually designed and crafted.

terracotta lightly fired red earthenware, usually unglazed.

throwing the technique of shaping ceramic vessels by hand on a rotating wheel.

tin glaze glassy glaze made opaque by the addition of tin oxide and commonly used on earthenware.

Toby jug 18th- or 19th-century jug representing a seated Englishman with a three-cornered hat and a mug of ale.

transfer *see* transfer printing.

transfer printing the process of transferring a single-colour image (a transfer), printed from an engraved copper plate on to tissue paper, on to the unglazed surface of a ceramic object.

tube-lining type of ceramic decoration in which thin trails of slip are applied as outlines to areas of coloured glaze.

underglaze colour or design painted before the application of the glaze on a ceramic object. Blue is the most common underglaze colour.

white ware white porcelain which has been glazed but not decorated, or white-glazed domestic earthenware.

WHERE TO BUY

Inexperienced collectors are advised to buy ceramics from the following sources: established auction houses; dealers who are members (in Britain) of the British Antique Dealers' Association or the Association of Art and Antique Dealers, or (in the USA) of the National Art & Antiques Dealers' Association or the Art and Antique Dealers League of America; and trade fairs organized by collectors' clubs.

BRITAIN

ASSOCIATIONS

British Antique Dealers' Association (BADA)
20 Rutland Gate, London SW7 1BD

Association of Art and Antique Dealers (LAPADA)
535 King's Road, London SW10 0SZ

MAJOR AUCTION HOUSES

Bonhams
101 New Bond Street, London W1S 1SR

Bonhams Chelsea
65–9 Lots Road, London SW10 0RN

Christie's
8 King Street, St James's, London SW1Y 6QT

Christie's South Kensington
85 Old Brompton Road, London SW7 3LD

Dreweatt Neate
Donnington Priory, Donnington, Berkshire RG14 2EJ

Sotheby's
34–5 New Bond Street, London W1A 2AA

Sotheby's Olympia
Hammersmith Road, London W14 8UX

MAJOR ANTIQUES SHOWS

Antique and Collectors' Fair
The Great Hall, Alexandra Palace, Wood Green, London N22 7AY

The Chelsea Antiques Fair
Chelsea Old Town Hall, King's Road, London SW3 5EE

West London Antiques Fair
Kensington Town Hall, Hornton Street, London W8 7NX

Fine Art & Antiques Fair
Olympia, Kensington, London W14 8UX

British International Antiques Fair
National Exhibition Centre, Birmingham B40 1NT

Buxton Antiques Fair
Buxton, Derbyshire SK17 6XN

The International Antique and Collectors' Fair
The Newark and Nottinghamshire Showground, Newark, Nottinghamshire NG24 2NY

Sunbury Antiques Market
Kempton Park Racecourse, Sunbury on Thames, Surrey TW16 5AQ

Antique and Collectors' Fair
The South of England Showground, Ardingly, West Sussex RH17 6TL

ANTIQUES MARKETS AND CENTRES

Alfies Antique Market
13–25 Church Street, London NW8 8DT

Antiquarius
133–41 King's Road, London SW3 4PW

Assembly Antique Centre
5–8 Saville Row, Bath, Avon BA1 2QP

Bath Antiques Market
Guinea Lane, Lansdown Road, Bath, Avon BA1 5NB

Bermondsey Market
Bermondsey Street, London SE1 3TQ

Camden Passage
Islington, London N1

Cloisters Antiques Fair
St Andrews Hall, Norwich, Norfolk NR3 0LH

Grays Antique Market
Davies Street, London W1

The Ginnel
Harrogate Antique Centre, The Ginnel (off Parliament Street), Harrogate, North Yorkshire HG1 2RB

Preston Antique Centre
The Mill, New Hall Lane, Preston, Lancashire PR1 5PE

NORTH AMERICA

ASSOCIATIONS

National Art & Antiques Dealers' Association of America (NAADAA)
220 East 57th Street, New York, NY 10022

Art and Antique Dealers League of America (AADLA)
1040 Madison Avenue, New York, NY 10021

MAJOR AUCTION HOUSES

Sanford Alderfer Auction Company
501 Fairgrounds Road, Hatfield, PA 19440

Bonhams and Butterfields
220 San Bruno Avenue, San Francisco, CA 94103

Christie's New York
20 Rockefeller Plaza, New York, NY 10020

Christie's Beverly Hills
360 North Camden Drive Beverly Hills, CA 90210

Doyle New York
175 East 87th Street, New York, NY 10128

Ken Farmer Auctions and Appraisals
105a Harrison Street, Radford, VA 24141

Freeman Fine Arts
1808 Chestnut Street, Philadelphia, PA 19103

Phillips-Selkirk
7447 Forsyth Boulevard, St Louis, MO 63105

David Rago Arts & Auction Center
333 North Main Street, Lambertville, NJ 08530

Skinner Inc.
63 Park Plaza, Boston, MA 02116

Sotheby's
1334 York Avenue, New York, NY 10021

Treadway/Toomey Galleries Cincinatti
2029 Madison Road, Cincinnati, OH 45208

Treadway/Toomey Galleries Oak Park
818 North Boulevard, Oak Park, IL 60301

Weschler & Son
909 E Street, NW, Washington, DC 20024

MAJOR ANTIQUES MARKETS AND SHOWS

Ann Arbor Flea Market
(April–November)
5055 Ann Arbor Saline Road, Ann Arbor, MI 48103-9722

Antiques Canada
(shows in Toronto)
Gadsden Promotions Ltd., Box 490, Shelburne, Ontario, Canada

**Atlanta Expo Center, Atlanta, GA
Columbus Expo Center, Columbus, OH
Florida State fairgrounds, Tampa, FL**
all managed by
Scott Antique Markets, P.O. Box 60, Bremen, OH 43107

Atlantique City
(at Atlantic City Convention Center)
F&W Publications, P.O. Box 547, Mays
Landing, NJ 08330

Brimfield's Heart of the Mart
(three big markets per year)
Tracey Healey, P.O. Box 26,
Brimfield, MA 01010

Hoosier Antiques Expositions
(four shows per year at Indiana State
Fairgrounds, Indianapolis)
Cox Shows, 1830 South Muessing Road,
Indianapolis, IN 46239

**Manhattan Antiques and Collectibles
Triple Pier Shows**
(several each year at Passenger Ship
Terminals on west side of Manhattan)

Stella Management Company,
151 West 25th Street, Suite 2, New York,
NY 10001

Metrolina Expo
P.O. Box 26668,
Charlotte, NC 28221

New York Ceramics Fair
(at National Academy of Design, 1083 Fifth
Avenue, NY)
Caskey-Lees, P.O. Box 1409, Topanga, CA
90290

**Renninger's Antiques and Collectibles
Markets**
(regular markets in Adamstown and
Kutztown, Pennsylvania; Mt Dora, Florida)
Renninger's Promotions, 27 Bensinger Drive,

Schuylkill Haven, PA 17922

Rose Bowl Fleamarket
(second Sunday of every month in the Rose
Bowl, Pasadena, California)
Canning Attractions, P.O. Box 400,
Maywood, CA 90270

Washington DC Antiques Fair
(in the DC Armory)
Sha-Dor Promotions & Pappabello, P.O. Box
12069, Silver Spring, MD 20908

ANTIQUES BUYERS' WEBSITE
www.ebay.com
Informs buyers of antiques received for
auction from many sources, and allows bids
to be made via the website.

WHERE TO VISIT

BRITAIN

Bramah Tea and Coffee Museum
The Clove Building, Maguire Street,
London SE1 2NQ

Bristol City Museum and Art Gallery
Queen's Road, Bristol BS8 1RL

British Museum
Great Russell Street, London
WC1B 3DG

Conwy Teapot Museum
25 Castle Street, Conwy LL32 8AY,
Wales

**Cheltenham Art Galleries
and Museums**
Clarence Street, Cheltenham, Gloucestershire
GL50 3JT

The Design Museum
Butler's Wharf, Shad Thames,
London SE1 2YD

**Royal Doulton Museum and
Visitors' Centre**
Nile Street, Burslem, Stoke-on-Trent,
Staffordshire ST6 2AJ

Geffrye Museum
Kingsland Road, London E2 8EA

Gladstone Pottery Museum
Uttoxeter Road, Longton, Stoke-on-Trent,
Staffordshire ST3 1PQ

Kirkcaldy Museum and Art Gallery
War Memorial Gardens, Kirkcaldy,
Fife KY1 1YG, Scotland

Leicester Museum and Art Gallery
New Walk, Leicester, LE1 6TD

Manchester City Art Galleries
Mosley Street, Manchester M2 3JL

Moorcroft Museum and Shop
Sandbach Road, Burslem, Stoke-on-Trent,
Staffordshire ST6 2DQ

National Museum and Gallery of Wales
Cathays Park, Cardiff CF1 3NP, Wales

People's Palace Museum
Glasgow Green, Glasgow G40 1AT, Scotland

The Potteries Museum & Art Gallery
(formerly City Museum & Art Gallery)
Bethesda Street, Hanley, Stoke-on-Trent,
Staffordshire ST1 3DW

**The Royal Pavilion and Brighton
Museum**
Pavilion Buildings, Brighton,
East Sussex BN1 1EE

Spode Museum and Visitors' Centre
Church Street, Stoke-on-Trent,
Staffordshire ST4 1BX

Victoria and Albert Museum
Cromwell Road,
South Kensington,
London SW7 2RL

Wedgwood Museum and Visitors' Centre
Barlaston,
Stoke-on-Trent,
Staffordshire ST12 9ES

NORTH AMERICA

Cincinnati Art Museum
(Rookwood Pottery)
Eden Park, Cincinnati
OH 45202

Dallas Museum of Art
1717 North Harwood, Dallas, TX 75201

Dedham Historical Society
612 High Street, Dedham, MA 02026

East Liverpool Museum of Ceramics
400 East Fifth Street,
East Liverpool, OH 43920

Everson Museum of Art
401 Harrison Street, Syracuse, NY 13202

Mint Museum of Art
2730 Randolph Road, Charlotte, NC 28207

National Road/Zane Grey Museum
(Ohio Art Pottery)
8850 East Pike, Norwich, OH 43767

New Jersey State Museum
205 West State Street, Trenton, NJ 08625

Ohio Ceramics Center
Crooksville, OH

COLLECTORS' CLUBS

BRITAIN

Antique Collectors' Club
5 Church Street, Woodbridge,
Suffolk IP12 1DS

Aynsley Collectors' Society
(collectors in Britain) Freepost (ST 1663),
Stoke-on-Trent, Staffordshire ST3 1BR

Aynsley Collectors' Society
(collectors outside Britain) Portland Works,
Longton, Stoke-on-Trent , Staffordshire
ST3 1HS

Carlton Ware Collectors International
PO Box 161, Sevenoaks, Kent TN15 6GA

Clarice Cliff Collectors' Club
Fantasque House, Tennis Drive, The Park,
Nottingham, Nottinghamshire NG7 1AE

Coalport Collector
PO Box 99, Sudbury, Suffolk CO10 6SN

Commemorative Collectors Society
Lumless House, Winthorpe, Newark,
Nottinghamshire N24 2NR

Susie Cooper Collectors' Group
PO Box 7436, London N12 7QF

Cornish Ware Collectors' Club
Tabletop Company, Lowmoor Road, Kirkby-
in-Ashfield, Nottinghamshire NG17 7RD

Goss Collectors' Club
31a The Crescent, Stanley Common,
Derbyshire DE7 6GL

Honiton Collectors' Society
112 Sylvan Avenue, London N22 5JB

Langley Collectors' Society
64 Hands Road, Heanor, Derbyshire DE75 7HB

Moorcroft Collectors' Club
Sandbach Road, Burslem, Stoke-on-Trent,
Staffordshire ST6 DQ

Moorland Pottery Collectors' Club
Moorland Road, Burslem, Stoke-on-Trent,
Staffordshire ST6 1DY

Pilkington's Lancastrian Pottery Society
Greenfields House, Hengoed, Oswestry,
Shropshire SY10 7EH

Poole Pottery Collectors' Club
Poole Pottery Ltd, The Quay, Poole,
Dorset BH15 1RF

Portmeirion Collectors Club
London Road, Stoke-on-Trent,
Staffordshire ST4 7QQ

E. Radford Collectors' Club
St Claver, Victoria Avenue, Kirby-le-Soken,
Essex CO13 0D

Royal Crown Derby Collectors' Guild
Royal Doulton, Minton House, London Road,
Stoke-on-Trent, Staffordshire ST4 7QD

**Royal Doulton International
Collectors' Club**
Sir Henry Doulton House, Forge Lane,
Etruria, Stoke on Trent, ST1 5NN

Royal Worcester Collectors' Society
Royal Worcester, Severn Street,
Worcester, Worcestershire WR1 2NE

Scottish Pottery Society
227 Wilton Street, Glasgow G20 6DE

The Shelley Group
228 Croyland Road, Lower Edmonton,
London N9 7BG

Spode Collector
Church Street, Stoke-on-Trent,
Staffordshire ST4 1BX

SylvaC Collectors' Circle
174 Portsmouth Road, Horndean,
Hampshire PO8 9HP

Studio Szeiler Collectors' Circle
The Finches, 2 Birchwood Gardens,
Mathern, Chepstow, Gwent NP6 6UF

Torquay Pottery Collectors' Society
Torre Abbey, The Kings Drive, Torquay,
Devon TQ2 5JX

**The Official International Wade
Collectors Club**
Wade Ceramics Ltd, Royal Victoria Pottery,
Westport Road, Burslem, Stoke-on-Trent,
Staffordshire ST6 4AG

Wedgwood International Society
Josiah Wedgwood & Sons Ltd, Barlaston,
Stoke-on-Trent, Staffordshire ST12 9ES

NORTH AMERICA

American Art Pottery Association
(club and magazine)P.O. Box 834, Westport,
MA 02790

Blue Ridge China
Frances Ruffin, 1050 Dogwood Hill,
Watkinsville, GA 30677

Boehm Porcelain (showroom and museum)
25 Princess Diana Lane, Trenton, NJ 08638

Cowan Pottery Museum Associates
P.O. Box 16765, Rocky River, OH 44116

Cybis (showroom and museum)
65 Norman Avenue, Trenton, NJ 08618

Dedham Pottery Collectors' Society
(quarterly newsletter)
Jim Kaufman, 248 Highland Street,
Dedham, MA 02026

Fiesta Club of America
P.O. Box 15383, Loves Park, IL 61132
Fiesta Collectors' Quarterly
P.O. Box 471, Valley City, OH 44280

Franciscan Collectors' Club, USA
(quarterly newsletter) 8412 Fifth Avenue NE,
Seattle, WA 98115

Frankoma Family Collectors' Association
94549 Frankoma Road, Sapulpa, OK 74066

Fulper *see* Stangl

Gladding-McBean *see* Franciscan
Collectors' Club

**The Glaze, Pottery
Collectors' Newsletter**
P.O. Box 4782, Birmingham, AL 35706

**Haeger Potteries Collectors'
Club of America**
Lanette Clarke, 5021 Toyon Way, Antioch,
CA 94509

Hall Collectors' Club (newsletter)
Hall China Collector Newsletter
Virginia Lee, P.O. Box 360488, Cleveland,
OH 44136

**Homer Laughlin China
Collectors' Association**
The Dish (quarterly magazine)
HLCCA, P.O. Box 721, North Platte,
NE 69103-0721

Hull Pottery Association
4 Hilltop Road, Council Bluffs, IA 51503

McCoy Pottery
The NM Express (monthly newsletter)
Carol Seman, 8934 Brecksville Road, Suite
406, Brecksville, OH 44141-2318
McCoy Pottery Collectors' Society
P.O. Box 5286, Delanco, NJ 08075

**Medalta Potteries,
Friends of Medalta Society**
713 Medalta Avenue S.E., Medicine Hat,
Alberta T1A 3K9, Canada

**National Autumn Leaf
Collectors' Society**
P.O. Box 7929, Moreno Valley, CA 92552-7929

Pickard Collectors' Club
300 East Grove Street, Bloomington, IL 61701

Potteries of Trenton Society
120 West State Street, Trenton, NJ 08608

Purinton Pottery
Lori Hinterleiter, P.O. Box 9394, Arlington,
VA 22219

Red Wing Collectors' Society
(bimonthly newsletter, local chapters)
John and Kim Key, Post Office Box 50,
Red Wing, MN 555066

Rumrill Society
P.O. Box 2161, Hudson, OH 44236

Shawnee Pottery Collectors Club
(newsletter, annual convention) PO Box 713,
New Smyrna Beach, FL 32170-0713

**Southern Potteries/Blue Ridge
Collectors' Club**
Phyllis Ledford, 245 Seater Road, Erwin,
TN 37650-329

Stangl/Fulper Collectors' Club
P.O. Box 538, Flemington, NJ 08822

Vernon Kilns
Vernon Views (quarterly newsletter)
Patricia Faux, PO Box 945, Scottsdale
AZ 85252

Eva Zeisel Forum
695 Monterey Boulevard, #203, San
Francisco, CA 94127

BIBLIOGRAPHY

BRITAIN

Beard, G. *Modern Ceramics*. Studio Vista, London, 1969

Buckley, Cheryl. *Potters and Paintresses: Women Designers in the Pottery Industry 1870–1955*. The Women's Press, London, 1990

Cameron, E. *Encyclopedia of Pottery and Porcelain: the 19th and 20th Centuries*. Faber & Faber, London, 1986

Charleston, Robert, J., ed. *World Ceramics*. Hamlyn, London, 1990

Cushion, J. P. *Handbook of Pottery and Porcelain Marks*. Faber & Faber, London, 1996

Forsyth, G. M. *20th Century Ceramics*. Studio Publications, New York, 1936

Godden, G. A. *Encyclopedia of British Pottery and Porcelain Marks*. Barrie & Jenkins, London, 1964

Jackson, Lesley. *The New Look Design in the Fifties*. Thames and Hudson, London, 1991

McCready, Karen. *Art Deco and Modernist Ceramics*. Thames and Hudson, London, 1995

Niblett, K. *Dynamic Design* (exhibition catalogue). City Museum and Art Gallery, Stoke-on-Trent, 1990

Savage, George and Newman, Harold. *An Illustrated Dictionary of Ceramics*. Thames and Hudson, London, 1976

Spours, Judy. *Art Deco Tableware*. Ward Lock, London, 1988

Stevenson, Greg. *Art Deco Ceramics*. Shire Publications, Princes Risborough, 1998

NORTH AMERICA

Cunningham, Jo. *The Collector's Encyclopedia of American Dinnerware*. Collectors Books, Paducah, KY, 1995

Denker, Ellen and Bert. *The Warner Collector's Guide to North American Pottery and Porcelain*. Warner Books, Inc., New York, a Main Street Press Book, 1982

Derwich, Jenny B. and Mary Latos. *Dictionary Guide to United States Pottery and Porcelain*. Jenstan, Franklin, MI, 1984

Duke, Harvey. *Official Price Guide to Pottery and Porcelain*, 8th edn. House of Collectibles, New York, 1995

Evans, Paul. *Art Pottery of the United States: An Encyclopedia of Producers and Their Marks*, rev. 2nd edn. Feingold & Lewis Publishing Group, New York, 1987

Kovel, Ralph and Terry. *The Kovels' Collector's Guide to American Art Pottery*. Crown Publishers, Inc., New York, 1974. (Subsequently published as *Kovels' American Art Pottery: The Collector's Guide to Makers, Marks and Factory Histories*. Crown Publishers, New York, 1993)

Lehner, Lois. *Lehner's Encyclopedia of U.S. Marks on Pottery, Porcelain and Clay*. Collector Books, Paducah, KY, 1988

KEY TO PRICES

The following list provides an estimate of the current value of each illustrated ware or group of wares, including those shown in advertisements; prices are not given for the advertisements themselves. An item may command a higher price in its area of origin.

KEY TO STAR RATING

★ newly collectable
★★ collectable
★★★ established or highly collectable

Conversion rate used: $1 = £1.6.

1	£50–150 $80–240 ★★	23	£25–100 $40–160 ★★
2	$350 £220 ★★★	24	retail price
3	£850 $1360 ★★★	25	retail price
4	£1000 $1600 ★★★	26	retail price
5	£850–2500 $1360–4000 ★★★	27	£50 $80 ★
6	£350 $560 ★★★	28	£25–50 $40–80 ★
7	see Clarice Cliff	29	£25–75 $40–120
8	£2000 $3200 for the set ★★★	30	£15 $25 ★
9	£25–45 each $40–70 ★★	31	retail price ★
10	£15 $10 ★	32	£25–35 $40–55 each ★
11	£100 $160 ★★	33	£50 $80 ★
12	retail price	34	retail price
13	retail price	35	£50–150 £30–95 ★★
14	£10–25 $15–40 ★	36	£100 $160 ★
15	retail price	37	£350 $560 ★★★
16	£5–15 $10–25 each	38	£250 $400 ★★★
17	£10–20 $15–30 each ★	39	$50 £30 each
18	retail price	40	£50–150 $80–240 ★★
19	£10–50 $15–80 ★★	41	£250 $400 ★★★
20	£50 $80 ★★	42	£30 $50 ★
21	£20 $30 ★	43	£35–65 $55–105 ★★
22	£75 $120 ★★	44	£50–150 $80–240 each ★★
		45	£35–75 $55–120 ★★
		46	retail price

47	retail price	69	£25–75 $40–120 ★
48	£50 $80 each ★	70	$150–750 £95–470 ★★★
49	£15–25 $25–40 ★	71	$125 £80 ★★
50	priceless ★★★	72	$25 £15 ★★
51	£100 $160 ★★	73	£50 $80 ★★
52	£50 $80 ★★	74	£250 $400 each ★★
53	£10–25 $15–40 ★	75	£30 $50 ★
54	£100–200 $160–320 each ★★	76	retail price
55	£20–40 $30–65 ★	77	retail price
56	£50–350 $80–560 ★★★	78	$30 £20 ★
57	£75–100 $120–160 each ★★	79	£500 $800 ★★
58	retail price	80	£75 $120 ★
59	$75 £45 ★★	81	£350–500 $560–800 ★★
60	£25–150 $40–240 ★	82	£15–50 $25–80 ★
61	£100 $160 ★★	83	£50 $80 ★
62	£35 $55 ★★	84	£60 $100 ★
63	retail price	85	retail price
64	retail price	86	retail price
65	retail price	87	retail price
66	£30 $50 ★★	88	retail price
67	£10–70 $15–110 ★★	89	£30–100 $50–160 ★
68	£5–50 $10–80 ★	90	£500 $800 ★★★
		91	£500 $800 ★★★
		92	£1500 $2400 ★★★

365 $25–50 £15–30
366 $10–30 £5–20
367 $150 £100 for the set ★★
368 £750 $1200 ★★
369 £25–250 $40–400 ★★
370 £50–150 $80–240 ★★★
371 £750 $1200 ★★
372 £25–75 $40–120 ★★
373 £25–75 $40–120
374 £500 $800 ★★
375 £150 $240 ★★
376 £2000 $3200 ★★★
377 £1000 $1600 ★★★
378 £250 $400 for the set ★★
379 £300 $480 ★★
380 £150 $240 ★★
381 £100–250 $160–400 ★★
382 retail price
383 $20 £12.50 with saucer
384 £100 $160 ★★
385 £75 $120 ★★
386 retail price
387 £50 $80 ★★
388 £30 $50 ★
389 £35 $55 ★
390 £25 $40 ★★
391 £10 $15
392 £15 $25 ★
393 retail price
394 £15–50 $25–80 ★
395 £25–100 $40–160 ★
396 retail price
397 £20–150 $30–250 ★★
398 £250 $400 ★★
399 £10–15 $15–25 each ★
400 £200 $320 ★★★
401 £350 $560 ★★★
402 £750 $1200 for the set ★★★
403 £100 $160 ★★★
404 £50 $80 ★★★
405 £250 $150 ★★
406 £60 £40 ★
407 £50 £30 ★
408 £25–70 £15–45 ★
409 $100 £60 each ★★
410 $200 £120 ★★
411 £65–70 £40–45 ★
412 £50 £30 ★
413 £250 $400 ★★★
414 £250 $400 ★★★
415 £350 $560 ★★★
416 £150 $240 ★★★
417 £400 $640 ★★★
418 £10–25 $15–40 ★
419 £150 $240 ★★
420 £20 $30 ★
421 £15 $25 ★
422 £10–15 $15–25 each
423 £10–25 $15–40 ★★
424 £5–25 $10–40 ★
425 £150 £95 ★★
426 $25 £15 ★
427 $400 £250 ★★★
428 $200–5000 £125–3000 ★★★
429 $250 £155 ★★★
430 $400 £250 ★★★
431 $225 £140 ★★★

432 $800 £500 ★★★
433 $120–400 £75–250 ★★★
434 $185 £115 ★★★
435 $225 £140 ★★★
436 $100 £60 ★★★
437 £20 $30 ★
438 retail price
439 £750 $1200 ★★★
440 £50–250 $80–400 ★★
441 £25–50 $40–80 ★
442 retail price
443 retail price
444 retail price
445 £25–75 $40–120 ★
446 £150 $240 ★★
447 £25–50 $40–80 ★★
448 £350–1000 $560–1600 ★★★
449 £2000 $3200 ★★★
450 £35 $55 ★★
451 £500 $800 ★★★
452 £150 $240 ★★
453 retail price
454 retail price
455 £5–25 $10–40
456 retail price
457 £10–15 $15–25 ★
458 £1250 $2000 for the pair ★★★
459 £400 $640 ★★★
460 £1000 $1600 ★★★
461 £50 $80 ★
462 retail price
463 retail price
464 retail price
465 £1000 $1600 ★★★
466 £2500 $4000 ★★★
467 £30 $50 ★
468 £500 $800 ★★★
469 £1000–2000 $1600–3200 ★★★
470 retail price
471 £15 $25 ★
472 £200 $320 ★★
473 retail price
474 £15–25 £10–15 ★
475 £75 $120 ★★
476 £150 $240 ★★
477 £25–35 $40–55 ★
478 £75 $120 ★★★
479 £50 $30 ★
480 £750 $1200 ★★★
481 £100 $160 ★★★
482 £100 $160 ★★★
483 £1000 $1600 ★★★
484 £100 $160 ★★
485 £250 $400 for the trio ★★★
486 £100–250 $160–400 ★★
487 $20 £12.50
488 $100 £60 ★★
489 $50–2000 £30–1250 ★★★
490 £75 $120 ★★
491 £75 $120 ★★
492 £350–500 $560–800 each ★★
493 £100 $160 ★★
494 £100–250 $160–400 ★★
495 £600 $960 ★★★
496 £400 $640 ★★★
497 £35 $55 ★★

498 £50 $80 ★★
499 £15–90 £10–55 ★★
500 £150 $240 ★★
501 £75 $120 ★
502 £50 $80 ★
503 £10–25 $15–40 ★
504 £50 $80 ★★
505 £5–15 $10–25 ★
506 retail price
507 £20 $30 ★
508 £5–15 $10–25 ★
509 £90 $55 ★★
510 £50 $30 ★★
511 £25–90 £15–55 ★★
512 £30 £20 ★
513 £75 £45 ★★
514 £30–60 $50–100 ★
515 £5–10 $10–15
516 £100 $160 ★
517 retail price
518 retail price
519 £5–10 $10–15
520 $50 £30 ★
521 $15–25 £10–15 ★
522 $15 £10
523 $50–75 £30–45 ★★
524 $30 £20 ★
525 £75 $120 ★★
526 £100 $160 ★★
527 £150 $240 ★★
528 £200 $320 ★
529 $15 £10 ★
530 $25 £15 ★
531 £10–25 £5–15 ★
532 £50–75 $80–120 ★★
533 £5–20 $10–30 ★
534 £5–20 $10–30 ★
535 £15 $25 ★
536 £20 $30 ★
537 $1250–7500 £780–4690 ★★★
538 $150–200 £95–125 ★★
539 $1750 £1095 ★★★
540 $100 £60 ★★
541 $75 £45 ★
542 $25–75 £15–45 ★
543 £75 $120 ★
544 £25–150 $40–240 ★★
545 £150–200 $240–320 each ★★
546 £15 $25 ★
547 £15 $25 ★
548 £5–75 $10–120 ★
549 £35–75 $55–120 each ★★★
550 £15–75 $25–120 ★
551 £5–15 $10–25 ★
552 £15–50 $25–80 ★
553 retail price
554 retail price
555 £5–10 $10–15
556 £20 $30 ★
557 £1000 $1600 ★★★
558 £1500 $2400 ★★★
559 £600 $960 ★★
560 £500 $800 for the set ★★
561 £750 $1200 ★★
562 £200 $320 ★
563 £150 $240 for the set ★★★

564 £350 $560 ★★
565 £50 $80 ★
566 retail price
567 retail price
568 $250 £155 ★★★
569 $800 £500 ★★★
570 $650 £405 ★★★
571 $175 £110 ★★
572 $175 £110 ★★
573 $350 £220 ★★★
574 $150 £95 for basin and ewer ★★
575 £150 $240 ★★
576 £2500 $4000 ★★★
577 $30–50 £20–30 ★
578 £5–100 $10–160 ★
579 £350 $560 ★★
580 £10 $15 ★
581 £75 $120 ★★
582 retail price
583 £15–50 $25–80 ★
584 £5–25 $10–40 ★
585 retail price
586 £300 $500 ★★★
587 £400 $600 ★★★
588 £50–350 $80–200 ★★★
589 retail price
590 retail price
591 £10–25 $15–40★
592 £5–20 $8–30 ★
593 £40–60 $60–100 ★
594 £20–30 $30–50 ★
595 £80–120 $125–200 for the set ★★
596 retail price
597 retail price
598 £50 $80 ★★
599 £20–60 $30–100★★
600 £50 $80 ★
601 £20–80 $30–125★
602 £5–25 $8–40 ★
603 £350 $550 ★★★
604 £500 $800 ★★★
605 £10–50 $15–80 ★
606 £500 $ 800 ★★
607 retail price
608 £500 $800 ★★★
609 £250 $400 ★★
610 £5 $8
611 retail price
612 £20–50 $30–80 ★
613 retail price★
614 retail price★
615 retail price
616 £150 $250 ★★
617 £1000 $1500 ★★★
618 £250 $400 for the set ★★
619 £20 $30
620 £50 $80 for the set ★
621 £250 $400 each ★★
622 £25 $40 each ★
623 £5–30 $8–50 ★
624 £50–250 $80–400 ★★★
625 £10 $15
626 £10 $15
627 £250 $400 ★★
628 £1000 $1500 ★★★
629 £1500 $2500 ★★★
630 retail price

Page numbers in *italic* refer to illustrations.

ACKNOWLEDGMENTS

AUTHOR ACKNOWLEDGMENTS
Thanks are due to all the factories, ceramics museums, dealers in ceramics and collectors' clubs who gave their time and expertise in the making of this book, and, in addition, to the City of Stoke-on-Trent Reference Library, Hanley, Staffordshire. The authors would also like to acknowledge the help of the following people: Barbara Almquist, Emma Bridgewater, Richard Dennis, M. R. Hadida, Rodney Hampson, Stephen Harrison, Kate and Greg Johnson, Mary Moorcroft, Cleota Reed, Michael and Delyse Rodwell, Polly Stetler, Ed Stump, Richard Vassil, Charles Venable, Gillian Vigus, Wendy Wort. Special thanks are due to the following for their assistance and support: Terry Batkin, Richard Dawes, Maria Gibbs, Jane Parry, Jason Smalley, Anthea Snow.

PICTURE ACKNOWLEDGMENTS
Key fc: front cover; bc: back cover; sp: spine; t: top; b: bottom; r: right; l: left; c: centre. **A:** Alfies Antiques Market 13-25 Church Street, London NW8; **AAC:** Afonwen Antiques Centre, nr Caerwys, Mold; **AAM:** Applied Arts Museum, Helsinki; **AC:** Aynsley China Ltd, Longton, Stoke-on-Trent; **AJ:** Andy Johnson, photographer; **AW:** Arthur Wood & Son (Longport) Plc, Longport, Stoke-on-Trent; **B:** Bridgewater, London; **BA:** Barbara A Almquist (USA); **BBA:** Beth & Beverley Adams, stall G043, Alfies Antiques Market 13-25 Church Street, London NW8; **BD:** Bert Denker, photographer; **BL:** Burgess & Leigh Ltd, Burslem, Stoke-on-Trent; **BLe:** The Collection of Barclay Lennie; **BM:** Bristol Museums & Art Gallery; **BP:** Bennington Potters, Bennington VT (USA); **BPS:** Boehm Porcelain Studio, Trenton NJ (USA); **BT:** Biltons Tableware Ltd, Stoke-on-Trent; **C:** Cybis, Courtesy of New Jersey State Museum (USA); **CB:** Christina Bishop; **CHB:** Chris Halton, photographer; **CHB:** CH Brannam Ltd, Barnstable, Devon; **CI:** Christies Images, London; **CR:** Cleota Reed, photographer (USA); **CS:** Cobridge Stoneware plc, Stoke-on-Trent; **CSA:** Church Street Antiques, 10 Church Street, Godalming, Surrey; **CSe:** www.ceramicsearch.co.uk; **CT:** Churchill Tableware Ltd, Tunstall, Stoke-on-Trent; **CW:** Carlton Ware; **DC:** Dunoon Ceramics Ltd, Stone, Staffs; **DCh:** Dennis Chinaworks, Shepton Beauchamp, nr Ilminster; **DG:** The Dudson Group, Tunstall, Stoke-on-Trent; **DL:** Douglas A Leishman, photographer; **DN:** Dreweatt Neate Auctioneers, Donnington, Berkshire; **DR:** David Rago Auctions, Lambertville NJ (USA); **ERC:** E. Radford Collectors' Club, St Claver, Victoria Avenue, Kirby-le-Soken, Nr Frinton-on-Sea, Essex; **:ET:** ET Archive / Stoke Museum, Staffs; **FMS:** Friends of Medalta Society, Medicine Hat, Alberta (USA); **FD:** Flying Duck Enterprises, 320-322 Creek Road, Greenwich, London SE10; **G:** Ginnel Gallery, 18-22, Lloyd Street, Manchester; **GC:** Goss Collectors' Club, 31a The Crescent, Stanley Common, Derbyshire; **GKJ:** Greg & Kate Johnson (USA); **GP:** Geoffrey Peake & Nick Jones at Susie Cooper Ceramics/Art Deco, G070-74, Alfies Antiques Market 13-25 Church Street, London NW8; **GSP:** Gordon & Suzanne Pfeiffer (USA); **H:** Hadida Ltd. Old Foley Pottery, Fenton, Stoke-on-Trent, Staffordshire; **HM:** Hudson & Middleton Ltd, Longton, Stoke-on-Trent; **HP:** Honiton Pottery Collectors Society, 12, Beehive Lane, Great Baddow, Chelmsford, Essex; **HPo:** Holkham Pottery, Holkham, Norfolk; **HRL:** Hanley Reference Library; **HS:** Highland Stoneware Ltd, Lochinver, Sutherland; **HW:** Henry Watson's Potteries Ltd, Wattisfield, Suffolk; **IB:** Ian Booth, photographer; **IHS:** courtesy of Indiana Historical Society (USA); **IT:** Ian Turner, photographer; **JH:** Joy & Edward Hallam; **JKa:** collection of / photo by James Kaufman (USA); **JK:** Jacqueline Kimball (USA); **JL:** collection of / photo by Jay Lewis (USA); **JN:** Jo Nelson, photographer; **JR:** John Rastall at Alfie's Antique Market, 13-25 Church Street, London NW8; **JS:** James Sadler & Sons Ltd, Burslem, Stoke-on-Trent; **JSm:** Jason Smalley, photographer; **JT:** John Tams Group Plc, Longton, Stoke-on-Trent; **JW:** Josiah Wedgwood & Sons Ltd, Barlaston, Stoke-on-Trent; **KU:** Keele University Library; **LA:** Laing Art Gallery, Newcastle upon Tyne; **LBA:** Lorna Bailey Artware, Stoke-on Trent; **LCA:** Lenox China Archives, Lenox Brands (USA); **MB:** Maureen Batkin; **MBDM:** Museum of Barnstaple & North Devon; **MC:** Mary Chappelhow at Wetheriggs Country Pottery; **MCa:** Mason Cash, Pool Street, Church Gresley, Swadlincote, Derbyshire; **MCo:** Miller's Collectables 1998-9; **MM:** Minton Museum, Royal Doulton Plc, Stoke-on-Trent; **MN:** Martin Norris, photograher; **MP:** Moorland Pottery, Chelsea Works, Burslem, Stoke-on-Trent, Staffordshire; **MY:** Martin Yates; **NB:** Neil Bingham; **NFM:** Newhaven Flea Market, Newhaven, Sussex; **NWM:** The National Museum of Wales; **OPG:** Octopus Publishing Group Ltd; **P:** Phillips Picture Library, London; **PA:** Prinknash Abbey Pottery, Cranham, Gloucester; **PAt:** Paul Atterbury; **PC:** Pamela Coates (USA); **PCo:** Private Collection; **PG:** Pottery Gazette & Glass Trade Review; **PGD:** Pottery Gazette Diary; **PGL:** Pottery & Glass; **PGR:** The Pottery Gazette Reference Book; **PM:** Portmeirion Potteries Ltd, Stoke-on-Trent; **PO:** Poole Pottery Ltd., Poole, Dorset; **PFP:** Pfaltzgraff Pottery (USA); **PP:** Purbeck Pottery Ltd, Purbeck, Dorset; **PTDP:** Petra Tilly at Dartington Pottery; **R:** Rennies, 13 Rugby Street, London WC1; **RD:** Royal Doulton (UK) Ltd, Stoke-on-Trent; **RDG:** Richard Dennis Gallery, 144 Kensington Church Street, London ; **RDM:** Royal Crown Derby Museum, Derby; **RDP:** Richard Dennis Publications, Somerset; **RDR:** Royal Doulton Room / Harrods Ltd; **RDu:** Rish Durka, photographer; **RP:** Rye Pottery, Rye, Sussex; **RS:** Robin Saker, photographer; **RST:** Royal Stafford Tableware Ltd, Burslem, Stole-on-Trent; **RT:** Raccoon's Tale, Mullica Hill, NJ (USA); **RW:** Royal Worcester, Severn Street, Worcester; **S:** Spode, Stoke-on-Trent; **SC:** Syracuse China (USA); **SH:** Samuel Heath & Sons Plc, Birmingham; **SI:** Southampton Institute Fine Arts Valuation Study Collection. curator Sharon Grigg; **DL/SIA:** © David Leach/Crafts Study Centre, The Surrey Institute of Art and Design 2005; **SIn:** Steelite International plc, Stoke-on-Trent; **SL:** Sotheby's Picture Library, London; **SP:** Stonies Pottery, London; **ST:** Staffordshire Tableware, Meir Park, Stoke-on-Trent; **SY:** The Studio Yearbook; **TG:** Thomas Goode Ltd (Caverswall China), Fenton, Stoke-on-Trent; **TI:** Tableware International; **TR:** The Resettlers (USA); **TRi:** Tim Ridley, photographer; **TTC:** Peter Pinnington at Tin Tin Collectables, G038-42, Alfies Antiques Market 13-25 Church Street, London NW8; **V&A:** Victoria & Albert Museum Picture Library; **VB:** Virginia Brisco / Torquay Pottery Collectors Society; **VH:** collection of Virginia Heiss (USA); **W:** Winterthur Library, Printed Book and Periodical Collection (USA); **WA:** Waterford-Wedgwood (USA); **WCA:** Wexner Centre for the Arts, Ohio State University (USA); **WM:** Trustees of The Wedgwood Museum, Barlaston, Staffs; **WS:** Wood & Sons Ltd, Burslem, Stoke-on-Trent, Staffordshire; **WW:** W. W. Winter Ltd, photographers.

fcl RD; fcr OPG/TRi /FD; fcc DG; fct PM; fccr OPG/IB/R; bcl CI; bcc CI; bcr RD; sp OPG/IB/NFM; 1 OPG/AJ/PCo; 2 RDP; 6t OPG/JSm/HRL/PG 1.11.1905 p1193; 6b LCA; 7t CI; 7b CI; 8t CI; 8b CI; 9t OPG/JSm/HRL/PG 1.4.29 p497; 9b CI; 10tl OPG/TRi /NB; 10b PCo/BD; 11t PO; 11c B; 11b RD; 12t OPG/JSm/ HRL/PG 1.4.13 p452; 12bl JW; 12br OPG/JSm/HRL/PG; 12.1946 p798; 13tr OPG/JSm/PCo; 13c RD; 14tr OPG/JSm/HRL/PG R 1952 p277; 14c OPG/JSm/PCo; 14b OPG/JSm/PCo; 15t PCo; 15b JH; 16tr JW; 16cr JW; 16b JW; 17t OPG/JSm/PCo; 17b OPG/JSm/PCo/PG 1.10.38; 18t OPG/JSm/HRL/PG 1.9.34; 18cr SI; 18b AC; 19t OPG/JSm/HRL/PG 1.9.19 p942; 19b OPG/JSm/PCo; 20t RST; 20b RT/BD; 21t DL/PCo; 21c OPG/CSK; 21b OPG/CSK; 22t BP; 22tr GKJ/BD; 22b CI; 23t RD; 23bl RD; 23br OPG/JSm/PCo/PG 1.3.94; 24tr CI; 24cr RD; 24b OPG/TRi /FD; 25tr BT; 25cr BT; 25br OPG/JSm/HRL/PG 2.2.20 p183; 26t OPG/JSm/HRL/PG 1.3.39 p1140; 26b BPS; 27tr OPG/JSm/PCo/SY 1953 p109; 27cr CI; 27b OPG/JSm/HRL/PG 1.9.34 p1009; 28t OPG/RDu/PCo; 28b OPG/JSm/ HRL/PG 10.56 p1472; 29t PCo; 29b DN; 30t CHB; 30b RT/BD; 31tr OPG/JSm/HRL/PG 1.9.21 p1289; 31bl PCo; 31br PCo; 32l OPG/RDu/B; 32tr B; 32bl OPG/RDu /B; 32br B; 33tl DL/PCo; 33tr DL/PCo; 33b OPG/JSm/HRL/PG 1.3.39; 34t OPG/JSm/HRL/PG 12.64 p1277; 34b OPG/JSm/PCo; 35t DR; 35cr PCo/BD; 35br PCo/BD; 36l OPG/JSm/PCo; 36tr OPG/JSm/PCo; 36br OPG/TRi/FD; 37tl BL; 37tr BL; 37c OPG/TRi/BBA; 37bl PCo/BD; 37br PCo/BD; 38t OPG/TRi/BBA; 38c OPG/RDu/BBA; 38b OPG/RDu/BBA; 39t OPG/JSm/HRL/PGL 10.60 p685; 39c CW/PCo; 39b OPG/TRi/BBA; 40b PCo; 41t OPG/JSm/PCo; 41c TG; 41b CT; 42t CT; 42b OPG/JSm/HRL/PGR 1952 p189; 43t CI; 43c OPG/TRi/BBA; 43b CI; 44t CI; 44b CI; 45tl CI; 45cl CI; 45cr CI; 45br OPG/TRi/BBA; 46t GKJ/BD; 46b OPG/JSm/HRL/PGD 1915; 47t OPG/JSm/PCo/PG 9.54 p1289; 47c OPG/RDu/BBA; 47b JW; 48t JW; 48cr JW; 48bl JW; 49t OPG/JSm/

PCo; 49b OPG/RDu/GP; 50t OPG/RDu/GP; 50b OPG/RDu/GP; 51tl OPG/RDu/GP; 51cl OPG/RDu/GP; 51b CI; 52t OPG/RDu/GP; 52c OPG/TRi/BBA; 52b OPG/JSm/HRL/PG 1.9.32 p1137; 53t PCo/BD; 53b PCo/BD; 54t OPG/JSm/HRL/PG 1.2.37; 54b PCo/BD; 55t OPG/JSm/HRL/PG 2.53 p268; 55c OPG/RDu/JR; 55b PCo; 56t RDP; 56b RDP; 57t C; 57b OPG/JSm/PCo/PG 10.53 p1443; 58t JKa; 58c RDP; 58b RDP; 59t RDP; 59b RDP; 60t RDP; 60b OPG/JSm/PCo; 61t DG; 61bl DG; 61br DG; 62tl DC; 62tr DC; 62b PCo/BD; 63t OPG/JSm/HRL/PG 1.6.39; 63b OPG/JSm/HRL/PGL12.60 p849; 64t OPG/AJ/PCo; 64b NWM; 65tr OPG/JSm/PCo; 65b H; 66t OPG/JSm/PCo; 66b PCo; 67tl OPG/RDu/GP; 67c PCo; 67br OPG/RDu/TTC; 68t OPG/JSm/PCo; 68b OPG/AJ/PCo; 69tl PCo/BD; 69tr PCo/BD; 69bl RT/BD; 69br RT/BD; 70t CI; 70c OPG/AJ/PCo; 70b CI; 71r PCo/BD; 71b PCo/BD; 72t PCo/BD; 72cl PCo/BD; 72cr RT/BD; 72b RT/BD; 73t BA/BD ; 73b RT/BD; 74t WA; 74c BA/BD; 74b PCo/BD; 75cl RT/BD; 75cr PCo/BD; 76tr RT/BD; 76cr RT/BD; 76b OPG/JSm/HRL/cat.ref.P738.94246; 77t OPG/JSm/HRL/PG 1.4.26 p509; 77bl GC; 77br GC; 78t OPG/RDu/BBA; 78c OPG/JSm/PCo; 78b OPG/TRi/BBA; 79t OPG/JSm/PCo/SY 1949 pxiv; 79c OPG/JSm/PCo; 79b OPG/TRi/BBA; 80tr OPG/MN/CB; 80c RDP; 80b RDP; 81t RDP; 81c RDP; 81b RDP; 82t RDP; 82b PCo; 83t OPG/JSm/HRL/PG 1.4.26 p515; 83c OPG/JSm/PCo; 83b OPG/TRi/BBA; 84t OPG/RDu/BBA; 84b PCo/BD; 85t RT/BD; 85c RT/BD; 85b RT/BD; 86t RT/BD; 86c RT/BD; 86b RT/BD; 87t RT/ BD; 87c RT/BD; 87b OPG/JSm/PCo; 88t PCo/BD; 88bl GKJ/BD; 88br PCo/BD; 89t PCo; 89c RT/BD; 89b RT/BD; 90t PCo/BD; 90c RT/BD; 90b JL; 91t SH; 91b OPG/JSm/HRL/PG 1.3.16 p208; 92t HP; 92cr HP; 92b HP; 93t OPG/JSm/PCo/PG 2.56 p213; 93c RDP; 93b OPG/RS/G; 94t OPG/JSm/PCo/PG 9.54 p1297; 94bl HM; 94br HM; 95t RT/BD; 95cl RT/BD; 95bl RT/BD; 95br RT/BD; 96t RT/BD; 96c PCo/BD; 96b PCo/BD; 97t OPG/JSm/HRL/Cat.ref.P738942.28; 97b OPG/JSm/HRL/PG 1.2.28 p193; 98t OPG/IB/NFM; 98c PCo 98b JW; 99t OPG/JSm/HRL/PGL 5.56 p138; 99b OPG/IB/NFM; 100t OPG/JSm/KU/PG 1.3.20 p331; 100c OPG/RDu/BBA; 100b PCo/BD; 101t PCo/BD; 101c PCo/BD; 101b PCo/BD; 102t OPG/JSm/HRL/PGL 7.60 p451; 102bl OPG/IB/PCo; 102br OPG/IB/PCo; 103t OPG/AJ/BBA; 103b OPG/JSm/PCo/PG 8.1953 p1197; 104t OPG/RDu/BBA; 104c OPG/JSm/HRL/PG R 1964 p9; 104b H; 105t H; 105b OPG/JSm/PCo; 106t PCo/BD; 106c PCo/BD; 106b PCo/BD; 107t W; 107c PCo/BD; 107b PCo/BD; 108t PCo/BD; 108bl TR/BD;108br TR/BD; 109t PCo/BD; 109cl PCo/BD; 109cr PCo/BD; 109b PCo/BD; 110t OPG/JSm/HRL/PGL 2.1957 pxvi; 110b W; 111tl RT/BD; 111c RT/BD; 111b RT/BD; 112t RT/BD; 112c RT/BD; 112b RT/BD; 113tr PCo/BD; 113cl OPG/AJ/RDR.; 113c RT/BD; 113b OPG/JSm/HRL/PGR 1952 p127; 114t OPG/JSm/PCo/PG 9.54 p1285; 114b LCA; 115t LCA; 115b LCA; 116t LCA; 116b LCA; 117t LCA; 117bl PCo/BD; 117br PCo/BD; 118tl John Giblin; 118t OPG/JSm/HRL/PGD 1915 p27; 118br PAt; 119tl PCo; 119bl PCo/BD; 119br PC/BD; 120t PCo/BD; 120c PC/BD; 120b RT/BD; 121t GKJ/BD; 121b OPG/JSm/PCo; 122t OPG/JSm/HRL/PG 7.37; 122b OPG/RDu/BBA; 123t OPG/JSm/PCo/PG 1.9.34 p1066; 123c MCo/CSA; 123b OPG/RDu/BBA; 124tl LA; 124tr OPG/TRi/BBA; 124b MCa/PCo; 125r PCo/BD; 125cl PCo/BD; 125cr PCo/BD; 125b PCo/BD; 126t OPG/IB/NFM;126c OPG/IB/NFM; 126b OPG/JSm/PCo/PGL 11.54, inside fc; 127t RDP; 127b FMS; 128tr BLe; 128cr DL/PCo; 128bl RT/BD; 128br RT/BD; 129t OPG/JSm/HRL/PG 1.2.37 p149; 129c OPG/JSm/HRL/PG 7.60 p837; 129b RDP; 130t RDP; 130c OPG/TRi/NB; 130b RDP; 131t OPG/RS/G; 131c OPG/IB/A; 131b OPG/RS/G; 132t OPG/JSm/PCo/PG 1.9.34 p1060; 132b CI; 133t P; 133b RD; 134t RD; 134cl PCo; 134cr MM; 134b OPG/TRi/BBA; 135t PCo; 135b RDP; 136t RDP; 136c RDP; 136b RDP; 137t RDP; 137c CI; 137b RDP; 138t RDP; 138b CI; 139t CI; 139c MP; 139b OPG/JSm/PCo; 140tl PCo/BD; 140tr PCo/BD; 140b VH/IHS; 141t PCo; 141c OPG/TRi/BBA; 141b PCo; 142t PCo; 142cl OPG/RDu/GP; 142br PCo; 143t OPG/TRi/ BBA; 143c OPG/JSm/HRL/PG 1.4.30 p615; 143b OPG/AJ/PCo;

144t OPG/JSm/HRL/ PG 1.2.21 p175; 144b DR; 145t V&A; 145c V&A; 145b SC/CR; 146t PCo/BD; 146c PCo/BD; 146b SC/CR; 147t SC/CR; 147b PCo/BD; 148t PCo/BD; 148tc PCo/BD; 148b PCo/BD; 149t RD; 149c OPG/JSm/HRL/PG 1.1.36 p62; 149b RDP; 150tl OPG/RDu/BBA; 150tr OPG/RDu/BBA; 150b OPG/JSm/HRL/PGD 1915 p19; 151t OPG/AJ/PCo; 151c PCo/BD; 151b GKJ/BD; 152t RT/BD; 152b PFP; 153t PFP; 153b PFP; 154t PFP; 154b PFP; 155t PFP; 155b PCo/BD; 155br PCo/

BD; 156t CI; 156b OPG/JSm/HRL/cat ref.P738742.12 plate v4; 157r CI; 157t OPG/JSm/HRL/cat.ref.P738742.12 v1; 158t OPG/JSm/HRL/PG 1.2.21 p69; 158b OPG/JSm/PCo/PG 1.55 fc; 159t RDP; 159c RDP; 159b CI; 160t MCo/RDG; 160b RDP; 161t OPG/IB/A; 161cl RDP; 161b RDP; 162t PO; 162cr BA/BD; 162b BA/BD; 163tr PM; 163cr PM; 163bl PM; 164t PM; 164b BM; 164br OPG/JSm/PCo; 165tr OPG/JSm/PCo; 165cl OPG/IB/NFM; 165b OPG/IB/NFM; 166t PA; 166c PP; 166b PP; 167t PP; 167 b MY; 168t ERC; 168b OPG/IB/NFM; 169t WM; 169c WM; 169b WM; 170t WM; 170b BA/BD; 171t BA/BD; 171c RT/BD; 171b RT/BD; 172t RT/BD; 172c RT/BD; 172b RT/BD; 173t PCo/BD; 173ct PCo/BD; 173cb CI; 173b CI; 174t OPG/RDu/GP; 174c CI; 174b OPG/RDu/GP; 175t OPG/RDu/GP; 175c OPG/ JSm/HRL/PG 1.2.30; 175b OPG/TRi/BBA; 176t OPG/JSm/PCo; 176tc OPG/TRi/BBA; 176cr OPG/JSm/PCo; 176b OPG/IB/NFM; 177t OPG/IB/NFM; 177b RD; 178t W; 178b RT/BD; 179t GKJ/BD; 179c W; 179b W; 180t GKJ/BD; 180b PCo/BD; 181t RT/BD; 181c RT/BD; 181b RT/BD; 182t RT/BD; 182c RT/BD; 182b JK/BD; 183t OPG/IB/NFM; 183c RD; 183b OPG/IB/NFM; 184t RDM/WW; 184b RD; 185t OPG/JSm/PCo/PG 1954 p1253; 185c RDM; 185b RDM; 186t RDM; 186b OPG/JSm/HRL/PG D 1915 p32; 187t PCo; 187c OPG/JSm/HRL/PG 1934; 187b CI; 188t CI; 188c OPG/IB/NFM; 188b RD; 189t CI; 189c RD; 189b OPG/AJ/RDR; 190t OPG/JSm/PCo/PG 11.1954 fc; 190c RST; 190b OPG/IB/NFM; 191t CI; 191b P; 192t RW; 192c OPG/IB/NFM; 192b RW; 193t RW; 193c RW; 193b OPG /IB/NFM; 194t CI; 194b CI; 195t OPG/JSm/PCo; 195c CI; 195b CI; 196t RP/JN; 196c OPG/IB/NFM; 196b ET; 197t JS; 197bl RT/BD; 197br RT/BD; 198t OPG/IB/NFM; 198c OPG/RDu/BBA; 198b OPG/IB/NFM; 199t OPG/IB/NFM; 199c OPG/IB/NFM; 199b RT/BD; 200t OPG/CH; 200c PCo; 200b OPG/RDu/GP; 201t OPG/RDu/BBA; 201b RD; 202t OPG/RDu /GP; 202c CI; 202b OPG/TRi/BBA0; 203t PCo/BD; 203cl WCA; 203c RT/BD; 203b PCo/BD; 204t OPG/IB/NFM; 204b OPG/IB/ NFM; 205t RDP; 205tc RDP; 205b OPG/TRi /BBA; 205bc RDP; 206cr PCo; 206bl PCo; 207t OPG/IB/NFM; 207c OPG/RDu / BBA; 207br OPG/RDu/BBA; 208tl RT/BD; 208tr RT/BD; 208b S; 209tl S; 209tr S; 209cl S; 209b OPG/IB/NFM; 210t PCo; 210tc OPG/RDu/BBA; 210b OPG/JSm/HRL/PGL 7.1960 p450; 211t ST; 211cl OPG/JSm/PCo; 211b OPG/JSm/PCo; 212t RT/BD; 212cl RT/BD; 212cr RT/BD; 212b RT/BD; 213tl PCo/BD; 213r PCo/BD; 213bl PCo/BD; 213br PCo/BD; 214t OPG/JSm/HRL/PG 10.1960 p702; 214b OPG/JSm/HRL/PGL fc; 215t OPG/JSm/HRL/PGD 1915 p5; 215c JT; 215b JT; 216t OPG/JSm/HRL/TI 2.87 p131; 216b RT/BD; 217t RT/BD; 217c RT/BD; 217b PCo/BD; 218tl RT/BD; 218tr PCo/BD; 218c VB; 218b VB; 219t OPG/RDu/JR; 219b MCo; 220t RT/BD; 220c PCo, Mullica Hill NJ, BD; 220bl PCo, Mullica Hill NJ, BD; 220br PCo/BD; 221tl OPG/RDu /JR; 221tr OPG/RDu/JR; 221b OPG/ JSm/HRL/PG 8.1947 p625; 222t OPG/JSm/HRL/PGL 3.1950 p5; 222c PCo; 222b PCo; 223t DR; 223b DR; 223br PCo/BD; 224t GSP/BD; 224ct RT/BD; 224cb RT/BD; 224b RT/BD; 225t OPG/RDu/BBA; 225c P; 225b OPG/RS/G; 226t OPG/IB/ NFM; 226c OPG/IB/NFM; 226b OPG/JSm/HRL/PGL 10.1960 p703; 227t OPG/IB/NFM; 227b OPG/JSm/HRL/PG 2.10.05 p1119; 228t PCo; 228cr OPG/JSm/HRL/PGL 8.53 pxxxiii; 228b HW; 229t HW; 229b OPG/JSm/HRL/PGL 2.1957 pxxx; 230t PCo; 230b SL; 231t PCo; 231c PCo; 231b PCo; 232t WM; 232c OPG/JSm/PCo; 232b WM; 233t PCo; 233c WM; 233b JW; 234t JW; 234c OPG/JSm/PCo; 234b PCo/BD; 235t PCo/BD; 235c PCo/BD; 235b GKJ/BD; 236t RT/BD; 236b GKJ/BD; 237t W; 237bl CI; 237br DL/PCo; 238t PCo/BD; 238tl PCo/BD; 238tr PCo/BD; 238b OPG/JSm/HRL/PG 2.10.1916 p981; 239t CI; 240t OPG/IB/NFM; 240c OPG/IB/NFM; 240b AW; 241t OPG/JSm/HRL/PG 2.1956 p250; 241cl WS/PCo; 241cr WS/PCo; 241b OPG/IB/NFM; 242t RDP; 242b LBA; 243tr CI; 243bl & br LBA; 244tl RDP; 244bl PAt; 244bc MB; 244br PAt; 245tl, tc & tr PAt; 245bl, bc & br BL; 246tr, tcr, tcl & tcr IT; 246 bcl & bcr MB; 246br PAt; 247tl PAt; 247tr RDP; 247bl, bc & br CS; 248c RDP; 248br CI; 249tl & tr PTDP; 249bl, cr & bc DCh; 250tl SIn; 250bl TG; 251tl PAt; 251cr & b HS; 252tl & tr HPo; 252cl & cr MBDM; 253c & cr DL/SIA; 253bl OPG/TRi/BBA; 254tl RDP; 254cl & cr PAt; 254bl & br MB; 255tl & tr SP; 255bl & br ERC; 256tl & tr, cl & cr MB; 256bl Top of the Hill Antiques 256br AAC; 257tl & tr RDP; 257bl & br MC.